Managing Sport Events

SECOND EDITION

T. Christopher Greenwell, PhD
University of Louisville
Leigh Ann Danzey-Bussell, PhD
Trevecca Nazarene University
David J. Shonk, PhD
James Madison University

HUMAN KINETICS

Library of Congress Cataloging-in-Publication Data

Names: Greenwell, T. Christopher, 1967- author. | Danzey-Bussell, Leigh Ann, 1965- author. | Shonk, David J., 1969- author.
Title: Managing sport events / T. Christopher Greenwell, Leigh Ann Danzey-Bussell, David J. Shonk.
Description: Second edition. | Champaign, IL : Human Kinetics, 2020. | Includes bibliographical references and index.
Identifiers: LCCN 2019004911 (print) | LCCN 2019005662 (ebook) | ISBN 9781492590668 (epub) | ISBN 9781492570967 (PDF) | ISBN 9781492570950 (print)
Subjects: LCSH: Sports administration. | Special events--Management.
Classification: LCC GV713 (ebook) | LCC GV713 .G65 2020 (print) | DDC 796.06/9--dc23
LC record available at https://lccn.loc.gov/2019004911

ISBN: 978-1-4925-7095-0 (print)

The web addresses cited in this text were current as of March 2019, unless otherwise noted.

Acquisitions Editor: Andrew L. Tyler
Managing Editor: Julia R. Smith
Copyeditor: Rodelinde Albrecht
Indexer: Andrea Hepner
Permissions Manager: Dalene Reeder
Graphic Designer: Dawn Sills
Cover Designer: Keri Evans
Cover Design Associate: Susan Rothermel Allen
Photograph (cover): Gareth Fuller/PA Images/Getty Images
Photo Asset Manager: Laura Fitch
Photo Production Manager: Jason Allen
Senior Art Manager: Kelly Hendren
Illustrations: © Human Kinetics, unless otherwise noted
Printer: McNaughton & Gunn

Printed in the United States of America 10 9 8 7 6 5 4 3 2 1

The paper in this book is certified under a sustainable forestry program.

Human Kinetics
P.O. Box 5076
Champaign, IL 61825-5076
Website: www.HumanKinetics.com

In the United States, email info@hkusa.com or call 800-747-4457.
In Canada, email info@hkcanada.com.
In the United Kingdom/Europe, email hk@hkeurope.com.

For information about Human Kinetics' coverage in other areas of the world, please visit our website: **www.HumanKinetics.com**

E7390

Tell us what you think!
Human Kinetics would love to hear what we can do to improve the customer experience. Use this QR code to take our brief survey.

To my supportive parents, Zack and Leigh, and my wonderful family, Donna, Sam, and Molly.

—T. Christopher Greenwell

To my family, Tim and Sophie Grace, you two are my reason for existing and my support system for pushing me to be the best I can be. To my parents in heaven, your love, support, and role modeling made me strive for excellence in all that I do. I am eternally grateful to all of my family, friends, and sport management colleagues for supporting this project. Finally, thank you to my coauthors, Chris Greenwell and David Shonk, for allowing me to continue to contribute to this amazing book.

—Leigh Ann Danzey-Bussell

To the great teachers in my life, Mom, Dad, Bob, Donna, Brother Bill, Uncle Jim, my mentor Chella, and my wonderful family, Jen, Ashley, and Ryan.

—David J. Shonk

CONTENTS

Preface ix

Accessing the Web Resource xii

CHAPTER 1 Understanding the Sport Event Industry 1

Career Paths in Sport Event Management 6 • Skills, Knowledge, and Traits for Success 7 • Sport Events Versus Nonsport Events 9 • Sport Tourism 10 • Relationship Between Sport Event Management and Sport Facility Management 13 • Types of Sporting Events 14 • Summary 20 • Learning Activities 21

CHAPTER 2 Event Conceptualization 25

Stages of Event Planning 27 • Event Leadership 28 • Decision-Making in Event Management 28 • Brainstorming in Event Management 29 • Project Management Approach to Event Planning 31 • Purpose of the Event 32 • Choosing the Type of Event 33 • SWOT Analysis 34 • Developing a Mission for the Event 35 • Setting Goals and Objectives 36 • Planning Logistics 36 • Thinking Creatively and Planning for Uniqueness 38 • Sustainable Sporting Events 39 • Planning Promotional and Ancillary Components 40 • Planning for Contingencies 41 • Operational Planning 42 • Event Planning Blunders 43 • Summary 44 • Learning Activities 44

CHAPTER 3 Event Bidding 47

Economic Impact 50 • Sports Commissions 52 • Bidding Process 52 • Feasibility Studies 53 • Bid Documents 54 • Summary 56 • Learning Activities 57

CHAPTER 4 Event Budgeting 59

Event Budgeting Process 61 • Types of Revenues 64 • Types of Expenses 69 • Controlling Costs 73 • Cash Flow and Cash Management 74 • Summary 74 • Learning Activities 75

CHAPTER 5 Event Sponsorship 77

Sponsorship 81 • Sponsorship Components 83 • Components of a Sponsorship Proposal 84 • Sponsorship Benefits 88 • Activation and Evaluation Techniques 89 • Summary 91 • Learning Activities 91

CHAPTER 6 Event Marketing 93

Marketing Sport Events 95 • Developing a Marketing Plan 95 • Market Research and Analysis 96 • Understanding Consumers 97 • Setting Marketing Goals and Objectives 99 • Market Segmentation and Target Markets 99 • Branding the Event 100 • Event Pricing 100 • Distribution 101 • Event Promotion 102 • Sales 105• Creating Community Support 105 • Summary 106 • Learning Activities 106

CHAPTER 7 Media Relations and Promotion 109

Symbiotic Relationship: Working Together to Achieve Greatness 112 • The Critical Rs of Media Relations 113 • Differentiating the Promotional Mix From the Marketing Mix 114 • Promotional Tools 115 • Social Media: Connecting Through Connectivity 117 • Evaluating Success 119 • Summary 120 • Learning Activities 120

CHAPTER 8 Contract Considerations 123

Contract Law 101 125 • Types of Contracts 126 • Tips for Negotiating Contracts 131 • An Attorney's Perspective on Contracts: Neil Braslow, JD 131 • Federal Legislation 132 • Technology and Contracts 134 • Summary 134 • Learning Activities 135

CHAPTER 9 Risk Management and Negligence 137

Risk Management Process 141 • Risk Management Planning 141 • Threats to Events 143 • Crowd Control 148 • Crowd Management Plans 149 • Negligence 150 • Summary 152 • Learning Activities 152

CHAPTER 10 Event Staffing 159

Organizational Chart 161 • Identifying Necessary Staff 162 • Scheduling Staff 163 • Considering Outsourcing Staff 165 • Managing and Motivating Staff 166 • Personal Management Style and Effective Leadership 168 • Management Meetings 170 • Communicating With Staff 172 • Volunteers 173 • Team Building 175 • Summary 175 • Learning Activities 176

CHAPTER 11 Event Services and Logistics 179

Event Timeline 181 • Event Registration 183 • Ticket Sales 183 • Food and Beverage Operations 184 • Hospitality Services 187 • Waste Management Services 187 • Custodial Services 187 • Transportation Services 188 • Lighting 189 • Vendor Relationships 189 • Event Facility Selection 190 • Customer Service 195 • Awards Ceremonies 196 • Summary 196 • Learning Activities 196

CHAPTER 12 Event Day Management 199

Managing Event Day 201 • Easily Missed Details 202 • Event Day Tools 202 • Managing Staff 205 • Managing Spectators 208 • Managing Participants 210 • Managing Sponsors 213 • Customer Service 214 • Event Day Technologies 216 • Summary 217 • Learning Activities 217

CHAPTER 13 Postevent Details and Evaluation 219

Postevent Promotions 221 • Postevent Media Coverage 221 • Sponsor Follow-Up 223 • Postevent Debriefing 224 • Event Evaluation 224 • Evaluating Outcomes and Objectives 230 • Measuring Economic Impact 230 • Summary 231 • Learning Activities 231

Glossary 235
References 239
Index 251
About the Authors 259

PREFACE

To have a successful career in sport, it is important to have some proficiency in sport event management because just about everyone involved in sport will be engaged in planning, promoting, or managing a sporting event at one time or another. Sport event management is unique among the many areas of sport management in that it integrates various areas of the sport industry, including marketing, sponsorship, budgeting, risk management, and personnel management. In addition, running a sporting event requires the skills to plan, organize, lead, and communicate. Users of this textbook should be able to demonstrate an understanding of event management principles unique to sport.

Managing Sport Events is written for those who are either working in or aspiring to work in the sport industry. One does not necessarily need to be working in event management per se; everyone working with sporting events should be able to draw something from this text, which is designed to familiarize readers with the principles and practices related to effective event management. It approaches sport event management from a practical standpoint, integrating theory to support suggestions for practice, and it takes readers through the entire process of organizing events, from conception through postevent evaluation.

Scope of the Book

Managing Sport Events covers a wide variety of competitions, from local grassroots events such as a youth soccer tournament to mega-events such as the Olympic Games. The reader should be able to glean relevant information that applies to events large and small, local and international. Further, the text accounts for the various purposes that events serve (e.g., competition, revenue, tourism, promoting a cause) and for the various stakeholders that sporting events may serve (e.g., athletes, governing bodies, sponsors, communities). This book is a resource for anyone involved in sporting events, whether in a parks and recreation department or in high school, college, amateur, minor league, professional, or international sports.

Organization

Each chapter begins with a profile of an industry professional, in the form of an interview. These profiles give an insider's perspective into the concept being discussed. Each chapter then covers key sport event management principles; relevant examples from the sport industry are woven into each principle to illustrate how it applies in practice. Finally, each chapter ends with learning activities that apply what has been learned in the text. Numerous checklists, templates, and worksheets are provided throughout the book to illustrate tools that can be used to successfully plan and implement events. Boldfaced terms and an end-of-book glossary highlight key terms.

Managing Sport Events covers the main topics necessary to plan, organize, implement, and evaluate an event. The book opens with an overview of the sport event industry and a chapter that educates readers on how to conceive and develop an event. The chapters that follow cover key planning areas such as bidding, budgeting, marketing, promotion, sponsorship, and legal concerns and risk management. These chapters illustrate how different disciplines within sport management apply specifically to planning sporting events. Key operational areas such as staffing, event services and logistics, and event-day management are then presented to encompass what happens during the event itself. The final chapter discusses what needs to happen after the event.

Updates to the Second Edition

The second edition includes several important additions. To keep up with the changing sport event landscape, new sections and real-world examples related to key issues such as project management, event management technologies, social media usage, and sustainability have been added throughout. To increase the book's scope, more examples related to recreational and small-scale events have also been incorporated. The end-of-chapter activities have been revised to focus more on practical skills and critical thinking. Each chapter also includes a case study based on actual sporting events, ending with a section designed to challenge readers to apply theory to practice. New profiles of industry professionals are also included. These profiles are designed to add a practitioner's perspective to the chapter and reinforce the concepts within.

Benefits of the Book

Managing Sport Events is intended for practitioners within the sport industry as well as for students preparing to enter the industry. It provides a strong conceptual, theoretical, and practical basis for understanding the sport event industry and for selecting, planning, implementing, and evaluating a sporting event. The textbook helps the reader better understand the conceptual aspects of a sporting event that form the basis of how the event will ultimately be run. Conceptual skills are vitally important to all managers, especially event planners, and help to differentiate top-level managers from middle- and staff-level managers and leaders.

Students

This textbook is written with the understanding that the primary audience will be undergraduate students, the majority of whom are studying sport management. However, the text is also applicable to students in any discipline of study who desire to learn more about the nuts and bolts of selecting, planning, implementing, and evaluating an event. Students interested in areas such as hospitality, entertainment, physical education, business, and nonprofit or public administration may also find the textbook useful.

Event management is an important course for almost every sport management program. More importantly, employers within the sport industry expect students to enter the field as young professionals with an understanding of event management and possessing the necessary skills to immediately engage in event production. Although not every student will have the title of event planner, every student within the sport industry will most likely be engaged in some type of event planning, even if it is only a meal function at your place of business. Our hope is that this will not be one of those books that students buy and sell back at the end of the semester. Instead, this text should serve as a continual resource as they graduate and enter the industry.

The web resource is a tool that students will find useful. Each chapter contains additional case studies with multiple-choice questions that provide immediate feedback. Each chapter also includes a key terms learning activity and a list of internet resources so that students can practice defining key terms and further explore examples discussed in the book. The web resource is available at www.HumanKinetics.com/ManagingSportEvents.

Professors

This textbook will assist faculty in teaching important practical and conceptual issues in the context of sport event management. These are important concepts that add to conceptual and cognitive skill development in each student. At the same time, the authors of the book recognize the practical nature of event management. We have extensive experience within the industry in the area of event management, and because we are also current faculty, we understand the challenges of bringing fresh and relevant practical material into the classroom.

Handy resources such as an instructor guide, test package, and PowerPoint presentation are included in the package for professors; these ancillaries are available at www.HumanKinetics.com/ManagingSportEvents. Specific instructions are provided should the faculty member want to engage the students in the process of putting on an actual event. Chapters are organized to follow the process of staging an event, and all chapters contain learning activities to assist the faculty member in engaging students. Each chapter summary offers a review of key concepts. Furthermore, each chapter provides a short biography of a current industry professional to assist professors in experiential learning by using case studies.

Current Industry Professionals

This text serves as an important resource for those currently working within the sport industry who may need a refresher course in event management. Those needing additional training or going back for a graduate degree will also find the textbook helpful. In addition, the text is useful as an independent study and as a resource for writing industry reports or proposals. It will help industry professionals brush up on key definitions and is a refresher for key theoretical concepts. All sport industry professionals should keep this text on their bookshelf because of its practical nature.

Need for the Book

Most of us who attend an event do so as an invitee, not fully understanding the vastness of what it takes to host an event. *Managing Sport Events* provides a comprehensive look at what it takes to produce a successful event from conception to fruition to evaluation. As a dynamic field, sport management encompasses traditional business segments (administration, finance, and marketing) requiring expertise. The uniqueness of the sport industry must be understood and applied to event management. This book marries the business side with the unique traits of sport to provide a fresh perspective on event management.

Marketing, risk management, staffing, budgeting, and sponsorship are just a few areas of concern for event managers. Being knowledgeable about these topics and the role each plays in the bigger picture is imperative for today's sport management students. This book provides a distinctive perspective on the how-to aspects of sport management and its intricacies. The years of experience expressed throughout this book and the industry profiles found in each chapter offer readers great perspectives and real-life examples to contemplate and critically analyze. Many textbooks focus on a single aspect of the sport management field, such as sport marketing, sport finance, or sport media relations, but this text represents an inclusive look at event management and how those individual aspects work together to provide a strong foundation for students considering careers in this segment of the industry. We have taken great effort to address all pertinent areas of event management. Upon completion of this course, readers will have a comprehensive knowledge of event management and will be prepared to accept the challenges of the field.

ACCESSING THE WEB RESOURCE

Throughout *Managing Sport Events, Second Edition,* you will notice references to a web resource. This online content is available to you for free upon purchase of a new print book or an ebook. All you need to do is register with the Human Kinetics website to access the online content. The following steps explain how to register.

The web resource offers learning activities that focus on key term comprehension, additional case studies with practice questions, and internet resources for each chapter. We are certain you will enjoy this unique online learning experience.

Follow these steps to access the web resource:

1. Visit www.HumanKinetics.com/ManagingSportEvents.
2. Click the second edition link next to the corresponding second edition book cover.
3. Click the Sign In link on the left or top of the page. If you do not have an account with Human Kinetics, you will be prompted to create one.
4. After you register, if the online product does not appear in the Ancillary Items box on the left of the page, click the Enter Pass Code option in that box. Enter the following pass code exactly as it is printed here, including capitalization and all hyphens: **GREENWELL-Q4LAG-WR**
5. Click the Submit button to unlock your online product.
6. After you have entered your pass code the first time, you will never have to enter it again to access this online product. Once unlocked, a link to your product will permanently appear in the menu on the left. All you need to do to access your online content on subsequent visits is sign in to **www.HumanKinetics.com/ManagingSportEvents** and follow the link!

Click the Need Help? button on the book's website if you need assistance along the way.

VANDERLEI ALMEIDA/AFP/Getty Images

CHAPTER 1

Understanding the Sport Event Industry

CHAPTER OBJECTIVES

After completing the chapter, the reader should be able to do the following:

- Appreciate the role of sporting events from a historical perspective.
- Identify various types of sporting events.
- Recognize the employment opportunities in sport event management and the skills and knowledge necessary for success within the industry.
- Compare and contrast sporting events versus nonsporting events.
- Understand the relationship of sport event management to sport facility management and sport tourism.

INDUSTRY PROFILE

Al Kidd, National Association of Sports Commissions

Al Kidd is President and CEO of the National Association of Sports Commissions, located in Cincinnati, Ohio. Kidd taught in Ohio and in Utah before entering the advertising world. His career eventually led him to San Diego, with several positions in advertising and venture capital investing. Starting in 2003 and continuing into 2011, Kidd helped with the financial turnaround of the San Diego Hall of Champions sports museum. As president of the San Diego Sports Commission, he led a merger effort to consolidate a number of the professional, collegiate, nonprofit sports organizations and governmental agencies under one roof to acquire and service sports events in San Diego. Most recently, he has served as a partner with BoldPointe Partners, a private equity firm specializing in middle market companies.

What is the mission of the National Association of Sports Commissions (NASC)? What else can you tell us about the organization?

The mission of the NASC is to be the essential resource and leading advocate for the sports events and tourism industries. We educate, advocate for, inform, and provide resources to our members to generate economic growth, create jobs, and to promote sports participation. We do so to enhance the quality of life through sports events and tourism.

As regards the composition of the association, we currently have 550 destinations as members: convention and visitors bureaus (CVBs), chambers of commerce, state associations, and sports commissions; 85 are industry partners (e.g., lodging industry, event services companies); 180 are rights holders (anyone who owns an event, e.g., NCAA, USOC). Of these 550 destinations, only 90 are true sports commissions (i.e., a freestanding incorporated business and not a division of a CVB). The trend line is consolidation of freestanding sports commissions into CVBs.

It is our goal to EARN the respect of our members every day through our four key pillars of excellence:

Education: Gain knowledge of industry trends and best practices.

Advocacy: Be represented on national issues and initiatives related to the sports events and tourism industry.

Resources: Access industry leading information, analysis, and trends you need to know to better conduct your business.

Networking: Reach a network of more than 2,000 sports events and tourism professionals.

Most of our efforts in the past focused on providing programming for sports commissions. Today, we focus on meeting the needs of all of our members (i.e., rights holders, industry partners, destinations, and sports commissions). We have opportunities to provide educational programming for all of these categories. We have recently added an event called the 4S Summit, a two-and-a-half-day educational symposium that emphasizes the four core activities of all of our members: strategy, sponsorship, sales, and servicing. We have also added a chief executive summit, open to a limited number of attendees, that delivers high-level content providing an up close and intimate perspective about the issues facing sport and recreation with our association top-level leadership. Finally, we also run a women's summit focusing on women's issues that takes place in conjunction with the NCAA Women's Final Four Championship.

How large is the sport event industry and how do you measure economic impact?

Having just completed our annual study, we project the youth pay-to-play sports tournament segment to be approximately $11.8 billion. Not captured in this number are the many facets of youth sport, which have led to hundreds or thousands of jobs across the United States, including everything from league administrators and coaches to clinicians and physical therapists. The business has created financial opportunities for municipalities to create new facilities, thus creating construction jobs, an increased tax base, and increased earned media.

In terms of economic impact measurement, a variety of tools have been available in the market with no real consistency among them. We have combined our resources with other organizations in order to offer sport modules that are far more robust, customizable, and detailed than ever before. Economic impact reporting has always been an imperfect analysis. However, combining the resources of the market segments that desire metrics with all the major tourism associations in the sport, CVBs, and facilities industries, produces a very consistent and detailed reporting module. Traditionally, measurement of economic impact has focused solely on events coming into the market. However, one of the fastest growing markets is the **O&O** (owned and operated) market comprised of those sports commissions or CVBs who own and operate their own events. The NASC has framed an agreement in collaboration with Destinations International to combine our economic impact calculators into one calculator that will also include information about indoor facilities and convention centers. The calculator will not just measure pure economic impact; in the future, we look to add analytical tools that will measure earned media as well as social and digital engagement.

How has the sport event industry changed over the years?

One of the big changes is the growth of sport facilities across America. Employees at these facilities need the same kind of professional development, skills, and activities that we provide to our general membership. Those facilities need to be developed because they will be competing for events with many of our members. Another change is the expansion of local events into the sports commission world. These are the O&O events; 37 percent of our markets now have these locally owned events.

Another change is a shift toward a higher level of skilled employees in the business. Because sport events are growing, there is a sophistication buildup of quality people. The concept of pay-to-play is so firmly entrenched that it will be difficult for the industry to shift away from it. We, as an industry, need to bring in a more sophisticated level of employees focused around sponsorship and marketing those who have vertical skills. These new career entrants will go beyond the involvement and development often associated with salespeople or event planners today.

Of course, we are always dealing with issues surrounding the obesity epidemic. To address these issues, we have partnered with the Aspen Institute's Project Play to deliver their toolbox focused around play to local markets. We are also deeply involved in various initiatives to encourage free play and physical fitness.

Specialization is another issue. We are starting to see a slight pattern away from complete specialization and toward realizing the importance of playing multiple sports. Many coaches want players to play multiple sports because they are more skilled, anticipate better, and have better instincts. I believe that a lack of physical education and of exposure to a variety of sports is partly why athletes do not play multiple sports.

Currently, Baby Boomers are the most neglected amateur sport market. They have discretionary income and are driving the craze for Pickleball. While the Boomers care less about paddleboarding, surfing, orienteering, and mud runs, the Millennials have brought adventure activities into being. This is the reason why the fastest-growing sports are the various color runs, fun runs, and similar types of events. Now it is better to talk about sports by these narrow demographic segments because they differ in terms of their sport interests.

What skills are most important for students who would like to work in the sport event industry?

I have seen two distinct types of people working in the industry. The first are those who are very detail-oriented; they are the event organizers, implementers, and executers. Second are those who are responsible for event development. These types of people are more

> *continued*

Al Kidd, National Association of Sports Commissions *> continued*

entrepreneurial; they can come up with activities and are able to develop an event that is sponsorable and generates revenue, and so they need to be good at marketing, creative thinking, and developing new events. Most sports commissions have very little staff and their growth is inhibited by lack of a funding mechanism. That is why people who can generate revenue are valuable.

There are a number of ways to gain marketable skills. Not everyone can work in professional sport, but there are thousands of sport facilities that need employees with development and management skills. Many corporations have a sport marketing arm where students can work and often make a lot more money. Many advertising agencies have a sport marketing and development arm as well. Colleges are also becoming more sophisticated in their marketing of events. Rights holders are looking for event managers. For example, BMX is now building a number of new tracks around the United States, with the infrastructure supported or even built by the cities. There will be a growing need for people to run these events. Finally, students should volunteer and seek to meet new people.

Is it possible to become a certified sport event planner? If so, how?

Yes, we are considering both member and nonmember education. In the future, we will have some changes to allow a larger number of people to have access to courses. The core courses focus on strategic planning, effective selling, and communication. More information is available on our website, www.sportscommissions.org.

One of the earliest documented examples of a sporting event, the Panhellenic Games of 776 B.C., attracted more than 40,000 spectators who traveled from all parts of Greece to attend (Weed and Bull 2004). This festival, held in Olympia, was celebrated once every four years in accordance with the Greek calendar, occurring after the crops had been gathered and there was a lull during which men could relax from a year's hard work (Swaddling 1999). Most cities in Greece had their own stadiums during this time, and touring was an important aspect of sport because athletes received awards for participating.

Today, sports participants as well as spectators engage in sport-related activities for several reasons. For active participants, playing in a softball tournament is a means of relieving stress; fans and spectators flock to professional sporting events on a weekend to relax after a long week of work. Even in the early years, stress relief was a motivational factor for those participating in various sport events. The word *sport* comes from the verb *disport*, meaning *to carry away from*; as a noun the word means *diversion*, *display*, or *amusement* (Struna 2009). The implication is that sports divert attention from the rigors and pressures of everyday life (Kurtzman and Zauhar 2003).

Many of today's contemporary sporting events derive from England's system of club sports managed by the wealthy elite (Masteralexis, Barr, and Hums 2015). When European settlers arrived in Virginia and Massachusetts, the only sports were those of the Native Americans, who participated in activities such as archery, running, horseback riding, and lacrosse (Gems, Borish, and Pfister 2008). However, as life became easier and values changed, the European settlers began to engage in various pastimes and later became concerned about health and fitness (Swanson and Spears 1995). The festive culture of 17th- and 18th-century Britain became a central component of sport in America (Rader 2009). Gambling became an important recreation, and many settlers in Virginia wagered on horses because of the excitement of the competition (Breen 2010). Harness racing soon became the sport of the common person and America's first national pastime and professional sport.

The outgrowth of the success of harness racing was the various profit-oriented **leagues** we see today. Organizations such as the

National Football League (NFL), the National Basketball Association (NBA), Major League Baseball (MLB), the National Hockey League (NHL), Major League Soccer (MLS), and others were created to develop a system for sport that would work in the United States. In addition, tournament sports such as tennis and golf evolved from England's system of club sport brought to the United States (Masteralexis, Barr, and Hums 2015).

Over the years, the modern sport industry has seen tremendous growth. The most recent estimated revenue of the sport industry in the United States is $498.4 billion (Plunkett Research 2018). Components of the industry include sporting goods, advertising and marketing, professional sport, fitness and recreation, golf courses, racetracks, amusement and recreation, other spectator sports leagues, and NCAA sports (Miller and Washington 2012). Revenues for the top four professional sports leagues (NBA, MLB, NFL, NHL) in the United States exceed $21 billion. Major sporting events such as the Super Bowl, the NCAA basketball finals, the World Series, the NBA Finals, and the Kentucky Derby attract millions of viewers. *Forbes* magazine assessed the value of professional teams such as the Dallas Cowboys (NFL) as $4.0 billion, the New York Yankees (MLB) as $3.4 billion, and the New England Patriots (NFL) as $3.2 billion (Miller and Washington 2012). In addition, professional athletes such as LeBron James, Tom Brady, and Mike Trout earn millions of dollars in salaries and endorsements for playing their respective sports.

The future of the sport event industry seems bright. As the nature of sport evolves, so do the various events that make up the industry. New sports such as Footgolf have recently entered the market with hopes of gaining popularity. According to the American Footgolf League (2018), Footgolf was first organized in the Netherlands in 2008; the sport combines elements of soccer and golf, but is more closely related to golf. The rules largely correspond to the rules of golf; players kick a regulation size 5 soccer ball at a golf course facility on shortened holes with 21-inch diameter cups in as few shots as possible.

Technology has changed how sporting events are marketed. Social media sites such as Facebook, Twitter, YouTube, and Snapchat are now used to promote and market many sporting events. New media technologies like GoPros, camera drones, and GPS tracking devices are being used by corporations, athletes, and everyday participants in action sports (Thorpe 2017). As new technologies emerge, sport marketers will continue to reach out to new consumers through these new media. The impact of the media allows sport marketers to promote their product to a global audience. In addition, as the sport industry continues to grow, there may be a greater focus on specialization within event management. Although many organizations currently employ a limited number of employees responsible for event planning, this may change as the roles and duties become more specialized in one or more areas within the industry.

Although the future is bright, there are also some concerns regarding the future of sporting events. One of the primary concerns within the sport event industry is the **dropout rate** of youth sports participants. Research suggests that many youth drop out because of injury or a lack of enjoyment. Sport event planners must continue to examine new ways to build sport identity in youth. Often, sport identity is carried throughout a person's life span, and parents pass the torch of a favorite sport or team to a child. The sport event industry is largely driven by the youth market and the growth of travel teams, which has led to some real challenges. In particular, young athletes and their parents encounter rising participation costs as well as increasing demands. In the United States, the average daily rate for a hotel room has risen from $101.73 in 2011 to $126.72 in 2017, an increase of 24.6 percent. Youth athletes are also being asked to specialize at an earlier age and are engaged in year-round training programs.

Opponents also note the commercial nature of sport and the ever-increasing need for sponsorship. As the number of events continues to increase, the competition for sponsorship dollars becomes more competitive, with the largest events having a considerable advantage.

OLIVIER MORIN/AFP/Getty Images

New technologies such as camera drones have changed the way sporting events are marketed.

The increasing level of commercialism in sport is also evident when we consider the impact of the media. Televised sporting events are now scheduled according to the timing of commercial breaks and for peak audiences. Moreover, this commercialism has led to the development of some sports at the expense of others. For example, in the United Kingdom, the top 10 sports receive 90 percent of all the money spent on sponsorships (Masterman 2009).

Career Paths in Sport Event Management

As the sport industry continues to grow, so do the number of sport-related event management jobs. Almost every professional sport franchise and collegiate athletic program hires some type of event manager. Jobs with titles such as special events coordinator, game operations coordinator, director of events, and associate athletic director for event management can commonly be found in an organization's marketing department, event department, or facilities management department. An increasing number of opportunities for employment are available to students seeking entry into event management in the sport industry. Almost every organization in the various segments of the sport industry recognizes the importance of individual employees who specialize in planning and implementing different types of events.

According to the National Association of Sports Commissions (NASC) website (2017), more than 300 cities across the United States currently have a sports commission or similar type of entity focused on attracting small-scale, youth, or amateur sporting events, and although many of these organizations are small, their employees spend a large amount of time involved in event planning. In fact, the NASC offers a certified sports event executive (CSEE) designation for those members who complete educational sessions related to sales and marketing, strategic planning, event management, technology, revenue generation, and the bid process. The enormous growth in the number of sports commissions is evident when we consider that in 1993 only 30 such organizations were in existence (Kelly 2000). Sport **governing bodies** and **international federations** offer potential applicants various event management opportunities. Organizations such as the International Olympic Committee (IOC), the United States Olympic Committee (USOC), U.S. Masters Swimming, USA Volleyball, USA Swimming, and U.S. Lacrosse employ event managers. Also, amateur sanctioning bodies such as high school state athletic commissions (e.g., the Ohio High School Athletic Association), Little League Baseball, the Babe Ruth League, the Amateur Athletic Union (AAU), Pony Baseball and Softball, American Youth Football, and American Youth Cheer are involved in planning events and championships.

Students and others seeking event management jobs should be flexible and think creatively as to the types of organizations to which they may apply and where to find these jobs. For example, organizations such as Disney's Wide World of Sports and Universal Studios in Florida offer sport event management jobs. Numerous nonprofit associations (e.g., the NCAA's national office, the National Association of Collegiate Directors of Athletics) hire people to plan their conferences and seminars. Recreational sport jobs are another consideration because almost every locality has a parks and recreation department, and most college campuses employ event managers at their campus recreation facility. Even insurance companies like Globe Life and Accident employ sport marketers who are responsible for the planning and preparation of event schedules and executing sport marketing advertising for the company. Some of the best free websites to consult for finding sport event management jobs include TeamWork Online, the NCAA Market, the National Association of Sports Commissions Career Center, NIRSA's Bluefishjobs, and the NRPA Career Center. In addition, there are a number of fee-based websites such as Sports Job Board and Work in Sports.

Skills, Knowledge, and Traits for Success

Beyond the sport- and event-specific knowledge necessary to run an event, a number of skills are critical for success in sport event management. Perhaps the most important skill is the ability to manage and maintain a strong personal life. The long hours required by many jobs in the industry can have a detrimental effect on an event planner's personal life. In fact, you may not be able to have a professional career if you cannot effectively manage issues such as interpersonal relationships and finances. The ability to organize, prioritize, supervise, and delegate is second to the ability to manage your time and professional resources efficiently and effectively (Goldblatt 2011).

Staging an event requires a multitude of management and business skills, and event managers encompass skills that derive from a multitude of disciplines. Among others, event managers may have backgrounds in law, marketing, accounting, and human resource management (Masterman 2009). Event planning requires a great amount of attention to detail, and event planners must have the ability to conceptualize, recognize, and implement all the key details of the event. More importantly, these details must be coordinated within a limited time frame. Thus, you must be able to manage your time and resources effectively. As new technologies continue to emerge, the ability to manage and use these technologies is critical for the implementation and marketing of an event. Event planners work within a network of people and companies and must effectively manage a wide variety of interpersonal relationships. This section highlights some skills that all students should work to further develop.

Interpersonal and Communication Skills

Interpersonal skills allow a person to work effectively with others. Vitally important is the ability to get along with others and to span diverse relationships. As will be discussed later in the chapter, event planners must network with a wide variety of people and organizations. As events continue to globalize, it is important that event planners have the ability to function and interact with diverse groups of people who speak multiple languages. Interpersonal skills also include written and verbal communication. Event planners are required to make numerous telephone calls and attend personal meetings. Developing written reports and proposals is a common task. The ability to listen is another important skill that allows the event planner to meet the needs and wants of a client more effectively.

Time Management Skills

When we suggest that event planners should be effective time managers, we are essentially saying they should be able to multitask. Graham, Neirotti, and Goldblatt (2001) claim that the most common traits of sport event managers include the following:

- Comfortable with preparing and managing a checklist of activities
- Projects a positive attitude
- Can work independently or as a member of a team
- Accurate and quick at details
- Articulate on the telephone and in written and oral communication
- Creative and flexible
- Capable of working under extreme pressure for long hours
- Good at working with all levels of people, including volunteers
- Effective at balancing multiple projects simultaneously
- Excellent time manager
- Effective negotiator
- Finance- and budget-conscious
- Possesses good typing, word processing, and other office skills
- Has leadership ability
- Quick problem solver
- Good motivator
- Has the desire to learn and grow

A number of these traits involve the ability to multitask and manage one's time. Many event planners enjoy their jobs because of the variety of duties for which they are responsible. For example, one day may entail traveling to a destination for a site visit, while another day consists of negotiating a contract, writing a proposal, or attending meetings. Because of this wide variety of duties and the deadlines imposed by an event, planners must be good managers of their time. Remember, once the date of the event arrives, an event planner is either prepared or not. At this point, it is often too late to arrange for busing, to order decorations, to prepare extra food, or to negotiate a hotel contract. These tasks must be done in advance and require strong organizational and time management skills.

Technology Skills

Students graduating from colleges and universities in the 21st century should possess proficient technology skills; moreover, they are often expected by their more senior coworkers to be highly advanced in these areas. Of course there are expectations that students will graduate with an advanced working knowledge of social media such as Facebook, Twitter, YouTube, and Snapchat. In addition, students should be familiar with software packages such as Microsoft Office and other types of media such as blogs, videoconferencing, and mobile applications. However, students may graduate without learning about the various software packages unique to their particular industry. For example, many sport organizations use ticketing packages such as Ticketmaster, SRO4, or Paciolan, which are not taught in detail by most college or university sport management programs. In addition, an event planner may need to be able to mine for data, use various project management and customer relationship management (CRM) software packages, manage and develop websites, and understand some aspect of information technology (IT) security.

Students who know the type of jobs they will be seeking after graduation should do some research while they are still in school to determine the technology skills required for their jobs of choice. Research can be done online through the Internet, by visiting trade journals, or even during informational interviews that many students are required to complete during their course work. Most of all, an event planner must be flexible and willing to adapt. New technologies are constantly being introduced in the industry. An example is the partnership between ShotTracker and Klay Thompson from the Golden State Warriors to launch a virtual basketball camp with his workouts and drills. ShotTracker manufactures wearable technology for players that analyzes the path of their shots by using two sensors, one of which is placed inside a wristband or shooting sleeve, and one of which attaches to the hoop itself (Barker 2016).

Sport Events Versus Nonsport Events

An event is a carefully crafted experience delivered to make an impact on the person in attendance. The event is staged and choreographed with such precision and polish that the mechanics are imperceptible to the consumer (Silvers 2004). Regardless of the type, event planning requires people who can design the event, manage human and material resources, plan strategically, conceptualize the logistics of the event, manage time effectively, and forecast and budget finances. People who have such skills can effectively manage a sport or a nonsport event. For example, event planners are needed for events such as corporate board meetings, business meetings, client appreciation events, executive retreats, fund-raising galas, incentive travel and premium programs, product launches, professional conferences, special events, teleconferences, webcasts, conventions and expositions, corporate shows, and trade shows (Allen 2009). The fundamental skills necessary for planning such events are no different from the skills needed for planning a sport event.

Sport events are different from nonsport events in the sense that some form of competition involving physical prowess is involved. They are planned and organized throughout the world for men and women, for those who are disabled and those who are not, using single and multisport formats. They offer varying competition formats (from one-day tournaments to year-round championships), cater to people of varying levels of ability (from elite athletes to recreational users), and are marketed to both active participants and passive spectators (Masterman 2009). The emotional element of sport is another unique characteristic that distinguishes it from other types of events. Sport marketers use this emotional element in their advertising by focusing on the drama of a sporting contest or matchup between star players. Depending on the type of sport, external factors such as the weather at an outdoor event may have a considerable impact on the success of the event. Sport is also a cultural phenomenon and can differ based on geography. For example, North Americans are apt to consider jogging and walking as recreational and fitness pursuits, whereas Europeans may consider them sporting pursuits (Weed and Bull 2004). In addition, geography and culture also dictate the types of sporting events that are popular in certain regions. Events such as skiing and snowboarding are likely to be more popular in mountainous areas, whereas surfing and fishing events tend to be more popular in coastal regions.

Unlike the case with the competitive and physical nature of sport, events such as meetings and conventions often revolve around a particular trade and are educational in nature. Most corporate meetings and events are discretionary and are held only if management deems them necessary. For example, incentive trips, recognition programs, and product introductions can be canceled if employees fall short of quotas, if nobody is worthy of recognition, or if products are not innovative enough to be introduced. In contrast, association conventions are obligatory and more predictable than corporate meetings and events. The bylaws for an association such as the National Association of Collegiate Directors of Athletics (NACDA) may require an annual convention for members that revolves around board and leadership meetings and concurrent educational sessions.

Depending on economic conditions, corporate and association meetings and events also differ. In tough economic times, fewer corporate events may be planned, whereas associations are more resilient and their events may be greater in number (Hoyle 2002). Although sporting events are not resistant to the challenges of tough economies, sport has often been considered recession-proof and a form of stress relief for active participants and spectators alike during tough times. Furthermore, in cases where governing bodies are involved, such as the Olympics, there are certain requirements for participation.

Sport Tourism

Sport tourism has become a global phenomenon and an increasingly important topic of study in the field of sport management. In the United States, sport tourism has become a significant economic activity for many regions (Kurtzman and Zauhar 1998; Eugenio-Martin 2003). In 2015, a state of the industry report by the National Association of Sports Commissions (2016) estimated visitor spending associated with sport events to be $9.45 billion. The revenue generated in the global sport tourism market in 2017 was estimated to be around $90.9 billion and analysts predict the global sport tourism market will grow at a compound annual growth rate (CAGR) of 41.45 percent between 2017 and 2021 (Research and Markets 2018; Statista 2018).

As suggested earlier in the chapter, sporting events have required some form of travel since the early days in Greece. Many current sporting events are family-oriented or youth events that travel between various destinations. Sport tourism is defined as leisure-based travel that takes people temporarily outside of their home communities to participate in or watch physical activities or to revere attractions associated with physical activities (Gibson 1998). Sport tourism has also been defined as "travel to and participation in or attendance at a predetermined sport activity" (Turco, Riley, and Swart 2002). The destination receives many economic, social, and psychological benefits from hosting an event.

At this point, it may be helpful to explain sport tourism by breaking it into two separate parts: one focused on sport and the other on tourism. Sport has been defined as a range of competitive and noncompetitive active pursuits involving skill, strategy, and chance in which human beings engage simply for enjoyment and training or to raise their performance to levels of publicly acclaimed excellence (Standeven and DeKnop 1999). It has also been described as a pursuit that builds character, teaches values, encourages healthy competition, provides an outlet for aggression, and promotes international friendship and understanding (Kurtzman and Zauhar 2003). Three characteristics are unique to sport: (1) Each sport has its own set of rules; (2) sport encompasses a continuum from elite competition to recreational sport or sport for all; and (3) sport is characterized by its playful nature (Higham and Hinch 2003).

Tourism has been defined in many ways, but it generally refers to travel away from a person's place of residence. Thus, tourism has the following four characteristics: (1) It entails traveling to and from a destination along with an overnight stay outside one's permanent residence; (2) a tourist's movement to and from a destination is temporary, is short term, and includes an intention to return to a permanent place of residence; (3) the destination is visited for purposes other than taking up permanent residence or employment; and (4) the activities the tourist engages in are distinct from those of the local resident and working populations of the place visited (Reisinger 2001). For the destination, there are a number of benefits such as enhancing economic impact and the social and psychological benefits of hosting an event.

Types of Sport Tourism

According to Gibson (1998), there are generally three types of sport tourism: (1) event sport tourism, (2) active sport tourism, and (3) nostalgia-based sport tourism. Event sport tourism generally refers to passive spectators attending an event. Examples of event sport tourism include mega-events such as the Olympic Games, the Pan American Games, the Super Bowl, the World Series, and the World Cup. It may also encompass tournaments hosted by the Professional Golf Association (PGA), the Amateur Athletic Union, or a college sport club. Active sport tourism refers to resorts and other segments of the hospitality industry such as golf courses, ski resorts, and country clubs. There has been a growing demand for active vacations since the 1980s, and the highest rates of participation for these activities generally stem from people between 25 and 34 years of age with household incomes between $50,000 and $75,000. The active sport tourist is likely to be male, affluent, and college educated; is willing to travel long distances to participate; tends to participate in the sport repeatedly; and is likely to engage in active sport tourism well into retirement. Nostalgia sport tourism includes sport-related attractions such as a hall of fame, sport museum, or stadium. According to Fairley (2003), nostalgia and memory are inextricably linked because you cannot have feelings of nostalgia without the memory or perceptions of how things used to be. Many professional sports teams market the concept of nostalgia with old-timers' games and nostalgic uniforms from days gone by in an effort to attract an older demographic of people who grew up watching those teams. Gordon (2013) notes that nostalgia sport tourism may include active travel to relive the nostalgia from a previous trip or celebrate a national championship team from years ago.

Types of Sport Tourism

Event Sport Tourism

Tourist is a passive spectator

- College football game
- FIFA World Cup
- MLB World Series
- NCAA Tournament
- NFL Super Bowl
- Olympic Games
- Pan American Games
- PGA Tournament

Active Sport Tourism

Tourist is an active participant

- Golfing at a resort in Phoenix, Arizona
- Rock climbing in Utah
- Running a marathon in Boston
- Skiing in Vail, Colorado
- Surfing in Hawaii
- Trekking in India

Nostalgia Sport Tourism

Tourist venerates sport attraction; memories of sport

- Memories garnered from uniforms at an old-timers' game
- Memories in traveling to a sporting place
- Touring Wrigley Field in Chicago
- Visiting a soccer museum in Brazil
- Visiting the Baseball Hall of Fame in Cooperstown, New York

Whether you realize it or not, you have probably consumed some type of sport tourism during the course of your life. Can you identify what type of tourism the following people are consuming?

- A fan traveling to Cooperstown, New York, to the Baseball Hall of Fame
- A marathon runner traveling to Massachusetts for the Boston Marathon
- A skier traveling to Vail, Colorado
- A spectator traveling to the Super Bowl in New Orleans, Louisiana
- An AAU basketball player traveling to Chicago, Illinois, to play in a tournament
- Parents of the AAU basketball player traveling to watch the tournament in Chicago

Motivation for Sport Tourism

A tourist's decision to travel may be influenced by a number of social factors such as family, reference groups, social classes, culture, and subculture (Moutinho 2001). Sport event planners should take these factors into account when marketing their events. For example, the sport of quidditch is marketed in a unique way based on its subculture. Although you will not often find this sport on television, it became popular because of the Harry Potter books and movies and is marketed to thousands of young people via Facebook (Carbonell 2012). Schools such as Harvard, UCLA, and Texas A&M have quidditch teams. Esport is also on the rise as it attracts a younger demographic and spectators who want to be part of a community that traditionally communicates online.

Tourists can also be segmented based on their purposes for traveling. Robinson and Gammon (2004) distinguish between *sport tourism*, where the major purpose of a visit is sport, and *tourism sport*, where the tourist engages in sport as a secondary pursuit. For example, many people travel to places like Miami or New Orleans with the primary purpose of attending the Super Bowl or to Augusta, Georgia, for the Masters Golf Tournament or to Churchill Downs in Louisville, Kentucky, for the express purpose of witnessing the Kentucky Derby. Other travelers may be visiting Chicago for a business convention but have enough discretionary time to attend a Chicago Cubs Major League Baseball game. Why a tourist consumes sport can be attributed to a wide variety of motivational factors, including stress alleviation, group affiliation, escape, drama, aesthetics, vicarious achievement, gaining knowledge, or interacting with family and friends.

Sport is also widely marketed as entertainment, and many spectators attend for reasons beyond just watching the players on the field. Major sporting events also include fancy halftime shows, on-field contests, and promotional giveaways. Relaxation and pleasure are common motivational factors for many tourists, and some fans use sport tourism as a way to escape from understimulation and boredom or from overstimulation and stress (Moutinho 2001; Wann, Allen, and Rochelle 2004).

Actors in Sport Tourism

Sport tourism has been described using a theatrical analogy suggesting that players represent the actors, sport spectators are the audience members, and the stadium or arena is the theater (Thwaites and Chadwick 2005). However, by digging deeper we find that a number of other actors engage in sport tourism, starting with the event planner. An event planner may be employed by a variety of different organizations, many of which include **rightsholder organizations (RHOs)** and **destination marketing organizations (DMOs)**. RHOs are organizations that own the rights to one or more events and are usually responsible for planning, organizing, and controlling the event. For example, the NFL owns the rights to the Super Bowl, and the American Cancer Society owns the rights to the Relay for Life event. A number of events rights holders are classified as governing bodies, which are sport organizations that have a regulatory or sanctioning function. USA Table Tennis is an example of a governing body that owns multiple events; this organization controls four events but sanctions more than 300 different table tennis competitions. DMOs are organizations that represent a specific destination and thus help the long-term development of communities through a travel and tourism strategy (Destination Marketing Association International 2012). DMOs include organizations such as sports commissions, convention and visitors bureaus, chambers of commerce, and other similar entities that serve as a link or point of contact for convention, business, and leisure travelers.

The integration of sport and tourism means event planners must be capable of collaborating with a network of different organizations or actors. These sport event networks may include event RHOs, DMOs, tourist attractions (e.g., local museums, battlefields), rental companies (e.g., rental cars), airlines, sport venues, accommodation providers (e.g., hotels, motels, campgrounds), local businesses, media, sponsors, stadium authorities, and sport governing bodies (e.g., IOC, USOC). This network of organizations must be committed to working together to plan and implement a successful event. To create a committed network, each organization within the network must provide resources and exhibit trust toward the others (Shonk and Bravo 2010).

All actors within the network seek to leverage the event. According to Chalip (2004), **leveraging an event** refers to the activities surrounding a sport event itself that seek to maximize the long-term benefit of the event. Chalip suggests that leveraging "begins by encouraging visitor spending and retaining the visitors' expenditures within the host economy by fostering the tourists' spending and lengthening their stay" (p. 230). For this reason, many events have other activities surrounding the larger event to encourage multiple-night stays and increased spending at restaurants and other attractions. For example, the NFL owns the rights to the NFL Experience, which they market as an exciting continuous event surrounding the Super Bowl. It has an interactive theme park offering participatory games, displays, entertainment attractions, kids' football clinics, free autograph sessions, and the largest football memorabilia show ever.

Relationship Between Sport Event Management and Sport Facility Management

All sporting events require a functional host facility. For event rights holders (e.g., AAU, NCAA), the event venue is the most important factor for determining the site of a nonfixed sporting event that travels between venues (O'Connor and Martin 2009). Event planners are often responsible for negotiating the type of venue to be used for the sporting event. As the event planner negotiates with potential host facilities, she must maintain a realistic image of the prestige of the event. Event venues are generally either public or privately owned facilities. The public facilities may include venues such as armories, municipal stadiums and arenas, convention centers, and fairgrounds, and they may be more flexible in negotiations (Supovitz 2005). An example of a public facility is the Kentucky Exposition Center. Privately owned facilities are generally in the business of making money and are less flexible. Joe Dumars Fieldhouse in Shelby Township, Michigan, is a good example of a privately owned sport facility.

Event planners spend a significant amount of time working with facility managers, who are key stakeholders in the sporting event network. A facility manager may work for a stadium authority, arena, convention center, armory, or any other of a number of facilities. He is responsible for coordinating all of the employees and entities involved in the facility to ensure they meet both short- and long-term goals. In some cases, the facility manager must work with outside vendors or government entities to secure permits. The facility manager may also be responsible for building design and thus may choose material color schemes or purchase new equipment. He may also need to ensure that contracts are fulfilled in addition to maintaining the building and all corresponding equipment (Fried 2009). Before an event, the facility manager may need to provide the event planner with certain field specifications and help coordinate the design and layout of the sport venue. In addition, the facility manager may discuss issues such as security and concession and merchandise layouts with the event planner, and may also be responsible for coordinating the walk-through for a site visit before the sporting event.

Types of Sporting Events

Because of the broad scope of sport, numerous types of sporting events can be planned. The various types of events may differ based on their scope and scale along with the type of market they target. In this section, we discuss the following types of sport events: action and extreme events, cross-cultural events, events for people with disabilities, family events, fixed and nonfixed events, international events, mega-events, multisport events, multiple-location events, senior events, small-scale events, and youth events. Table 1.1 provides an overview of these types of events.

Action and Extreme Events

New action and extreme sport events have emerged in recent years. These types of sports are traditionally outside the mainstream and the athletes often assume considerable risk. In 2018, the Red Bull Cliff Diving World Series made stops in Texas, United States; Bilbao, Spain; São Miguel, Azores, Portugal; Sisikon, Switzerland; Copenhagen, Denmark; Mostar, Bosnia and Herzegovina; and Polignano a Mare, Italy, with athletes free-falling from up to 27 meters (90 ft) with awe-inducing acrobatics. Other popular extreme sport events include the Dew Tour and the X Games. The Dew Tour hosts five multisport skateboarding, BMX, and motocross events across the United States. The Winter Dew Tour features freeskiing and snowboarding events. The X Games are an Olympic-style extreme sport event hosting annual summer and winter competitions. The focus on emerging extreme sports makes these events attractive to a new generation of sports fans.

What is more important to event organizers is that these events provide a valuable connection between sponsors and young, active consumers. For example, Gatorade is the naming rights sponsor for the amateur extreme sports tour, Gatorade Free Flow Tour. Gatorade has the opportunity to extend its brand beyond traditional sports through 50 summer and 10 winter competitions (Mickle 2009).

Cross-Cultural Events

Cross-cultural events involve interactions between members of different cultural groups. The Olympic Games are the greatest example of a cross-cultural event. Such events bring people of different backgrounds together or give people of one culture an opportunity to experience another culture. When staging a cross-cultural event, it is important to understand the cultural norms of the participants and the location. Event organizers need to appreciate differences between cultures because something that is acceptable in one country may be unacceptable in another. For example, religious differences may prohibit play on certain days or limit dietary options.

Events for People With Disabilities

A variety of sporting events exist for persons with either physical or intellectual disabilities. Some are traditional sports adapted for people with physical disabilities (wheelchair basketball and sledge hockey), while others have been created specifically for disabled participants (goalball and torball).

The preeminent event for persons with physical disabilities is the Paralympic Games, a multisport, multicountry event governed by the International Paralympic Committee (IPC) and held in conjunction with the Olympic Games. Originally staged for rehabilitation, the Paralympics have grown into a major international sporting event featuring the top disabled athletes in the world. In the PyeongChang 2018 Paralympic Games, 567 athletes from 49 delegations competed in 80 medal

TABLE 1.1 Overview of Types of Sport Events

Type of event	Definition	Example
Action and extreme sports	Sports that are traditionally outside the mainstream and where the athletes often assume considerable risk	Red Bull Cliff Diving World Series Dew Tour Gatorade Free Flow Tour
Cross-cultural events	Sport events that involve interactions between members of different cultural groups	Olympic Games
Events for people with disabilities	Sports that are adapted for people with physical disabilities, or sports created specifically for disabled participants	Paralympic Games Deaflympics Extremity Games Special Olympics Goalball Torball
Family events	Events that provide families with opportunities to gather and enjoy sport	Fishing Derby All-American Soap Box Derby
Fixed and nonfixed events	Fixed events: events that occur each year in the same place Nonfixed events: annual sport events that take place at a different location each year	Fixed events: Kentucky Derby, Masters Golf Tournament, Little League World Series Nonfixed events: AAU Basketball Tournament, NCAA Men's and Women's Final Four
International events	Sport events involving more than one country	Olympic Games Asian Games Pan American Games Commonwealth Games Tour de France British Open
Mega-events	Large short-term, high-profile events capable of having a significant impact on their host community or country	Olympic Games FIFA World Cup
Multisport events	Sport events that feature competitions in a variety of sports in a host city or host region	Olympic Games Pan American Games Maccabiah Games World Police and Fire Games
Multiple-location events	Sport events where competition takes place in several different cities or in the same city but in multiple venues	FIFA World Cup Olympic Games
Senior events	Sport events specifically targeting older adults	National Senior Games Senior League Softball World Series
Small-scale events	Regular-season sport competitions that use existing infrastructure and need less public support for hosting	Salem Red Sox vs Frederick Keys baseball game
Youth events	Sport events targeting children 18 and younger	Columbia Invitational Memorial Day soccer tournament Little League World Series

BOB MARTIN FOR OIS/IOC/AFP/Getty Images

A variety of sporting events exist for persons with either physical or intellectual disabilities, such as the Paralympics.

events across six sports. Athletes compete in 26 different summer and winter sports in six different classifications according to their disability: amputee, cerebral palsy, visual impairment, spinal cord injuries, intellectual disability, and a group that includes all those who do not fit into the aforementioned groups.

Similarly, the Deaflympics is an elite sport competition for people with hearing impairments. Summer and winter games are held every four years, and athletes compete in 25 sports. According to the International Committee of Sports for the Deaf, the 23rd Summer Deaflympics in Samsun, Turkey, in 2017 attracted 2,873 athletes from 86 countries competing in 18 sports with 21 disciplines.

The Extremity Games are an extreme sport competition for people with physical impairments. Organized by the Athletes With Disabilities Network (ADN), the Extremity Games have many of the same sports you would find in other extreme sport events. The Extremity Games 4 (eX4) in Michigan included competitions in skateboarding, rock climbing, wakeboarding, kayaking, mountain biking, and motocross.

The most prominent event for people with intellectual disabilities is the Special Olympics. Founded as a series of summer camps by Eunice Kennedy Shriver in 1962, the event grew into an international competition by 1968. Today there are local and national competitions in more than 160 countries, with more than 2.5 million athletes competing in 30 different sports. The events are based on a philosophy that people with intellectual disabilities can learn and benefit from participation in sports.

Family Events

Family events provide families with opportunities to gather and enjoy sport. In these events, family togetherness and educational components often take precedence over competition. An example of an event often designed with family in mind is a fishing derby, where adults and youth spend time together fishing. Many of these events have games, contests, and educational components on water safety and fishing techniques. Another good example is the All-American Soap Box Derby. Since 1934, children have built and raced nonmotorized cars (All-American Soap Box Derby 2009). Winners of local events can move on to race in the world championship finals. In addition to the races, there are several educational and entertainment programs for families.

Some organizations have added family-friendly elements to their events in order to widen their appeal. The National Soccer Festival, a collegiate soccer event in Fort Wayne, Indiana, draws some of the top collegiate soccer teams in the country. Organizers have turned this into a family event by adding activities attractive to youth soccer participants and their families. To appeal to families, the event features live music, youth soccer clinics, activities for kids, and a variety of food vendors in addition to autograph and photo sessions. This combination of activities has created an event that draws large crowds in addition to quality competition (Bogle 2008).

Fixed and Nonfixed Events

Fixed events are sport events that occur each year in the same place. For example, the Kentucky Derby occurs on the first Saturday in May every year at Churchill Downs in Louisville, Kentucky. Annual sport events that take place at a different location each year are called nonfixed events. Examples are the NCAA Men's and Women's Basketball Final Four, which occur every year, but at a different location.

International Events

Many major sporting events are international in nature. It is now easier than ever for athletes to play in other countries and for fans to access events taking place in other countries (Lizandra and Gladden 2015). Some international events, such as the Olympics, the Asian Games, the Pan American Games, and the Commonwealth Games, have different countries competing in multiple sports. Others bring together multiple countries competing in one sport, such as world championship events. Still others, such as the Tour de France and the British Open, feature the best individual athletes from around the world.

From a marketing standpoint, the global appeal of these sports can be very attractive to broadcasters and sponsors. For example, Formula One, an auto racing series featuring drivers and race teams from around the world, can be watched either live or by tape delay in more than 200 countries. Races attract millions of viewers across Europe and in other major markets such as China and Brazil.

International events can also be used to promote a sport or sport entity. American sports have extended their reach beyond borders through international exhibitions or tournaments. The World Baseball Classic, created by Major League Baseball in 2006 and sanctioned by the International Baseball Federation, provides a format for the top players from around the world to compete while promoting the sport internationally. The National Football League hosted international exhibitions, called the American Bowl, from 1986 to 2005 in countries such as Great Britain, Ireland, Germany, Japan, Spain, Australia, and Canada to promote the sport abroad. Since then the NFL has hosted regular-season games in Mexico City and London.

Mega-Events

Mega-events are large short-term, high-profile events capable of having a significant impact on their host community or country (Hiller 2000). Such sporting events as the Olympics and the FIFA World Cup are large enough to qualify as mega-events because of their size in terms of prestige, public involvement, social and political influence, media coverage, and economic impact (Getz 2005). These events are generally referred to as first-order mega-events.

While events like the Commonwealth Games, the World Military Games, and the World University Games are also international in scope, Cornelissen (2004) refers to them as second-order mega-events because they are smaller in terms of their extent and level of participation than first-order events. Sport mega-events that are still more limited in scope are called third-order events and may include regional or continental tournaments.

Mega-events can have a significant economic impact through tourism, infrastructure improvements, and economic development. Mega-events also attract interest far beyond the event itself. For example, it is estimated that 50,000 people who will not attend the game travel to the Super Bowl's host city each year (Super Bowl XLVII New Orleans Host Committee 2012). These people go there to attend meetings, parties, and other festivities that surround the event. Beyond the economic impact these events generate, mega-events often create a legacy in the city or country where they are held. For example, local organizers of the 2010 FIFA World Cup in South Africa hoped the event would leave a lasting legacy much more important than soccer. According to Danny Jordan, executive director of the organizing committee, the event was about nation building and country branding. Through the event, they hoped to drive trade, investment, and tourism to the country (Allmers and Maennig 2009). Even prior to the 2018 FIFA World Cup in Russia, the organization had put out facts and figures regarding its impact and legacy, including 12 stadiums, 96 training sites, 27 new hotels, 13,000 people involved in the construction and renovation of 10 stadiums, and 100,000 jobs created and supported by the event (FIFA, 2018).

Events of this nature involve extensive logistical planning and require significant political and taxpayer support to be successful. For example, the bidding process for the Olympic Games is lengthy and costly. The Olympic Games are normally awarded by the International Olympic Committee (IOC) either seven or eleven years prior to the event. According to Vomiero (2018), the cost of hosting both the Summer and the Winter Games has gone up consistently since 1960. The 2012 London Games were the most expensive Summer Games, costing $15 billion; and Sochi 2014 was the most expensive Winter Games, costing over $20 billion. Beijing was awarded the 2022 Winter Olympic Games only after six cities dropped potential or official bids, mostly on account of these enormous costs.

Multisport Events

Multisport events feature competitions in a host city or host region in a variety of sports. These events often bring together participants from different sports competing under a common theme or organized for a specific community. Although the Olympics are the most notable multisport event, numerous others exist to serve different purposes. Examples of multisport events include the following:

- Amateur Athletic Union's Junior Olympic Games: the largest national multisport event for youth in the United States
- Maccabiah Games: an event for Jewish athletes
- Pan American Games: an event open to countries in North, South, and Central America
- World Police and Fire Games: an event for active and retired police officers and firefighters

Hosting a successful multisport event requires long-term planning, a variety of competition venues, available hotel space, and willing community partners. Although the logistics of managing several different sporting events can be daunting, the advantages of having all the athletes competing in one location can be substantial. Specifically, these events tend to draw more participants and spectators, creating a more exciting event and a better economic return for the host (Chavis 2008). The Mediterranean Games are a multisport competition, featuring Europe, Asia, and Africa, organized within the Olympic Movement. The XVIII Mediterranean Games held in Tarragona, Spain, featured 33 sport disciplines. During the ten days of competition, the games attracted 4,000 athletes from 26 different countries, 1,000 judges and representatives of the International

Federations and the International Committee of the Games, 1,000 journalists from all over the world, 3,500 volunteers to cover the needs of the organization, more than 150,000 spectators (which will impact more than 3,000 indirect jobs), and 70 to 80 professionals working for the organizational structure of the games.

Multiple-Location Events

Events that span multiple locations present special challenges. Competition may take place in several different cities (e.g., soccer's World Cup) or in the same city but at multiple venues (e.g., the Olympics). Smaller events can also take place at multiple venues. For example, a volleyball tournament may be staged in multiple gyms while ancillary events such as practices, banquets, and awards ceremonies take place in additional facilities. The complexity of managing multiple sites makes it difficult for one person, or one group of people, to efficiently manage all operations at once.

To manage multiple-location events, organizers often assign a management team to each venue, creating events within an event. This type of structure allows for more immediate decision-making and tighter control over activities. Venue-specific staffing allows the flexibility to deal with issues unique to that location or activity. Typically, venue staff are given the authority to deal with local issues. Larger issues are the responsibility of the main event staff.

Senior Events

Numerous senior events exist for older participants. The Summer National Senior Games are the largest multisport event in the world for seniors. The games are organized by the National Senior Games Association, a nonprofit member of the United States Olympic Committee. The 2019 Senior Games in Albuquerque, New Mexico, took place over a two-week period, attracting 10,000 athletes age 50 or older who competed in 20 different sports. The 2009 National Senior Games in San Francisco attracted more than 10,000 athletes over the age of 50 to participate in 18 medal and 7 demonstration sports. Organizers estimated that 20,000 visitors attended the games, generating $35 million in economic impact (Dremann 2009). In addition to the national games, the organization supports and sanctions member-state competitions.

According to the Louisville Senior Games organizers, senior events are lucrative because senior athletes tend to have high incomes, eat at upscale restaurants, and take advantage of local attractions (Shafer 2007). Even smaller senior events can have a significant impact on the local economy. The Senior League Softball World Series costs $225,000 to organize and operate, but it delivers an estimated economic impact of $1.2 million (Shortridge 2009).

Small-Scale Events

Small-scale sport events include regular-season competitions that use existing infrastructure and need less public support for hosting (Gibson, Kaplanidou, and Kang 2012). An example of a small-scale event would be a minor league Class-A baseball game between the Salem Red Sox and the Frederick Keys. The city of Frederick, Maryland, benefits from the Keys' 70 home game schedule when spectators and visitors attend games and purchase hotel rooms, meals, gas, merchandise, and other items from local businesses. Some research on small-scale events suggests that net expenditures associated with small-scale sport events benefits not only the host economy, but it also spurs the production of goods and services directly demanded as well as the production of supplier activities (Amador et al. 2017).

Youth Events

The youth sport market has been steadily growing over the last decade, making youth sports a lucrative industry. While statistics in 2017 from the Sport Fitness Industry Association and the Aspen Institute Sports & Society Program suggest that the percentage of kids playing sports continues to decrease in the United States, the total number of kids playing

As the youth sport market continues to grow, youth sports is becoming a lucrative industry.

continues to increase because of population growth (O'Connor 2018). In addition to the participants themselves, youth sports also tend to attract significant numbers of coaches and family members, which can generate important business for restaurants and hotels as well as for the organizers. For example, the Columbia Invitational Memorial Day soccer tournament attracts approximately 9,000 youth athletes to Maryland, generating a sizable economic impact (Sharrow 2009). From 2009 to 2011, Indianapolis attracted 155,000 visitors for amateur sport events who paid for approximately 62,000 hotel room nights and spent an estimated $62 million (Cutter 2009).

Sponsors also see opportunities with youth sports. In 2017, Target committed $14 million to local youth soccer through two national initiatives: an $8 million local soccer grant program, and a $6 million partnership with the U.S. Soccer Foundation to build 100 new soccer spaces by the year 2020 (Target 2017). The inaugural ESPN Rise Games featured competitions for athletes 10 to 19 years old in the sports of baseball, basketball, field hockey, and track and field at Disney's Wide World of Sports Complex in July of 2009. Media companies such as ESPN, along with sponsors Target, Champion, Powerade, and Under Armour, saw this event as an opportunity to reach young consumers while they are making brand decisions (Mickle 2009).

Management of youth sport events can differ significantly from adult sporting events. Martens (2001) identifies several issues that affect sport programs. First, the needs of the participants must be balanced against the needs of the adults. Although the events are for the young athletes, it is often the parents or the coaches who make the events possible and make decisions as to whether or not their athletes or their teams participate. Second, the role of competition can vary greatly across youth sport events. Each event has to address whether the focus is competition, with winning being the ultimate reward, or whether the event is recreational, emphasizing participation over winning. The following is a list of some of the larger youth sport governing bodies:

- Amateur Athletic Union
- American Junior Golf Association
- American Youth Soccer Association
- Babe Ruth Baseball
- Little League Baseball
- Pony Baseball and Softball
- Pop Warner
- U.S. Youth Soccer
- USA Football
- USA Hockey

Summary

Sport event management has evolved from the early days of athletes celebrating the end of the harvest by traveling from city to city within ancient Greece, to the lucrative and specialized industry it is today. As the sport industry continues to grow, so do the number of sport-related event management jobs. Almost every professional sports franchise and collegiate athletic program hires some type of event manager. Today's sport event planner must be able to manage his personal life along with having strong conceptual, interpersonal, technical, and time management skills. The event planner must also be able to negotiate with sport event venues and recognize the importance of sport tourism and the need for collaborating with a wide variety of network organizations.

Sporting events can also be quite diverse, and each type of event presents its own opportunities and challenges for event organizers. Events vary in size from small-scale and local events to mega-events such as the Olympics and the FIFA World Cup. Events also vary in the groups they reach, because competitions for young participants, seniors, and disabled spectators each appeal to a different demographic. The challenge for event organizers is to be mindful of the needs of different groups and different sports.

LEARNING ACTIVITIES

TIME MANAGEMENT SKILLS

The chapter describes a number of time management skills that are critical for sport event managers. The skills listed include projecting a positive attitude, working independently or as a member of a team, being accurate and quick at details, articulate on the telephone and in written and oral communication, creative and flexible, capable of working under extreme pressure for long hours, good at working with all levels of people, including volunteers, effective at balancing multiple projects simultaneously, being an excellent time manager, effective negotiator, being finance- and budget-conscious, possessing good typing, word processing, and other office skills, leadership ability, being able to solve problems quickly, being a good motivator, and having the desire to learn and grow.

Now, choose three of the skills listed above. *In detail*, write one paragraph for each of these three skills. For example, you could start the first paragraph with the words "I am very effective at balancing multiple projects simultaneously." Then you need to show how you have done this in the past. You might start by saying, "This summer I did an internship where I was responsible for recruiting volunteers and registering participants at a soccer event. I received both multiple volunteer forms and multiple registration forms every day. I had to multitask so I could process all these forms." Your paragraph should be at least four or five sentences long and offer insight into how and why you are good at the skill. This information can also be used in a cover letter or a resume for a future job application.

THE SPORT OF KABBADI

Kabbadi is a combative sport that has been played in India for many decades. There is currently a Pro Kabaddi League in India. However, most people could not describe the sport if you were to ask them. Do an internet search to learn more about Kabaddi. Based on what you have read, describe Kabaddi and some of the rules of the game. What are some ways you might market the sport of Kabaddi to tourists? What are some other sports you might include along with Kabaddi in a multisport event?

CASE STUDY: SPORTS AND INDIA

India is a country of about 1.3 billion people in South Asia. While the most popular sport in India is cricket, other sports have garnered interest in recent years. According to the firm of Ernst & Young (2017), seven new sports leagues were developed between 2012 and 2016, including a Premier Badminton League, Pro Kabaddi League, International Premier Soccer League, Indian Super League (soccer), Universal Basketball Alliance, Pro Wrestling League, and Premier Futsal League. Perhaps the largest growth can be seen in the Indian Super League (ISL), for which television viewership grew from 207 million in 2015 to 224 million in 2016. Star India, which owns the digital rights of the ISL, has seen viewership more than double from 41 million in 2015 to 110 million in 2016 on its Hotstar mobile streaming app. In addition, viewership for the Pro Kabaddi League grew 51 percent from 2012 to 2016.

Adventure and action sports are also popular in India. For example, white water rafting is popular in the ancient town of Rishikesh, known as the Gate to the Himalayas, and the best place for rafting the Ganges River. Auli, located in the northern part of India, is one of the major skiing destinations in the Himalayas. Hang gliding is popular in the State of Himachal Pradesh, and the mountain ranges of the Himalayas are popular spots for trekking and ice climbing. The white sandy beaches and clear blue waters of the Andaman and Nicobar group of islands are great places in India for scuba diving (Tourism on the Edge 2014).

Rahul Bhatnagar is the director general of the Sports Authority of India (SAI), which is part of the government of India. The SAI exists to promote capacity building for broad-basing sports and to achieve excellence in various competitive events at both the national and international levels as well as to plan, construct, acquire, develop, take over, manage, maintain, and utilize sports infrastructure and facilities in the country. Bhatnagar notes that sport has traditionally been given very low priority in India, thus there has been a lack of an evolving sports culture. Of the more than 700 million children and youth in the country, less than 50 million have access to organized, competitive sport (Ministry of Youth Affairs and Sports 2018).

While historically India has not been noted for hosting sport events, the Indian Olympic Association announced in April 2018 their plans to bid on three major sport events: the 2026 Youth Olympics, the 2030 Asian Games, and the 2032 Summer Olympics. In 2017, the capital city of New Delhi hosted the International Shooting Sports Federation's World Cup, which included the three shooting disciplines of pistol, rifle, and shotgun that are included in the Olympics. New Delhi also hosted the International Table Tennis World Tour in 2017. For the third time, the Asian Athletics Championships (a continental athletics event) were hosted in New Delhi at Ranchi's new Mega Sports Complex. Finally, Kochi, Kolkata, New Delhi, Goa, Guwahati, and Navi Mumbai played host to the 2017 FIFA U17 World Cup with athletes from 24 nations and 6 soccer confederations. The 2010 Commonwealth Games in Delhi were the largest international multisport event in India. The games were host to 6,081 athletes from 71 Commonwealth nations competing in 21 sports and 272 events. The opening and closing ceremonies were held at the Jawaharlal Nehru Stadium, the main stadium of the event. It was the first time that the Commonwealth Games were held in India and the second time they were held in Asia after Kuala Lumpur, Malaysia, in 1998.

Case Study Application

1. Your task is to market India as a sport tourism destination. Create a short promotional flyer that would appeal to either an event sport tourist, an active sport tourist, or a nostalgic sport tourist, or all three.
2. The chapter describes a number of types of events (e.g., multisport events, multiple location events, cross-cultural events). Choose one of the events outlined in the case study and discuss how it falls under one or more of these types of events.

3. In the case study, Rahul Bhatnagar (the sports secretary of India) suggests that less than 50 million of the more than 700 million children in India have access to organized, competitive sport. Describe three to five activities or initiatives that you would suggest for enhancing youth sport in India.
4. According to the case study, India would like to bid on the 2032 Olympic Games. Do some further research on India and outline two or three ways you would promote India as the host of this type of first-order mega-event. Also, outline the two or three largest obstacles you believe India will face in terms of bidding on the Olympics.

Ben Ryan/SOPA Images/LightRocket via Getty Images

CHAPTER 2

Event Conceptualization

CHAPTER OBJECTIVES

After completing the chapter, the reader should be able to do the following:

- Understand the process involved in conceptualizing and developing an event.
- Adopt a systematic approach to event planning.
- Identify the various stakeholders in event planning.
- Outline the steps in developing a SWOT analysis.
- Identify a purpose and develop a mission, goals, and objectives.
- Develop timelines, manage logistics, and plan for contingencies.

INDUSTRY PROFILE

Michael Clemons, Louisville Sports Commission

As race manager for the Louisville Sports Commission (LSC), Michael Clemons is responsible for planning, organizing, and executing multiple running events. Prior to joining the LSC, he was the senior event planner for JAM Active, planning and organizing traditional running events as well as fun runs around the country.

What do you want to accomplish when you create or host events?

For each of our events, we try to create an ROO, or return on objectives. The first thing that we try to accomplish is making money, although that doesn't mean every event has to make money. We're a nonprofit organization and our events are our main source of funding for our annual operating budget. We have a few events that lose money and the whole point of one of those is we know that it's benefiting the city in some way other than financially. Second, we ask if it is meeting one or multiple parts of our mission. Our mission is threefold; it's to promote sports in Louisville, to promote the city of Louisville, and to make the city more active. Third, we ask whether it is providing something good back to the community, if it's making the community a better place.

When you're running an event, how do you begin your planning process?

The planning process is year-round. It's not an overnight thing, especially for running races. People think they just kind of come together, but there's so much that goes into the planning of the event. The first thing that we look at is the feasibility of the event. For our running races, we have to look at the route that we want to run and determine if it's possible. That requires going to the city and getting the city to approve of it. We have to go to our major sponsors and ask if they would be willing to come on board. Those are the early stages of the planning process. Then it's just going through a checklist that we create and seeing if the operation is set. Do we have social media coverage? Do we have the marketing side of it set? Are the permits and the volunteers and staff ready?

How do you go about creating new events?

Last year we created a new event called the Parkway Mile. It started from seeing other cities hosting mile races around the country. Other cities were having success with them so we thought it could happen here. I had to put down on paper how this event would look, which came from looking at other cities' events, seeing what worked, and evaluating what the return on objectives would be. From that we had discussions with our partners about getting their input.

How do you develop timelines and how do you stick with those?

Timelines are always evolving and always changing. Our checklist keeps growing year after year, and a lot of that comes from constant communication among our staff. We ask what still needs to be done this week that hasn't been done and where we were at this point in the process last year.

What are some of the biggest logistical issues you run into?

One of ours is weather, as most of our events are outdoors. We can plan all year for all kinds of different emergencies, but weather is something we can never really predict. For weather we go through what-if scenarios and bounce ideas around about what we would do if different weather events happen. Another one is just handling the footprint of the event. For a lot of our events, it's not a contained area. Our races are on up to thirteen miles of roadway and we have to handle all of the logistics within those thirteen miles, from road closures to setting up water stops to making sure barricades are handled. To do that, we divide up our race into segments, so there's a Cherokee Park area of the course, there's a downtown area of the course, and there's a neighborhood area of the course, and there's somebody who's in charge of each of those areas.

What are some of the main challenges you face?

Making sure we have enough resources, whether it's financial such as the cost of road closures, or personnel such as having knowledgeable staff and volunteers, is always challenging. Another challenge is differentiating ourselves within the event space. Not only are there thousands of events in town, there are hundreds of road races every year in the region. We are constantly having to battle for participants who are only going to do a certain number of events each year, so making them choose our event over a half marathon in Indianapolis or the Flying Pig in Cincinnati comes down to making our events stand out.

What is the key to success in organizing events?

One of the keys to success in organizing events is communication. There is a lot of communication with everybody involved, making sure that every possible scenario is thought through and we have everything to the smallest detail planned. Even if there's only a one in a hundred chance of something happening, we've planned out what we would do if that one in a hundred happened, and we've communicated that to each other, so there's not just one person who knows what to do.

When you run a sporting event, you want everything to go smoothly while accomplishing all of your goals. For this to happen, you need to plan. Extensive planning is necessary in order to do the following:

- Define direction
- Empower decision-making
- Identify risks and opportunities
- Improve performance
- Prepare for challenges

Planning for sporting events can be quite complex when you consider the number of decisions that have to be made and the number of people involved in those decisions. Specifically, multiple **stakeholders** (local organizing committees, participants, sanctioning bodies, facilities, sponsors, and so on) are involved and multiple tasks have to be undertaken (event logistics, budget, marketing, operations, risk management). Therefore, this chapter focuses on what happens in the early stages when the event is conceptualized and formal planning begins. Specifically, the event planning process addresses key issues such as decision-making, goal setting, and logistics. As such, the topics covered in this chapter reflect issues that will affect event organizers throughout the event management process.

Stages of Event Planning

Events go through multiple stages, and event planning takes on different roles at each stage. When it comes to sporting events, there are four basic stages: conceptual planning, operational planning, implementation, and assessment.

- *Conceptual planning*. At the conceptual stage, event organizers envision an event and champion the intention to hold an event. Planning is focused on the feasibility of the event and decisions are made as to whether or not it is suitable to go forward. An event organization is established to facilitate the planning process at this stage.
- *Operational planning*. After a decision to proceed, detailed plans are developed in order to turn the planners' vision into reality. It is at this stage that activities are prioritized and budgeting, marketing, and logistical decisions are made.
- *Implementation*. As the event approaches, tasks are shifted to resource allocation and staff training. Leadership, timing, and coordination become more important. Project status is constantly compared against plans to ensure tasks are on schedule. It is important at this stage to be flexible, because incidents may occur or

situations may alter, necessitating changes to the plan. If mismanaged, great ideas can fail if event organizers do not understand what it takes to effectively implement the event.

- *Assessment.* Throughout the event, results are matched with objectives to ensure the event is going as planned. Event organizers assess various activities during and after the event to make sure the desired results are being achieved. If things are not going as planned during the event, the plans may need to be readjusted. If at the end of the event the results do not match the objectives, organizers may need to amend, modify, or completely change the plans for the next event. Event planners should always be asking how they can make the event better. This is vital because customers will expect more, better, or different experiences from the next event.

Event Leadership

Strong leadership is frequently the key to a successful event. Without good leadership, event planners can be left directionless and unmotivated. Therefore, it is important to understand the differences between being a manager and a leader. Goldblatt (2013) explains that managers are people who make decisions, assign tasks, allocate resources, and solve problems. Leaders, on the other hand, motivate and inspire others to achieve the event's goals. A leader is able to provide a vision of how to achieve the event's outcomes and is able to collaborate with others to achieve those outcomes.

Large events will frequently utilize a **local organizing committee** (LOC). These groups are often made up of members from different stakeholder groups and are enlisted with the task of planning and managing an event. For example, an LOC that includes a variety of stakeholders with a wide range of experiences hosting events was created for the 2020 World Masters Athletics Championships, with former Olympian John Craig serving as the CEO. The other members of the committee include

- the president of Ontario Masters Athletics,
- the director of the Toronto Office of Partnerships, an arm of the city that seeks strategic partners for initiatives,
- local corporate executives,
- local government officials, and
- representatives from Athletics Canada, the governing body for track and field in Canada.

Decision-Making in Event Management

Some event leaders prefer to be very hands-on, focusing on every task and every decision. Others may prefer a more democratic or collaborative process. The effectiveness of each style often depends on the type of staff and organization. A staff with little experience or direction, such as new employees or volunteers, may need more direction, requiring more control from people in leadership positions. Conversely, leaders with a staff of experienced or more qualified people are more likely to give them more control so as to utilize their skills and engage them in the planning process. This is especially true of large-scale events, where the tasks are too large for one person or even a small team to handle on their own. In such cases, leadership has to be more collaborative, giving more control over decision-making to others in the organization.

Given the complexity of the decision-making process and the importance of making good decisions, it is essential to understand what goes into making collaborative decisions. Successful events can be seen as partnerships between stakeholders, athletes, and spectators. Making decisions is much easier when event organizers understand what each party wants from the event. Each stakeholder may have expectations of what the event will generate for them in terms of revenue, goodwill, or experience. Further, each stakeholder is risking something in terms of money, time, or support. Understanding each party's expected benefits and risks will facilitate the decision-making process.

Organizers also need to define levels of authority and determine how both short- and long-term decisions are made (Supovitz 2014). Organizers have to ascertain who will have authority in making decisions—the event manager, event staff, committee, or task force. Defining roles and responsibilities for key decisionmakers allows for a better understanding of the authority each unit possesses; for example, whether this person or committee will have the authority to hire personnel, commit to purchases, sign contracts, and so on. Further, event organizers must define which stakeholders—the sanctioning body, local government, the host, or the committee—will have input into decisions.

These questions can often be addressed by developing an organizational chart that shows how different units are related. Organizational charts also define reporting structures by illustrating who reports to whom. Figure 2.1 shows a sample organizational chart.

Brainstorming in Event Management

Brainstorming is a useful technique for generating new ideas or addressing difficult problems. In a typical brainstorming session, a group of people comes together to participate in a free flow of ideas. This team effort allows members to encourage and stimulate each other's thinking. For sporting events, brainstorming sessions often incorporate multiple stakeholder groups. For example, a championship golf event may include representatives from the local sports commission and tourism board in addition to the local organizers.

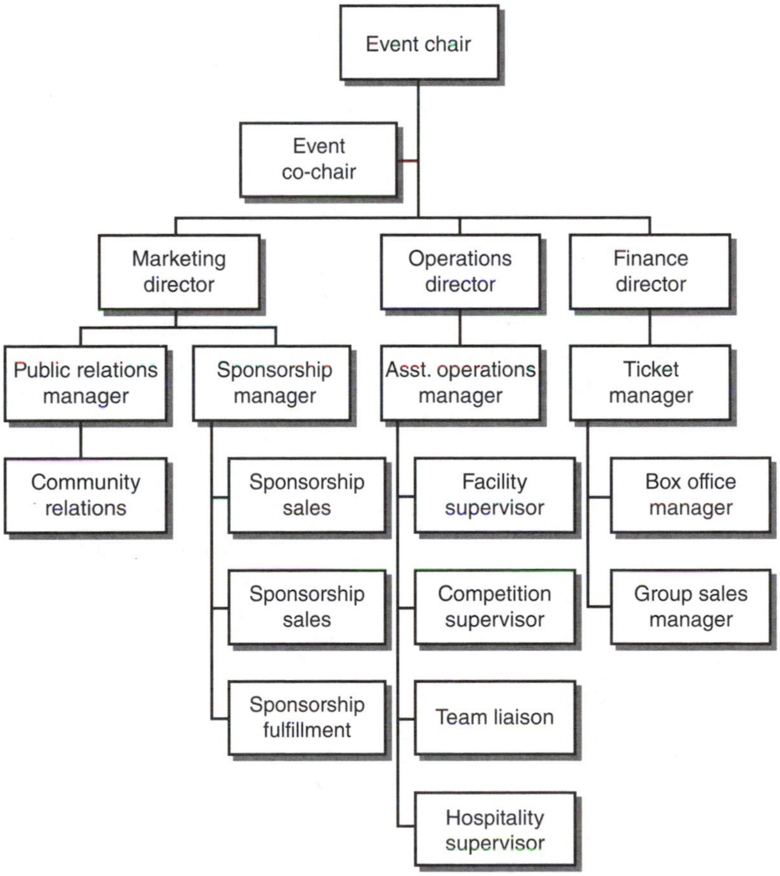

FIGURE 2.1 Sample event organizational chart.

While some would argue that there are no rules for brainstorming, you can do some things to make your brainstorming sessions more effective.

- Have clear objectives in mind about what you want to accomplish. This approach will help keep the group working toward solutions.
- Ask challenging questions. Challenge members to think openly and critically.
- Think big. Most often, brainstorming sessions are designed to generate new or creative solutions, so don't limit yourself to conservative ideas.
- Welcome unusual ideas. Sometimes unusual suggestions lead to good ideas; therefore, it is important to be open to all ideas, leaving feasibility questions for later.
- Avoid negativity. Your goal is to reach solutions, not to get bogged down by existing problems.
- Postpone criticism. If you criticize ideas too early, you run the risk of stifling creativity.
- Give everyone an opportunity to speak. Don't limit your discussion to the most outspoken members of your team.

Brainstorming sessions are often initiated because of a specific issue or a crisis. For example, high school athletic directors faced with tight budgets might get together to brainstorm ideas to cut budgets without cutting sports. Or a new event may bring people together to develop a name and a logo for the event. The following is a list of potential issues that could be resolved through brainstorming.

- Creating an event brand
- Planning an effective event program
- Developing a SWOT analysis
- Creating ideas for promotional programs
- Formulating effective pricing programs
- Identifying sponsorship prospects
- Conceiving additional sponsorship benefits
- Finding new target markets
- Categorizing event risks
- Identifying ways to recruit and reward volunteers
- Devising methods of developing community support
- Suggesting ways to maximize revenues
- Locating areas to cut costs
- Recognizing areas for contingency planning
- Generating customer service initiatives
- Conceptualizing a promotional campaign

Project Management Approach to Event Planning

In many ways, event conceptualization and planning is analogous to project management, a process organizers use to ensure events meet their desired purposes. The Project Management Institute (PMI) defines **project management** as the "application of processes, methods, knowledge, skills and experience to achieve the project objectives." The following list illustrates the planning process that projects go through.

- Project management starts with defining the event's scope. At this point, organizers need to identify the project's purpose and the stakeholders served. This analysis will dictate the type of event.
- After careful situational analysis of the organization and environment, planners can define the mission and set goals and objectives for the event.
- Once the event's direction has been determined, more detailed planning can take place. These plans may cover event logistics, thematic elements, auxiliary elements, and contingencies. These decisions will lead to more decisions about budget and personnel.
- Most sporting events have numerous functions and multiple tasks needing to be accomplished at different points in

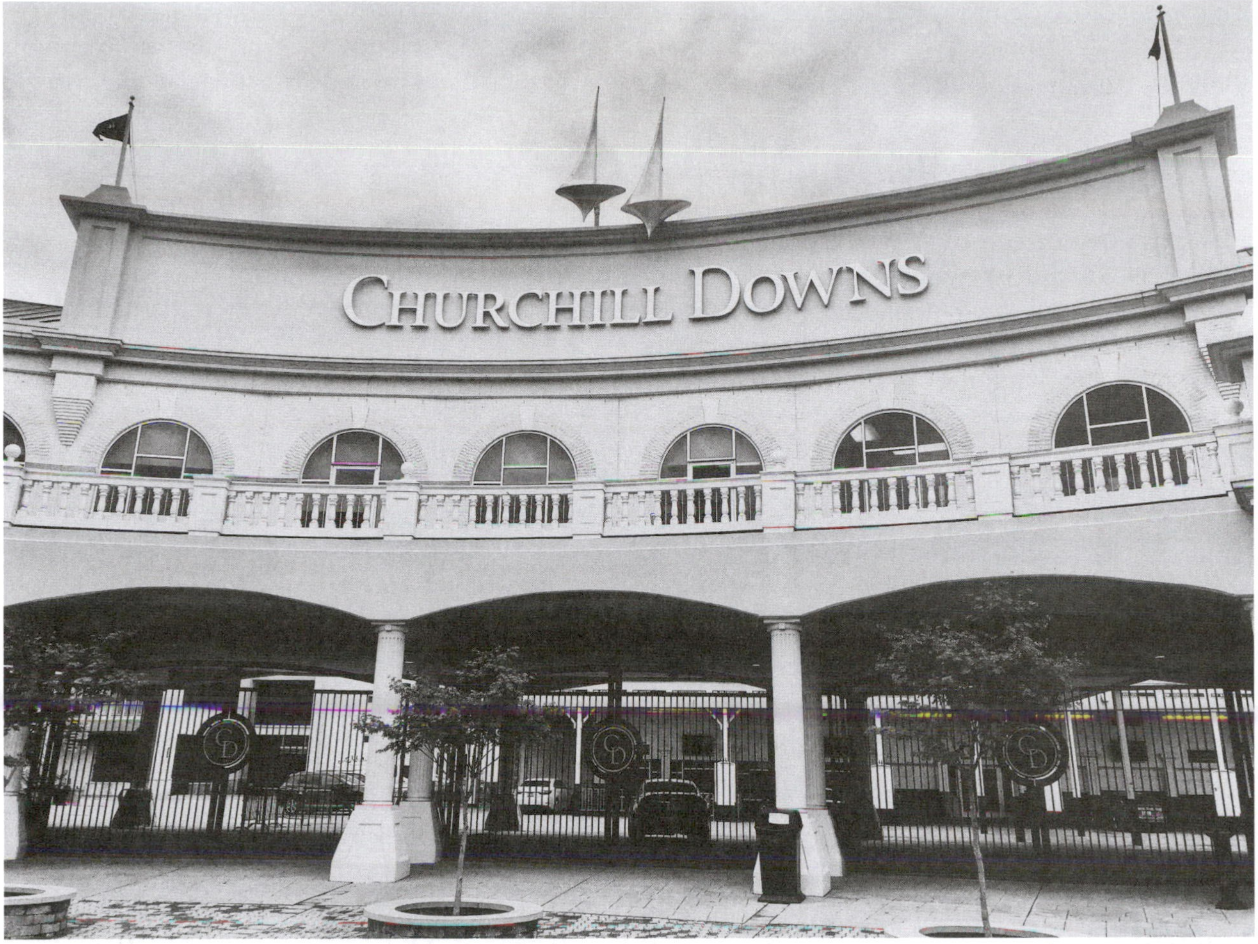

© Chris Greenwell

Planning the Kentucky Derby requires careful project management.

time. These tasks may involve multiple people and resources, all while being constrained by time and budget; careful operational planning needs to take place in order to ensure everything gets accomplished on-time and on-budget (Bladen et al. 2018).

When you consider how many tasks need to be completed to stage an event, the different timelines for each task, and the variety of people working on those tasks, keeping event planning on schedule can be overwhelming. For that reason, many event managers use various technologies to help manage the process and increase productivity. Among the technologies event planners use are the following:

- *Communication tools*. Communication is often cited as a key to project success, so many organizations will incorporate software allowing team members to chat in real time, provide updates, and share critical information. These tools range from apps that manage group texts to web conferencing software.
- *Collaboration tools*. These applications allow planners to collaborate on documents or tasks so that individuals can work together from different locations. Allowing people to work together, whether they be across town or across the globe, greatly increases the speed in which tasks can be accomplished.
- *Project tracking software*. Project tracking software allows planners to follow the progress of different tasks. By tracking progress, planners can identify bottlenecks and reassign resources to keep things moving.
- *Scheduling software*. Scheduling software helps planners keep the planning team organized by managing staff meetings, progress

milestones, and deadlines. These technologies can greatly improve the planning team's time management.

Purpose of the Event

The purpose of the event will drive many decisions related to event design and event planning. Events can serve many purposes; it is therefore important that event organizers clearly identify what they want to accomplish. Is the purpose of your event to make money, create an image for your community or cause, attract tourists, or provide memorable experiences? Purposes vary widely from event to event. Beyond competition and revenue, some of the other common purposes include the following:

- *Promoting an issue*. The Didi Hirsch Suicide Prevention Center organizes a 5K walk/run to bring attention to issues related to suicide prevention in addition to raising money for the cause. Through this annual event, they hope to educate people about the services the organization provides to help those considering suicide.
- *Raising funds for a cause*. Fire Up a Cure, an event involving Chicago firefighters competing in events like tug-of-war and dodgeball, raises money for pediatric cancer research. Organizers have been able to raise more than $250,000 from the 2011-2016 events (Fireupacure.com 2018).
- *Promoting an image for an organization*. The U.S. Army All-American Bowl is an all-star game showcasing the top high school football players. Event organizers must create the best possible experience for both players and fans. The broader purpose, however, is to promote the Army's positive brand attributes.
- *Driving tourism and promoting economic impact*. The Rose Bowl football game in Pasadena annually matches two of college football's top teams; however, the game's original purpose was quite different. The event was started by members of Pasadena's Valley Hunt Club to attract tourism by showcasing the region's great weather.
- *Meeting sponsorship objectives*. The Burton US Open Snowboarding Championships is the longest-running snowboarding event. Burton, one of the top snowboard manufacturers, originally organized the events to help legitimize snowboarding as a sport, which helped drive the sales of snowboards (D'Ambrosio 2014).
- *Promoting a sport*. In 2017, Major League Baseball put on the MLB Little League Classic, in which the St. Louis Cardinals met the Pittsburgh Pirates in a regular-season game in Williamsport, Pennsylvania, the home of the Little League World Series. The game and the surrounding ancillary events were designed to promote youth baseball (Sanchez 2017).

Event organizers should also consider for whom the event is planned, because different groups may have different reasons for supporting an event. It is imperative to understand your stakeholders and their primary needs. For example, each of the following stakeholders may have different needs.

- *Sponsors*. Sponsors seek multiple benefits, including increasing sales of their products,

Questions to Ask When Assessing Your Stakeholders

- Who are your key stakeholders? Do you have multiple stakeholders? If so, who are the primary stakeholders?
- What resources do your stakeholders possess?
- What are your stakeholders' needs? Expectations?
- What can you do to meet stakeholders' expectations?
- How can you positively influence stakeholder outcomes?
- How can you avoid negatively influencing stakeholder outcomes?
- Are there conflicts of interest between stakeholders?

generating awareness of a brand, building an image for a brand, reaching target markets, and providing hospitality for key customers or employees.

- *Broadcast partners*. Broadcast partners seek to maximize viewership in order to maximize value for advertisers or subscribers.
- *The local community*. Community partners seek to generate economic impact, attract tourism, create opportunities for residents, and promote their community.
- *Charitable causes*. Given that many events have charitable connections, it is important to understand the charity's needs, which may range from promoting its cause to raising funds for the organization.
- *Sport governing bodies*. Governing bodies offer a regulatory function by providing oversight, setting rules, and sanctioning events. The mission of these organizations is to provide competitive opportunities or promote the sport. Examples of governing bodies include the National Federation of State High School Associations, USA Triathlon, the United States Equestrian Federation, and the United States Youth Soccer Association.

Consider an NCAA championship event. These events have multiple stakeholders including the governing body, the community hosting the event, the host committee, and sponsors. The governing body, the NCAA, may be concerned with providing an elite competitive environment and an excellent experience for participants. The community's primary purpose for supporting the event is most likely to be to generate tax dollars and economic impact through tourist spending. Sponsors may be most concerned with product exposure or product sampling. Event organizers have the task of identifying their stakeholders, their stakeholders' objectives, and how to deliver results.

Choosing the Type of Event

Considering the many purposes for staging events and the many different beneficiaries events serve, it is important to choose an event that will best meet relevant stakeholders' needs. For some purposes, a large full-scale event may be necessary, while other purposes may be best served by smaller, local events. There are also several different formats for sporting events. Will it be a tournament or a single-game event? Will it be competitive or recreational? Will it be for young participants? Will it include participants with special needs?

For example, a local high school may need to develop an event to raise funds for a building project. Hosting a high-profile professional golf tournament would have the potential to attract a lot of attention and revenue; however, it would not be feasible considering the limited resources available to the school. Instead, the school would be better off planning an intimate golf scramble to attract local donors. Such an event would meet their purpose while making use of available resources.

In addition, event managers need to consider whether or not they have the resources (time, money, people, and facilities) necessary to make the event a success (see table 2.1).

TABLE 2.1 Event Planning Resources

Resources	Key questions
Time	• Does your organization have enough time to devote to planning the event? • Is there enough time to complete all of the tasks between conceptualization and execution?
Money	• Will the event deliver a return on your investment? • Do you have the appropriate capital to produce the event to appropriate standards?
People	• Do you have access to enough people to execute the event? • Does your organization have the expertise to deliver the event?
Facilities	• Are available facilities appropriate for the event? • Is the location appropriate?

SWOT Analysis

Information may be the most important resource during event planning. A valuable strategic planning tool is a **situational analysis**, or SWOT analysis. (SWOT stands for **s**trengths, **w**eaknesses, **o**pportunities, **t**hreats.) The goal of this type of analysis is to identify factors to exploit (strengths and opportunities) or minimize (weaknesses and threats). A well-developed SWOT analysis helps you analyze the state of your event or organization and prepares you to make better decisions as you plan your event.

Strengths and weaknesses are internal and may include factors such as resources (human or financial), structure, and marketing efforts. Strengths are resources, competencies, and advantages your organization or event possesses. Weaknesses, on the other hand, are often direct opposites of strengths.

Opportunities and threats are external to the organization and may include factors related to the economic, social, technical, legal, or competitive environments. Opportunities often represent areas for increased efficiency or new growth. Threats are incidents or entities that may endanger your event's success. See the sidebar SWOT Analysis Considerations for examples.

It is not enough to merely identify your strengths, weaknesses, opportunities, and threats. You should also thoroughly analyze each factor in order to appreciate any potential

SWOT Analysis Considerations

Potential Organizational Strengths

- Event characteristics
- Financial capacity
- Staff experience
- Community support
- Brand strength and awareness
- Existing technology
- Available planning time
- Facility and location
- History and tradition
- Leadership skill

Potential Organizational Weaknesses

- Event limitations
- Financial restrictions
- Untrained staff
- Lack of community support
- Weak brand image
- Lack of technological competence
- Short planning cycle
- Unsuitable facility and location
- Lack of history
- Leadership inexperience

Potential Environmental Opportunities

- Potential sponsors
- Potential partners
- Untapped resources
- Underserved target markets
- Copromotional opportunities
- Economic conditions
- Social trends
- Technological advances
- Political and legal environment
- Industry trends

Potential Environmental Weaknesses

- Competitors
- Inclement weather
- Environmental concerns
- Community dissent
- Labor, supplier, or transportation disputes
- Unfavorable economic conditions
- Political or legal uncertainty

implications. A SWOT analysis requires an honest assessment of each factor. All too often, event organizers choose to focus on the good and trivialize the bad. This shortsightedness leads to poor planning and, ultimately, poor results. For instance, your area may experience heavy rainfall in the month of May. If you were planning the golf tournament in the previous example, this would be a serious threat. You could choose to ignore this and hope for good weather, or you could take the threat seriously, making contingency plans for bad weather. If event organizers believe weaknesses or threats are minor, these may be ignored. But if these weaknesses or threats are major, appropriate steps should be taken to minimize them. Figure 2.2 gives a brief example of implications associated with a SWOT analysis for a regional amateur golf tournament.

Developing a Mission for the Event

The event's mission provides it with direction. Without direction, planning and decision-making can become difficult and ineffective. Given that events can have many purposes and serve many different stakeholders, it is vitally important for event organizers to identify and communicate their mission to ensure that decisions and activities related to the event serve the purpose of the event. To communicate the event's mission, organizations often develop mission statements. A mission statement is a brief declaration that describes who the organization is, explains what the organization does, and communicates the organization's purpose, philosophy, and values (Hums and MacLean

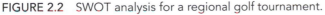

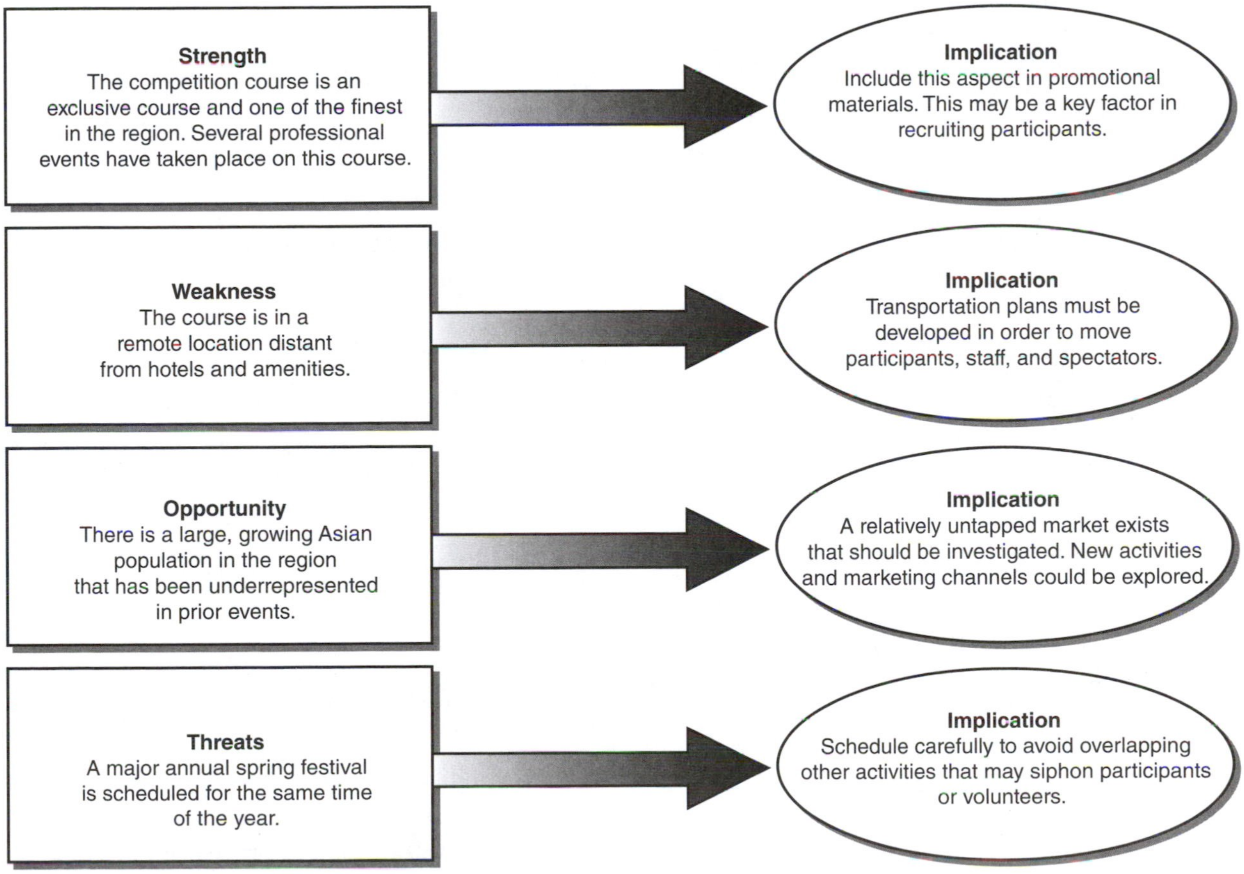

Strength
The competition course is an exclusive course and one of the finest in the region. Several professional events have taken place on this course.
Implication
Include this aspect in promotional materials. This may be a key factor in recruiting participants.
Weakness
The course is in a remote location distant from hotels and amenities.
Implication
Transportation plans must be developed in order to move participants, staff, and spectators.
Opportunity
There is a large, growing Asian population in the region that has been underrepresented in prior events.
Implication
A relatively untapped market exists that should be investigated. New activities and marketing channels could be explored.
Threats
A major annual spring festival is scheduled for the same time of the year.
Implication
Schedule carefully to avoid overlapping other activities that may siphon participants or volunteers.

FIGURE 2.2 SWOT analysis for a regional golf tournament.

2017). Good mission statements convey a concise message understandable by everyone in the organization. Every word should have a purpose. That said, mission statements often take a considerable amount of time to write and finalize.

Women's Tri-Fitness is a competition that features female athletes competing in fitness routines, fitness skills, and an obstacle course. Their mission outlines who they are and what they promote:

To present a women's sporting event with a foundation based on dedication to health, fitness, and the competitive spirit; and an event which embodies a realistically attainable level of athleticism that could be readily identifiable to the general public as well as to the most ardent sports enthusiast.

Sometimes an event's mission can be short while still effectively communicating what the event should be all about. For example, the mission of the United States Tennis Association (USTA) is direct but still communicates enough to guide event planning:

To promote and develop the growth of tennis.

Setting Goals and Objectives

Goal setting is a very important part of the planning process because goals and objectives provide direction. Without direction, it is possible to waste important resources on activities that do not serve the event's mission or stakeholders. Further, **goals** and **objectives** define expectations for the event as well as how the success or failure of an event will be measured. Once individual objectives have been defined it is possible to develop strategies and tactics to support them.

At this stage of the process, it is important for event organizers to envision the future of the event, thinking about what needs to be achieved in order to realize the event's mission. Although the terms are often used interchangeably, the following examples define *goals* as broad statements and *objectives* as quantifiable statements that support individual goals. Examples of goals include the following:

- Maximize attendance or participation.
- Create value for sponsors.
- Create a positive image for the host community.
- Attract tourists to the region.
- Raise money for charity.
- Promote the sport and generate goodwill.
- Increase overall customer service.

Good objectives are specific, measurable, achievable, realistic, and timely (SMART). The following is an example of some goals and objectives that a high school basketball tournament organizing committee might use.

Goal 1: Increase average attendance for the tournament.

Objective 1: Retain 90 percent of last year's all-tournament package purchasers.

Objective 2: Sell 200 new all-tournament packages two weeks prior to the event.

Objective 3: Sell 1,200 single-session tickets per session.

Goal 2: Attract the highest-quality basketball teams in the state.

Objective 1: Recruit at least four teams ranked in the top 20 in the state.

Objective 2: Recruit at least four local teams.

Objective 3: Recruit at least two teams with a recognizable star player.

Planning Logistics

Several issues related to **event logistics** need to be addressed at the planning stages, specifically decisions related to date, time, location, and duration. Remaining logistical issues will be addressed as the planning process proceeds.

• *Date*. Event organizers should consider major local events, competing sporting events, weather conditions, or important holidays when scheduling. For example, few major events are scheduled around Super Bowl weekend because the game tends to dominate media coverage and attract most Americans' attention. Holidays can be a help or a hindrance. Some events will avoid holidays such as Memorial Day or Christmas because potential consumers' attention will be elsewhere. However, in the auto racing industry, the Indianapolis 500 and NASCAR's Coca-Cola 600 both take place over this time period because the three-day weekend makes travel to these big events more convenient. For outdoor events, the time of year is especially important because weather can be either an advantage or a major deterrent to an event's success (the weather is great on the Gulf Coast, except during hurricane season).

- *Time*. When setting the time for events, event managers need to consider how long each contest will take. For events with multiple matches (e.g., tournaments), managers need to consider the number of contests, the time necessary to prepare the facility between contests, and the amount of rest competitors need between contests. Similarly, they have to consider constraints their target market may face. Schedule too early in the day and it may be difficult for some to attend because of work, school, or other commitments. Schedule too late and some may not be able to attend because of tomorrow's work, school, or other commitments. The media play a role in start times for televised events because broadcasters seek to maximize viewers and fill available time slots.

- *Location*. Location involves issues with the host city and host facility. The host city is an important factor in determining whether or not people will attend. Organizers need to consider both the attractiveness and the convenience of the host city's location. Several issues influence the choice of facility such as size, occupancy, playing surface, participant services, spectator amenities, accessibility, parking and transportation, lease terms, and cost. Organizers may also be faced with the decision of whether to stay in one location year after year or to change locations. Each choice has its own set of advantages and disadvantages (see the sidebar Event Location on page 38).

- *Duration*. Although many events last only one day, others (e.g., an NCAA basketball tournament, the Olympics, various sports festivals)

© Chris Greenwell

Winter in Minneapolis presented additional logistical issues for the Super Bowl.

Event Location

Major Events With Fixed Locations
- Kentucky Derby
- Little League World Series
- Masters Golf Tournament
- Wimbledon
- FA Cup Final
- Monaco Grand Prix

Advantages of Fixed Locations
- Reputation
- Existing fan base
- History and tradition
- Community support
- Event management expertise
- Staffing and volunteer base
- Client relationships
- Vendor relationships
- Media relationships

Major Events That Change Locations
- Breeders' Cup
- Olympic Games
- Ryder Cup
- Davis Cup
- UEFA Champions League Final
- WrestleMania

Advantages of Changing Locations
- New consumers and markets
- New sources of revenue
- Healthy competition among sites
- Increased media coverage
- Community enthusiasm
- Larger scope
- Event novelty
- Flexibility

may last weeks or months. When deciding on duration, event managers need to consider the type of competition, participants' travel needs, facility availability and cost, availability of officials and staff, and flexibility if delays due to weather or unforeseen events occur.

Thinking Creatively and Planning for Uniqueness

Considering the competition for spectators, participants, and sponsors, sporting event organizers need to be unique to attract attention and separate themselves from the competition. Why is it that some events consistently draw more spectators, participants, and sponsors than others? Quite often, it is because organizers have developed or highlighted special elements that make the events desirable. Here are some examples:

- The Pinstripe Bowl is a college football bowl game held in New York's Yankee Stadium. The uniqueness of playing a football game in a baseball stadium in a cold weather city provides an additional attraction beyond the game itself, which helps organizers set their game apart from the numerous other bowl games being played during that time period.
- Location and timing contribute to the many holiday basketball tournaments held in Hawaii or Puerto Rico. Spectators plan vacations around these games regardless of who is playing their favorite team.
- Polar bear plunges are fundraisers for various charitable events. What sets them apart from other fundraisers is that instead of walking or running, participants swim in icy water. One of the largest of these events, the Long Beach Polar Bears Super Bowl Splash, attracts approximately 8,000 participants to raise funds for the Make-a-Wish Foundation.
- In a crowded marketplace, Cincinnati's Flying Pig Marathon sets itself apart from the jam-packed race calendar by focusing on the fun nature of the race.

In addition to the pig theme, organizers incorporate a variety of events into the weekend such as an awards ceremony, kids' races, a family fun festival, and a race for dogs called the Flying Fur Run.

Sometimes uniqueness starts with the name. El Clásico is the name given to football matches between rivals FC Barcelona and Real Madrid. This name incorporates the history and rivalry among two of Spain's largest clubs. The name Super Bowl is another great example. Although its former name, AFL-NFL World Championship Game, was accurate and descriptive, it did not quite communicate the grandeur of the game. The name *Super Bowl* is consistent with what colleges traditionally call their big games while communicating the size and importance of the event.

Sometimes a simple idea can lead to great results. In 2003, the National Hockey League (NHL) decided to hold an outdoor regular-season game featuring the Edmonton Oilers and the Montreal Canadiens. The creativity of putting an indoor sport into an outdoor football stadium generated significant attention and delivered huge results. More than 57,000 fans attended the game (a lottery to allot tickets attracted more than 750,000 entries), and the Canadian television broadcast attracted more than 2.75 million viewers, setting records for a regular-season game (Ramshaw 2014). Since then, the league has hosted an annual Winter Classic at a large outdoor stadium every year on or around New Year's Day. The event's popularity pushed them to add additional outdoor games drawing 50 to 70 thousand fans each.

It is not just high-profile or big-budget events that try to stand out; smaller events can benefit from creative planning, too. In recent years, mud runs have emerged as an alternative sporting event. Mud runs are running events where competitors must negotiate hills, obstacles, and mud to test their endurance as well as their mental stamina. These events provide a unique challenge that differentiates them from other running events. Another example is snow golf, where golfers compete in the snow using orange golf balls. The greens are referred to as *whites*. In many tournaments, golfers are encouraged to wear costumes as a way to focus on the fun element of the event.

Sustainable Sporting Events

Recently, sport event planners have put an increased focus on planning for more environmentally friendly events. Sporting events typically draw large numbers of participants or spectators who can have a large impact on the host community's environment because such events tend to create a lot of trash, consume power and water, and generate pollution from vehicle transportation.

By planning for a "green" event, organizers can help achieve **sustainability** by conserving resources, reducing waste, and protecting air and water quality. Further, greener practices can benefit event organizers by reducing costs and decreasing waste. Such events also appeal to eco-conscious consumers and can further differentiate your event from those of competitors. The following is a list of some of the ways event planners can incorporate greener practices.

- Use digital communication (websites, social media, e-tickets) rather than printed materials (flyers, programs, paper tickets).
- Use electric vehicles for staff, participant, and spectator transportation.
- Maximize public transportation to and from event venues.
- Incorporate eco-friendly cleaning products and practices.
- Use recyclable or compostable food ware and utensils.
- Provide recycling bins next to or in place of trash receptacles.
- Buy locally sourced food and beverages.
- Reuse supplies and equipment.
- Use sustainable materials for products and supplies.
- Use renewable energy to power venues.
- Conserve water and other natural resources.

Some events stand out for their emphasis on green practices. In 2012, the Waste Management Phoenix Open launched the Zero Waste Challenge with the goal of minimizing waste sent to landfills. This event attracts more than 600,000 spectators over the weeklong event and is able to divert 100 percent of its waste through reuse, donation, recycling, composting, and material recovery. The organizers claim that this is the largest zero waste event and the most sustainable sporting event in the world (Boteler 2018).

Similarly, the NFL instituted the Rush2Recycle program at the 2018 Super Bowl in Minneapolis. The program was able to successfully recover 91 percent of the game day waste that would have ordinarily ended up in a landfill. To do so, they had their concessionaire swap plastic food containers, utensils, and cups for compostable ones and had ambassadors posted at recycling stations to direct fans on how to separate recyclable waste from compostable waste (Danigelis 2018).

Planning Promotional and Ancillary Components

In addition to the main event, **ancillary events** such as fan expos, music festivals, contests, youth clinics, and interactive activities are often planned to further organizers' objectives such as promoting the event, adding value for participants, contributing to the community, or adding to the spectacle of the event. Every event is going to have different ancillary components based on what organizers hope to accomplish. For example, the NBA introduced more interactive fan events surrounding the 2016 All-Star Game in Toronto. NBA Centre Court involved skills competitions, instructional clinics, and a Special Olympics game and clinic in order to celebrate the game of basketball and engage basketball fans (NBA 2016).

Many organizations host multiple smaller events and activities surrounding their main event in order to achieve multiple objectives. World Wrestling Entertainment (WWE) hosts a full week of activities before WrestleMania, their signature event, in order to support multiple initiatives and further engage their fans. These ancillary activities add to the grandeur of the event while making the destination more attractive to fans traveling to the big show. In 2017 alone, WWE hosted a number of activities in Orlando, Florida, including the following:

- WrestleMania Axxess, a fan fest comprised of autograph signings, performer Q&A sessions, memorabilia, and exclusive matches
- Hall of Fame Ceremony, an event honoring their greatest performers of the past
- WM Pro-Am Golf Tournament
- Susan G. Komen Yoga, an event featuring WWE Superstars to support the breast cancer charity
- NXT TakeOver, a special wrestling event featuring up-and-coming performers

In addition to four days of basketball, a number of activities were planned for the 2018 Phillips 66 Big 12 Men's Basketball Championship to add to the experience of visiting Kansas City.

- *Spirit Rallies* prior to the start of each session
- *Big 12 GameDay Fan Experience*, an interactive experience with games, music, giveaways, and autograph sessions
- *Miller Lite Basketball Fan Fest*, an all-day party experience with live entertainment, pep rallies, and watch parties
- *Big 12 Run*, a downtown road race designed to kick off the event

The National Wheelchair Basketball Tournament (NWBT) creates additional events designed to advance the sport, including the following:

- *Junior Girls' Player Showcase*, a scrimmage for female players hoping to be noticed by national teams and college coaches
- *High School Senior Boys Game*, a scrimmage for male players hoping to be noticed by national teams and college coaches
- *Junior Division Banquet*, with awards ceremonies and speeches from members of the U.S. National Teams

- *3V3 Tournament*, a series of competitions for athletes competing across different competitive divisions

Planning for Contingencies

Odds are that something planned will not go off as expected. Therefore, event managers should identify what could go wrong and develop **contingency plans** to address any possibilities. Contingency plans are alternative plans you develop to tackle uncontrollable, but foreseeable, events. The goal of a contingency plan is to create a level of preparation so that you can minimize issues and reduce the inconvenience to participants and spectators. You need to have a backup plan for your backup plan.

Identify Potential Issues

When developing contingency plans, you should first identify areas of concern. Try to think of what can go wrong. It is also useful to involve your staff in helping identify potential issues. Typical situations needing advance preparation may include the following:

- Fire, gas leak, or other emergency
- Bad weather
- Power failure
- Equipment failure
- Scoreboard or scoring system failure
- Larger than expected crowd
- Hostile crowd
- Late-arriving team or official
- Staff shortage
- Ticket irregularities
- Medical emergencies
- Food and beverage issues
- Parking and transportation problems

Although some occurrences are unlikely, they should be planned for if the severity of the occurrence would have a major impact on the event. Consider a scoreboard failure at a college basketball game. This rarely happens, but if it does it could bring an event to a close.

Prepare Action Plans

Once areas of concern have been identified, managers need to develop action plans detailing what to do in each case. If these eventualities cannot be prevented, plans need to be developed to minimize their effects. Plans should consider the staff, budget, time, training, and resources needed to deal with each situation. Some plans will be more complex than others depending on the likelihood and the severity of the problem being considered. Contingency plans may include procedures for emergency access, evacuation, communication, security procedures, staff responsibilities, and plans for dealing with the media.

Many events have contingency plans for weather-related issues. For outdoor events, weather is an important concern, since rain, wind, and snow (or lack of snow for a winter event) can significantly alter event plans. In 2016, heavy rains from Hurricane Matthew moved across the East Coast, forcing numerous changes to college and professional football schedules. Given the hurricane's uncertain path, multiple plans had to be developed to address threats to playing conditions, fan safety, and damage to surrounding areas, based on when and where the storm would hit. For some games, it was as easy as moving kickoff times, while other games were moved to different locations, rescheduled to other dates, or canceled altogether. Even good weather may need contingency plans. For the 2017 Winter Classic at Busch Stadium in St. Louis, forecasts of unseasonably warm temperatures created the need to develop contingency plans in case the ice was not playable for the outdoor game. To deal with this issue, the NHL created plans for when the game could be played if it needed to be rescheduled and how the game would be decided if the game were started and unable to be played to its completion ("The NHL" 2017). Considering the different types of weather, managers may need to have plans to provide rain gear for staff, procedures to protect equipment, public address announcements to inform participants and spectators, evacuation plans, and procedures for rescheduling or cancelation.

Update Plans

Contingency planning should be a dynamic process. Continual review and revision are necessary to identify additional risks and alternative ways to deal with those risks. This phase involves reviewing existing plans and developing new plans defined in the project scope.

Operational Planning

Events may take months or even years to plan and execute, with each logistical area having its own needs and timelines. For example, the 2017 PGA Championship in Charlotte, North Carolina, was only a weeklong event, but planning started when the city was awarded the event in 2010. Tickets went on sale more than a year before the event, with renewed marketing pushes over the winter holiday period eight months before the event. Two hundred separate structures, ranging from souvenir shops to hospitality areas, started to go up more than two months ahead of the event. Logistical plans for parking and transportation took months and had to be completed well in advance of the event so that ticket buyers would know their transportation options. Food service locations and menus needed to be addressed. This planning was in addition to the landscaping that needed to be done to accommodate the golf itself (Spanberg 2017).

Project management techniques apply to event planning in that larger tasks need to be broken down into smaller units. These smaller activities can then be assigned to appropriate work groups and time and cost can be effectively budgeted (Bladen et al. 2018).

When developing operational timelines, the keys to success are to start early, identify important tasks, and budget an appropriate amount for completion. Important tasks left to the last minute add time, costs, and stress. Further, tasks must be scheduled in relation to each other (e.g., promotional materials cannot be printed until the date and site have been confirmed).

The following is a sample event timeline. Keep in mind that every event will have different needs, and the length of time to complete tasks will vary according to the event. Small events may require only a few weeks to a few months of planning, but larger events may require years of planning.

Initiation (18 months to 2 years out)

Needs assessment and feasibility analysis

Bidding process

Early planning (1 to 2 years out)

Develop mission, vision, and purpose

Select date and location

Secure venues

Create organizing committee

Detailed planning (6 months to 1 year out)

Generate budgets

Assess staffing needs

Develop marketing plans

Develop contingency plans

Produce event program

Pre-event (3 to 6 months out)

Seek event sponsors

Begin promotional campaign

Create internet presence

Arrange for security, parking, transportation, and vendors

Order supplies and equipment

Sell tickets and register participants

As the event approaches (1 to 3 months out)

Follow up with teams or participants

Confirm officials

Event week

Perform on-site checks

Install equipment and set up venue

Finalize event day timelines

Continue staff and volunteer training

Ramp up media activity

Schedule transportation for VIPs and guests

Event day

Perform equipment checks

Conduct pre-event briefings

EVENT!

Postevent

Postevent review

Aftermarketing

Begin planning cycle for next event

Another tool that can help with operational planning is a **Gantt chart**, which will give you a visual of how tasks are scheduled over time. These charts specify start and end dates for each task, allowing organizers to see what tasks need to happen, how long each task will take, and who is working on each task. Figure 2.3 is an example of a basic Gantt chart covering sales, promotion, and operations functions.

Event Planning Blunders

Strong event planning is necessary to ensure your event is successful. Details that may seem small can cause big problems. Think about how these seemingly minor issues can derail your event. You've scheduled your championship game on a religious holiday, meaning you will be losing potential participants or spectators. Your big volleyball tournament is ready to begin, but no one brought the game balls. There is a misspelled word on the sign welcoming your attendees. The following is a list of common errors you should strive to avoid.

- *Lack of focus.* Not being specific about your purpose and mission leads to disorganization and waste. Everything you do should be directed toward achieving your mission.

- *Limited concept.* Trends in producing sporting events are constantly changing, as are customer expectations. Just because something has been done before does not mean it is necessarily going to work now. Event planners have to keep up with trends and identify how to make their events different from the competition.

- *Overlooked details.* Considering the number of things that have to happen to execute a successful event, it is easy to overlook details. Details such as the intricacies of the venue and complexities of contracts may seem small at first, but if not dealt with may create large problems as the event approaches.

- *Lack of depth.* The best way to ensure you are successful and to reduce the risk of things going wrong is to plan every element of the event. Merely hoping things work out is not a plan but an invitation for failure. Further, a lack of planning tends to create issues needing attention at the last minute, adding to unnecessary stress and expense.

- *Overlooked contingencies.* Things don't always go as planned. Don't be surprised if something takes longer than expected or does not turn out as you hoped. Good event planners plan for these occurrences so that they don't ruin their events.

Task	Group	5/7	5/14	5/21	5/28	6/4	6/11	6/18	6/25	7/2	7/9
Sponsorship sales	Sales	■	■								
Group sales	Sales			■	■	■	■				
Individual sales	Sales					■	■	■	■	■	■
Create website	Promotion	■									
Ad campaign	Promotion		■	■	■	■	■	■			
Media blitz	Promotion								■	■	
Order equipment	Operations	■	■	■							
Event setup	Operations								■	■	
Staff training	Operations									■	
Event day	Operations										■

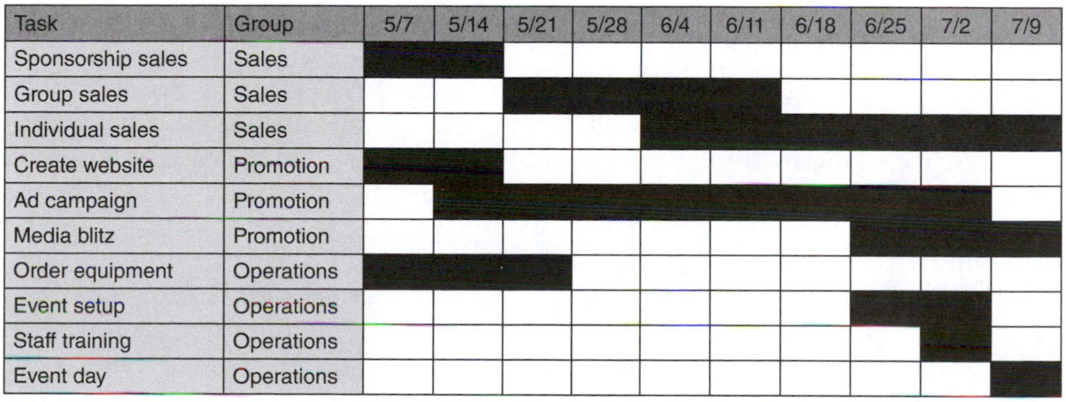

FIGURE 2.3 Sample Gantt chart.

Summary

Event planning can be a time-consuming and complex process involving numerous decisions. Event planning goes through multiple stages, involving many individuals. As such, leadership and decision-making are vital to success.

A project management approach can help with working through the planning process. This process starts with understanding and defining the event's purpose and stakeholders. An understanding of each stakeholder's interest in the event assists in decision-making. Many of these decisions will be driven by the purpose of the event, such as raising funds for a cause, promoting an image, driving tourism, promoting sponsors, or promoting sports.

A significant part of the planning process is the SWOT analysis. A frank assessment of an event's strengths, weaknesses, opportunities, and threats enables organizers to make informed decisions. The event's mission, goals, and objectives provide direction so that organizers can prepare strategies and plan logistics to meet the event's purpose efficiently. Once the major issues have been identified, logistical issues such as date, time, and place are determined, and operational timelines are developed to ensure everything that needs to be done is accomplished at the right time. Considering the number of things that could change or go wrong, contingency plans are developed to deal with deviations from the plan.

LEARNING ACTIVITIES

Assume you have decided to stage a 5K mud run. Mud runs are races through trails, hills, and other assorted obstacles (especially mud). There is no standard course; each event host plans unique and creative obstacles to challenge competitors' stamina and mental discipline. Further, mud run organizers usually add ancillary events such as awards ceremonies and postevent parties to create an exciting event.

1. Who would be the key stakeholders? What would be the primary purpose of the event?
2. Assess the event's strengths, weaknesses, opportunities, and threats (you may have to do some research to complete this task).
3. What would be some appropriate goals and objectives for an event such as this?
4. If you were to host an event like this, what would you call it? What would you do to make it unique?
5. What could go wrong with this event? What contingency plans would you have to make?

CASE STUDY: WOMEN'S ICE HOCKEY

Since the first indoor game was played in 1875, ice hockey has been a popular sport for both participants and spectators. Considered Canada's national pastime, the sport has also grown across the world with 76 countries participating as members of the International Ice Hockey Federation (IIHF). Since 1904, professional men's ice hockey has been played in North America at the highest level with other professional leagues competing in several European countries, Australia, and Japan.

While overall participation by youth in team sports has been declining, participation in ice hockey has seen an increase. Canada leads the way with more than 600,000 registered players, and there were more than 550,000 players in the United States in 2017, up from fewer than 195,000 in 1991 ("Countries by number" 2017). Participation is also especially strong in Czechia, Russia, Finland, and Sweden. Much of this growth has been attributed to television exposure of professional leagues and the visibility of Olympic and Paralympic competitions. These events give the sport's organizers great opportunities to showcase the sport (Townley 2017).

One of the biggest areas of growth has been among female participants, with participation by girls and women in ice hockey at an all-time high. In the United States alone, the number of girls and women playing, according to USA Hockey, was up 32 percent from 2007 to 2017 (Lissau 2017). High schools and colleges are adding teams, and youth developmental programs have popped up around the United States and Canada.

While women have played the sport since the 1980s, the first IIHF championship was not until 1990, and it did not debut as a medal sport in the Olympics until 1998. Since then, teams from the United States (1998 and 2018 Gold Medals) and Canada (Gold Medals in 2002, 2006, 2010, and 2014) have dominated the competition. The first intercollegiate championship for women in Canada was in 1998 and the first NCAA Women's Ice Hockey Championship was contested in 2001. In 2016, NCAA hockey players came from 13 different countries, 9 Canadian provinces, and 35 U.S. states (Haase 2017).

There are still some obstacles to participation. First, the sport still tends to be male dominated, with approximately 85 percent of all players being male. Further, the sport is still considered by many to be a masculine sport, which can marginalize female players. Second, the sport demands a lot of resources because equipment can be very expensive and ice time can be difficult to find. Additionally, the lack of local teams often forces teams to incur significant travel costs to play appropriate competition. Third, women's teams lack the exposure the men's sport receives, which limits opportunities for young girls to be introduced to the sport outside of the Olympics every four years.

Case Study Application

When creating sporting events, it is important to consider that the type of event will be different based on its purpose. Below are three different purposes for creating sporting events. Your task is to envision an event that could be created featuring women's ice hockey for each of the purposes described below.

1. Many events are created to promote a cause. What kind of hockey event could you create to promote a cause encouraging girls to participate in sport? How could you construct an event to get more girls playing sport? How could you make this event unique?
2. USA Hockey has made promoting the sport of women's hockey a priority. What kind of hockey event could you create to promote the sport? How could you construct an event to maximize this purpose? How could you make this event unique?
3. Participant events are often created to bring visitors to a community to generate economic impact (spending on local hotels, restaurants, and attractions). What kind of hockey event could you create to bring visitors to your community? How could you construct an event to maximize this purpose? How could you make this event unique?

© Chris Greenwell

CHAPTER 3

Event Bidding

CHAPTER OBJECTIVES

After completing the chapter, the reader should be able to do the following:

- Appreciate the reasons why host communities bid on sporting events.
- Calculate economic impact and identify issues with economic impact calculations.
- Understand the role of sports commissions and how events work with sports commissions.
- Outline the steps in the bidding process for sporting events.
- Create a competitive bid document.

INDUSTRY PROFILE

Jennifer Stoll, Greater Grand Junction Sports Commission

Jennifer Stoll, executive director of the Greater Grand Junction Sports Commission (GGJSC), has been with the GGJSC since 2013. The GGJSC is a nonprofit agency that attracts new sporting events and enhances existing sporting events in western Colorado, hosting numerous events, including the USA Cycling Collegiate National Championships, the Colorado Special Olympics, the Junior College World Series, and the Rim Rock Marathon. Prior to coming to Grand Junction, Jennifer worked with the Professional Golf Association (PGA) of America, specifically with the 2008 Ryder Cup and the 2010 Senior PGA Championship.

What are you trying to accomplish through your work with the Greater Grand Junction Sports Commission?

We're really just trying to improve our community through sport and outdoor recreation. Our mission is really to build events, recruit events, or enhance events that contribute to our community and to our economy. We use sport and outdoor recreation as a platform to expose our community to individuals who might not be aware of it. Small events with a low overhead to the community can have a good economic return in terms of visitors staying in hotels and driving economic expenditures. Secondarily, we consider what we do very much woven into the culture of our community. From a local perspective, we want to create a community that has fun things going on that offer an opportunity for health and wellness participatory and spectator-driven activities.

How do you choose whether to bid on outside events or build events yourself?

Small and midsize markets might not have the financial resources to spend on recruiting or paying bid fees, so we're very judicious about what we choose to place bids on versus events we build ourselves and operate. For events we build ourselves, it's very valuable to us to have the revenue from an event stay within our community versus going to an outside third party. Not every sports commission is that way, but our operational background lends itself to being able to do that. Some sports commissions just recruit events and put them in contact with a venue, but we can actually plan those events ourselves.

What criteria do you use to decide whether to take on an event?

From a broad perspective, we look at the calendar in the community and what's already in place. We look at the community's hotel capacity, we look at the sport to see if it fits the culture of our community, we look at venue usage to see if there are underutilized or creative venues we could use, and we look at sport trends for up and coming events that are trending upward in participation. Then we look at the financial side to see if we could generate revenue, we look at what participation would look like, and what sort of risk we would take on as a community. We look at the pros and cons to see if it is the right fit for our community at that time. Our venues and the number of available hotel rooms limits us on the scope of events that we can host. We can't hold a three-hundred team lacrosse tournament, but we can host a really solid regional tournament on a championship quality field.

What is your niche?

There are hundreds of destinations that are vying for traditional team sports events. Our culture is very outdoor-centric, so we try to play to that strength as much as possible. We want things that fit with the Colorado culture, whether it's cycling, archery, paddle boarding, or others that are more outdoor-centric than your traditional sports.

How are you competitive in attracting and keeping events?

We try to flip the script. Instead of a bland bid with a visitor's guide and a description of the venue, we approach it from a personal side. We really want it to be a partnership where it is a win for our community and a win for their organization. That separates us from other bidders.

How do you keep people coming back?

We try to be yes people. We want to help their events succeed. We try to blur the lines between their organization and ours. It's about the hospitality and the experience. If they don't have a good experience interacting with all of the people in our community it is all for a lost cause.

For events without fixed locations, one of the first tasks for event organizers is to identify the best location to stage their event. Mega-events such as the FIFA World Cup, the Olympic Games, and the Super Bowl are staged in different locations each time. Other events, ranging from international championships to youth tennis tournaments, seek locations that best suit their needs. In order to select the best location, event organizers should solicit bids from interested parties who will submit proposals outlining why they should be chosen. The bid process is competitive, encouraging interested parties to detail how they would present the best possible event.

Hosts for sporting events are often local sports commissions, convention and visitors bureaus (CVBs), civic organizations, or colleges and athletic conferences (for many intercollegiate athletic events). For larger mega-events, a city or country may serve as the host. Potential hosts are willing to bid for events for a variety of reasons.

- Enhancing the local economy by attracting spectators, participants, and officials who will spend money on hotel rooms, in restaurants, and at local attractions.
- Providing a catalyst for improving the host community's infrastructure and facilities.
- Enhancing community image and providing an increased quality of life for local citizens.
- Promoting the community or organization by showcasing its attributes and benefits.

Different cities seek different benefits from attracting events. For example, Birmingham, United Kingdom, bid to host the 2022 Commonwealth Games with the goal of using the games to celebrate diversity, drive business links, and showcase Britain to the world (Commonwealth Games 2017). Las Vegas, Nevada, on the other hand, hosts numerous college basketball tournaments, knowing that fans of participating schools will fill hotel rooms and spend money in casinos, restaurants, and nightclubs (Markazi 2018).

Table 3.1 includes examples of some events seeking bids for a host. As you can see, each of these events has the potential to bring a large number of athletes, coaches, and spectators to a community.

This chapter introduces several concepts related to why and how locations bid for various sporting events. Specifically, issues such as economic impact, the bidding process, and preparation of bid documents are addressed in order to help the reader understand how to make wise decisions related to which events to seek and how to make the most competitive bids for those events.

TABLE 3.1 Examples of Events Seeking Bids

Event	Length	Participants	Room nights	Rights fee
USA Roller Sports National Championship	28 days	2,500 athletes	15,000	$200,000
NAIA Football National Championship	1 day	150 athletes 3,000-8,000 spectators	200	$30,000
Strongman Corporation North American National Championships	3 days	300 athletes 500-5,000 spectators	2,000	$20,000
Quidditch Cup	2 days	1,800 athletes	900	$35,000
Timbersports Canadian Championship	3 days	34 athletes 2,000-5000 spectators	224	$70,000- $100,000
Professional Masters Disc Golf World Championships	3-4 days	200 athletes	124	Competitive

Economic Impact

One of the primary reasons communities seek to host events is to improve their local or regional economy. **Economic impact** refers to the net change in the economy that occurs as a result of hosting a sporting event. A great example of how major sporting events can affect a region comes from the greater Phoenix area, which estimated a $1.3 billion economic impact by hosting the Super Bowl, the College Football Playoff, and the NCAA Final Four over a three-year period. They estimated that visitors for the 2017 Final Four spent an average of $487 per day over a four-day period, and people who bought tickets to the 2016 College Football National Championship game spent an average of $467.93 per day (Economic Impact 2018). Smaller events typically generate economic impact by attracting athletes, along with coaches and families, who travel to participate in events. For example, the United States Bowling Congress (USBC) Youth Open Championships has a sizable impact on the community, attracting approximately 3,500 athletes and their family members who fill more than 10,000 hotel rooms over a two-week period (Walton 2014).

Given that many sporting events require financial support from the local community, it is important to calculate an event's economic impact. Communities want to demonstrate an economic return in exchange for their investment. Howard and Crompton (2014) provide a simple formula for estimating the economic impact of visitor spending.

$$\text{economic impact of visitor spending} = \text{number of visitors} \times \text{average spending per visitor} \times \text{multiplier}$$

The first step in this equation is to accurately estimate the number of visitors, whether they be participants or spectators. It is also important to distinguish between visitors and locals, since locals most likely are not bringing new money to the local economy, or are spending money that would have been spent elsewhere in the community anyway.

Average visitor spending is the amount of money the typical visitor brings to the community when attending an event. Visitor spending is generated by a number of sources.

- Hotels and other lodging
- Food and beverages
- Retail purchases
- Entertainment and other activities
- Parking
- Rental cars
- Taxes and charges (hotel taxes, car rental taxes, sales taxes, and airport fees)

Multipliers account for the direct spending and the additional spending facilitated by this direct spending (Bladen et al. 2018). For example, a visiting team spends money in a restaurant. The restaurant uses that income to buy goods and services from suppliers (e.g. restocking their inventory, paying employees, paying taxes), the suppliers then spend that income on goods and services, and so on. Multiplier effects vary by industry and location. A sales multiplier coefficient can be calculated by estimating the direct, indirect, and induced effects. Direct effects refer to visitor spending on goods and services in the local economy. Indirect effects are from the recirculation of money generated through the direct effects. Induced effects are from the spending by employees impacted by direct and indirect effects. The multiplier can be calculated by the following formula:

$$\text{multiplier} = (\text{direct spending} + \text{indirect spending} + \text{induced spending}) / \text{direct spending}$$

It is important to note that economic impact numbers are estimates, because many different approaches are used to derive numbers. Overall estimates often vary according to how the geographic region is defined (local, regional, national), the number of industries affected (e.g., venues, tourism), and the methods used to collect and measure data. The following are some examples of economic impact estimates across a variety of events.

- Indianapolis, Indiana, was awarded the 2022 College Football Playoff National Championship game. They expect the event to generate more than $150 million for the city and draw approximately 100,000 visitors (Bartner 2017).

- The Horsemen's Benevolent and Protective Association estimates that the Kentucky Derby drives $217 million in economic impact to the Louisville community, from visitor spending on lodging, local transportation, shopping, restaurants, and bars in addition to wagers on the races (Lyons 2018).
- The St. George Tourism Office estimates a $7 million economic impact from hosting the Ironman 70.3 St. George Triathlon, with 12,000 visitors traveling to Southern Utah for the race (DeMille 2018).
- The Taipei 2017 Summer Universiade was estimated to generate $152 million in economic impact to the local economy. The event attracted 7,377 athletes and 127,200 spectators to Taipei City over a 12-day period (Etchells 2018).

Organizers often overstate economic impact, however, in order to justify their activities. The following are some common ways they overinflate their estimates.

- *Lack of objectivity*: Event planners may overstate effects to justify support or investment in events.
- *Not accounting for leakage*: Leakage refers to the portion of spending that does not remain in the local community (e.g., goods and services purchased from outside the community).
- *Counting spending by locals*: Spending by locals is most often just reuse of money already in the local community.
- *Inflating the multiplier*: Providing a higher multiplier coefficient is one of the easiest ways to overstate overall economic impact.
- *Only counting benefits and not costs*: Often communities incur significant costs in hosting events, and those costs should be accounted for.

Joshua Duplechian/ NCAA Photos via Getty Images

Indianapolis won the bid to host the 2010 NCAA Final Four Division I Men's Basketball Championship at Lucas Oil Stadium.

Sports Commissions

The host organization bidding on the event might be a local organizing committee, a chamber of commerce, a CVB, or a sports commission, among others. A **sports commission** is normally a nonprofit or governmental entity designed to attract and assist sporting events. Today, almost every large city has a sports commission or someone in the CVB specifically assigned to sell to the sport market.

According to the National Association of Sports Commissions (NASC), most sports commissions have a small staff (10 or fewer full-time staff) and are overseen by a board of directors. More importantly, all sports commissions depend on volunteers to execute their missions, and most depend on public funding to support their budget (NASC 2018).

The benefits of having a sports commission are both economic and social. For example, the Detroit Sports Commission seeks events that will enhance the image of the city, generate community pride, and improve quality of life in addition to impacting the local economy (Krupa 2017). Here are some examples of mission statements illustrating their role.

The mission of the Louisville Sports Commission (LSC) is to promote active lifestyles and enhance economic vitality by attracting, creating, and hosting quality sporting events in the Louisville area.

The Durham Sports Commission's mission is to create economic and social impact by leading the community's efforts to attract, support, and promote youth, amateur, collegiate, and professional sporting and recreational events.

The mission of the Utah Sports Commission is to help enhance Utah's economy, image, and quality of life through the attraction, promotion, and development of national and international sports, and to be a catalyst for Utah in its Olympic legacy efforts.

Bidding Process

The event owner will specify bid procedures and timetables for the bid. Every organization has different criteria for selecting a host site, and much of this information will be outlined in a **request for proposal** (RFP). RFPs provide information about the event, including specifications, and outline the expectations for the event. Organizations may have very specific requirements, such as facility specifications, playing surface, spectator capacity, locker rooms, and amenities. Minimum requirements may also relate to dates, event staff and officials, and any fees or revenue guarantees.

The minimum requirements to bid for the USA Weightlifting (USAW) National Championships include the following:

- Availability for preferred dates
- 20,000 square feet of competition space
- 7,000 square feet of training space
- Seating for 600 spectators
- Complimentary wired Internet
- Hotels within walking distance of the venue
- 850 room-nights for an estimated 500 participants
- $5,000 rights fee

However, it is rarely sufficient just to meet the minimum requirements to win a bid. Bidders have to identify what will make for an ideal partnership. For example, the USAW outlines what they expect from an ideal partner in their RFP.

- Proximity to a major airport and available transportation
- Strong local weightlifting community
- Strong media and marketing plan to promote the event in the host city
- No or low rental cost for the venue
- Complimentary rooms for USAW staff and discounted rooms for referees

In addition to checking the minimum requirements, organizations requesting bids also assess a host location's suitability for an event by evaluating bidders' other attributes such as their experience in hosting events, financial strength and abilities, level of community support, and support services such as transportation, housing, and meals. Bidders must therefore include information illustrating their suitability across several areas.

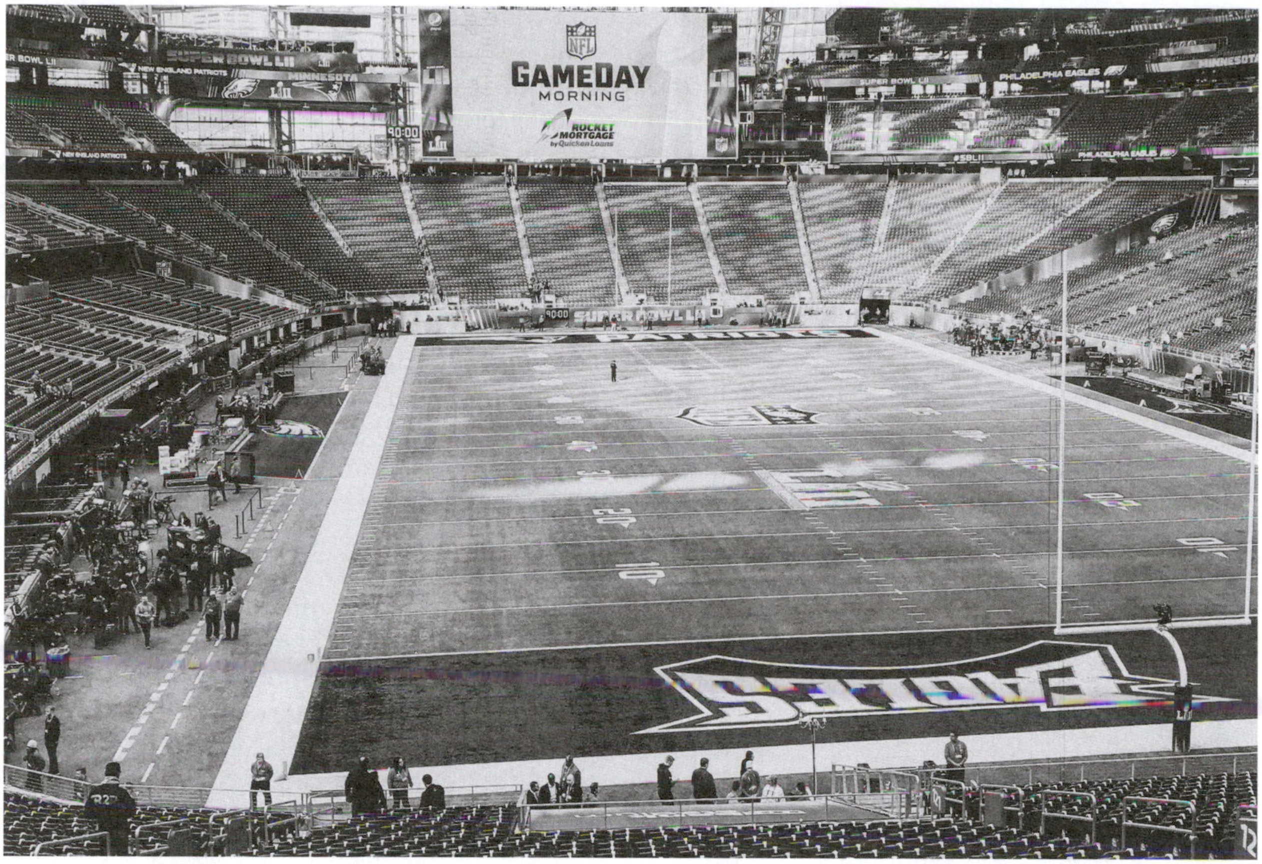

© Chris Greenwell

Minneapolis won the bid for Super Bowl LII.

For example, in requesting bids for their 2019 PDGA Professional Disc Golf World Championships, the Professional Disc Golf Association (PDGA) required bidders to address the following:

- *Host organization*: past events hosted, volunteer support, and community support
- *Host course*: location, layout, length, type of tees, type of targets, signage, and other assets
- *Course amenities*: parking, pavilions, Wi-Fi capabilities, and security
- *Host hotel*: location, capacity, room rates, restaurants in close proximity, pool, exercise room, and meeting space
- *Budget*: revenues (sponsorship, merchandise, food and beverage), expenses (staff, supplies, payout), and expected profit or loss
- *Publicity and marketing plan*: connections with local and regional communities
- *Proposed event schedule*: competitive program and ancillary events

The financial aspects of a bid cannot be overlooked. Many host communities extend considerable financial considerations in order to attract an event that will generate a significant economic impact. For example, host cities do not charge the National Football League rent when they host the Super Bowl. In fact, the NFL gets most of the revenue from the event, while the host city absorbs most of the costs. Communities often offer financial incentives for smaller events as well, in the form of bid fees or in the form of shared or reduced operational costs.

Feasibility Studies

Before bidding, host committees usually conduct some sort of **feasibility study** to make sure that the benefits of hosting the event outweigh the costs. Feasibility studies involve detailed forecasting and analysis of the pros and cons of hosting an event. If benefits outweigh costs, and the local organizing committee is confident they can deliver what the organization requires, the local organizing committee may proceed to put together a bid. For smaller events, feasibility studies may be quite informal, but for major events, these studies can be quite extensive.

There are many questions to ask in a feasibility study.

- Do we have facilities that are appropriate and available?
- Do we have the financial resources to host?
- Do we have the human resources to host?
- Do we have support from necessary stakeholders (community, governmental, business)?
- What will be the costs (financial costs, environmental impact, opportunity costs)?
- Is there a market (participants and spectators) for the event?
- What revenues may stem from hosting?
- What will be the economic impact on the community?
- What other opportunities may arise from hosting (e.g., new business, enhanced image, improved infrastructure)?
- What risks are associated with hosting the event?
- Do we have the time to execute the event appropriately?

Given the time and expense related to bidding for events, communities must be careful about which events they bid on. Careful analysis of a community's strengths and weaknesses allows cities to be selective about which events they bid on, choosing events that best meet their strengths. Dauphin Island, Alabama, is an example of a smaller community that leverages its key strength, beach access, to attract events such as the Extreme Volleyball Professionals (EVP) Island Championship. By identifying their key assets, they can choose to bid on events that would be a great fit for what they have to offer. Similarly, Sioux Falls, South Dakota, illustrates how communities can use their strengths to show how they can be attractive to certain types of events. Sioux Falls touts its large number of venues such as its Sanford Sports Complex which is home to a 3,200-seat arena, a field house with 62,000 square feet of playing space, an indoor tennis facility, and an iceplex with three rinks. These facilities and its location in The Heart of America makes Sioux Falls attractive to youth and amateur events (Swenson 2017).

Cities bidding for mega-events like the Olympic Games and the FIFA World Cup have started to look more closely at the bottom line when considering when to bid. For example, Boston, Budapest, Hamburg, and Rome either withdrew bids or decided not to bid for the 2024 Summer Olympic Games, citing fears of sizeable cost overruns. Similarly, Munich and Stockholm dropped out of bidding for the 2022 Winter Olympic Games, and London withdrew its bid to host the opening of the 2017 Tour de France. In the past, bidders were eager to attach themselves to major sporting events for the international attention and prestige associated with hosting, but now cities are more hesitant to take on the huge financial commitments and risks (Zhukovsk 2017).

Bid Documents

If the host decides to bid on an event, a **bid document** is produced. Bid documents are thorough accountings of the site's key assets and how they conform to bid requirements. These documents may contain information about the host committee to illustrate their expertise and credentials, information about community and sponsor support, and other facts about the community (e.g. population, weather, accommodations, media, attractions) making the location attractive. Table 3.2 is a list of categories commonly found in bid documents.

Considering that the bid process is open to multiple suitors, bidders need to make their bids as competitive as possible. In addition to meeting requirements, host committees should include information that highlights the key strengths of their bid and their competitive advantages over other bidders. The following examples show that criteria may differ from event to event.

TABLE 3.2 Information Commonly Found in Bid Documents

Purpose statement	• Why is the host committee bidding on the event? • What do they hope to achieve through hosting this event?
Host organization	• What experience does the committee have hosting events? • What community or governmental organizations are supporting the event? • Who is filling key positions, and what experience do these people bring to the event?
Budget and finances	• What are the costs associated with the facility, labor, equipment, supplies, printing, etc.? • What are the estimated revenues from registrations, ticket sales, sponsorship, media rights, merchandising, concessions, etc.?
Staff and volunteer support	• Is there an experienced staff available to support the event? • Is there a sizable volunteer base available to support the staff? • What experiences does the host committee have in recruiting and training volunteers?
Competition venues	• What facilities will be available for the event? • What are the facility specifications (seating, parking, restrooms, locker facilities, etc.)? • What amenities exist for players and coaches?
Support facilities	• What other facilities can be used to support the event (meeting space, exhibitor space, space for social events)? • What workspaces are available for staff and volunteers? • What are the arrangements for concessions and merchandise sales?
Transportation	• Where is the nearest airport, and how accessible is the event to air travel? • How are participants able to access competition sites and accommodations? • How can spectators and participants get around the city when not participating in or watching the event?
Accommodations	• What accommodations are available near the site? • How are accommodations priced, and what is the availability during the time of year when the event will take place? • What other lodging options exist?
Health services	• How will the host committee provide for the health and safety of participants and spectators? • What clinical services will be provided to players? • Where are the nearest hospitals and ambulance services?
Public relations and media coverage	• What are the opportunities for media coverage? • Who will be handling public relations for the event?
Environmental sustainability	• What will be the impact on the environment? • How will supplies be properly disposed of?
Geography and climate	• What is the typical weather during the planned event time? • What contingencies exist for adverse weather?
Security	• What is the security plan for players and spectators?

- Glasgow, Scotland, was awarded the 2019 European Athletics Indoor Championships based on their success hosting similar prior events. Enthusiastic crowds and strong venue operations at prior events were cited as assets to Glasgow hosting the event (Carp 2018).
- Even though the Atlanta Braves sought to have the 2020 Major League Baseball (MLB) All-Star game in their new stadium, the league chose 56-year-old Dodger Stadium in Los Angeles, citing that the Dodgers had not hosted since 1980 while the Braves had hosted as recently as 2000 (Tucker 2018).
- After not hosting the NCAA men's basketball tournament games since 1992, Cincinnati was awarded first and second round games in 2022. The Sports Commission noted that renovations to their arena and a revitalized downtown scene were key to winning the bid (Watkins 2017).
- Paris won the 2024 Olympic Games after having fallen short in three earlier bid attempts. They cited a shift in focus away from politics and toward the sports and the athletes. They also placed an emphasis on showing how their event will be greener and cheaper than prior events (Peltier 2017).

Summary

Sporting events can be catalysts for a variety of positive outcomes, both economic and noneconomic. Sporting events can bring participants, spectators, coaches, and officials who generate revenue through local spending on lodging, food, and entertainment. Communities often create sports commissions to attract and assist sporting events.

To make sure that the best possible site is chosen, event organizers often put their events up for bid. To win a bid, sports commissions, or other interested parties, must be able to create bid documents showing not only how they meet the needs of event organizers but also how their location or host organization may be more attractive than others.

Tips for Winning Bids

The following tips illustrate how to make bids more competitive.

- *Demonstrate your capabilities.* Detail how you have the capability and resources to host the event successfully. Show how you have successfully hosted events in the past and how that expertise will contribute to their event.
- *Do your research.* Be sure to understand the event's history, needs, and requirements so that you address each of the requester's questions.
- *Demonstrate support from stakeholders.* To illustrate the strength of your organization, show how you are working with local and regional sport organizations, governmental entities, the corporate sector, and the tourism community.
- *Utilize community resources.* Maximize the expertise of your community partners to incorporate the best data and information into your proposal.
- *Demonstrate your motivation to host.* Be clear about why you are bidding for the event and what you want to get out of it. This approach helps show your commitment to the event and to delivering positive outcomes for all parties.
- *Illustrate why you should be chosen.* Remember, this is a competitive process, so it may not be sufficient to meet the event's requirements. You should provide additional reasons why your location is the best.

LEARNING ACTIVITIES

For this example, assume your community is looking to attract sporting events.

1. Think about what your community has to offer in terms of facilities, amenities, attractions, and infrastructure. What does your community have that would be attractive to events looking for a location? What makes your community more attractive than other competing communities?
2. Based on what you have identified in the prior section, what types of events would you bid on?

CASE STUDY: WHEELCHAIR RUGBY

Wheelchair rugby is a unique sport for people with physical disabilities, combining features of rugby, basketball, ice hockey, and handball. Originating in Winnipeg Canada in 1977, it was created by athletes looking for an alternative to wheelchair basketball. Because of its physical nature, the sport was originally called *murderball* but is now more commonly known as *wheelchair rugby* or *quad rugby*. In 1993, the International Wheelchair Rugby Federation (IWRF) was formed, and a year later it was recognized by the International Paralympic Committee (IPC) as a paralympic sport. It debuted as a full medal sport in the 2000 Sydney Paralympic Games and more than 40 countries either now participate in international competition or are developing the sport.

Wheelchair rugby teams consist of up to 12 players with four on the court at any time. Games consist of four 8-minute quarters played with a ball similar to a volleyball; teams score by carrying the ball across their opponent's goal line. Cones are used to mark the goal lines. Wheelchair rugby is a contact sport, and physical contact between wheelchairs is a fundamental part of the game. Players compete in manual wheelchairs. Competitive players typically use lightweight sports wheelchairs which have to meet certain safety and competitive specifications.

Players are both male and female, with physical disabilities ranging from spinal injuries to amputations to neurological conditions. To allow players with different functional abilities to compete, players are classified based on their abilities on a 0.5 to 3.5 scale, and the four players on the court may not exceed 8 points at any time.

Games are played on surfaces (preferably hardwood) the size of a basketball court, and facilities that can be used for wheelchair basketball are sufficient for wheelchair rugby.

Case Study Application

1. Assume you are organizing a wheelchair rugby event that will attract 30 teams over the course of five days. What would be your primary requirements when soliciting bids? What would be the most important factors in choosing a location?
2. Based on the event in question 1, assume that sports commissions from each of the following three cities have bid on your event. Which of the following would you choose, and why?

   Metropolis

   - Large city with 7,000 hotel rooms
   - 66,000 square foot convention center that can hold five basketball courts
   - Home to numerous attractions (amusement parks, museums, etc.) and restaurants
   - A history of hosting sporting events for all age groups

Middlesboro

- Medium-sized city with 1,200 hotel rooms
- 204,000 square foot convention center that can hold 12 basketball courts
- Centrally located, with easy highway and airport access
- A history of hosting large recreational events for different types of sports

Smallville

- Small city with 600 hotel rooms
- 100,000 square foot convention center that can hold six basketball courts
- Home to a nationally recognized adapted sports training center
- A history of hosting small sporting events for physically handicapped athletes

© Chris Greenwell

CHAPTER 4

Event Budgeting

CHAPTER OBJECTIVES

After completing the chapter, the reader should be able to do the following:

- Understand the budgeting process and develop event budgets.
- Identify appropriate revenue streams.
- Identify appropriate expense categories.
- Understand how to control costs and manage cash flows.

INDUSTRY PROFILE

Scott Crawford, Kansas Collegiate Athletic Conference

Scott Crawford became commissioner of the Kansas Collegiate Athletic Conference in August of 2007. He is responsible for organizing championship events for 23 different sports in addition to various special events. Since becoming commissioner, he has expanded the conference to 13 full and 7 associate members, implemented a statewide radio network, established a live video streaming network, and hosted multiple National Association of Intercollegiate Athletics (NAIA) national championships. He was the recipient of the NAIA's Charles Morris Administrator of the Year Award in 2012-2013.

How do you go about developing your budgets?

I always try to come close to even when it comes to revenues versus expenses. We have an expectation of a certain amount of gate receipts from fans and family that come. Over time, I've built up a process where I use five years of comparable data, which gives me a really good idea about what to expect for gate receipts and gives me an idea of what to expect for expenses. Comparable data really is the foundation for any budget plan that I establish for any events that I run.

How do you control costs?

You have to say no a lot. I try to aim very conservatively on revenues and I try to project rather high on the expenses. We then work toward having expenses come in lower than expected and revenues come in higher than expected. That usually accounts for the adjustment in our margins.

What are some things that pop up that most people overlook?

You had better budget for extra equipment in the event the equipment that you currently use fails. I budget to acquire additional equipment over time, such as over a three-year period. If you can account for that in your budgeting, then you shouldn't really have that big of a surprise in a given year.

How do you save money promoting your events?

We spend the bulk of our time promoting events using our social media accounts. We drive people to our conference website. We also work with the visitors bureaus to fund radio, television, or newspaper advertising. We also try to stay in the same community as much as possible and get as much word-of-mouth advertising as possible by having stayed in those communities.

How do you deal will staffing costs?

If you're not able to acquire volunteers, then your budgets will get rather large. So, my advice is to find some things that the volunteers are willing to work for such as a small thank you gift, conference apparel, or souvenirs that only they have access to. Those kinds of things help them to feel good about giving up two, four, six, eight hours of their time in return for very little compensation. I always plan for having as good a hospitality room as possible for my volunteers. Feeding people well seems to be a great way to reward them.

What other advice would you give people who are planning events?

If you think it might happen, you had better plan for it, because if you think it might happen, it very well could.

An early and important step in the event planning process involves developing an event budget. An **event budget** is an estimate of revenues and expenditures over the life of the event, which helps align financial activities with the organization's overall strategy. Additional benefits of budgeting include:

- Helps event organizers recognize and maximize revenue streams
- Reduces waste by identifying and scrutinizing expense categories
- Communicates financial limitations to management and employees
- Empowers management to make good decisions with their available funds

A budget provides event organizers with realistic estimates of upcoming revenues and expenses associated with the event. Good budgeting requires managers to project all potential revenues and anticipate relevant expenses, and the budgeting process requires significant information gathering and planning.

Event organizers should create two budgets during the budgeting process: a **preliminary budget** and a **working budget**.

- *Preliminary budget*. As the name suggests, preliminary budgets are constructed during the earliest phases of the event planning process. Event organizers spend time gathering information about projected revenues and expenses as they plan for the event. The preliminary budget represents a work in progress; event organizers continue to gather additional information and modify the event budget over time.

- *Working budget*. When organizers believe the numbers presented in the preliminary budget reflect their most informed and accurate estimates, the budget becomes a working budget. The budget numbers in this document should include more specific and expected revenues rather than just estimates. For example, sponsors may have signed contracts detailing that they will receive specified sponsorship benefits and pay a specified amount in return. Participants may have paid registration fees, and spectators may have purchased tickets. Similarly, event organizers may have signed contracts with vendors, agreeing to pay the suppliers a certain amount in exchange for the requested products. This document will help track how actual financial performances compare to detailed estimates. For instance, if incoming revenues are lower than expected, organizers may attempt to identify ways to increase the number of paying participants or spectators. If staffing costs are too high, organizers may look for ways to supplement staff through the use of volunteers.

Event Budgeting Process

The budgeting process is an in-depth and necessary exercise typically involving five basic steps: Align with organization goals, research, estimate revenues, estimate expenses, and project profits and losses.

Align With Organization Goals

Because budgets differ according to what the organization is trying to accomplish, organizers should set performance targets that are consistent with the organization's overall goals. The anticipated size, scope, and purpose of the event will dictate the budget.

Research

A budget is only as good as the information collected. Having good information helps organizers make more informed estimates and projections as they begin constructing a budget. Information gathering typically comes from both internal and external sources.

Sources of internal information

- *Historical information (past events and similar activities)*: Information from prior events can inform you about what to expect as you go forward.
- *Financial statements*: Look at revenues and expenses from previous events; notice where estimates varied from actual charges, and identify potential reasons for those variations.
- *Management and staff feedback*: Often, your own staff can be your best resource. Each department probably has a good idea of

what they need in order to accomplish their tasks.

Sources of external information

- *Current and potential vendors*: Contacting vendors regarding goods and services needed for the event can generate initial cost estimates. Event organizers can also use online sources to investigate prices for various goods and services and gather information on credit terms, payment processes, and available discounts in order to make more accurate estimates.
- *Industry trends*: An examination of industry trends may help organizers identify potential opportunities and threats that could directly affect future activities. Opportunities include new customers, products, channels, and price increases, which could have a positive effect on sales. Threats include competitors and accompanying price wars, government regulations, and challenging economic conditions, which could have a negative effect on sales. Have new competitors or events arisen since the last time the organizers hosted the event? Do economic indicators show evidence of spending by spectators and participants on sporting events similar to this one?
- *Professional associations and trade publications*: Professional associations often provide information to members related to operating costs, participation numbers, industry trends, and other topics that can help organizers make more accurate estimates.
- *Competing events*: Examining how competitors are running their events, the services they offer, and the prices they charge can help provide benchmarks for comparison. Learning from other competitors may also help event organizers avoid potential mishaps and account for previously unexpected occurrences.

Estimate Revenues

Revenues represent funds coming into the event or organization through an exchange of money for goods or services. Most events will generate revenues from a variety of sources. The challenge for event organizers is to identify where money will come from and estimate how much will be generated in each category. Historical sales information can provide insights into the latest financial trends and seasonal patterns, will give organizers perspective regarding the types of sales generated from past events, and will help them make estimates about potential sales associated with the newest events.

When budgeting, event organizers have to forecast revenues and make projections about how much the event will generate. As part of these projections, organizers should consider using scenario analysis—estimating a best-case, worst-case, and most likely scenario. These scenarios allow event organizers to see the range of projected sales figures and make decisions based on several potential outcomes.

Estimate Expenses

Expenses represent money flowing out of the event or organization and are the costs associated with generating revenues. Organizers will incur expenses as they attempt to generate revenues. For example, the event may create sales through parking. Organizers will hire or contract employees to manage those parking transactions—collecting parking fees, directing traffic, and helpings fans get to the event quickly and safely. Event organizers can calculate expense items by employing the same process used for forecasting revenues, such as reviewing historical data and examining how much was spent on similar events in the past. Have costs increased over time? What costs have other event organizers incurred related to operating or hosting the same or similar events? Do opportunities exist to minimize or reduce costs with the upcoming event? What other information can be gleaned from organizational financial information or external trade journals and economic indicators that may factor into expense projections? The opportunities and threats identified during the sales forecasting process may also provide insights into related expenses. For example, marketing and promotion expenses may increase with an influx of new competitors or waning economic conditions.

Event organizers can use this pool of information to develop an expense-related scenario analysis, projecting best-case, worst-case, and most likely scenarios that now incorporate revenues and expenses. The planning process should focus on getting the most out of every dollar spent, because every expense dollar represents a cost to the event and the organization and reduces the event's profit potential. Yet the adage "it takes money to make money" remains true. Event organizers must spend money on a variety of expenses, from paying staff and other personnel to preparing the site for the event to promoting and marketing the event. These expenses may reduce the event's overall profit potential. The goal is to make sure that the event generates the biggest bang for its buck, meaning that each dollar spent leads to an accompanying increase in sales and profit generation.

Project Profits and Losses

After estimating revenues and expenses, event organizers should develop an event budget, which includes expected revenue projections and expense projections. A comparison of revenues and expenses will give organizers a snapshot of projected net income or net loss. Net income occurs when revenues exceed expenses, while net loss occurs when revenues do not cover the incurred expenses. Depending on how this budget matches performance targets, organizers may need to identify new revenues, look for ways to cut costs, or adjust their planning. A sample budget template is presented in figure 4.1.

Income category	Estimated income	Actual income
Entry fees (price × number of teams)		
Sponsorships		
Donations		
Silent auction		
Merchandise sales		
Food and beverage sales		
Totals		

Expense category	Estimated expense	Actual expense
Venue rental		
Board rental		
Participant gifts		
Staffing		
Awards		
Website hosting		
Printing		
Cost of goods sold		
Totals		

Revenues		
Expenses		
Net profit (loss)		

FIGURE 4.1 Sample budget template for a fundraising cornhole tournament.

After projecting profits and losses, event organizers should examine industry data where possible, and use this information to determine whether the event estimates are in line with, or similar to, the competition. Did other events incur similar expenses related to this event's marketing and operating expenses? Did other organizers bring in similar sales on the number of athletes and spectators forecast for this event? Event organizers should feel greater comfort with their budgets when the estimates are similar to those of other events. Still, in some cases, event projections may not reflect the numbers of similar events. A thorough review may be required to determine where the differences lie and what justifications there may be for those differences. Differences from industry norms are not necessarily negative. Instead, they simply merit a second look, so that event organizers can provide adequate support or rationale for the variances.

Types of Revenues

Revenues represent money coming into an organization, resulting from an exchange of goods or services. Although high revenues do not necessarily guarantee financial success, they represent the cornerstone of, or the pathway toward, a more profitable event. Event organizers should understand their available revenue streams and determine where they will focus their revenue generation efforts for upcoming events. This section provides a listing of common revenue streams with examples from various sporting events.

Tickets, Registrations, and Memberships

Tickets, registrations, and memberships from attendance at or participation in an event are often the main source of an event's revenue. Spectator events such as a boxing match or a professional baseball game generate revenues from spectators purchasing tickets to attend the event. Participatory events such as the Chicago Marathon and Ironman generate revenue through participants paying registration fees. Other organizations such as USA Triathlon and the U.S. Tennis Association receive revenues when sporting event participants pay membership dues as part of their entry into the events. When estimating this source of revenue, it is important to adhere to the following steps. See table 4.1 for an example.

- *Define your inventory*. For a spectator event, your inventory may be limited by the number of seats you have or the space available to hold customers. For a participant event, you may be limited by how many participants you can effectively accommodate. For example, 18-hole golf scrambles are often limited to 144 players because any more players would significantly slow down the pace of play.

- *Classify your inventory*. Not all tickets have the same value, so you need to identify

TABLE 4.1 Sample Registration Revenue Projections for a Tennis Competition

Registration type	Registration price	Capacity	Maximum revenue	Expected registrations	Expected revenue
Regular	$45.00	48	$2,160.00	40	$1,800.00
Youth	$25.00	24	$600.00	18	$450.00
Senior	$30.00	24	$720.00	18	$540.00
Team	$150.00	8	$1,200.00	6	$900.00
Totals			$4,680.00		$3,690.00

how much inventory you have available at each price point. For example, you may have 40 front row seats that sell for $100 each, 800 seats that sell for $50 each, and 400 seats that sell for $25 each. Similarly, participant events may break into price tiers with different benefits for each tier.

• *Estimate sales at each price point*. Use sound research to estimate how many sales you will make at each price point. Numerous factors such as the type of event, where it is located, the type of consumer it attracts, and when it is scheduled will affect event sales. Given the uncertainty of event sales, it is usually best to be conservative with your estimates to avoid overestimating revenues in this area.

Sponsorships

Spectator and participatory sporting events often generate revenues through sponsorship rights by partnering with corporations and other organizations. Event organizers may agree to create signage, booths, or other displays promoting the sponsorship. In exchange for a sponsorship fee, the sponsor has the opportunity to reach a desired target market attending or participating in the event. Brands typically have different reasons for sponsoring events, for example:

- Red Bull sponsors extreme sporting events in order to connect with young consumers who have an affinity for those types of events (Collier 2018).
- Adidas sponsors the World Outgames, an LGBT-focused sporting and human rights event to reach out to the LGBT community (Kell 2017).
- Piper-Heidsieck, a French champagne house, signed a multimillion-dollar sponsorship with tennis's Australian Open in hopes of expanding champagne consumption beyond moments of celebration (Tabakoff 2018).
- Northwest Mutual sponsors NCAA championship events in order to engage with key consumer groups and generate business leads (Vladem 2018).

Merchandising and Licensing

Sport organizations view sales of merchandise and licensing rights as another revenue opportunity. These products satisfy fans looking for ways to commemorate their attendance at various sporting events and to show their affiliation with a specific athlete, team, league, or sport. Spectators and participants alike appreciate the opportunity to purchase related merchandise. Event organizers can benefit financially from this revenue stream by offering a range of licensed products and merchandise to interested consumers. The following are some tips for maximizing merchandise sales.

- Location is key to maximizing sales.
- Know what customers are looking for and have those items in stock.
- Create souvenir and collectible items that would appeal to customers wanting to commemorate their attendance.
- Have sufficient space available for merchandise sales.
- Train your sales team to process sales quickly and efficiently.
- Have adequate staffing for high-volume sales windows (e.g., when fans enter and exit the facility).
- Use mobile credit card readers so you are not limited to selling only to consumers with cash.
- Prevent illegal sales of unlicensed merchandise in and around your facility.

Food and Beverage Sales

Food and beverage sales can be a major revenue stream for sporting events. While concession operations take a lot of time and effort, they can be very profitable if managed correctly. Issues related to menu, inventory, equipment, staffing, risk, and service can all cut into profits without strong planning. For this reason, many organizations choose to outsource their concessions to organizations that often can provide management expertise and purchasing power event operators may not have.

In addition to classic fan favorites like hot dogs, nachos, popcorn, and beer, concessionaires are expanding their offerings in order to provide a better, and more profitable experience (White 2017). Some of these trends include the following:

- High-end items such as sushi, crab cakes, stir-fry, and cappuccinos to appeal to more affluent consumers.
- Novelty items such as chargrilled octopus at San Francisco 49ers games, lobster poutine at Boston Red Sox games, and cricket tacos at Atlanta Hawks games.
- Locally sourced options to appeal to consumers preferring authentic food experiences.
- Healthy options including fruit, salads, and gluten-free items.
- Craft beers from local breweries.
- Upscale mixed drinks with specialty cocktails.
- Self-service options where consumers can grab items quickly without waiting in long lines.

Additionally, more event organizers have incorporated technology to better serve consumers interested in purchasing concessions. Using a mobile app, fans can place orders from their seats, enter their credit card information, input their seat locations, and wait for their items to arrive. This type of technology has the benefit of providing convenience to consumers and making them feel special, and at the same time providing an additional point of sale for the concessionaire (Attwood 2014).

Concession items typically have large markups because consumers at sporting events don't have other options and are typically willing to spend more on themselves when they are attending a sporting event. On the other hand, Mercedes-Benz stadium, home of the Atlanta Falcons and many other major events, went the opposite way by offering what they called Fan First Menu Pricing, charging 50 percent less for food and nonalcoholic beverages. As a result, they saw an overall increase in fan spending of 16 percent because fans arrived at games earlier and ate inside the stadium rather than in the surrounding area (Belson 2018).

Parking

Parking is a major revenue driver at many events. In addition to the traditional pay-per-car model, many events now maximize revenue through premium parking where consumers can receive a variety of amenities such as prime locations, shuttle service to the facility, on-site security, and dedicated facility entrances. In addition, many organizations have created special lots designed for tailgating or camping to provide additional benefits, at a cost, for consumers.

Publications

Many events derive revenue from the sales of souvenir or commemorative publications. For example, Churchill Downs creates special programs for its annual Kentucky Oaks and Derby events (Kentucky Derby 2018). These programs sell for a premium over the usual price on a non-Oaks or non-Derby day, and provide customers with memorabilia that may appreciate in value over time. Keeping in mind that not everyone will be interested in purchasing a program, some events choose to give away programs in order to put the materials in the hands of more consumers and to provide more value for program advertisers.

Corporate Hospitality

Corporations and other large organizations may express interest in corporate hospitality, whereby sport organizations or event organizers set aside seats and space for a group of company employees plus their families, friends, and customers. These corporate hospitality packages provide benefits both for the event organizers and for the corporations purchasing them. Event organizers can work with a larger group of confirmed ticketholders, ensuring a large block of tickets sold. They also have the opportunity to upsell the event by offering additional amenities not always offered to individual ticketholders, such as dedicated support staff catering to the guests. In turn, corporations can use these offerings to provide incentives to productive employees, thank current customers for their support, or attract new customers.

- The Ryder Cup, a golf competition between teams from Europe and the United States, earns a significant amount of revenue off hospitality packages. The host organization sells a variety of packages such as chalets, suites, and reserved tables in hospitality tents. These packages are all-inclusive, providing a premium on-site experience with parking, food and beverage, and concierge service (Kirchen 2018).
- The NFL offers hospitality packages for the Super Bowl ranging from pregame parties and concerts to access to in-stadium clubs and field access for the postgame trophy presentation. Tickets for these special experiences range from $5,000 to $17,500 per person (Tucker 2018).
- At Formula One races, consumers can experience races through private viewing facilities in addition to accessing pit tours, driver appearances, and exclusive entertainment (F1 Corporate Hospitality 2019).

Donations, Grants, and Subsidies

Depending on the size and type of event, additional funding may be necessary to make the event feasible. In such cases, events often reach out to public and private sources to acquire additional revenue. Sources include donors, grants, sports commissions, and government **subsidies**.

- *Donors*. Through capital funding campaigns, organizers can attract donors who express an affiliation with the organization and a willingness to contribute. The donors may reside in the same community where the organization is located and witness firsthand the event's or the organizer's impact. Donors also may share similar interests with the event or support the event's activities and feel excited to contribute to its longevity.
- *Grants*. Financial grants may be available to help fund events. Many governmental and private foundations will consider funding events that align with their initiatives or their missions. For example, funding organizations may support events that reach underserved populations, at-risk youth, or people with disabilities.
- *Sports commissions*. Sports commissions often help fund events that will facilitate business growth in their communities.
- *Government subsidies*. Regional and national governments often subsidize sporting events and sport facilities in hopes of driving tourism, increasing employment, or enhancing the community's profile. The willingness of governments to subsidize sporting events varies from community to community.

Media Rights

The media can provide significant revenues and promotional opportunities. Event organizers may negotiate with various media outlets, exchanging the right to broadcast their events for contracted revenues. The largest and most popular events, such as the Olympic Games, the Super Bowl, and the World Cup, tend to command the largest media rights contracts. However, event organizers of regional and local levels may also have the opportunity to reach broadcasters and provide their events to a smaller but more targeted audience. Media rights exist for a variety of channels, including television, terrestrial and satellite radio, and the Internet.

- *Television*. The biggest sporting events typically negotiate media rights. Outlets for television include local broadcast, national broadcast, cable, satellite, and subscription networks.

- *Internet.* The Internet continues to expand its reach as a medium by which consumers can access sports. Organizations generate revenue by broadcasting on their own sites as well as through streaming sites or social networks. The Internet especially has given smaller events a chance to showcase their offerings to dedicated and potentially curious audiences alike.
- *Terrestrial radio.* Radio is the oldest of the media offerings. Television and the Internet typically capture more media attention, yet radio still plays a sizable role in broadcasting sporting events. Sport organizations and event organizers continue to use radio to reach fans, whether at home, in the office, or on the road.
- *Satellite radio.* Coupled with terrestrial radio, satellite radio is another way consumers access information about and tune in to various sporting events.

Event organizers can choose from a variety of agreement types and associated fees. These decisions are largely contingent on the size, scope, and popularity of their events. One of the more lucrative is a rights fee. A **rights fee** is an agreement whereby a broadcaster pays for the rights to broadcast an event and its associated content. The broadcaster is gambling it can sell enough advertising or generate other revenues to offset the cost of the rights fee.

Traditional broadcasters pay large sums to televise big events. The following are a few examples.

- ESPN and Turner pay a combined $2.6 billion per year to televise NBA games (Ourand 2018).
- Sky Sports pays nearly £200 million per year to televise Formula One events in the UK (Benson 2018).
- ESPN pays $40 million per year for the US rights to broadcast Wimbledon (Kaplan 2017).
- Sky Germany and EuroSport share the rights to broadcast the Bundesliga, paying €1.159 billion per year (New Bundesliga 2016).

Nontraditional broadcasters have also entered the market. The following are examples of rights agreements between streaming companies and sporting events.

- Verizon agreed to pay the NFL about $500 million per year to live stream on digital platforms (Adgate 2018).
- Amazon Prime pays up to £10 million per year to air ATP events in the UK (Sweeney 2017).

Other types of agreements include the following:

- *Time buy.* A time buy is different from a rights fee agreement. In a time buy, the event property buys the airtime and broadcasts the event itself. In this situation, the event assumes the risk of selling advertising and sponsorship, while keeping the revenue. Many smaller organizations choose this option when they need the exposure to promote their sport or to provide value for their sponsors.
- *Barter.* Barter agreements, or partnerships, involve some sort of split in advertising revenues between the event property and the broadcaster. This type of agreement reduces the risk for each party.
- *Syndication.* Event organizers can sell media rights to have their events broadcast simultaneously on multiple television and radio stations in different markets. This opportunity expands an event organizer's reach beyond a single channel or station, and it meets consumer sport consumption demands beyond a local market.
- *Pay-per-view.* Pay-per-view is an agreement whereby cable or satellite television providers offer the event, and viewers pay the provider a fee for the right to access the event. Pay-per-view is typically used for events that may attract a smaller but more passionate audience willing to pay a premium for access to the event. Mixed martial arts, boxing, and professional wrestling have made efficient use

of pay-per-view, and other events have also found a use for this method.

Types of Expenses

Expenses represent money flowing out of an organization, or the costs incurred to generate revenue. The old adage that it takes money to make money best summarizes the concept of expenses. Event organizers need to incur expenses such as hiring staff or promoting the event in order to provide superior service and encourage potential attendees to purchase tickets. Having said that, event organizers should proceed with caution, because expenses can quickly erode the event's bottom line. Carefully planning and tracking expenses will also help ensure that the revenues generated lead to a financially more successful and viable event. Expenses typically fall into two categories: variable costs and fixed costs.

- *Variable costs* are costs that change in proportion to the event's activities. For example, a local YMCA hosting a youth soccer tournament may purchase T-shirts for each participant. At $5 per shirt, the organization would pay $500 to a T-shirt supplier if 100 children participate, but only $250 if 50 children participate. In this situation, the cost varies according to the number of children participating.
- *Fixed costs*, on the other hand, remain the same, whatever the organization's activities. For example, the YMCA may hire a tournament director for $1,000. This cost is a fixed cost because the tournament director will receive the same amount no matter how many children participate in the event.

This section provides a listing of the various expenses event organizers should expect when planning for and putting on events. Event organizers should consider these expense items and take a strategic approach in determining which of these expenses, and how much, to incur in their efforts to generate revenues for the event.

Event Operations

Event organizers have to budget for the expenses directly related to organizing and operating the event itself. These costs are basically the cost of doing business and vary according to the size and type of event. The challenge is to anticipate which expenses the event will incur and budget for them so that there are no surprises. Some typical event operations costs to consider are:

- *Administrative expenses*: accounting, phone and internet service, office supplies, legal services, office space, postage, software, storage, etc.
- *Staffing costs*: full-time staff salaries and benefits, part-time worker salaries and benefits, volunteer expenses, uniforms, training, travel, etc.
- *Medical costs*: first aid supplies, athletic trainers, physicians, emergency services, etc.
- *Officials*: referees, timekeepers, and statisticians, etc.
- *Competition equipment*: balls, goals, nets, specialized playing surfaces, whistles, signage, etc.
- *Competition services*: towels, laundry service, catering, water, ice, snacks, waste management, tents, tables, chairs, etc.

Facility or Venue Costs

Facility rental fees are often one of the larger costs an event incurs. Careful planning, site selection, and lease negotiation is necessary to ensure facility rental fees do not overwhelm the budget.

Estimating facility expenses will present different challenges based on the type of rental agreement. With a straight rental agreement, the event typically pays a flat fee for the use of the facility. In this case, the fee stays constant regardless of the number of participants. Some rental agreements may include a percentage of ticket sales or registrations rather than a flat fee. In that case each additional participant

© Human Kinetics

Additional equipment required for a golf scramble.

increases the fee paid to the venue. Other venues may include a combination of the two. For example, an organization renting a golf course for a fund-raiser may pay the course a $1,000 guarantee plus $45 for each golfer registered to participate. In cases such as this, event organizers have to consider both fixed and variable costs.

In addition to facility rental fees, event organizers may have to budget operation expenses required by the facility. Following is a list of fees you may incur in addition to rental fees.

- Taxes
- Setup and teardown
- Security or police
- Ushers and guest services
- Ticket takers and box office
- Ambulance and emergency medical services
- Traffic and parking
- Maintenance and janitorial services
- Electrical and HVAC services
- Utilities
- Physical plant and labor
- Concession and merchandise fees
- Administrative fees
- Use of concession or kitchen areas
- Use of auxiliary facilities (e.g., practice room, driving range)

Insurance

Most events and facilities require some sort of insurance coverage to guard against potential damage to the facility, loss, or injury. Other types of insurance may be purchased to guard against cancellations, weather, or labor shortages. The amount and type of insurance you need will vary according to the event. For example, a mixed martial arts event, with a relatively high likelihood of injury, will have different insurance needs than a golf tournament. Similarly, events serving alcohol will likely incur more risks than those not serving alcohol.

Player-Related Costs

Player costs will vary by event and may include items such as appearance fees, prize money, transportation and accommodations, equipment and supplies, and player services. For example, in addition to prize money, many professional tennis tournaments offer sizable appearance fees to ensure their events have enough star power. Even if you are not compensating players, you may incur expenses related to food, lodging, travel, and any associated perks.

Capital Investment

Event organizers may purchase physical assets for use over multiple events. Large-scale sporting events such as the Olympic Games and the World Cup make major capital investments in their host cities and countries, including improvements to transportation and other community-wide infrastructure, in conjunction with investments directly associated with their events.

Traveling or tour sporting events may also make major capital investments, which may be used numerous times across multiple locations during the tour. For example, an extreme sporting event may have to invest in ramps and skate bowls. A bike race would need portable race clocks, cameras, and course markers. A rodeo tour may need to invest in portable gates, security walls, and seating. Further, event organizers who operate traveling events should also consider the logistical costs associated with transporting these capital investments and include the projected expenses in their budget.

Marketing and Promotion

Event organizers often have to incur significant costs to market their events. Sport organizations and events large and small regularly incur these expenses to generate interest and excitement, which eventually translates into ticket sales and registrations. Some potential marketing expenses include:

- Creative fees to develop logos, advertisements, and publications
- Advertising costs (outdoor space, space in print publications, radio and television time, and social media targeting)
- Promotional materials and giveaways
- Website hosting and management
- Social media content production and management
- Photography
- Media costs (credentials, media room, hospitality)
- Marketing staff

Sponsor Fulfillment

Event organizers must make sure they deliver on the terms of their sponsorships, fulfilling what they promised sponsors. Costs associated with sponsorship fulfillment involve everything promised to the sponsor, and these expenses should be included in the budget and tracked as they are incurred. Providing this level of service can be costly in terms of manpower, tickets, media, data, and other amenities. However, sponsorship fulfillment is a critical element in ensuring that sponsors are retained for future events. Common expense categories for sponsorship fulfilment include:

- *Activation*: All of the signage, vendor space, promotions, and advertising promised to the sponsor
- *Tickets and hospitality*: Free or discounted tickets to attend the event plus special access and hospitality while in attendance
- *Sponsor liaisons*: Designated staff to guide corporate sponsors during the event and attend to their special requests or needs
- *Postevent reporting*: Summaries of what the sponsors received in exchange for their monetary or product commitments, which may include detailed information about event viewership and attendance, the time and duration of their commercials, and the estimated number of potential consumers who saw or responded to promotional activities

Guest Management and Hospitality

Event organizers work with a variety of stakeholders to organize and host their events. These stakeholders may include participants, spectators, corporate sponsors and other corporations, staff and volunteers, and VIP guests. To keep this varied group happy, you may consider providing special amenities and services as part of your guest management and hospitality offerings. For example, the Olympic Games organizers traditionally have an athlete village for participants, where they can access a variety of services from housing to medical assistance to food and beverages.

Guest management may also come in the form of corporate hospitality, whereby event organizers make special arrangements for corporate sponsors and other corporate guests. These groups may use the hospitality offerings to reward employees and current customers, plus meet and attract potential customers. Event organizers often provide hospitality for coaches, volunteers, and officials to thank them for their assistance. These services also come

Tom Pennington/Getty Images for HONOLULU MARATHON

Participants enjoying post-race snacks, which added to their event experience.

at a cost, and organizers should consider the number of people required to staff the hospitality area and what items will be provided (e.g., food, beverages, seating).

Event Presentation

One of the largest financial considerations is presenting the actual event from the opening ceremonies to the competition itself to the closing ceremonies. The opening and closing ceremonies are extensive events in and of themselves and require a detailed level of planning and budget forecasting. For example, the World Flying Disc Federation outlines cost considerations for its awards, ceremonies, and social events. These expenses include securing venue space and accounting for associated rental expenses, security and other personnel, tables and chairs, catering food and beverage costs, trash collection and disposal, lighting, entertainment, and a players' lounge. Additional expenses required for the closing ceremonies include medals and trophies awarded to players and teams (WFDF 2018). Event organizers should consider the complete costs associated with these activities. These activities will leave a lasting impression on the event stakeholders, including participants, spectators, sponsors, staff, volunteers, and other guests.

Miscellaneous Expenses

Miscellaneous expenses are those costs that are typically too small to need their own category. Event organizers should include a line for miscellaneous expenses in their budget to cover these costs.

Contingency Allowances

Contingency allowances are funds reserved for emergencies or cost overruns. With most events, there are additional or unanticipated costs, such as those incurred because of bad weather or price increases from suppliers. Plan

Tips for Budgeting Success

The following tips outline how to make budgeting more successful.

- *Do your research.* The more information you have, the better chance you have to make good estimates. Look at similar events, contact suppliers, and involve employees in the process to make sure you have the most realistic and accurate information.
- *Be conservative in your revenue estimates and liberal in your expense estimates.* It is easy to balance a budget by nudging your revenue estimates up and underestimating expenses, but you are setting yourself up for failure. It is better to be realistic in expectations rather than to create an untenable budget.
- *Monitor income and expense.* It is important to monitor activities to identify where the organization is over- or underperforming.
- *Reforecast.* Actual revenues and expenses are likely to vary from estimated revenues and expenses. Therefore, organizations need to periodically reforecast their estimates. Reforecasting allows organizers to reassess and reallocate funds.
- *Maximize revenue.* Develop and implement plans to obtain all income.
- *Control costs.* Identify ways to save money and avoid unnecessary expenses.
- *Be prepared for the unexpected.* Budget for emergencies and contingencies. Anticipate additional costs and be prepared to cover those costs.

for a contingency amount of 5 to 10 percent of your overall expenses.

Controlling Costs

The process of controlling costs is an important facet of event management. Event organizers may spend significant time making meticulous budgetary estimates and forecasts. However, it becomes equally important to control costs throughout the event to ensure those estimates become a reality. Cost overruns can quickly turn a potentially successful event into a financial nightmare.

Event organizers are encouraged to follow a few recommendations to keep costs under control. They should take advantage of cost procurement procedures by finding low-cost goods and services through auctions, bids, or negotiations. They can use their working budget in conjunction with a spreadsheet-based tracking system to monitor their expenses. A spreadsheet may take some time to create, but once a suitable template is created, event organizers can more readily make changes in one section of the budget and have those changes update across the spreadsheet.

Spreadsheets can also be used to estimate expected costs. Updating the spreadsheet throughout the event allows for tracking revenues and expenses in real time, allowing event organizers to make changes quickly to various line items or to examine the effects of adjusted estimates. Adding additional columns to the spreadsheet allows organizers to input actual costs and calculate the variances between forecast and actual expenditures. This exercise will help organizers quickly see where cost overruns exist and determine ways to rein costs in for future expenditures. This information may prove useful during the postevent process as you assess the successes of your events and highlight best practices and improvement opportunities for future events. Spreadsheets also create a paper trail and critical documentation for future events.

Controls should be put in place to determine who can make spending decisions. Event organizers should limit who makes these decisions and the spending amounts they can authorize. Restricting spending authorizations and amounts to relatively few people will help make sure that spending is monitored and will leave fewer chances for spending to spiral out of control. Similarly, controls should be established for who can use the organization's credit card or submit purchase orders. These spending options typically have higher authorization limits and allow users to make larger purchases. Organizers should have proper knowledge of products and be authorized to purchase them to ensure that spending remains in control.

In conjunction with limited use, event organizers should create spending checks and balances with proper controls and oversight. For example, if one person uses the event or organization credit card or submits a purchase order, someone else in the organization should examine this cost to determine whether this was a necessary and approved expense. Once purchases have been made, organizers should ensure adequate documentation of this spending through credit card receipts and bank statements. This documentation creates a paper trail from the original approval of the expense to evidence of its occurrence. Additionally, event organizers should retain this documentation, inputting the appropriate numbers into the spreadsheet, so others can easily see what has been spent thus far and determine whether spending is on track.

Finally, organizers may utilize a petty cash fund (typically $100 or less in loose currency) to make small purchases. A tracking mechanism should exist for these funds as well. People using the petty cash account should submit receipts, and this spending should be documented in the tracking spreadsheet. Guidelines for spending—who can use petty cash and for what items—should be determined in advance and carefully monitored throughout the event. Proper tracking and documentation of spending will help organizers keep costs under control and may help with related cash flow and cash management considerations.

Cash Flow and Cash Management

Cash flow and cash management address the timing of revenues and expenses. Event organizers often incur expenses before they receive adequate revenues to cover them, especially early in the event planning process. For example, a 5K organizer may need to purchase flyers and other promotional materials to market the upcoming event, but athletes are not likely to register until they learn about the event through these marketing activities. In this case, there is a delay between when the organizers incurred expenses to market the events and when they received revenues in the form of registration fees to offset the marketing expenditures. This means that event organizers may face a cash flow problem, where they need to pay their vendors but wonder where they will get the funds to do so. Organizers may need to seek out government agencies, sponsors, private sources, and financial institutions to help defray the costs. Providing evidence of a clear budget, cost controls, or previous event and organizational financial statements may help in the effort to secure funds if organizers can show a clear connection between these expenditures and subsequent revenue opportunities.

Summary

Event budgeting begins early in the event planning process and is key to making sure the event's financial activities align with the organization's mission. An event budget is an estimate of revenues and expenditures over the life of the event, and good event budgeting empowers management and staff to make sound financial decisions.

Budgeting requires significant information gathering and planning in order to identify and project revenues and expenses. An organization's net profit (net loss) will be the difference between actual revenues and expenses, therefore it is vital for organizations to identify and maximize revenue streams by simultaneously accounting for associated expenses and controlling costs.

In conjunction with putting together the budget, organizers are encouraged to compare the estimated figures to the actual numbers after the events take place. This exercise will give them the chance to see where their estimates were correct and where variances existed. Taking time to examine these variances will provide a valuable reference when planning future events.

LEARNING ACTIVITIES

1. Research event bid proposals from sport events and examine their revenue requirements and anticipated expenses. Where could they be making more money? How could they control expenses?
2. Identify a local sporting event and develop a preliminary budget. How would you go about estimating revenues? How could you estimate expenses?

CASE STUDY: FUND-RAISING GOLF SCRAMBLE

Golf scrambles are popular fund-raisers for organizations. For these events, organizers rent a golf course for a day and charge golfers to participate for fun and prizes. Well-organized events can raise a lot of money, but poorly organized events can struggle to make money.

Assume your organization has taken over operations for an annual golf scramble. The organizing committee has asked you to investigate probable income and expenditures and prepare a budget for next week's committee meeting. After some initial investigation, you have come up with the following information:

Revenues

- *Entry fees*: Each player is charged an entry fee to play. The organization has total control over how much to charge. The challenge is to charge enough to maximize revenue but not so much as to inhibit participation. Your research suggests that the most someone would pay for an event like this is about $120.
- *Sponsorship*: Organizers sell sponsorships for the event. In the past, they have been able to generate between $1,000 and $3,000 for this event.

Expenses

- *Facility Rental*: To secure the golf course for the event, the facility charges a $1,000 fee, which allows players access to the driving range and pro shop.
- *Promotion*: The event organizers promote the event via the local media (newspaper, radio, and television advertisements plus social media sites).
- *Equipment and rentals*: Not much equipment is needed for the actual event because the golf course provides most everything. However, organizers do usually need to rent items such as wireless radios, tents, umbrellas, etc.
- *Supplies*: Organizers need to budget for supplies to run the event, such as printing, office supplies, postage, etc.
- *Insurance*: A short-term accident and general liability policy covers organizers from risks.
- *Photographer*: Organizers hire a photographer to document the event and to provide photos to the participants.
- *Awards and trophies*: Trophies are provided for first-, second-, and third-place teams.
- *Greens fees*: The golf course charges $45 per player. There is a 72-player minimum and a 144-player maximum.
- *Food and drink*: Lunch is provided for the players. To make the event more hospitable, organizers provide water, soft drinks, and snacks on the course. The golf course charges $12 per player to provide these items.
- *Participant gifts*: A goody bag is provided to each participant. Goody bags include balls, tees, and a gift commemorating the event. In the past, the event has provided logoed water bottles, shoe bags, hats, and T-shirts. This past year, each participant received a shot glass engraved with the event logo and date. The cost per participant was $8.

Summary of 2018 Event

The 2018 event registered 100 players at a price of $100 per player. They were able to generate $2,000 in sponsorship.

Entry fees ($100 per player x 100 players)	$10,000
Sponsorship	$2,000
Total revenues	$12,000
Facility rental	$1,000
Promotion	$650
Equipment and rentals	$400
Supplies	$150
Insurance	$250
Photographer	$200
Awards and trophies	$350
Greens fees ($45 per player x 100 players)	$4,500
Food and drink ($12 per player x 100 players)	$1,200
Participant gifts ($8 per player x 100 players)	$800
Total expenses	$9,500

Case Study Application

1. What was the event's profit (loss) last year?
2. What was the break-even entry fee?
3. Based on the same number of players and the same amount of sponsorship, how much would the entry fee have to be increased to make a profit of $4,000? What would be your concerns with increasing the entry fee?
4. Based on the same entry fee and the same amount of sponsorship, how many players would have to be recruited to make a profit of $4,000? What would be your concerns with adding more players?
5. Other than increasing entry fees or adding players, how could you generate additional revenue?
6. How could you reduce expenses?

LIU JIN/AFP/Getty Images

CHAPTER 5

Event Sponsorship

CHAPTER OBJECTIVES

After completing the chapter, the reader should be able to do the following:

- Define sponsorship and comprehend the relevance of the event triangle.
- Identify the various components of sport sponsorship.
- Recognize and relate the benefits of sponsorship to potential partners.
- Develop a sponsorship proposal.
- Identify sponsorship implementation strategies and evaluation techniques.

INDUSTRY PROFILE

Patrick Scully, NFL Tennessee Titans

Patrick Scully is in his fourth season in the NFL and his third with the Titans. As sponsorship sales coordinator, Scully's primary responsibility is to establish strong working relationships with local, regional, and national companies and to understand individual marketing and business goals and initiatives so as to create lasting partnerships with the Tennessee Titans. Among other duties, he develops customized proposals and sales presentations for new business prospects, identifies and researches key open sponsorship categories as prospective new business leads, and works to grow existing corporate sponsorships and media partnerships through service and communication.

A native of Hoffman Estates, Illinois, Scully graduated from DePaul University in 2014 with a degree in sports management and a minor in marketing. He spent time working with Learfield Sports, the Green Bay Packers, and the Chicago Fire prior to joining the Titans in 2016. He resides in Nashville, Tennessee.

Tell us how you ended up working with sponsorship and the Titans.

I went to DePaul University in downtown Chicago where I studied management with a concentration in sports management and a minor in marketing. I started my professional career with Vivid Seats, a secondary ticket marketplace based in Chicago (with a business model similar to StubHub). I was their first-ever intern, and after my internship I joined the sales staff where I would receive inbound calls and help people process their ticket orders. From there I took an unpaid internship with the Chicago Fire (MLS) in the corporate partnerships department. After my summer internship was completed, they were able to create a position for me while I finished up my senior year. I was working with the team Mondays, Wednesdays, Fridays, and some weekends and going to school Tuesdays and Thursdays. I always knew I wanted to work in the NFL, so after I got my degree I took another internship with the Green Bay Packers. After my internship there was completed I went to work for Learfield Sports, where I was in charge of selling and managing sponsors for Northern Illinois University Athletics. I wanted to get back in the NFL and when an opportunity opened here in Nashville I called my friends with the Packers and asked them to put in a good word for me.

What was the attraction for you to work in the area of sponsorships?

I took a class at DePaul that focused on sponsorship sales and I really enjoyed it. At that time, I knew I wanted to work in sports but wasn't sure exactly what area I wanted to focus on. I fell in love with the idea of partnering with organizations to create meaningful experiences for fans. The challenge of gaining the fans' attention while making a natural connection to the brand that has a lasting impact is one that I enjoy facing every day. There is also the thrill of sales and the eat-what-you-kill mentality that makes going to work every day enjoyable.

What is a typical day like for someone in sponsorship or sales for an athletic department?

Depending on the time of year, I am generally doing one of the following things:

- Prospecting potential partners to see who I should reach out to
- Calling or emailing those prospects and trying to set up a meeting
- Meeting with the prospect to discuss what their needs are and discover if the Titans are a fit for their organization
- Building a proposal of sponsorship elements based on that meeting
- Pitching that proposal to the prospect and answering any questions or concerns
- Negotiating back and forth with the prospect on different assets, investment levels, term lengths, and so on
- Creating, adjusting, and signing the final contract
- Executing the contract and making sure the client is happy with all aspects of their partnership

- When it comes time for renewing their partnership, discovering what we did well, what we didn't do well and how we can improve, what other things they would like to try

How do you determine what type of sponsorship to pitch to a potential client?

You must do your research on the prospect and their industry before you meet with them. Sponsorship is about finding the right asset mix that turns them from just being a sponsor to becoming a partner of the organization. Certain brands may have very large budgets and just want their logos everywhere. Other brands have smaller budgets and are more interested in different areas while still maximizing their spend. One thing that is consistent is that people want to feel important and want to know that you care about more than just getting their money.

What is one of the most unusual sponsorship deals you have negotiated?

I will give you a few:

- *Rackley Roofing*: a roofing company based 45 minutes outside of Nashville that has never spent a dime on marketing. They wanted to prove to people that they were a legitimate business, drive digital traffic to their new website, and have an opportunity to entertain some of their VIP clients while also providing fans with an unforgettable experience. I was able to put together a package that addressed all those objectives with the following assets:
    - *Trademark rights*: Official Roofer of the Tennessee Titans
    - *Banner ads and logo placement on TitansOnline.com*: helps with SEO when an established site has their advertisements on it
    - *Suite*: great opportunity to host guests in a controlled climate with food and drinks just steps away
    - *Rackley Roofing zip line at the pregame tailgate*: a once-in-a-lifetime experience that fans can enjoy for free, and Rackley Roofing can tell the story that the harness that you use when riding the zipline is the same harness that is securing a Rackley employee when she is up on a roof
- *Permobil*: a company that makes wheelchairs, both manual and automatic, based about 30 minutes outside of Nashville. They have a very specific target that they are trying to hit, and they want to show that they are a valued member of the community here in Tennessee. Nissan Stadium has the most ADA platforms in the NFL and we rebranded all of them with Permobil branding. We also added Permobil signage to our existing handicap parking spaces. In addition to all that, every year we pick a winner and surprise them on the field with a custom Titans-branded wheelchair. In 2018 we honored a young man who suffered a horrific football accident and has been a big Titans fan his whole life. In 2019 we will honor a wounded warrior during our Veterans Day game against the New England Patriots.
- *Ole Smoky Moonshine*: simply because we are the only team in NFL history to have a deal with a moonshine company!

It seems everyone wants to work in professional sports these days. Do you have any advice for someone who is looking into the marketing or sponsorship area as a career?

I got my job with Vivid Seats through a job application website that DePaul had set up for us students. I met my future boss from the Chicago Fire at a networking event. I was able to get this job here with the Tennessee Titans because of connections I had made at the Green Bay Packers. Connecting with people is the most important thing you can do and when you do connect with them, make sure you stick out in some way (send a follow up e-mail). Everyone wants to work in sports, but if you're able to have a clear vision of what you want to do within sports and you can tell people "I want to sell sponsorships in the NFL" at a young age, you will stick out when compared to your peers.

It is fascinating to ponder the impact that marketing has had on society. Years ago, when television was in its golden phase, commercials were estimated to reach about 70 percent of the population (Johnson 2006). With the advent of digital cable and the ability to bypass commercials, one might assume that commercials lost their ability to reach an audience. But with all the new technology and means for reaching an audience wherever they are, by today's advertising standards, it has been estimated that each of us is exposed to between 4,000 and 10,000 messages a day. Stop and think about that for just a second. In fact, in that second you stopped, another media platform was launched and it is safe to say you were exposed to yet another advertisement on Facebook, Twitter, e-mail, Instagram . . . you get the picture. Have you ever considered that abundance of messages you are exposed to on a daily basis and the impact they have on you? Or how much we are now addicted to social media and how it has impacted our lives and our consumption habits? The technology and the methods may be new, but the concept of communicating a message is not. Magazines, billboards, newspapers, direct mail, television, radio, the Internet, phone apps, and virtual placement are all viable media to convey a message to a specific audience. Some of these messages are advertisements and some are sponsorships. In this chapter we will focus on the idea of soliciting sponsorship as a means to financially support and market your event.

Mullin, Hardy, and Sutton (2014) define **sponsorship** as the "acquisition of rights to affiliate or directly associate with a product, person, organization, team, league, or event for the purpose of deriving benefits related to that affiliation or association" (p. 231). Solomon's (2002) simplified definition states that sponsorship is one company paying a fee to a promoter to endorse the event and promote its products. The 2015 Plunkett Research report on industry statistics and trends asserts the sport industry weighs in at a healthy $1.5 trillion. The International Events Group (IEG), a leading expert in sponsorships, reported that global spending on sports sponsorship in 2018 topped 65.8 billion (Ukman 2018).

Advertising and sponsorship are kindred spirits, but their intent is very different. Kokemuller (n.d.) explained the relationship best: "sponsorship is typically regarded as a stronger and deeper relationship than a simple advertising exchange of value. An advertisement is a singular message placement while sponsorship is an ongoing arrangement" (para. 1).

To fully understand the role of sponsorship, we must first identify its place in the promotional mix and define various terminologies associated with the traditional marketing mix and promotional mix. The traditional marketing mix consists of the four Ps: product, price, place, and promotion (McCarthy 1960). The promotional mix (discussed in chapter 7) encompasses advertising, public relations, personal selling, and sales promotions.

What is the lure of sponsorship? Why sport sponsorship? And how can seeking sponsorship help you manage your event? Much of the growth can be attributed to the growing desire (and need) for corporations to be affiliated with sport entities to help them achieve their strategic goals. Sport is consuming, sport is exciting, and sport provides an avenue for businesses, large and small, to reach their target demographics and to grow and maintain relationships with customers through mutually beneficial interactions. Sport and sport-related properties (fitness centers, apparel, equipment, and shoes) are a constant for most people; daily interactions are almost a given. These interactions come in many different shapes, sizes, and methods, but the common denominator is the link to sports and the opportunities that are present through sponsorship.

Keep in mind that sponsorship is a triad, a dynamic connection of the event, the fans, and the sponsors. As Ammon, Southall, and Nagel (2010) present, this relationship triangle "represents important stakeholders who must be satisfied for the event to be a success" (p. 14). SponsorMap (2008), a marketing research firm, describes the **event triangle** as "the emotional connection" between an event and the fans that turns emotion into a reaction that ultimately benefits the sponsor. In essence, the relationship the event has with the sponsor encourages fans to take action, purchasing the product or service offered by the sponsor. The relationships within the event triangle can be described in three distinct but related parts.

First, the event delivers the opportunity to attract fans and provide exposure for potential sponsors. Second, fans seek entertainment from the event and are exposed to the various promotional activities during an event. And third, sponsors exploit the opportunity to leverage fans through what we call borrowed equity, or marketing through sport.

These connections and actions allow a sponsor to achieve its anticipated **return on investment (ROI)** or **return on opportunity (ROO)**. ROI and ROO refer to the effectiveness of the investment either in monetary terms (ROI) or in accomplishing the goals set for the sponsorship (ROO). The National Association for Stock Car Auto Racing (NASCAR) provides great examples of how the event triangle is utilized to a sponsor's advantage. Having great success with fan loyalty, NASCAR has been the subject of many marketing studies. One such national study by Performance Research, an analytical sport and event marketing firm, randomly surveyed NASCAR fans, revealing "71 percent [of them] elected to purchase products that were involved in NASCAR over one that is not" (Performance Research n.d.), ranking NASCAR the number one sport for brand loyalty.

Sponsorship

Sponsorship is a give and take process. One side says, "show me the money" (Jerry McGuire) while the other says "show me your audience" (Kear 2017). As our own definition states, this is a formalized relationship involving an exchange that is designed to offer benefits to both parties who "use sport, entertainment, and other forms of lifestyle marketing to send messages to a targeted audience" (Mullin, Hardy, and Sutton 2014, p. 231). Over the past 23 years we have seen the definition of sponsorship evolve from simply communicating an association (Cornwell 1995) to an avenue for achieving organizational goals (Shank 2009) to exploitation for commercial potential (Ukman 2012). We have seen the results go from mass broadcasting of relationship to very targeted attempts to reach certain demographics.

For event planners, sponsorship is a means to an end in terms of funding their endeavor. Many organizations rely on funds raised from sponsorship sales to achieve their event goals. In fact, many events exist solely as fund-raisers for a specific cause. Even high school sports teams still rely on fund-raising (selling of sponsorships) to augment their increasing expenses and decreasing federal funding. Nolensville High School (Tennessee), which is only in its third year of existence is one such example. The athletic committee at Nolensville hosts two events each year benefiting their athletic department. In the fall they host a 5K event cosponsored by the local running club and in the spring they put on "Boots and Bling," an event that connects the Nashville music scene with the school, bringing musicians and songwriters to the campus for an acoustical performance while the attendees are treated to a buffet meal that is sponsored (donated) by local restaurants. These two events raise over $25, 000 for the athletic program.

Sponsorship has found its roots and is now firmly entrenched in sport, and sport has clearly welcomed this partnership and the benefits it provides. Sponsorship opportunities within the sport industry have attempted to bridge the gap between needs and wants, tempting the sports fan through enticing promotional campaigns, direct selling strategies, and heightening emotions. Ultimately, businesses associate with sport to achieve sales goals, while sport organizations view the relationship as necessary to support the escalating costs of fielding a team (Stotlar 2005). Making sure you have the right fit, philosophically and demographically, is also critical. Conflicting philosophies or values could produce negative outcomes. For example, the X Games, more directed at the young adult market, might not be a good fit for Johnson & Johnson's Bengay line but would align better with their Clean & Clear products.

For event managers, sponsorship is a means to an end, if you will, generating the necessary funds to create a memorable event, thus satisfying customers. Sponsoring an event can range from a simple advertisement in the program to full-blown naming rights, and various levels in between. As event planners map out their plans for creating, planning, and executing a successful event, they create manageable components that become targeted sales pitches to businesses and organizations. Golf tournaments provide an excellent example of the various types of sponsorships you can create. A typical golf fundraiser might offer the following sponsor opportunities: event, hole, cart, range, lunch, long drive, hole in one, closest to the pin, beverage cart, raffles and prizes. A kind of if-you-can-tag it-you-can-sell-it mentality.

Companies seek these unique ways to engage potential customers. Traditional methods such as advertising, public relations, and promotions are still utilized, but adding sponsorship to that mix provides myriad opportunities to communicate a message. **Integrated marketing communications (IMC)** create a symphony of promotional efforts that work in concert, linking all promotional pieces. This unified effort increases the likelihood that marketing will be successful, leading to consumer action. This process aligns with Lavidge and Steiner's (1961) hierarchy of effects model (see table 5.1.), which suggests there is a force that

TABLE 5.1 Applying the Hierarchy of Effects Model

Stage	Application
Awareness	If your target market is unaware of your product or service, then the first order of marketing priority is to achieve awareness within your target market. To test awareness, you might ask "Have you heard of our firm?"
Knowledge	Awareness can answer the question of whether or not a prospect knows of your firm; however, she may not know the context in which she heard your name and thus cannot accurately describe what you do or what you sell, nor can she determine whether or not she would ever do business with you. To test for knowledge, you might ask "Do you know what our company does for organizations like yours?"
Liking	When a prospect knows what your firm does and what you might do for him, he begins to form opinions about your firm. Perhaps, because of his heightened awareness, he now seems to notice you in the newspaper and in trade journals, and he now receives your newsletter. He's forming an opinion of whether or not he likes you. Perhaps you provide valuable thought-leading wisdom in the industry, and he likes you for that fact. To test for liking, you might ask "What is your overall perception of our firm?" His response might range from favorable to unfavorable.
Preference	The preference stage is where we begin to see the real value of the hierarchy of effects. A prospect in the preference stage has a clear definition of why she would want to do business with your firm or purchase a product or service in the category you serve. To test for preference, you might ask "What criteria will you use to make your decision about XYZ?" Marketers also gauge interest through trials, surveys, and other means to better understand the customer at this stage of the buying cycle.
Conviction	At the stage of conviction, the prospect is in a state of already being convinced that you are the right choice for whatever problem he needs you to solve. He believes, through your credible demonstration of capability, that you're the right fit and that you've done everything right to this point. Testing for conviction is now a matter of moving the conversation to purchase. However, in long sales cycles, maintaining conviction is also important. Any lead-nurturing activities you have in progress should not cease once you believe you've reached the conviction stage.
Purchase	Ultimately, the work to move the prospect through the hierarchy will result in her purchasing your offering. However, beware of the purchase or signal to purchase from a customer who has not gone through the various stages. Nor should you try to induce a customer purchase without recognizing the aforementioned stages. A customer purchase without the rigor of traversing the hierarchy of effects can lead to postpurchase dissonance.

Reprinted by permission from D. VanDen Heusel, *The Hierarchy of Effects* (Green Bay, WI: MarketingSavant), 3-4.

guides people through the six-step (stages) model. The six stages of consumer evolvement range from thinking to feeling to *I must have* (VanDen Heuvel 2009).

As event manager, you can leverage this information by presenting the various marketing opportunities you can offer to potential sponsors. Sometimes a potential sponsor does not immediately see the need to become a sponsor. This presents you with the opportunity to help them see the bigger picture. Realize that you may be the guide on the journey that will take a potential sponsor through the hierarchy of effects to become your partner.

Sponsorship Components

As you begin to consider the idea of soliciting sponsors for your event, first make your marketing goals and objectives clear to ensure that potential sponsors know, understand, and relate to them. Consider sponsorship a three-step process of identifying (research), securing (selling), and maintaining (servicing) (Skildum-Reid and Grey 2008).

Once you have planned your event and established your goals, you can turn your attention to developing the components of your sponsorship program. These components allow you (or your sales team) to give companies various opportunities to be associated with your event. Kim Harrison, author, consultant, and founder of CuttingEdgePR.com, asserts that it is up to event managers to identify what a company needs and to package event sponsorship opportunities in a way that will provide the company "with value for money" ("Focus on What" n.d.). Typical sponsorship components are identified in the sidebar Typical Sponsorship Components.

Typical Sponsorship Components

- Access to property mailing lists or databases
- Inclusion in event promotions
- Category exclusivity
- Link on the event website
- Complimentary advertising
- Right of first refusal
- Displays and sampling
- Right to purchase additional tickets
- Distribution rights
- Right to use event trademarks and logos
- Free tickets
- Signage
- Hospitality areas
- Other items as determined by contract

Costs of Sponsorship to a Corporation

When a company is considering a sponsorship opportunity, they have two available options, **in-kind** donations or traditional monetary support. In-kind sponsorships are nonmonetary partnerships that provide a service or product to an event in exchange for sponsorship recognition. In-kind contributions can include such items as gift bags, basket giveaways, prizes for raffles, entertainment services, volunteers, food and beverages, photography services, and T-shirts, to name a few. Our Nolensville High School example earlier in this chapter shows how in-kind donations are appreciated. In 2017, Leigh Ann Danzey-Bussell's event management class at Trevecca Nazarene University partnered with the Nolensville Athletic Committee and the Nolensville 5K event to provide several in-kind services. First, the class was charged with creating an operations manual for the event; second, they were to volunteer during the event; and finally they were divided into groups representing the various logistical and management functions associated with running the event. For the group assigned to sponsorship and hospitality, an in-kind donation of granola bars, bagels, and chocolate milk was secured from Trevecca Nazarene University's dining services and made available to the participants at the end of the event. In return, Trevecca Nazarene University was identified as a sponsor of the event and the students were recognized for their outstanding efforts.

Although in-kind donations are great for helping eliminate many of the expenses you might have with that support, it is still necessary to secure funding to host an event. Your financial needs are identified during the planning phase, presented in your proposal, and secured during active selling. This monetary involvement entails the exchange of cash for the right to associate with an event. You must first know your inventory and your available sponsorship opportunities and then you must craft your proposal with your vision and mission in mind.

Components of a Sponsorship Proposal

You have planned your event's mission, goals, and objectives; defined your sponsorship levels; and identified potential companies to approach for sponsorship. Selecting companies entails a carefully crafted plan of attack based on market research and acumen. With these elements in place, you are ready to construct your proposal—a carefully crafted and tailored packet that will address all the questions necessary for a company to decide whether to participate or not. Skildum-Reid (2010) boldly stated that "sponsorship is not about your need; it's about achieving the sponsor's objective" (p. 2). You can draft a **sponsorship proposal** after you have identified the various items you have to "sell" to potential sponsors. As this is a mutually beneficial process, it can best be described in terms of a partnership or relationship. You are looking for those potential sponsors who will best fit your needs while accomplishing theirs.

There is no magic formula for a proposal, but certain elements are necessary in order to properly ask for sponsorship. According to Singh (2009), event managers should keep these questions in mind when writing the proposal:

- Why should I sponsor this event? (benefit)
- Who is going to attend the event? (audience)
- Why will they come?
- How do I target the audience?
- What is the credential of the organizer?
- Who else is sponsoring the event?
- What is the cost, and does it justify the benefit?

These questions will help you construct a proposal that will garner attention. It has been stated that potential sponsors look at two segments first: what you are offering and how much it will cost them.

Your first step is not just to put together and mail the proposal. You must first secure the name of the person responsible for making sponsorship decisions. With technology, you may be able to acquire this information on the company's website. If not, a simple phone call will do the trick. It is imperative that your proposal reach the right person for full consideration. In her blog, Skildum-Reid (2010) professed that most sponsorship proposals are "total crap" because someone failed to do adequate research.

Constructing your proposal in a sensible order, presenting your case professionally, and keeping the proposal as brief as possible is a great strategy (Skildum-Reid 2011). Various authors suggest that the following information be included:

- Provide a concise overview of your organization, including your location, main activities, and goals and a brief history.
- Include the benefits your organization can offer a sponsor and demonstrate how these benefits relate to the sponsor.
- List the credentials of your organization and key personnel. Sponsors need to know they will be dealing with experienced and reputable people.
- Supply a list of current and past sponsors (if applicable). This allows potential sponsors to check for competition.
- Outline any benefits you are prepared to offer the sponsor.
- Explain the nature and extent of potential media coverage.
- Supply a realistic estimate of the number of people who might participate in the event.
- Demonstrate the current level of community support and awareness for your

project. Sponsors have a strong interest in supporting projects that have wide community support.

According to Stotlar (2005), the sponsorship submission should include the following elements:

- *Cover letter*: address it to the appropriate person, focus on tailored benefits for specific partners, be specific, let them know when to expect a follow-up
- *Description of the event and the program*: location, duration, size, media plan, promotional elements, and demographic profile
- *Sponsor's benefits*: signage, hospitality, pre- and postevent activities, on-site opportunities, cross-promotions, rationale for partnering, evaluation methods, and VIP opportunities
- *Sponsorship investment amount*: include levels or categories of sponsors, parameters, and a list of former sponsors
- *Deadline for decision*: this is critical for keeping the event on schedule

Sponsors are looking to determine the viable benefits of this relationship. Stotlar (2005) contends that sponsorship bridges the gap between how people want to be reached and how marketers want to reach them. Keeping these things in mind will help you craft a proposal that will land you the partnership.

Mullin and colleagues (2014) suggested an eight-step sponsorship process that includes research, a meeting with the decision maker, listening to the potential sponsor's needs during the meeting, taking the information and looking for a fit, creating a proposal, presenting the ideas (tailored to their needs) to the potential sponsor, negotiating if necessary, and handing off to an activation team. The proposal is your offer to the potential sponsor that outlines what you are offering, the worthiness of the offer, and what you would like in return. Specifics such as demographics, exposure, cost, and benefits are outlined in your proposal (McCue, 2016). As we mentioned earlier in this chapter, there are various ways you can package your offerings. In the next section we discuss one popular way to present sponsorships through different levels of support.

Sponsorship Levels

Keep in mind that what you are creating with your sponsorship opportunities is value. The value varies for each potential sponsor, and sponsorship packages neatly represent the various **sponsorship levels** that can be purchased. Most classic sponsorship values are presented as gradual levels (packages) of involvement ranging from minimal investment to full-blown rights of ownership. These levels allow you to address your own needs and the potential sponsors' needs at a level that is comfortable for both. For years the standard levels for many events were gold, silver, and bronze, following the ever-popular Olympic medal model. But the increased desire by corporations to be associated with sport has driven event managers to cast aside cookie-cutter models and creatively construct unique levels for their events. Still, some distinctive categories have emerged, such as the following:

- Contributing
- Corporate
- Hospitality and food
- Major
- Media
- Naming rights
- National
- Presenting
- Supporting
- Title

Depending on the event, event planners develop specialized categories that represent the available opportunities. For example, a golf tournament might have tee, hole-in-one, or hydration station levels, while Little League organizations might offer levels such as uniforms and fields. The differentiation of these levels from greatest involvement down to minimal involvement allows potential partners to see what level they can afford and helps them identify the best fit (Ukman 2012). Table 5.2 shows an example of sponsorship levels for a local Little League organization.

TABLE 5.2 Example of Sponsorship Levels

Package	Fee	Details
Teamwork *Fall only*	$175	Company banner on walkway fence, team sponsorship, listed on seasonal all-sponsor recognition banners throughout park, and fall season team plaque *Copy for banner, logo, or sign must be submitted before March 1*
Teamwork **PLUS** *Fall Only*	$275	Company banner on infield fence, team sponsorship, listed on seasonal all-sponsor recognition banners throughout park, and fall season team plaque *Copy for banner, logo, or sign must be submitted before March 1*
Single *Spring Only*	$350	Company banner on walkway fence, team sponsorship, listed on seasonal all-sponsor recognition banners throughout park, and spring season team plaque *Copy for banner, logo, or sign must be submitted before March 1*
Single **PLUS** *Spring Only*	$450	Company banner on infield fence, team sponsorship, listed on seasonal all-sponsor recognition banners throughout park, and spring season team plaque *Copy for banner, logo, or sign must be submitted before March 1*
Double Play *Spring and Fall Combo*	$500	Company banner on walkway fence, team sponsorship, listed on all-sponsor recognition banners throughout park, website listing, and spring and fall season team plaques *Copy for banner, logo, or sign must be submitted before March 1*
Double Play **PLUS** *Spring and Fall Combo*	$650	Company banner on infield fence, team sponsorship, listed on seasonal all-sponsor recognition banners throughout park, and spring season team plaque *Copy for banner, logo, or sign must be submitted before March 1*
Manager	$600 each; $1200 all	One garage door signage at barn for both seasons (painted artwork, lasting a minimum of two years) **Up to three garage door sponsorships available** *Approx. 3' × 3' space reserved for color artwork to be painted on garage door(s)*
Power Play	$750	All three golf carts sponsorship for both seasons (metallic sign on front of each cart) *1' × 2' color sign affixed to each golf cart*
Triple Play	$750	Signage on all three storage sheds around the park for entire year *18'' × 36'' color sign affixed to each storage shed*
On Deck	$750 ea. $1500 all	Signage on any batting cage for entire year **Up to three batting cage sponsorships available** *2' × 4' color sign to be suspended from each cage facing walkways*
Cracker Jack	$1000	Signage on a concession stand at the park for entire year *2 ' × 6' color sign to be affixed to concession stand below windows*
Clubhouse	$1250	Walkway naming rights for entire year, with one street sign to be affixed to post at each walkway juncture
MVP	$1000 to $2500 each	Official naming rights for entire year; field uses sponsor name in all league documents *4' × 8' color sign suspended above top of each backstop* *Rates are as follows:* $2,500: fields 2, 6, and 13 $2,000: fields 1, 3, 4 and 12 $1,500: fields 5, 7, 8, and 9 $1,000: fields 10 and 11
Packages are available on first come, first served basis, depending on availability.		

All sponsorships automatically include company name listing on
- company-specific recognition banner along one of our three entrance paths
- OYO's website, where we will link listing to your company's website

Reprinted by permission from Oaklandon Youth Organization (Indianapolis, Indiana).

Event managers are limited only by their creative energies as to the types of levels they can offer. But take note: You don't want to overwhelm the client with your offerings; your goal is to create interesting opportunities that will provide the potential sponsor with the greatest ROI. This is why researching potential partnerships is the first step in drafting your proposal; know your audience.

Naming Rights

As one of the fastest-growing segments of sponsorship, **naming rights** have truly come into their own as of late. Burton (2008) identified three distinct naming rights options:

1. Rights to a legacy gift
2. Rights to be a title sponsor of an event
3. Rights for a long-term partnership

Legacy gifts are best exemplified by names such as Rockefeller and Kennedy and the many buildings that bear these names (Burton 2008). Since many of the events in the sporting world do not require such grandiose names or funding, of particular importance to you is what to name your event. The extent of the financial undertaking to produce an event has become so great, why not explore new opportunities to augment out-of-pocket costs for your event?

Golf tournaments have had a long tradition of using naming rights for their events. Some tournaments have gone so far as to utilize a legacy right, an event sponsor, and a course name (Bissell 2011). A cursory glance at the PGA Tour schedule is evidence enough that events do draw large sponsors. Names such as AT&T, FedEx, Honda, Sony, Waste Management, and Wells Fargo stand out (PGAtour.com 2012). BB&T, a leading financial services holding company, has truly bought into sport sponsorships, leaving an imprint on collegiate sport (official bank of the Atlantic Coast Conference and 10-year naming rights to the Wake Forest University Football Stadium), motorsports (official sponsor of Jeff Burton, NASCAR driver number 31), and its

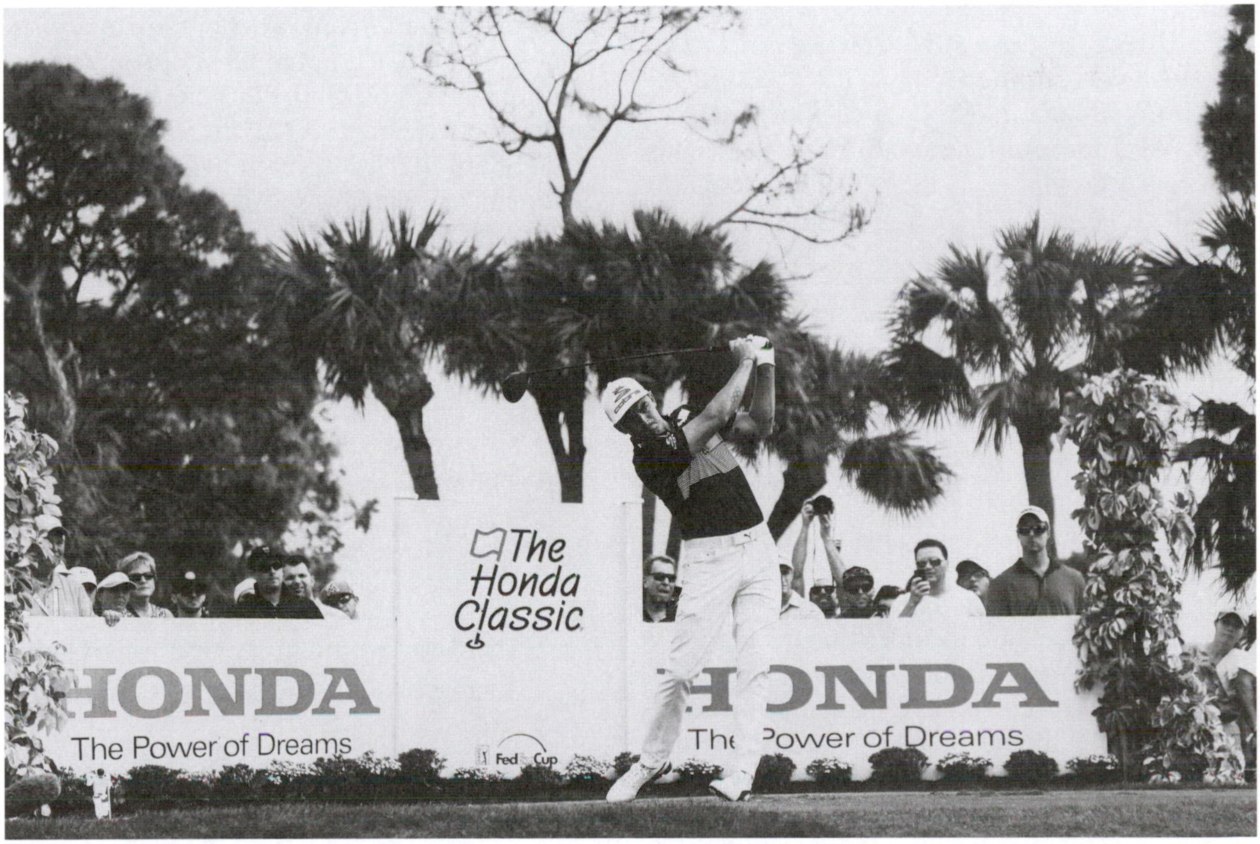

Mike Ehrmann/Getty Images

Golf tournaments, such as The Honda Classic, have had a long tradition of using naming rights for their events.

latest acquisition, the Atlanta Tennis Championships (Limpert 2012; USTA.com 2012).

Don't underestimate the power your event may hold for a potential sponsor. Reach for the stars, and you just might get what you want. You must be willing to accept whatever response you get. Sometimes that response is yes, we would welcome the opportunity to partner with your event; other times, it will be no. But perseverance and belief in your event will ultimately pay off.

Cost of Sponsorship for Event Organizers

Harrison ("How to Calculate" n.d.) maintains that the investment you seek from potential sponsors is a uniquely crafted formula of identifying the cost to fulfill the sponsorship multiplying by two. In simplified form, Harrison presents the formula this way:

> Total investment asked = cost of providing the benefits offered; admin staff costs + sales costs + servicing costs = total cost to deliver the package + 100 percent margin = sponsorship fee.

To illustrate this, let's refer to the Little League levels outlined in table 5.2. Oaklandon Youth Organization (OYO) is seeking a teamwork-level sponsor for the fall. The costs break down as follows:

Company banner	$18
Team sponsorship	$12
Sponsor-recognition banner	$30
Plaque and administration fees	$17
Sales fees	$10
Total OYO cost	$87 + 100 percent margin = $175 (rounded)

Harrison adds the need to include both direct and indirect costs associated with staff, noting their involvement from conception to fruition of sponsorships. She concludes that event planners should not just think selfishly about what it will take to run the event but must consider what is most valuable to the potential sponsor. It is also important to consider the competition (i.e., what they are offering and charging) to ensure you are operating within the boundaries of what the local market will support.

Sponsorship Benefits

Inevitably, when a potential sponsor is approached, they want to know the details of what's in it for them. To have that conversation, you need to understand what you have to offer. Ukman (2012) contends you must take inventory of your assets before moving forward. She identifies your potential offerings as follows:

- An audience
- Database information
- Hospitality opportunities
- Marks and logos
- Media coverage
- Merchandise
- Possible broadcast package
- Printed materials
- Signage
- Talent
- Venue
- Website and social media outlets

Familiarize yourself with the benefits that sponsorship—or maybe a better term is *partnership*—offers to each potential sponsor. Various authors have outlined the benefits of sport sponsorship (Ukman 2012; Lawrence and Wells 2009; Shank 2009; International Events Group 2018; Mullin, Hardy, and Sutton 2014; Logh, Irwin, and Short 2000; Schmader and Jackson 1997); their consensus is as follows:

- Award presentation (perpetual trophy naming)
- Change in or reinforcement of image
- Community engagement
- Differentiation
- Exclusivity
- Fresh, nontraditional promotional strategies
- Increased brand awareness and loyalty
- Increased sales and achievement of sales goals
- Merchandising opportunities
- Naming rights
- Narrowcasting (targeting a niche market)
- Philanthropy

- Product promotion
- Publicity
- Showcasing of products through samples or displays

Remember that you are not the only horse in the race. Your ability to understand these elements, package them to fit your potential sponsors, and then deliver on your promises will not only reduce the clutter of traditional marketing mechanisms but also generate greater opportunities for you, your sponsors, and the fans (event triangle) (Ukman 2012). Your success, according to deLisle (2009) is based on two principles: understanding your product and understanding your audience. Understanding your product (event) requires that you grasp the appeal it will have and how it is unique compared with alternatives. This allows you to differentiate your offerings, creating that necessary appeal. To understand your audiences, deLisle suggests that you consider marketing to be like dating (p. 135). Growing the relationship requires nurturing and effort. It also requires that you do your homework, researching and preparing for that initial experience in hopes that it leads to a "long term and mutually beneficial relationship" (deLisle 2009, p. 135). As with any other relationship, it needs close monitoring to ensure that you are both providing the necessary elements initially prescribed in the arrangement. Shank (2009) concluded that sponsorship provides benefits to all involved and produces the proverbial win-win partnership (p. 333).

Activation and Evaluation Techniques

The old adage *What's in it for me?* absolutely rings true in sponsorship. Each partner is looking for the win-win scenario that satisfies their needs in terms of exposure, recognition, ROI, and ROO (Stotlar 2005). **Activation** of a sponsorship refers to the process of actively marketing and managing the sponsor's partnership with an event. Technology has greatly

Brian Bahr/Getty Images

Taco Bell's 'Ring the Bell' promotion is an example of activation.

changed the way sponsorships are being activated. Twitter, Facebook, and YouTube have (literally) virtually enhanced the way marketers interact with target markets. With the advent of quick response (QR) codes, the speed at which a fan can connect to a sponsor is fractional. Butcher (2010) reported that Swiss watch manufacturer Tissot added a QR code to the hood of NASCAR driver Danica Patrick's race car.

Activation closely aligns with advertising—creating public awareness of a product and its association with an event. This process requires more than simply putting a logo on a sign at your event; it requires action. As the term implies, activation refers to stimulation, stimulation translates into action, and action is what the sponsor desires. The relationship you build with the sponsor will help identify the methods of activation you select for your event. Coca-Cola, a longtime supporter of the Olympics and one of 11 companies designated as part of the Olympic Partners (TOP) program, continually shines in the area of activation. Most recently, the Youth Olympic Winter Games saw Coca-Cola sponsoring the Youth Olympic Torch Relay and utilizing red London-style double-decker buses in Innsbruck's city center to provide music and giveaways in conjunction with the Coca-Cola Happiness Truck that traveled the city handing out Coca-Cola products (Mickle 2012).

Concepts such as **cross-promotions** and **cause-related marketing** are exciting activation techniques. Cross-promotion is a *partnership* where two (or more) businesses join forces to engage in joint promotion (Jones 2018). For instance, Donnor uses the example of the recent cross-promotion of the Dodgers Pride Night tickets on sale at a Los Angeles Kings game. He contends that the leader in cross-promotion is MSG Holdings; the organization that operates Madison Square Garden utilizes cross-promotions for the seven professional teams it services.

Cause-related sponsorship, better known as **cause-related marketing (CRM),** is relatively young in comparison to other forms of marketing. Essentially, CRM brings together not-for-profit and for-profit entities that share mutually beneficial goals in an effort to increase attention and facilitate action. American Express was the first company to enter into such an arrangement when it offered to donate a portion of each of its transactions to the fund to restore the Statue of Liberty in 1983 (GrantSpace 2012). Some may call this double-dipping—promotion of products or services while raising money—but for event planners, it ultimately comes down to the idea that the show must go on, in any way and by any means possible. Regardless of how you spin it, activation is critical to a sponsorship opportunity. Donna's Hope is a non-profit foundation for breast cancer survivors started by Donna Ward, wife of Turner Ward, the hitting coach for the Los Angeles Dodgers. Turner, a former MLB player, is the recipient of Yasiel Puig's kisses in the dugout after a successful at bat. Using that as a parody, Donna's Hope partnered with BreakingT, a company that creates fan T-shirts, to create a Pucker Up Puig T-shirt. The shirt depicts Turner doing the kissing this time, and a portion of the proceeds are being filtered to Donna's Hope.

After you have implemented your marketing plan, you must have a means of evaluating the success of your efforts. For an event, this can be as simple as whether you sold all the tickets. But **evaluating sponsorship** can be accomplished in various other ways, such as on-site distribution of products; website traffic before, during, and after the event; and an increase in sales after activation. How you establish the success of your event relies heavily on what you are offering and how you will track it. International Events Group (2012), a leader in sponsorship research, asserts that event managers must consider both the tangible and the intangible benefits of sponsorship when determining value and success. Tangible benefits are easily noticed elements such as the use of a logo on goods. The intangible benefits, such as name awareness, loyalty, and the collection of names for a contact database, are more elusive.

At the close of your event, you should generate and distribute a report encompassing the various components of each sponsor's package. This report, according to Spoelstra (1997), should contain samples of all materials that utilized the sponsor's name and logo. This will aid in determining ROI and ROO. Return on investment relates to the idea of tangible benefits because it asks patrons to recall the sponsors. Built-in expectations can be quantified through data gathering to allow sponsors to determine if their investments were profitable. But what about the qualitative aspect of sponsorship, those intangible benefits discussed earlier? In terms of return on opportunity, the qualitative information that can be gathered from interviewing patrons or conducting focus groups can better answer whether objectives were met through sponsorship affiliations. Both ROI and ROO are effective in valuing and evaluating sponsorship success. These data also justify the relationship between the sponsor and the event (Stotlar 2005).

Summary

Sport is big business thanks in part to the immense sponsorship deals that are carved out by major corporations. The billions of dollars spent annually on sponsoring sport entities is quite astounding. You may be wondering why anyone would want to sponsor your event. Do not get caught up in the idea that your event may seem small or insignificant compared with others. There are companies and organizations out there that are seeking an event just like yours to sponsor.

Events are created with the goal of at least breaking even financially. In today's tough economic environment, it is becoming increasingly more difficult to pull that off. To help defray the cost of planning and implementing an event, event managers turn to sponsorship as a lucrative and viable option to raise the necessary capital. Knowledge of the sponsorship process and the event triangle will help ground your efforts. Do your research, identify those entities that will benefit the most from an association with your event, and go out there and clinch the deal!

LEARNING ACTIVITIES

Assume you work for an athletic department at a local high school. Because of recent budget cuts that have plagued interscholastic sport, you are looking to raise money for the department. Golf tournaments are a great way to secure funding from various sources, including sponsors. The local golf course has donated the use of the course for your event. You must now solicit your sponsors.

1. You begin the process with goal setting. What are your goals for this event?
2. How would you begin to identify potential sponsors? Are there any sponsors you should be leery of approaching? (Remember your product.)
3. Identify the parties of the event triangle. What are the investments of each?
4. Categorize the levels of sponsorship you will utilize. (This may require you to research similar golf tournaments for ideas.)
5. What benefits will you provide to sponsors (i.e., what differentiates the levels you have established)?
6. How will you present the ROI and the ROO to the potential customer? How will you evaluate?

CASE STUDY: THE NAME GAME PAYS OFF

Over the past 15 years there has been a steady decrease in federal education funding to states. When the federal monies are cut, the states have to either find a way to make up the funds or pass the cuts along to the state department of education. In lean times, it is customary to turn to a pay-to-play plan to help fund the various sports teams. But following the precedent set by college and professional teams, high schools looked to sponsorship deals, specifically naming rights, to raise the necessary operating funds.

In 2006, Noblesville High School (Indiana) was struggling to find the funds they needed to complete some renovations to their football stadium. Athletic director Steve Hurst decided to seek corporate funding to help pay for the installation of the new $575,000 turf field.

Hurst approached Dave Cox, owner of Hare Chevrolet, a local car dealership with strong ties to the community. Cox and Hurst came to an agreement on the terms of a 10-year deal; for the sum of $125,000, Hare Chevrolet, secured the naming rights deal for the football stadium. This agreement was the first of its kind in Central Indiana, but it would not be the last. A one-year, $12,000 extension was awarded for 2017. In August 2018, it was announced that another local company, Beaver Materials, has secured a 5-year, $83,000 deal to put their name on the stadium.

In 2008, the Hamilton Southeastern School District (HSE), the district just south of Noblesville, struck a deal with a local farm supply company, Reynolds Farm Equipment, to provide funding for their turf campaign. The $400,000 deal would place the Reynolds name on the stadiums of both HSE high schools, Hamilton Southeastern High School and Fishers High School. Westfield Washington Schools, the neighboring system to the west of Noblesville, landed a 10-year, 1.2-million-dollar naming rights deal with Riverview Health in 2014, which allowed them to build a new stadium.

It is becoming the norm for high schools to seek naming rights deals as a means for making improvements across all campuses and for all programs, not just for sports. Jerry Thacker, superintendent of Penn-Harris-Madison School Corporation in Mishawaka, Indiana, commented: "We have a parking lot we could name, the middle school gymnasiums, every single classroom could be supported by some organization."

Case Study Application

1. Every time there is an event in one of these stadiums or the media covers a football game, those corporate names are mentioned, and the sponsorship investment pays off. Some might say that these schools were selling out to the highest bidder just to make sure sports were adequately funded. How would you defend striking a deal with a local company for naming rights to a local high school?
2. Is this idea a positive one for all involved? Or is this a disaster waiting to happen?
3. What types of conditions would you place upon a naming rights deal if you were to negotiate one?

© Chris Greenwell

CHAPTER 6

Event Marketing

CHAPTER OBJECTIVES

After completing the chapter, the reader should be able to do the following:

- Understand why event marketing provides different challenges and opportunities than traditional marketing.
- Understand the role of the marketing plan and the marketing planning process.
- Utilize multiple methods of identifying target markets for events.
- Identify the key issues of developing an event brand.
- Understand multiple tools available for promoting events.

INDUSTRY PROFILE

George Barbetto, University of Louisville

As senior marketing manager for the University of Louisville athletic department, George Barbetto is responsible for marketing and sales for multiple college sport programs. In this role, he oversees various sales and engagement initiatives and develops marketing plans to increase attendance and maximize fans' experiences. Prior to coming to Louisville, George worked in event and game operations for the New York Jets, overseeing a variety of marketing and event initiatives.

What are some unique challenges in marketing college sporting events?

We have 23 NCAA Division I sports here and each sport is different. Marketing tennis is obviously different than marketing men's basketball or football. We want to make an engaging atmosphere for fans while they are at the event, but you have to get the fans there to do so.

When you put together your marketing plan, how do you identify the direction you want your marketing efforts to take?

You have to set goals based on what the team wants, what the coaches are looking for, and what goal the athletic department as a whole has for the sport. We work with the team to set those goals and then create the plan and marketing efforts to reach those goals.

Who is your target customer?

Each sport's consumer is different. Our football and basketball fans have a similar overlap, but our women's basketball and volleyball fans are completely different. Through our social media analytics and through our customer relationship management databases, we have information on who our season ticket holders are, where they live, and their demographic information. We tailor our messaging to those demographics. We know what time they are most active on social media and if they are opening our e-mails. We build an outline of our customer so that we know who you are without knowing exactly who you are.

What methods do you use to promote your events? What is most effective for you?

Over the last five years it has been heavy social media interaction. Some of the newest, most engaging things are Instagram stories and Snapchat stories. Our go-to is e-mail marketing. We are heavy on that for all sports. Paying a small amount to advertise on Facebook, Twitter, and Instagram always has the best return on investment. Social media is our best bet to target our audiences.

What makes someone successful in event marketing?

What makes someone successful in event marketing is having a passion to learn and constantly grow and push yourself and the events; to be new, innovative, interactive, and thinking of how it can be more fun for the fan. Pushing yourself to be creative, whether it is brainstorming every day with your team or being actively involved in other events and active in how other people do things. You never know when the next best idea is going to come.

What are some tips you would offer to others marketing events?

You can never plan too far in advance for an event. Having plan B, C, and D prepared will get you a long way. There are things in events that you may never anticipate happening. Being able to react on the fly, be a quick thinker, and adjust on the move are definitely skills people in event management and event marketing need to have.

Marketing Sport Events

Sporting events are unique products; therefore, marketers must consider differences between marketing sporting events and marketing other goods and services. Mullin, Hardy, and Sutton (2014) and Wakefield (2007) provide a series of differences between sport marketing and marketing other goods and services. Many of those differences can be applied to the marketing of sporting events.

- Sport consumers tend to be highly identified with the sport or the event. Spectators may travel great lengths and spend more than they should to attend events featuring their favorite athletes or teams. For example, a college student may stay up all night for tickets, skip class, and spend a week's salary to see his team play in the NCAA basketball tournament. You do not see that type of behavior with the purchase of toothpaste or socks. Similarly, event participants may also be highly identified with the sport in which they participate. Given sport is part of their identity, they may follow it more closely, be more aware of upcoming events, and be more willing to invest their time and resources to participate in a specific event.
- Every sporting event is a unique experience for the spectator and for the participant, adding an element of unpredictability for the event marketer. Event marketers cannot promise a close game, a competitive tournament, or good weather. The implication here is that participants and spectators typically consume sporting events for the experience instead of some tangible factor. Therefore, event marketers have to focus on the experiential nature of the event in order to attract and retain customers.
- Sporting events may consist of core offerings (e.g., basketball game, volleyball tournament) as well as extensions (e.g., halftime show, awards ceremony, music, tailgating). The challenge for an event marketer is to develop an acceptable mix of activities to meet the needs of participants and spectators. Consider the Circle City Classic, a college football game featuring two historically black institutions. Although the game itself may be the central product, fans often attend the games for the entire experience, which includes a fan fest, a parade, and a postgame concert, in addition to a number of community activities that take place during game week.
- The cost of attending an event is often much greater than just the ticket price. Spectators attending sporting events may also incur expenses for travel and lodging, food and beverages at the event, and souvenirs and entertainment surrounding the event. For example, the average ticket cost to Super Bowl LI in Houston was $4,652; however, when airfare, lodging, local transportation, parking, and meals were figured in, the total cost was $6,820 for fans traveling from Atlanta and $7,467 for fans traveling from Boston (Kaylor 2017). Clearly, event organizers have to consider these total costs when setting their prices for tickets, registrations, and other goods and services.
- Sporting events are social in that most consumers prefer to attend or participate with other consumers. Sport consumers like the idea of being part of a crowd, and event participants tend to prefer the events with more players or more teams. In other words, sport spectators help create the environment, and other participants help create the competition. Considering the technological changes that make it easy to stay home, sporting events represent opportunities to be social and be a part of a community (Morrison 2014).

Developing a Marketing Plan

The **marketing plan** is the document detailing the marketing activities that need to happen for an event to reach its objectives. In other words, it is the blueprint you create to outline your marketing activities. Developing a marketing plan is a step-by-step process whereby organizations first consider their objectives, analyze relevant data, and then develop tactics accordingly. A typical marketing plan contains the following sections.

• *Data and analysis.* This section encompasses the information necessary to make wise marketing decisions. It should include detailed analyses of the event, current and potential customers, and the external environment.

• *Marketing goals and objectives.* Using data from the analyses, event marketers should set performance goals consistent with the organization's overall goals.

• *Target markets.* In this section, target markets are identified and described. Target markets are selected based on careful analysis of consumer data, and should be consistent with overall objectives.

• *Marketing tactics.* Sporting events are no different from other businesses in that effective use of the marketing mix is important for reaching marketing objectives. Traditional definitions of the marketing mix consist of elements related to the sport product, price, promotion, and place. Tactics based on the marketing mix are typically developed with the specific needs of each target market in mind.

• *Implementation.* This section of the plan includes a thorough detailing of what needs to take place to successfully implement the marketing plan. Having good ideas is not enough to be successful; marketers have to execute those ideas. Planners should identify and address issues related to budget, organizational support, leadership, resource acquisition, resource allocation, coordination, and timing (Mullin, Hardy, and Sutton 2014).

• *Assessment.* In this section, organizers describe how they will measure and assess results. At this point, organizers can address how plans can be modified in the future.

Market Research and Analysis

Effective decision-making depends on having good information. In order to make these decisions, event marketers need to collect and analyze information across a variety of areas such as the internal environment, the external environment, current and potential customers, and the competition. Table 6.1 illustrates some of the methods that can be used to collect data.

TABLE 6.1 Market Research Techniques

Method	Description
Internal data	Information such as sales records, consumer inquiries, attendance figures, and web traffic that can easily be collected to learn about your organization and consumers.
Secondary research	Published data. The advantage of secondary research is that it has already been collected and produced. The drawbacks are that the data may not be specific to your research questions, the data may be dated, and some data can be quite expensive.
Surveys	Lists of questions that can be distributed by mail, e-mail, or phone, or face to face. Surveys are good for collecting a lot of quantifiable data from a large number of consumers.
Personal interviews and focus groups	Qualitative research involving discussions with consumers designed to get feedback about issues or ideas. These methods are used to get more in-depth information about consumers' perceptions, attitudes, and beliefs.
Social media research	Collecting data from social media sources, which can be used to follow trends or to follow what your consumers are saying in real time.
Participant observation	Observing behavior of consumers and employees in their natural setting. This method is appropriate for measuring direct behavior rather than reported behavior (which can often be unreliable).
Mystery shopper	Using staff to pose as consumers in order to evaluate your own staff and facility.

- *Internal Environment*: What is it that makes the event or location unique, attractive, and exciting to potential participants or spectators? What are the event's strengths and weaknesses?
- *External Environment*: External influences such as social trends, technological advances, legal restrictions, demographic trends, and economic issues should be analyzed so that you understand factors that may affect your marketing strategies (Shank 2014).
- *Customers and potential customers*: Who are our customers and what are their needs?
- *Competition*: Who are our competitors? What gives us a competitive advantage?

Understanding Consumers

Understanding your consumers' wants and needs is at the core of the marketing plan. Knowing this information allows you to create events appealing to consumers and craft messages to communicate effectively with consumers. Regardless of whether you are marketing to spectators or to participants or both, addressing the following questions will go a long way toward understanding your consumers.

- What is important to consumers?
- Why are they are attending?
- What is keeping people who want to attend from doing so?
- What do consumers expect from the event?

To address what is important to consumers, you must identify what consumers want and what they value. Do they want to see the top athletes? Be a part of history? Enjoy time with family and friends? The following is a list of aspects of sporting events that commonly influence spectators' decisions to attend. The event marketer's task is to identify which aspects of an event are relevant to your consumers, to highlight the appealing aspects, and to illustrate how this product is different from other entertainment options.

- Amenities offered
- Atmosphere
- Attractiveness of teams and players
- Convenience and accessibility
- History and tradition
- Level of excitement
- Popularity of the sport
- Pregame and in-game entertainment
- Significance of the event
- Social opportunities
- Special offers

In addition to identifying event characteristics that are important to spectators, event marketers need to identify why consumers attend their events. The *why* is often addressed by identifying the consumer's **motivation**, the internal drive that leads to behavior. Motives to attend may differ by type of consumer. For example, youth teams might travel to a volleyball tournament to challenge themselves against the best competition, while older adults might participate in volleyball tournaments for the social aspects. Participant motivation may also differ by type of event. For example, runners in a charity road race are likely participating to support a cause or just to have fun, while competitors in a triathlon are more likely to be participating to challenge themselves and to gain a sense of achievement. It is important for marketers to identify what it is about their respective sports that motivates consumers to watch and attend. Some of the more common sport event motives are:

- Achievement and performance
- Affiliation
- Escape from daily life
- Excitement and drama
- Family togetherness
- Fun and entertainment
- Health and fitness
- Learning and discovery
- National pride
- Socialization

In some cases, consumers may want to attend but are prevented by one or more barriers to participation. These barriers are referred to as **constraints**. For example, some individuals may want to attend events but not have the time to attend or anyone to attend with. Or, a tennis player may want to play in a local tournament, but may feel that he cannot afford the entry fee or that he is not skilled enough to participate. While not all constraints can be removed, marketers can try to design programs that will eliminate or lessen potential constraints. Some of the more common constraints are:

- Economic
- Environmental
- Lack of someone to attend with
- Lack of success or skill
- Lack of support
- Location and access
- Social restrictions
- Time
- Weather

Sport consumers have most likely attended other events and therefore have expectations of what their experience should be like. For example, a marathon runner has likely entered marathons across the country and will have expectations of what amenities should be offered and the level of service she should receive. When her experiences meet or exceed expectations, she is likely to be satisfied. Satisfied customers are likely to come back and

© Chris Greenwell

Professional soccer is growing in popularity among U.S. fans.

tell others about their experience (positive word of mouth). When experiences fall short of expectations, they will be dissatisfied. Not only are dissatisfied customers unlikely to return; they will tell others (negative word of mouth). Therefore, you need to make sure you understand why people are participating and what they hope to get. From that knowledge, try to turn your event into an unforgettable experience.

Setting Marketing Goals and Objectives

If the organization's goal is to generate revenue, the marketing plan should be designed to maximize the amount of money that comes in through registrations, ticket sales, sponsorships, and so on. The plan will be much different if the focus of the event is to promote a cause. Typical marketing goals may be related to revenue, attendance, participation numbers, media coverage, fund-raising targets, or room nights. Specific, measurable objectives define targets that need to be reached to achieve each marketing goal. For example, a local runners' organization may set the following goal and objectives for its annual event:

Marketing goal: Increase participation in the annual Spring Fun Run.

Objective 1: Retain 95 percent of last year's participants.

Objective 2: Recruit 50 new runners.

Objective 3: Recruit 10 more organizational groups.

Objective 4: Increase number of youth participants by 15 percent.

Market Segmentation and Target Markets

No event can provide all benefits to all people. Even the Super Bowl, with an average audience of almost 100 million viewers in the United States, reaches less than half of the population. Think about an extreme sport event. Would it make sense to try to market the event to the entire community? Given that most people in the community would not be interested in the event, a broad marketing campaign would be wasteful because many resources would be expended on people with no intention of ever attending the event.

Instead of marketing to everyone (mass marketing), events should be tailored to meet the needs of specific segments of the population (target marketing). **Market segments** are groups of consumers or potential consumers with similar attributes, attitudes, or behaviors. By segmenting the population into groups with similar attributes, event marketers are able to develop efficient marketing plans to reach those groups. Segments are often identified using the following criteria:

- *Demographic segmentation*: identifying groups based on population characteristics such as age, gender, ethnicity, geographic location, income, and education
- *Psychographic segmentation*: identifying groups based on psychological characteristics such as lifestyle, personality, opinions, and values
- *Product usage*: identifying groups based on how often or how much the consumers use the product
- *Product benefits*: identifying groups based on the benefits consumers seek from an event

After identifying segments, event marketers select **target markets**, that is, the segments to which the event will be marketed. These markets are selected based on the segment's interest in the event, the likelihood of buying, size, and accessibility. Once targets have been selected, event marketers can develop specialized marketing activities and messages designed to appeal to and meet the specific needs of the target.

One common mistake is to target overly broad segments or to target segments based solely on size. Think of an extreme sports event. Organizers may have identified a large segment of senior citizens in the community. Although this segment may be large, it would not be appropriate to target this group because they would not be interested in the event, and no amount of marketing genius would be sufficient to get them to attend. This example illustrates that just because a segment is large, it may not necessarily be the best one to target. In fact, smaller, well-defined segments are often the more attractive targets. **Niche markets** are typically small, focused segments whose needs may not be currently served by larger events. A good example of this strategy comes from the cable television industry. Although ESPN and Fox Sports Net reach wide audiences with a variety of events, smaller networks such as The Golf Channel, The Tennis Channel, and The Outdoor Channel have emerged and have experienced success in marketing to smaller, focused audiences. Another example of catering to niche markets comes from the Arizona Diamondbacks, who create unique promotions and concession items to appeal to their Hispanic consumers. According to them, it is not enough just to translate content from English to Spanish, they have to create content specifically for their Hispanic fan base (Diaz 2015).

Branding the Event

A **brand** is the combination of names, symbols, slogans, or logos identifying a product and distinguishing it from other products (Aaker 1991). Brands also communicate an identity or image of a product. Events' brand names (e.g., the Olympic Games, the Ashes, the Super Bowl, the Masters, the Ironman Triathlon) and marks (e.g., the Olympic rings, the Ashes urn, the Super Bowl logo, the green jacket, the Ironman M-Dot) help consumers identify the event and differentiate it from competitors.

A strong name is especially important because it is often the center of marketing and promotional campaigns. For example, in 2006 the Senior LPGA Tour, a series of golf events for professional golfers 45 years of age and older, changed its name to the Legends Tour. Whereas the former name was effective in describing the event, the new name communicates an image more attractive to consumers.

Beyond having a strong name, events have to continue to build their brands in order to differentiate themselves effectively from the competition. The first step is by building brand awareness. Target consumers need to be aware of the brand and be able to recognize the brand's marks. Once consumers are aware, efforts shift to managing a brand's image. At this step, marketers associate the brand with attributes important to the consumer such as quality, tradition, reputation, success, and prestige. High levels of brand awareness and a strong brand image should generate brand equity, or the added value attributed to the brand. For example, the Spartathlon, a 246-kilometer race from Athens to Sparta, draws upon tradition to build its brand image. The race follows the path of Pheidippides, who ran from Athens to Sparta before the Battle of Marathon in 490 BCE.

Event Pricing

Price is what you ask your customers to pay in order to watch or participate in your event. Pricing decisions are important to event managers because price balances attractiveness and value with organizational revenue. Setting the price is especially difficult for sporting events because in this case price is associated with an experience rather than with a tangible good. Because of the subjective nature of intangible benefits, it is difficult to determine what the experience is worth to the customer.

To make effective pricing decisions, event marketers need to consider factors such as the cost of producing the event, consumer demand (what people are willing to pay), and competitors' prices (how your event compares with others). Event marketers also have to consider organizational objectives when setting price. Events may set their prices to maximize profits, to generate exposure, to meet competitive threats, or to provide participation (Shank 2014). For example, each of the following events would use different pricing strategies to meet different objectives.

- *Championship boxing event*: Set a high price to maximize revenue.
- *Charity fun run*: Set the price at a level that would encourage people to attend and give to the cause.
- *Volleyball tournament*: Set a price that would be comparable to other tournaments.
- *Intramural softball tournament*: Set a low price to encourage as many people as possible to participate.

Sporting events have many pricing options to meet these objectives. Some common pricing tactics are illustrated in table 6.2.

Distribution

Distribution relates to important issues of time (when is the event) and location (where is the event). Marketers can make events more attractive by making them more accessible and convenient. Time of the year, day of the week, and time of the day each influence consumers' ability to participate. In regard to location, event marketers need to consider access, perceived safety, and proximity to transportation when designing marketing efforts. Distribution is particularly important for sporting events because if tickets go unsold or teams don't register, the tickets can't be shelved and sold later.

A great example of how place can influence the perception of an event was the Battle at Bristol, a college football game between the University of Tennessee and Virginia Tech University. Rather than playing at one of the home stadiums, the game was played at Bristol Motor Speedway, which lies approximately halfway between the two schools. Thanks to the unique setting and the proximity of the two schools' fan bases, the game set a record of 156,990 for the highest attendance at a college football game (Cole 2018).

Distribution is often improved by working with various intermediaries (also called distribution channels) that make the event available to consumers. Examples of these intermediaries

TABLE 6.2 Common Pricing Tactics

Pricing Tactic	Description
Single ticket pricing	Each person is charged for admission or participation.
Group pricing	Teams or groups rather than individuals are charged. Group pricing takes advantage of the fact that consumers are often motivated to participate for social reasons.
All-inclusive pricing	Provide multiple benefits (e.g. admission, food, and parking) under one price. This method has the advantage of providing the consumers with extra perceived value.
Package pricing	Create packages that include multiple events, such as all-tournament passes or multiday passes. Rather than paying per game or match, consumers pay for access to multiple events. This method encourages consumers to attend more events or less attractive events.
Variable pricing	Set higher prices for the more attractive times and locations and lower prices for the less valuable inventory.
Dynamic pricing	Change prices as demand changes. If demand increases, prices increase to capture more revenue. When demand is low, prices drop to stimulate purchases.
Complimentary tickets or admissions	Free admission can be profitable if you can generate revenue through sponsorships or media. In addition, customers attending for free may generate revenue through concessions, parking, merchandise sales, or, depending on the type of event, donations.

include the venue where the event is held, the media that broadcast the event, ticket agents, web hosts, and retail partners. While working with intermediaries may add costs, it can also help make it easier for consumers to access your event.

Event Promotion

Promotion embodies the methods marketers use to communicate with customers. The keys to effective event promotion are to define what you want to accomplish, choose messages that appeal to your target audience, and use the right methods to communicate with that audience.

First, event marketers need to define what they want to accomplish through their promotional program. For a new event, promotional objectives may be to inform people about the event and make them aware of what the event offers. For events people are already aware of, promotional objectives may focus more on persuading people to attend or participate. Popular events may focus on reminding people about the event and reinforcing consumers' commitment to the event. Ultimately, the objectives should result in some action.

Second, the right message will go a long way in meeting promotional objectives. Effective messages will appeal to the target market and give that market a reason to listen. Marketers must therefore carefully identify what they want to promote and to whom. This is often accomplished by focusing on the needs of the consumers. For example, an event targeting families will be most effective if it focuses on issues relevant to families, such as opportunities for family fun at a low price. The message also depends on the type of event. Think about what makes the event exciting or attractive. Is it the history of the event, the location, or the participants? What makes this event relevant to the target market? Demonstrating the key benefit of the event is another characteristic of an effective message. For example, the PGA Tour used the message "These Guys are Good" for 20 years, because it emphasized the most important attribute of their events, their athletes' skills. In 2018, they decided to incorporate more of a focus on their players' personalities. Their new slogan, "Live Under Par" refers to life on and off the course (Klara 2018).

Third, the event marketer has to choose communication tools that will achieve the promotional objectives. An event marketer typically uses multiple tools to communicate the event but should take care to make sure the same message is getting across regardless of the tool being used. An integrated marketing communication (IMC) approach means the event will utilize several promotional elements to deliver a consistent message about the event.

Website Marketing

Event marketing often starts with a good website because consumers now depend on the Internet for information about events and activities surrounding them. Further, organizations depend on the Internet to build their brands, generate sales, and collect consumer feedback. Advances in technology now demand professional skills to develop sites that look and function at a level your visitors expect. In fact, a poorly designed website may suggest a poorly organized event in the minds of many consumers. When designing your web presence, keep the following in mind:

- *Think about the end user*: Take time to identify what your visitors may be seeking from your site.
- *Stay updated*: Make sure your site has the most up-to-date information. New content added on a regular basis keeps consumers coming back.
- *Add unique content*: The advantage of websites is that you can provide information, video, and archival material that may not be easily found in other places.
- *Be interactive*: Interactive activities help you build relationships with your consumers.
- *Make it mobile friendly*: Most consumers use mobile devices to access content, so your site should transfer easily to different devices.

- *Generate leads*: Capture information on your visitors, such as name and e-mail address.
- *Collect feedback*: Don't just focus on putting out information; identify ways to collect feedback in order to learn about your consumers.

Social Media

Successful sporting events embrace social media to connect with customers and promote events. Social media allow organizations to bypass traditional media and communicate directly with consumers before, during, and after events. Social media also allow events to engage their fanbase and develop personal connections with their consumers.

- *Have a strategy*: It may seem easy to just post on various platforms, but good social media campaigns are well thought out and planned. Be specific about what you want to accomplish.
- *Create content that aligns with your strategy*: What you say and how you say it should align with your overall strategy.
- *Understand your audience and the platforms they use*: Are your target consumers using Facebook? Twitter? Snapchat? Use the platforms that best align with your target consumers.
- *Create unique content for each platform*: Each platform has its own advantages and disadvantages.
- *Listen to your audience*: By following your audience, you can learn how you are being perceived and identify issues your consumers may be having.
- *Engage with the audience*: By responding to your audience, you can build relationships and show your customers that they are a priority.
- *Research your competition*: It is important to understand what they are doing and identify tactics you could be using.
- *Measure what is important*: Are you trying to reach new consumers? Build loyalty? Drive people to your website? Generate sales? Effective measurement allows you to adjust and adapt your strategy.
- *Convert social media engagement into sales*: Build in offers and incentives to drive consumers to action. Don't settle for merely reaching consumers; identify opportunities to generate leads, acquire new customers, and increase customer loyalty.

The following are a few examples of how social media can be used to promote events.

- ONE Championship, an Asian martial arts promotion, boasts a global Facebook fanbase of over 7 million, allowing the organization to reach consumers and promote their events in more than 130 countries (Mazique 2018).
- The National Basketball Association uses Snapchat to create exclusive 3- to 5-minute shows revealing what goes on behind the scenes. The platform allows them to create content appealing to their younger consumers (Wagner 2017).
- The National Hockey League and NBC Sports partnered to create a Snapchat lens that added a playoff beard (a hockey playoff tradition) and an animated Stanley Cup to their photos. The goal was to market the playoffs by creating shareable content that would keep fans engaged (Perez 2017).
- Wimbledon uploads content to 10 different social media sites (they reached 157 million people on Facebook alone in 2017) in order to make their event more accessible and immersive to a younger, tech-savvy audience (Hartnett 2017).

Viral Marketing

Viral marketing refers to techniques designed to encourage consumers to share information with other potential consumers. The goal is to get your consumers talking to others in their own social circles. These tactics can be very successful as consumers are more likely to trust their friends' and families' opinions. These effects can be generated by working with other organizations to get their members talking about your event, providing recruiting incentives to current customers who spread the word and enlist new customers, giving coupons or premium items to customers to pass along to new customers, and creating videos or games consumers share with each other. Social media also provides a good platform for encouraging word-of-mouth. For example, the University of Florida launched their #GatorAlways campaign to encourage fans to share their stories about becoming a fan. By sharing their stories, the most passionate fans are spreading the organization's message to others in their networks (Clapp 2017).

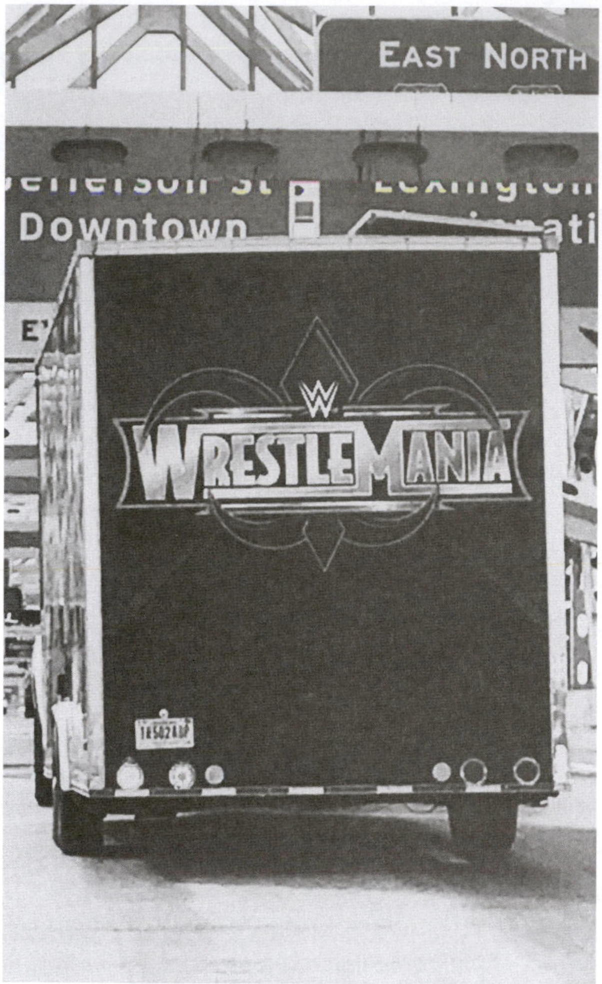

© Chris Greenwell

A mobile billboard for Wrestlemania.

Advertising

Advertising is a paid, nonpersonal, clearly sponsored message (Mullin, Hardy, and Sutton 2014). Choosing the right media is critical to the success of advertising. In choosing media, it is important to consider whether it is appropriate for your message, whether it reaches your target market, and how much it will cost to reach your target market. Although we typically think of advertising as newspaper print ad, a television commercial, or a billboard, a variety of other media such as newsletters, transportation ads, and yard signs can effectively reach target markets. In addition, new technologies have changed advertising. For example, events trying to reach younger markets are finding that advertising on websites and through social media may be more effective than traditional newspaper advertising. Table 6.3 provides a list of some of the media commonly used to promote sporting events.

TABLE 6.3 Advertising Media

Type of media	Examples	Advantages
Electronic media	Television, radio, podcasts	The use of sight and sound makes these options good if you need to appeal to consumers' senses
Internet	Websites, mobile devices	Messages can be customized and can reach very specific targets
Print media	Newspapers, magazines, newsletters, trade publications	Can be more cost effective than other advertising options
Outdoor media	Billboards, buses, benches, posters, fliers	Good for repeat exposure and low message competition

Sales Promotion

Sales promotion consists of many different techniques used to engage the consumer such as discounts, special offers, coupons, samples, premiums, contests and sweepstakes, demonstrations, and exhibitions.

In event management, sales promotion is often used to create interest or generate purchases through reduced-price or value-added incentives. When your consumers are price sensitive and will respond to price changes, you may consider a price incentive such as a ticket discount, a coupon, or a free trial. If price is not an issue with customers, or you are concerned about cheapening your product, adding value may be the best option. Numerous types of sales promotions can be used to promote an event. The key is to identify which types of promotions will resonate with your target market and deliver results. See the Sales Promotion Techniques sidebar for some common techniques.

Sales

Sales is where we directly facilitate the exchange of goods and services. Often the key to sales is the list of prospective customers, or prospects. Sales activities rarely work unless you are contacting the right people. Smaller and less frequent sporting events do not have the luxury of full-time sales staff, so they use multiple techniques to facilitate sales. Table 6.4 on page 106 presents a list of typical sales techniques and the advantages of each.

Creating Community Support

Another good way to promote your event is through partnerships with community organizations that can be utilized to create community support, promote your event, and involve the community. Community leaders and local politicians can provide high-profile support, and your work together is likely to generate media attention. Local agencies such as sports commissions, convention and visitors bureaus, and chambers of commerce are in the business of promoting economic activity; therefore, they are likely to have the networks, capabilities, and know-how to promote events. In addition, local businesses that cater to tourism such as restaurants and tourist attractions make good partners because they also stand to benefit from your success.

To better engage the community, organizations will often create advisory boards made up

Sales Promotion Techniques

Price promotion

- Buy one, get one free
- Coupons
- Discounts
- Family packages
- Group discounts
- Loyalty programs

Value-added promotion

- Camps and clinics
- Contests and sweepstakes
- Exhibitions
- Honors and celebrations
- Interactive experiences
- Meet and greet events
- Premium item giveaways (hats, T-shirts, collectible items)
- Product sampling
- Special attractions (postgame concerts, autograph sessions)
- Theme nights

TABLE 6.4 Sales Techniques

Type of sales	Uses
Personal selling	Used for larger purchases such as season tickets, premium seating, sponsorships, and group sales
E-mail and mobile marketing	Good for creating highly targeted offers or reaching large numbers of contacts at a low cost
Direct mail	When used with targeted mailing lists, direct mail can be effective in putting offers in consumers' hands
Telemarketing	Can be inbound or outbound and is particularly good for business-to-business sales
Volunteer sales	Using your own customers to sell or refer new customers in exchange for exclusive rewards or perks

of local leaders to help them promote the event. Advisory boards bring contacts and knowledge of the community to the table and play a role in advising event organizers on these matters. Advisory boards can also establish legitimacy for events lacking awareness or recognition in the community. By utilizing trusted and respected community leaders, advisory boards can emphasize the significance of the event (Supovitz and Goldwater 2014).

A great example of an event that generates considerable community support is the PGA's St. Jude Classic. This PGA Tour event benefiting St. Jude Children's Research Hospital has been held in Memphis, Tennessee, since 1958 and has an undeniable bond with the city. FedEx, a local company, has supported the event since 1986, and according to tournament organizers, about 1,850 volunteers contribute more than 25,000 hours of service to the event each year. Youth Program, Inc., an organization made up of local business and political leaders, serves as the host organization. As of 2017, the event's 60th anniversary, the tournament has raised more than $35 million for St. Jude Children's Research Hospital.

Summary

Effective event marketing does not happen by accident. Merely getting the word out is not enough to meet most marketing objectives; it takes extensive planning and forethought. Marketers need to identify what their customers want and systematically develop marketing plans to meet those customer wants. Effective marketing plans require careful analysis of internal and external influences, meaningful goals that support organizational objectives, selection of appropriate target markets, carefully planned tactics, and a plan for implementation. Event marketers have numerous tools at their disposal. A strong event brand and various promotional tools allow marketers to communicate that their events will meet consumers' needs.

LEARNING ACTIVITIES

Assume you are in charge of marketing a senior women's professional golf tournament in your town. The organization's goal is to maximize ticket sales to make sure the event is a financial success.

1. Describe your target market.
2. What benefits or attributes would be most attractive to this target?
3. What would be your marketing message?
4. How would you reach potential ticket buyers?

Now assume you are in charge of marketing an amateur junior women's team golf tournament in your town. The organization's goal is to maximize the number of junior golf teams that register for the event. You have to recruit teams to participate in this event.

1. What would be your selling points to attract teams?
2. How would you reach these teams?

CASE STUDY: URBAN BOURBON

The Urban Bourbon Half Marathon (UBHM) is a road race staged every October by the Louisville Sports Commission. Created in 2011, the event grew to over 3,200 participants by 2017. The 13.1-mile race begins downtown and weaves through historic and scenic parts of the city. Event organizers have three primary goals: create an experiential destination event that will attract affluent consumers to the community, promote healthy lifestyles in the community, and generate revenue to support the organization's mission of attracting sporting events to the community. Based on its quality course, accessible destination, and unique theme, the race was voted the best half marathon in the US in the BibRave 100.

Half marathons are popular and growing in the US, with more than 2 million runners and walkers finishing events each year. While most half marathons attract the majority of their participants from the local market (80-85 percent), the UBHM has exceeded expectations by attracting a large percentage (43 percent) of out-of-town consumers from 45 different states and six different countries. In addition, the event's demographics are attractive, with 56 percent of participants being female, 80 percent being between the ages of 21-49, and 75 percent having incomes between $75,000 and $200,000.

Much of this appeal has been attributed to the event's bourbon theme. By limiting the event to participants 21 and older, organizers are able to deliver the bourbon experience before, during, and after the race. Sponsor Jim Beam hosts a VIP packet pick-up at the Jim Beam Bourbon Stillhouse and provides a bourbon tasting at the regular pick-up location. During the race, runners pass Louisville's historic Whisky Row, and after the race runners celebrate at the Bourbon Bash with bourbon tasting, food, and other race amenities.

In terms of prior marketing efforts, almost all of the event's participants sign up online, enabling the organizers to collect key data on their consumers and communicate with them on a regular basis. Part of their strategy has been to add unique events to enhance the experience of current participants, attract potential participants, and engage community partners. Word of mouth is responsible for attracting the majority of participants, either by having a friend or family member involved (43 percent) or by hearing about it through a past participant (28 percent). Attendance at race expos (9 percent), running publications and websites (8 percent), and social media (5 percent) were the other ways participants learned about the event.

Case Study Application

The sports commission has a plan to continue to grow the race to 7,500 runners over the next ten years. Given their limited budget and the number of other races competing for participants, they have to be very strategic in their marketing efforts.

1. What could you do to make the event more attractive to potential runners?
2. Whom would you target to increase participation?
3. How would you reach these participants?
4. What would be your selling points to attract these participants?

CHAPTER 7

Media Relations and Promotion

CHAPTER OBJECTIVES

After completing the chapter, the reader should be able to do the following:

- Understand the role of the media, media promotion, and media relations.
- Understand the symbiotic relationship between the media, sport, and events.
- Recognize the critical Rs of media relations: relating, retaining, and repairing. Value the role of the promotional mix with regard to marketing.
- Appreciate the value of social media in event management.
- Understand how to evaluate the success of a promotion and media relations campaign.

INDUSTRY PROFILE

Chris Richards, PGA TOUR

As a journalism student at Michigan State University, Richards was a four-year intern in the Sports Information Department and worked more than 100 games for the basketball, football, hockey, wrestling, and golf teams. He completed summer internships with the Game of Your Life Foundation, a junior golf tour in Michigan, as well as with the American Junior Golf Association (AJGA) and spent a summer term studying environmental journalism at Macquarie University in Sydney, Australia.

After graduating in 2007, he began his career at the AJGA, where his responsibilities included media relations, social media strategy and production, website production, event management, and sponsor activation. He was with the AJGA for seven years and with U.S. Kids Golf for two years before accepting a job as manager of the PGA Tour.

Can you explain your role on the Champions Tour?

I work up to 20 tournaments a year as a media official on PGA Tour Champions. Overall, my objective is to enhance the exposure for the tour and help tell the stories of our players and tournaments. I provide the information and access to players that journalists need to cover our tournaments. I work closely with players, tournaments, and title sponsors to understand their key messages, and I pitch stories to local and national media in hopes of earning media coverage that tells those stories.

What was it about media relations and promotions that enticed you to this field?

I've always been a writer, but I never aspired to be a traditional journalist. Public relations seemed like a natural fit because I could blend my writing skills with strategic communications.

What special skills are necessary to compete for jobs in this field?

Relationship building is the most essential skill for a communications professional because you will work with the same people your entire career, even if you change industries. Being trustworthy and reliable aren't flashy traits, but people remember those qualities for many years.

Curiosity is an intangible characteristic that sets people apart. Storytelling is a big part of my job, and good stories are much deeper than birdies and bogeys on a scorecard. Thoughtful questions lead to thoughtful answers, and usually good stories.

Jobs that require travel sound very exciting, a new adventure each week. In your position, your travel is international. Does this present a challenge? If so, how?

Whether it's international or domestic travel, it can be a challenge to adapt to a local media market, especially because I work in nearly 20 markets a year. A storyline that resonates in Raleigh may fall flat in Phoenix. Journalists in Tokyo have different expectations than those in New York City. Not only do I need to recognize these differences, I also need to communicate these differences to players. For instance, in Tokyo, the media wanted to talk with Tom Watson every day, regardless of what he shot, because they wanted the Hall of Famer's impressions on the golf course, the fans, and how he's enjoyed his trip.

Golf events are the same week to week: play 18 holes and post your score and repeat two more times on the Champions Tour. How do you keep each week unique and fresh?

While the tournament structure is repetitive, every tournament has a different personality and there are new stories to be told every week. Every tournament is an opportunity to build a new relationship, have a new conversation, and add to my mental index of stories.

How have the social media impacted your job? What platforms work best for promoting an event versus promoting an individual player?

The social media have given us an opportunity to tell more fun and creative stories. Players can take advantage by telling their own stories in their own voices, while tournaments share the fan experience. Social media are also a way to create new connections with influencers who can share their experiences at tournaments with people outside our existing core audience. In all cases, it's important to find the platform that best matches the story to the target audience.

Working with the media has its challenges. What would you say is the most difficult challenge you have encountered thus far in your career?

One challenging part of the job is when I'm forced to be reactive, such as managing negative news stories. Those situations test every PR skill, especially problem solving, clear and effective communication, and relationships with the media. Other times, the challenge is making sure I'm proactive. For instance, some writers may have an agenda and the challenge is to identify the potential pitfalls ahead of time and make sure I prepare accordingly.

Describe a typical day for you in the office and then also at an event.

It may be counterintuitive, but Tuesdays through Thursdays at tournaments are often busier than competition days. I schedule and moderate pretournament press conferences; I pitch and fulfill media requests for the current tournament as well as for future events; and I help create or produce content for the tour's social media channels. Early in the week, player schedules are much more fluid than during tournament rounds. On competition days, I coordinate postround interviews with players and compile tournament notes that I distribute to the local and national media. In the office, I manage stats and records, update media guides, recap past events, and plan for upcoming events.

What is the most important thing someone entering this career field should know?

Communications is constantly evolving. The job I will have in five years may not exist yet. It's important to be a problem solver and a critical thinker because those skills will survive any evolution, and they will make you valuable beyond how well you fulfill your day-to-day functions.

What particular skills or talents are most essential to be effective in your job?

The skills I value most are writing and editing. Good writers are efficient communicators, and good editors ask questions that make people better writers.

Any final thoughts?

There's a certain amount of luck involved in finding a job you love in sports, but you also make your own luck by being ready to take advantage of an opportunity. Find a professional mentor who will tell you what you need to hear, not what you want to hear. Be humble and be open to criticism and feedback. Ask good questions and be a good listener. Make mistakes, but only make them once.

After reading this chapter you will have a better understanding of media relations and promotion, and how you can create a win-win relationship with the media. Media relations and promotion are two highly visible avenues utilized by companies, and event organizers specifically use these tools to help them accomplish their marketing and promotional goals. Sport organizations and events engage in these two forms of communication as means to reach their target market. To better understand what is meant by these two terms, we will define **media promotion** as the integrating of various communication strategies to convey the organization's message, and **media relations** as the give-and-take relationship that must be groomed and nurtured by the sport organization in an effort to maintain a favorable position with the media outlet. When managed properly, the relationship affords both parties positive outcomes (such as the event being broadcast). This relationship is discussed later in the section "Symbiotic Relationship: Working Together to Achieve Greatness".

At the end of the day when people leave an event, the main goal for event management is for people to have had a pleasant experience and to have connected with the event on some level so that they will be repeat customers. Success, for a sport event, depends on several factors, but none is more critical than the ability to engage your audience, provide a memorable experience, and have positive feedback. Engaging an audience is a three-fold process: before the event, during the event, and after the event. Clever advertising, catchy phrases, giveaways, and sales promotions are just a few of the ways we can generate interest before the event. Generating hype through both traditional and new media is the most cost-efficient way an event planner can reach the target audience, potential sponsors, and possible participants. Identifying ways to communicate with your target audience will provide them with the necessary information to make an informed decision to purchase tickets, attend, and participate or, at a minimum, to increase chatter about the forthcoming event. This communication can take many forms and falls in line with the marketing concepts discussed in the previous chapter. Whether functioning independently or in unison, the traditional elements of the **promotional mix** (also known as integrated marketing communication) have been categorized as advertising, direct marketing, personal selling, public relations, sales promotions, and sponsorship (Mullin, Hardy, and Sutton 2014; Shank 2009; Irwin, Sutton, and McCarthy 2002). We contend that **social media** are now a necessary promotional consideration, and they will also be addressed here. The goal of promotion, according to Mullin, Hardy, and Sutton (2014) is to move the consumer through four phases: first, we increase awareness, next their interest grows, from there we hope to spark their desire, and finally, we hope they take action (make a purchase). This is referred to as the **AIDA** process. The ways in which we can motivate people to action are limited only by our creativity.

Symbiotic Relationship: Working Together to Achieve Greatness

The adjective *symbiotic*, derived from the root word *symbiosis*, is defined as a cooperative relationship between two entities. For event managers, the **symbiotic relationship** shared between the media and an institution or an event planner is critical to the success of the event. The relationship is best described as one that garners the most benefit for both the media and the organization or event, despite the fact that both could function independently. In other words, media outlets and the sport industry form a very lucrative partnership. This partnership is fed through the advent of sporting events that need media relations tactics and promotional efforts to fulfill their potential. The partnership blossomed in harmony, each using the other through the years, sport as cultural unifier and the media reporting feel-good stories, both functioning as a means of distraction during difficult times, first with newspapers, then with radio and television, and now with social media. Blogger Anjelique Kyriakos summed up this social connection as: "It is readers who drive the media, and fans who drive the sports" (Kyriakos, 2015, para. 7). In order to better understand this, let's look at some examples of media relations in action.

In all levels of sport we see the need to build and maintain a healthy relationship with media outlets. The Kansas State High School Activities Association *Media Relations Guide* explains the value of a positive working relationship. The guide clearly states that "positive exposure is often the result of good preparation and providing media representatives with information and/or ideas they need and then allowing them to do their job" (Kansas State 2012 , p. 2). This is why it is critical to know the media assigned to cover your event and to forge a working relationship. Remember, the media need content to fill the pages of their newspapers and the segments of their broadcasts. They rely on you just as much as you rely on them. You must be diligent in distributing your information in a timely manner and respecting the media's deadlines (Kansas State 2012).

In the *Encyclopedia of Sports Management and Marketing*, Bussell (2011) states:

> *As one element of the public relations equation, media relations, when combined with the other element, community relations, provides organizations with powerful tools for creating positive exposure. Organizations must be proactive in establishing media relations by providing information for them to scrutinize and utilize. The media possess a powerful influence over public opinion so great care must be taken in providing timely and accurate information. Open, honest communication will help to build this relationship.*

The Critical Rs of Media Relations

Three processes that are critical to the success of an organization's media relations efforts are the relationship with the media, the retaining of that relationship, and the repairing of any issues that arise that could negatively affect the relationship. Their status in the **critical Rs** of media relations shows the importance of the role of the media in the sport industry.

Relating

According to Stoldt, Dittmore, and Branvold (2012), media relations are the most popular form of public relations in the sport industry. The goal of media relations is to develop positive relationships with members of the media and the sport organization (Mullin, Hardy, and Sutton 2007). Tuckwell (2011) described this as the process of garnering public support and acceptance. Media relations are founded on the principle of generating positive publicity while lessening the impact of negative publicity for a sport entity (Stoldt, Dittmore, and Branvold 2012). Publicity is a free form of communication for an organization, and since a legitimate media outlet is reporting the information, consumers believe what they hear (Tuckwell 2011).

Zhong Zhi/Getty Images

Retaining favor with the media requires special care.

Event managers rely on publicity to spread the word about their events. Depending on the setting, this could be as simple as a sports information director producing a press release, a facility manager listing upcoming events on a billboard or a marquee, or an event manager setting up an interview to discuss her event and how it will affect the local community. In an effort to relate to the media, practitioners must be willing to work at building a relationship with the local media that is above reproach. This requires providing the media with access to information. Practitioners have multiple tools that allow for this flow of information, such as press releases, feature articles, press conferences, and Internet sites.

Retaining

Retaining favor with the media requires special care. The extending of courtesy is not only required but also expected. Remember, a media outlet is your friend until you do something to tarnish that friendship. The same rules that apply to a friendship such as mutual respect, honesty, fair treatment, and openness are essential for maintaining a positive relationship with the media. You must supply accurate and timely information both in good times and during controversy. People are very much aware of the flow of positive information when things are going great. Nowhere is the process more evident than in the role of the college **sports information director (SID)**. In a constant fight to garner media attention, SIDs work feverishly to create press releases, media guides, and feature articles that provide the media with much-needed content for little effort on their part. The constant flow of information from the SID to the media outlets establishes a positive rapport and, in most cases, captures the attention of the media so that the story is reported.

Mavros (2015) suggested five considerations that will aid a sport organization looking to enrich their media relationships:

1. Be timely and have relevant information
2. Remember your competition
3. Don't be discouraged if you don't hear back
4. Manage expectations cooperatively and with honesty
5. Know the media who cover you and keep up with what they are covering

These tips will allow you to better pitch to the media and to grow your relationship.

Repairing

Media relations can be tricky. Sport and its ancillary parts (events, facilities, athletes) are not above media scrutiny. Even a minor miscue or bad timing can thwart all of the time and energy you have put into building your relationship. Building a positive relationship requires an investment of time and energy; repairing a severed relationship will require even more. In times of crisis, the media can turn on you if you don't respond accordingly. Often this is a result of a breakdown in communications. Take care to manage your relationships properly and to be proactive in times of crisis. DeMarco (2014) acknowledged that being proactive requires that you have a thorough plan that predicts possible crises, that you have prepared a plan of response to those predicted issues, and that your plan offers protection for your reputation (event or facility). Crisis communication sets the tone for your relationships. Having a designated spokesperson and open communication will help to rebuild any trust issues that might arise from the crisis.

Differentiating the Promotional Mix From the Marketing Mix

In chapter 6 you were introduced to the concepts of marketing and promotion as they relate to the sport industry. As it applies to sport, marketing has been defined as "the specific application of marketing principles and process to sports products and non-sports products through association with sport" (Shank 2015, p. 5) and as "consisting of all the activities designed to meet the needs and wants of sport consumers through exchange processes" (Mullin, Hardy, and Sutton 2007, p. 11). Chapter 6 also describes the process of capturing the four Ps (product, place, price, promotion) with the intent of creating products at acceptable prices, and in appropriate places, that can be promoted to target consumers (Masterman 2009).

Pitts and Stotlar (2002) expanded on the traditional Ps of marketing, stating that sport marketers must address elements outside the four Ps if they are to create and implement a successful marketing plan. They devised a two-tier, 10-step approach to the sport marketing process that identifies strategies and tactics to help us better understand the uniqueness of marketing the sport product. Their **10 Ps** include purpose, product, projecting the market, position, players, package, price, promotion, place, and promise (Pitts and Stotlar 2002). Of the 10 Ps, positioning, promoting, placing, and promising are key in media relations and promotion. These four concepts most directly relate to the dissemination of information.

Shank (2009) defines **positioning** as "fixing your sports entity in the minds" of those people you are targeting with your product or service (p. 198). A sporting event must compete with other events and attractions for consumers' discretionary funds. Positioning your event in a way that creates a memory and thus action on their part to participate in or attend your event over other options is the desired outcome. This process requires some creative strategies and careful planning.

As discussed in chapter 6, promoting is how marketers communicate with customers. Kaser and Oelkers (2008) define the promotional mix as the blending of the promotional elements of "advertising, sales promotion, publicity, and personal selling" (p. 246). Kotler (1975) labeled it a form of communication dedicated to persuading. For our purposes, we define **promotion** and the promotional mix as the communication process that uses varied communication tools such as advertising, publicity, public relations, community relations, media relations, selling, and sponsorship to convey a message and entice action. As you work through this chapter, you will begin to see the important role the media play in fulfilling the expectations of a sport organization's promotional goals. The media are critical for success because event marketers cannot rely on an "if you build it, they will come" approach to marketing.

In traditional terms, *place* refers to the distribution strategies (Shank 2009). But we contend that placing also relates to the various media used in promoting an event. Identifying the optimal channels for promoting an event is critical. Technology continues to shape how we engage with others and obtain information. The various social media such as Facebook, Twitter, YouTube, and smartphone applications have reshaped how we disseminate information. These, as well as traditional media communication channels, are discussed later in this chapter.

The final P to consider is the promise. Typically, the promise refers to evaluating. How well did you do what you said you were going to do? How well did you follow your plan for doing it? In terms of the media, built-in mechanisms such as ratings and shares help determine both return on investment (ROI) and return on objectives (ROO). ROO measures the achievement of goals and objectives and is a viable alternative to ROI (Silvers 2007). Yes, money—specifically a profit—is an indication of financial success, but sometimes we seek more than just monetary gains; we seek attainment of marketing plan goals and objectives. ROO will provide this information.

Sport entities rely on these processes to convey their offerings to fans to entice and inform. Successful promotional efforts will take the fan through the hierarchy of effects model discussed in chapter 5. This process moves the intended consumers through the phases of awareness, interest, desire, and action so that they go from being in the target group to being a purchasing consumer. In terms of the event, the goal is that the experience be enjoyable and that fans become repeat customers. Media relations and promotional efforts are significant tools in achieving this desired outcome for event managers.

Promotional Tools

Promotion is all about persuasion. Your intent is to drive customers to want to attend your event. With a firm knowledge of media relations, you can turn your attention to developing and designing those tools that will help promote your event. What does it need in order to be successful, aside from the typical patrons and performers? Do you need to generate interest, or has interest already peaked? What is your target audience, and how will you best reach them?

Creativity in your promotions will help to establish your event in the minds of your target market. Truettner (2017) suggested that event promoters consider varied strategies and tactics when creating their promotional objectives and plans. She emphasizes that establishing and knowing your goals will help drive your promotional efforts. Preevent activities should encompass all departments that will be involved in promotion and making sure the goals are attainable and measurable; knowing what you want to accomplish and measure and how you measure. These will help determine your target market and your best means for reaching them.

Next, Truettner presented the idea of omnichannel marketing. In a Forbes article, Rigby (2011) addressed the idea of omnichannel retailing as a way to "interact with customers through countless channels; a sort of reaching them where they are scenario; email, social media, websites, direct mail and PR to name a few." (The use of social media will be discussed later in this chapter.) Rigby's final three suggestions encourage you to (1) maintain any traditional marketing approaches as well, (2) promote during your event (by tweeting, blogging, and streaming) to help to "keep it live, keep it relevant" (para. 33), and (3) use postevent marketing to gather items (photos, videos, feedback) that will help for your next event.

Using these questions and Truettner's suggestions as a starting point will help you devise your promotional plan. This promotional plan represents the promotional goals, strategies and tactics, budget, and evaluation processes you have defined during your planning stage. This is when your advertising, direct marketing, personal selling, public relations, sales promotions, and sponsorship ideas are fashioned (Shank 2009; Mullin, Hardy, and Sutton 2007; Irwin, Sutton, and McCarthy 2002). Chapter 5 introduced you to sponsorship, while chapter 6 discussed marketing and its related components, including promotion. Chapter 6 also described two types of sales promotions, those associated with price and those that are value-added. Let's take a look at some specific examples of each.

Price promotions include such things as discounts, coupons (money off or buy one, get one free), family or group discounts, and bundling of amenities (tickets plus parking pass). Value-added enticements such as premium giveaways, sweepstakes, meet-and-greet events, theme nights, pre- and postevent entertainment, autograph sessions, interactive experiences, and fan appreciation promotions are fan lures. No other sector of the sport industry relies on these promotions the way minor league baseball does.

> *Fans at minor league baseball games have come to expect the added value of a special event or giveaway when they attend a minor league game. Minor league ball clubs are aware of this expectation. Most of them provide fans on a regular basis with more than just a baseball game. They offer entertainment activities, free souvenirs, or ticket and concession discounts. (Hixon 2005)*

For example, the Nashville Sounds have what they call the Band Box located in right field. This area not only offers unique food options and a bar area but is full of other entertainment options like ping-pong, cornhole, foosball, shuffleboard, and a mini golf course.

NASCAR, the one sport in which you can actually see sponsor activation before, during, and after the event and even hear it in the winner's circle, is a huge marketing success. What a tremendous visual a car is as it tools around the track or visits the local grocery store for a meet and greet. Because of NASCAR's integrated approach to marketing, its promotional efforts have paid off, literally. NASCAR fans are more likely to be loyal purchasers of products "their" driver represents. Ukman (2012) reports that more than 70 percent of NASCAR fans would purchase a sponsor's product over the product of a competitor who was not affiliated with NASCAR. That is powerful!

The ability to extend the excitement and grow fan support through promotional efforts is endless. Limited only by your creativity, you are able to use the various promotion mix tactics to fit your needs and your target audience. Bobbleheads, T-shirts, fireworks, win-a-car night, and social media gaming are just a few of the popular promotional gimmicks that can drive excitement for your event.

Social Media: Connecting Through Connectivity

As mentioned earlier, omnichannel marketing involves various social tools to reach an intended audience. The growth of social media usage confirms the need to address its use for promoting your event. As Jackson (2012) boldly claimed, "social media and sports are natural teammates" (para. 1). Who can argue that? You would be hard-pressed to find a sport entity that has not jumped on the social media bandwagon. Jackson further contends that baseball was slow to migrate to the new medium, but once MLB tested the waters, it too was hooked. He stated, "the New York Yankees, with an estimated marketing worth of $340 million, are becoming as aggressive online as they are on the field. With more than 500,000 Twitter followers, nearly 5 million Facebook fans . . ." (para. 7). This comment refers to sports teams but holds true for sport events as well.

In 2009, Qualman proclaimed that "social media transforms the way you live and do business" (p. 278). He also professed that using social media is not wasting time; instead, it motivates productivity. Social media allow us to live and work transparently in a world that can be summed up in 280 characters on Twitter (up from the original 140 when the application launched), or in Facebook posts or YouTube videos or Instagram stories. We no longer seek information; information finds us. Social media have infected our lives, and we are gracious hosts. In his 2018 video *Social Media Revolution* Qualman reaffirmed "we don't have a choice to digitally transform, the choice is how well we do it."

Sports teams and athletes understand the importance of social media. Perez (2017) stated that "social media provides many aspects of marketing and engagement previously unavailable to teams—it changes how teams and their fans can interact and affects how often fans are exposed to content from the teams they follow. Today, teams can receive feedback from fans immediately as well as respond to questions from fans." The power of social media was very evident when NBA superstar Lebron James publicly announced his move to Miami on ESPN. His newly created Twitter account went from 18,000 followers to more than 90,000 within a few hours.

How do you harness the power of social media for your event? You take your message to the people. Frost (2012) identified the following 10 reasons why you should engage in social media.

1. *Cost-effectiveness*. There is little to no cost to use the established social media platforms. A great example is the Texas Christian University (TCU) volleyball program. Reibel (2010) highlighted the impact of Facebook on the TCU program and summer camps. TCU utilized Facebook as a research tool, searching for and identifying more than "50,000 people within 50 miles of the Fort Worth campus on Facebook that stated in their profile they liked volleyball" (para. 7). From this information they began a campaign to reach out to those people, and in the first year they generated more than 7,000 fans on Facebook, increased attendance by 85 percent, and grew summer camp registrations by 30 percent.

2. *Reach*. In the previous TCU example, the impact of reach is easily seen. Reach, as defined by Shank (2009), is "the number of people exposed to an advertisement in a given medium" (p. 308). Utilizing social media to connect with current and potential customers is just one of its benefits. It makes even greater sense when you consider the following statistics: Bullas (n.d.) offers that Facebook reaches more than 850 million people per month online and 425 million mobile users; Twitter has 465 million established accounts, with another 1 million added daily; and YouTube has more than 2 billion views a day. Now do you get it?

Social media's reach is far greater than public releases, but the social media augment rather than replace the traditional media.

3. *Connectivity*. Better yet, get personal with customers. What better way to stay in touch during the off-season or downtime? The WWE has positively exploited this engagement tool. In an effort to maintain emotional hype between events, the WWE and its members began tweeting so that the plots and the conflicts among the Superstars would not fizzle (Cummins 2012).

4. *Timeliness*. The social media deliver instantaneous information. Just as sport is a unique product (produced and consumed at the same time), social media can be produced and disseminated just as quickly (Frost 2012; Mullin, Hardy, and Sutton 2007). In 2008, the University of Utah, in a last-ditch effort to sell its remaining 500 football tickets, posted to Facebook, and within two hours the tickets were sold (Steinbach 2010).

5. *Flexibility*. The ability to share more than you would with traditional avenues such as advertising creates a more flexible promotions approach. Giving updates, altering information, and offering supplemental information are possible within seconds when you use social media. Many schools have turned to social media as a way to extend their sales promotions. For example, Louisiana State University has capitalized on their mascot, Mike the Tiger, by creating Facebook and Twitter accounts that allow students to interact with the feline (Tomko 2011).

6. *Promotional opportunities*. Mass distribution of your promotional efforts is now more accessible with social media. Two such promotions come to mind. First, the National Football League's Carolina Panthers held a citywide scavenger hunt fashioned after *The Amazing Race* to engage fans. According to Hepburn (2010), participants met at Bank of America Stadium, followed clues to prescribed points, and checked in with location-based applications such as Foursquare. Participants had fun and earned points for each check-in, businesses that participated experienced an influx of people, and prizes were awarded at the end. The second example comes from Bowling Green State University's Stroh Center grand opening. In an effort to generate hype for the new facility, BGSU students created a music video chronicling the funding of the building. Kielmeyer (as cited in Goss 2011) reported that the school was looking to do something different that would create a lasting impression for BGSU students, fans, and supporters. I think they hit this one out of the park! You can watch the video at www.youtube.com/watch?v=Yx-NJJgs08Xg.

7. *Easier referrals*. The social media let you engage in a more global outreach through word of mouth, or as Qualman (2018) puts it, "world of mouth."

8. *Increased web traffic*. The various forms of social media allow you to cross-promote all the outlets you use, thus driving web traffic, smartphone application downloads, and virtual retail opportunities.

9. *Branding opportunities*. Honigman (2012) stated it best when he said that "most of the time, only fans interested in your athlete or brand will see your content on Facebook or Instagram since it's their choice to follow you or not, giving you the opportunity to connect with your real brand advocates" (para. 11). In February 2012, the Philadelphia Wings, a National Lacrosse League (NLL) franchise, decided to spice things up a bit by using the players' Twitter monikers on their jerseys instead of their last names (Olenski 2012). The hashtag craze is still going strong as well. In 2013, AT&T launched their #BeTheFan promotion that married a Hollywood name with College Game Day in order to promote college football (Beese 2014). The result was an astonishing 200 million people interacting across several social media platforms, driving their usage as well as increasing AT&T's social clout. Today, we see hashtags everywhere from college recruiting events that want you post to social media while on campus to youth sport organizations like the Little League World Series (#LLWS) using hashtags as a promotional element.

10. *Hiring*. Actively using social media engages potential employees who are also utilizing the media. This allows you to identify highly qualified employees and also to screen their social media etiquette.

It's evident that the social media are an integral part of the integrated promotions mix. Using social media is not outside-the-box thinking, nor is it a fad as Qualman (2011) stated; social media offer a powerful tool that must be embraced and utilized to its fullest potential.

Evaluating Success

Assessment of your event will help you determine success, but feedback from customers (positive and negative) is also valuable. We can't make important decisions regarding our event if we are not poised to seek and utilize feedback. Feedback in its many forms allows us to know whether our intent was received, understood, and appreciated. Actions such as purchasing tickets, apparel, or other sport-related products are the most tangible forms of feedback (Shank 2009). Intangible forms of feedback such as attitudinal changes and nonverbal cues speak just as loudly as a lack of purchasing.

As you began your journey into the field of media relations and promotions, you established specific goals in your planning phase. Now those goals need to be measured against your actual performance.

Keep in mind that along the way you have picked up new fans and (hopefully) maintained your previous ones. The goal now is to retain all those customers. According to Mullin et al. (2014), you must view customers as assets (p. 174). Listen to what they are saying, change if necessary, and keep the lines of communication open. If this sounds cyclical, it is. Planning, executing, and evaluating are constants in business and sport. To maintain the attention of fans, you must constantly engage them at every opportunity. Communication and transparency are critical.

Super Bowl XLVI in Indianapolis is a great example of how the flow of information and the transparency of the host committee helped create a spectacular mega-event without incident. Utilizing all forms of the promotional mix, the host committee was committed to

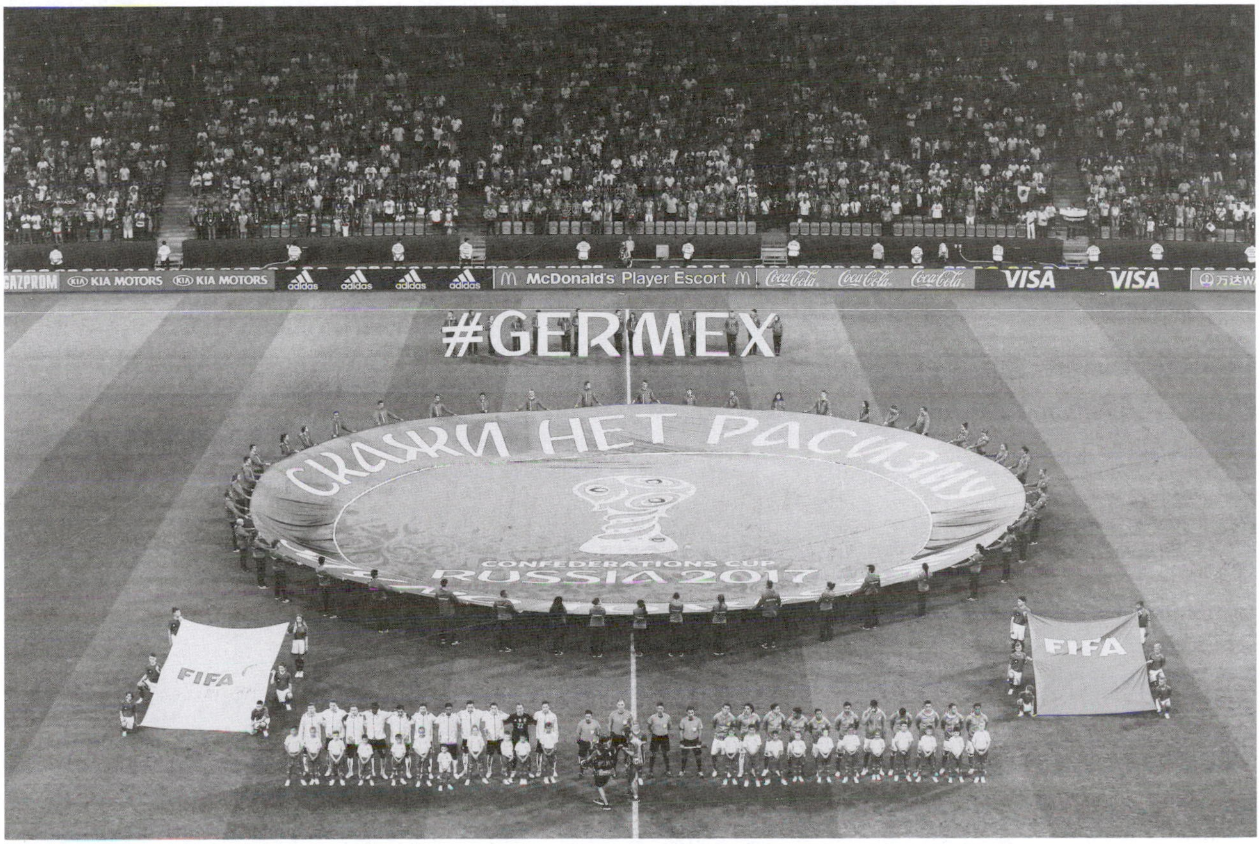

Simon Stacpoole/Offside/Getty Images

Hashtags are an example of how social media can be used as part of the integrated promotions mix.

keeping residents, volunteers, tourists, and the media abreast of the happenings in Indianapolis and the surrounding communities (Schoettle, 2012). Billboards, signage, mall kiosks, smartphone applications, and Twitter were all utilized to help with everything from the events of the day to which restaurant had the shortest waiting line. For Indianapolis, the real promotional plan was not realized until well after the actual game, which was won by the New York Giants. Indianapolis is hoping that its Hoosier hospitality wowed the visitors to the city to the point that they will return some day.

Summary

We create events because we want to share with the public what we have to offer. These events may be as simple as a fund-raiser for a charity or a carnival at a local elementary school, or they could be mega-events such as the Super Bowl. Regardless of the size of your event, developing a presence through positive interaction with the local media and through your own promotional efforts is a must for event planners. Media relations are fundamental to an organization's ability to maintain public support, support that builds a reputation (Bussell 2011). It is important to engage the media early and often before, during, and after your event. Setting the tone for a positive relationship will be more than just a media win for you, it will also be a financial win. We have all heard the adage that reputation is everything. Reputation—what others think about you—is critical to an event's survival. Making sure that what you have to offer is a quality product and that your efforts to raise awareness are creative and unique will help to promote your event.

Remember, never underestimate the power of the press; keep them happy and seek their partnership. Using social media is now a necessity, not just a fad. Know your target audience, engage your audience where they are (by virtue of smartphones), and present an event that will keep them talking, texting, and tweeting long after it is over.

LEARNING ACTIVITIES

1. Select an event to review.
2. Gather as much information about that event as you can.
3. Create a promotional chart to identify the vehicles or channels used to promote the event.

PROMOTIONAL CHART

Medium	Description
Television	
Radio	
Newspapers	
Magazines	
Billboards	
Posters and fliers	
Direct mail	
Social media	

Once you have decided on the event and created your chart, answer the following questions.

1. How did you hear about the event?
2. Once you selected the event, what was your first impression of the promotional efforts of the organizers? Did the advertising catch your attention, or was it more low key?
3. On a Likert scale (1 to 10, 10 being the best), rate how well you think the promoters did in enticing customers to attend. What did they do well? What could they have done better?
4. What forms of media were utilized to deliver the message?
5. If this had been your event, what would you have done differently and why?
6. What lessons from this event can you take and use in a future event you may host?
7. How did the event staff determine whether their efforts were successful? If they did not assess their performance, how would you evaluate the success of a media relations and promotion campaign?

CASE STUDY: CLEVELAND ROCKS THE NO-PROMOTION PROMOTION

Since 2014 the Cleveland Browns had posted a 4-49 record. It was December 2016 the last time the Dawg Pound celebrated victory. But on Thursday, September 20, 2018, the Cleveland Browns, after a 635-day waiting period, finally posted the long-awaited W, beating the New York Jets 21-17.

The 2017 season started with a blazing preseason run as the Browns went 4-0, beating the Saints, the Giants, the Buccaneers, and the Bears. Then came the regular season, the fire fizzled, and the team finished the year 0-16. There were opportunities to post the W; four of their first seven games were decided by three points, but that W was never to be posted.

As the city of Cleveland patiently waited for their beloved Browns to win another football game during that 2017 season, the Philadelphia Eagles made an impressive run for the title and ultimately were crowned World Champions in Super Bowl LII. Along the way to the title, Eagles o-lineman Lane Johnson took to social media to build some hype and maybe a peace offering (he had been suspended the previous season for PED use), stating he would buy beer for everyone if they won the Super Bowl. Bud Light saw his Tweet and responded with a proposition of their own: they would cover his offer of beer for everyone if the team won.

It was such a unique promotional gimmick for them in 2017, that this year they upped the ante, so to speak. Bud Light offered to give Cleveland free beer when the Browns got that illusive win. One might think this was making fun of the Browns' misfortune, but what it did was unify a city, a city that already supported their team, but now had an additional incentive to cheer them on. To set the promo in motion, beer fridges filled with Bud Lights had been scattered around the Cleveland metropolitan area, secured with chains, and adorned with the motivational phrase "When the Browns win, Cleveland wins" (Maskeroni 2018). Each fridge contained 200 16-ounce cans of beer. Ohio law does not allow for such promotion, so the location of the coolers was not disclosed. The gimmick paid off, again. Anheuser-Busch paid and Cleveland won, on the field and off.

Case Study Application

1. This could have gone a very different route (like the 2017) season. What gamble did Anheuser-Busch take in crafting this promotion?
2. Research this promotion further to identify the ROI for Anheuser-Busch.
3. How might they use this in subsequent years with other teams?
4. Does it have to be a gimmick for it to work or is it just as successful as a traditional promotion?
5. This could not be done in intercollegiate or high school sports, but brainstorm potential gimmick promotions that you might be able to implement.

© Human Kinetics

CHAPTER 8

Contract Considerations

CHAPTER OBJECTIVES

After completing the chapter, the reader should be able to do the following:

- Comprehend the legal environment as it relates to event management operations.
- Understand the contract law fundamentals and the importance of contracts in event management.
- Develop negotiation strategies for various event contracts. Identify typical contractual arrangements for events.
- Comprehend the federal laws that must be a consideration for event managers.

INDUSTRY PROFILE

Erica Zonder, Eastern Michigan University

Erica Zonder J.D., M.S., is a sport management professor at Eastern Michigan University where she teaches classes in sport risk management and sport finance, and coordinates and supervises internship experiences. She is co-chair of the university-wide Title IX Education, Prevention, and Advocacy Committee, as well as a Title IX Review Panel member. Prior to Eastern Michigan, she was a sport law and business law professor at Adrian College, where she also served as the faculty athletics representative (FAR), co-created the Master of Arts in Sport Administration and Leadership program, and taught both graduate and undergraduate facility planning and management classes. She is an active member of the Sport and Recreation Law Association, the North American Society for the Sociology of Sport (where she has served on both the finance committee and the diversity committee), and the North American Society for Sport Management. A graduate of University of Michigan law school, she previously spent 10 years working in the entertainment industry, where she specialized in literary talent management.

What would you say are the top legal considerations for someone who is planning an event?

Obviously, safety is a top consideration for any event, particularly in sports. Not only do venues and organizations that are responsible for events want to keep participants and attendees safe from harm, but they also want to limit their exposure to liability. Therefore, necessary contractual language includes waivers and indemnification clauses. Other legal considerations for events include language clarifying the use of trademarks and logos, and the commercial use of name and likeness and right of publicity. The rise of social media necessitates special attention to these areas.

Contract negotiations are critical to events. What advice would you offer an event planner with regard to this process?

Event planners are typically not lawyers, and often the use of lawyers can be expensive, so the less use, the better. Event planners need solid boilerplate contracts with standardized language and common provisions for each area of the event, such as facilities, vendors, and concessions, to use as a starting point for negotiation. Paying an attorney for this initial step is well worth it, as it can lead to fewer problems down the road. Contracts with this type of language can be modified for specific circumstances or tailored to meet specific needs, but they give a planner a jumping off point and the ability to save money and time by not requiring the use of an attorney for each event. And while this standardized language can often be downloaded from the Internet or copied from other sources, a nonlawyer will not necessarily be able to distinguish nuances in the language; using a lawyer, at least initially, is strongly recommended.

We have all heard the adage "the devil is in the details." Discuss this in terms of legal liability for event managers.

As I touched on above, many in the event business will cobble together an agreement from the Internet or from previous contracts. As a responsible event planner or manager, you are tasked with making sure each step of the event is carried out in accordance with the agreement. And because of this responsibility, it is important that the contract language is clear and not vague; don't say "reasonable" time or effort when you can spell out exact wants and needs. And be sure to address *all* aspects of an event: Which party is providing the referees for the contest? Is the facility or event providing security? Who is responsible for cleanup and breakdown of the event? So, while there might be industry standards that are not explicitly stated, or boilerplate language used, it is still important to get it in writing, and get it right.

What legal advice would you offer for someone looking to plan or host an event?

Risk management! Identify and assess risk and then address it if necessary. For instance, if alcohol will be served, you need a strategy to prevent liability. Too much alcohol can lead to illness, violence, injury, and so on. The smart event host addresses this risk, whether creating policies such as a two-drink maximum, training entrance searchers and ticket takers to spot intoxicated patrons and preventing entrance to the event, transferring the risk to outsourced concessionaires, or ultimately eliminating the risk by deciding not to serve alcohol. The most successful event is often the most legally uneventful event.

How do your sport management students benefit from your legal background?

My students, many of whom are future event planners and managers, are taught to think about liability first, and then think about it repeatedly as they add flourishes and entertainment options to sporting events. We often go over legal cases in the classroom, and the students are able to apply similar fact patterns and details to their real-life event issues, leading to anticipation of potential pitfalls and prevention of loss and liability. Additionally, we review appropriate contract language and samples. While the great majority of my students will not attend law school, the hope is that most, if not all, of them will be able to negotiate simple standard agreements such as participant waivers for their event, spot problems and issues before signing, and ultimately know when they had better call a lawyer!

Organizing a great event starts with planning. When we are effective at planning our event, the outcome is one of satisfaction not only for our customers but for our employees, vendors, sponsors, and others affiliated with our event. Efforts to create such a satisfactory outcome start with the forming of partnerships that will add value and excitement to what we have planned. To this end, great care must be taken in selecting those to partner with and what the relationship is based on must be taken into consideration; make sure that all potential legal considerations have been addressed appropriately during planning. The legal concerns that an event must consider require intricate details to be identified and documented for the protection of the event, the facility, the attendees, the vendors, and the workers. From the hiring of staff to the serving of food to the actual contract negotiations, each process must be exhaustive and designed for the event and the facility involved. Throughout this chapter and in chapter 9 (Risk Management and Negligence), we explore the contractual elements that are critical considerations before, during, and after an event, identifying who is responsible for what in an effort to offer protection from legal recourse and to be proactive in providing a safe, secure, and fun event.

With any endeavor, having clearly defined goals and objectives sets the tone for your expected outcomes. In the event management field, we need to take those preparations a bit further to consider all of the potential ramifications of our intended event. In an effort to lay the groundwork for event planning, Goldblatt (2008) identified four steps to making sure you have covered the requisite laws and regulations for a quality event: (1) protect your legal interest, (2) operate ethically, (3) provide a safe and secure environment, and (4) protect your financial investment. To assure your event meets the four proposed criteria, a formal agreement should be established between and among the various entities involved in producing the event. The simplest way to achieve this is by means of a contract. Black's Law Dictionary defines a contract as "an agreement, upon sufficient consideration, to do or not do a particular thing; a promise made on one side and assented to on the other." In essence, a **contract** is a tool that protects your interests and helps foster partnerships between the various entities critical for producing events.

Contract Law 101

Agreements between events and facilities, events and vendors, and events and ancillary contractors must be negotiated and formalized by creating the various contracts necessary for producing an event. Van Der Wagen and Carlos (2005) contend that the "effectiveness of the contracts between the parties involved in an event is crucial" (p. 56). Contracts must be concisely written, avoiding the arbitrary, and agreed upon by all parties involved. Matthews (2008) states that contracts consist of two parts: (1) the specifics of the terms and conditions that establish the relationship and (2) the clauses that provide more specific details. In simplistic terms, a contract is a "legally enforceable promise" (Brickley and Gottesman 2017).This promise requires that an offer be presented and accepted, that there be some form of consideration, that the parties have the capacity to enter into a relationship, and that it be legal (Cotten and Wolohan 2012; Sharp, Moorman, and Claussen 2014; Spengler et al. 2016).

- *Offer*. This is the initial promise made by one party to another to either do something or not do something; it usually has a price tag attached. For example, event tickets are contractual; you give up something in order to get something (e.g., you exchange $40 for a ticket to attend a University of Alabama nonconference football game).
- *Acceptance*. Only the person to whom the offer was extended may accept the offer. Should the offer not be accepted, it is voided (Ammon, Southall, and Nagel 2016).
- *Consideration*. In order to be binding, a contract must offer consideration (Ammon, Southall, and Nagel 2016); both parties must give to get. Consideration involves one person offering something of value in exchange for something of value from the other person. In most instances, the exchange is a product or a service traded for money.
- *Capacity*. Each party to a contract must have the capacity to enter into the contract. Capacity is determined by such factors as being of legal age (minors cannot sign) and being mentally capable of understanding the conditions of the promise.
- *Legality*. The promise must be based on a legal transaction. Sharp, Moorman, and Claussen (2014) emphasize that neither state nor federal laws may be broken in the formation of a contract.

There are two types of contractual agreements: bilateral and unilateral. A **bilateral contract** involves two parties engaging in a promise; both parties have expectations. A **unilateral contract** represents the offering and accepting of a promise; it is one-directional, with an offer being made without an acceptance; the party does not have to agree to the terms. As a precautionary measure, Spengler et al. (2016) propose the following tips for managing contracts:

- Get it in writing.
- Read the contract thoroughly.
- Keep copies of all contract documents.
- Use good faith when negotiating contracts.
- Note deadlines for performance.
- Ensure the performance of third parties.
- Share contract information with those who need to know, and educate staff on the consequences of contract breach.
- Resolve ambiguities as quickly and fairly as possible.

Types of Contracts

With regard to events, many potential partnerships will need to be negotiated via contractual agreements. Both Allen and colleagues (2011) and Bladen and colleagues (2012) discuss the typical contracts associated with an event. They conclude that those contracts related to the facility, game or entertainment, sponsorship agreements, media, security, vendors and suppliers, food and beverage, and waivers and releases. A facility contract is the most complex contract to negotiate (Bladen et al. 2012). Essential elements of such a contract are the following:

- Parties involved
- Game or event details
- Governance
    - Eligibility
    - Rules
    - Regulations

- Financial consideration
  - Guarantee
  - Additional negotiated financial arrangements
- Cancellation
  - Weather
  - Force majeure
- Tickets
- Broadcasting rights
  - Radio
  - TV
- Game management
- Insurance
- Miscellaneous

The football game contract from the Georgia High School Association in the web resource has an example of a game contract that covers these particulars. It is also an example of one of the games that is the focus of the Case Study found at the end of the chapter, in which the force majeure (superior force) clause was implemented. Game contracts are established so there will be no discrepancy in the terms of the agreement between teams participating in a single game or a series of games. Many state high school associations have created fillable forms for their schools to utilize.

WWW Go to the web resource for an example of a football game contract from the Georgia High School Association.

Because most facilities do not put on their own events, they look to lease or rent their facilities to event managers and planners in order to utilize their space as often as possible. Million-dollar multipurpose facilities do not want to stand idle; a vacant building serves no purpose and costs money in terms of upkeep, insurance, and even opportunity cost (Fried 2015). Selecting the facility for an event can be a cumbersome task. The type of facility depends on the type of event you are producing: sports, entertainment, or charity. What makes it complex are the various clauses and addenda that are specific to your needs for your event. For example, Allen et al. (2011) list indemnification, security deposits, signage, and change orders (additions or alterations to the original contract) as possible clauses. Bladen et al. (2012) add to that list of clauses payment terms, security, food and beverage, and any additional facility staff that might be required and at what cost. Lawrence and Wells (2009) offer ancillary clauses that include any activities associated with the event but not part of the main attraction, such as banquets, awards presentations, and autograph signings scheduled around the event.

The main attraction of your event can be a game, a concert, or a performance. Regardless of the type of entertainment, you need to formalize a contract for participation. Entertainment contracts contain the common elements just discussed, but they also carry two unique items: an exclusivity clause and a rider. The **exclusivity clause** protects the event manager from the talent's scheduling another event close by that could affect your event's success (Allen et al. 2011). Exclusivity would potentially offer a geographic boundary from which to work. The **rider** is an amendment that spells out the requirements of the talent (Allen et al. 2011). The rider can involve any items the talent insists on, such as specific food or beverage items, transportation requirements, and dressing room necessities.

Chapter 5 outlines the various sponsorship opportunities for event managers. Sponsorship agreements and contracts are specific to the events and the parties involved, so a standard fillable form for the agreement is not advised. Each sponsorship agreement (contract) is established to "protect the best interests of all parties involved" (Ammon, Southall, and Nagel 2016, p. 116). Expectations, rights, benefits, fees, terms, governing laws, marks and logo usage, and duties should be expressed in the contract. Any items unique to the relationship should be spelled out, especially the critical component of establishing liability. When you review a sponsorship agreement, you begin to realize its complexity as well as the need to involve legal counsel to ensure the protection of each party.

Go to the web resource for an example of a sponsorship agreement. WWW

As you have learned, there are other types of sponsorships besides financial investments. Agreements can include trades between the parties or in-kind donations. Such instances do not preclude the need for a contract. As Lawrence and Wells (2009) indicated, this is a "mutually beneficial partnership" (p. 50) and should be carefully crafted.

Should you have the fortune of negotiating a media contract, you will find yourself involved in an intricate and complex negotiation that could result in a sizeable financial gain for your event. Because your event likely will not garner national or international media attention, you should consider the relationships with local media outlets and how you can partner with them to air your event. Solomon (2002) claims that "the growth in television means that what once was not even thinkable is today at least a possibility" for broadcasting (p. 133). Networks, regional and local stations, pay-per-view, and streaming over the Internet could all be viable options as many media outlets look for content to broadcast. Your "event is a tool" for a media outlet "as much as television is a tool for you" (p. 137). Initial negotiations should include the air date, the time slot for airing, the length of the event, and whether you will have it aired live or have it recorded for future broadcasting (Solomon 2002). Once those particulars are finalized, you can start discussing finances. You can pursue various financial options in an effort to televise your event. You can negotiate rights fees; you can barter your way on; or you can pay for the production, which is risky and pricey (Solomon 2002).

According to Allen et al. (2011), you should address some important clauses in your media and broadcasting contracts such as reach (region or territory), access, credits, and merchandising. Solomon (2002) also stresses that you need to secure the proper **clearance** for any music or video you want to include in your event. Many times an event will contract with a third party for goods or services. You want to spell out the arrangements with this third party in a contract. According to Kuse (2012),

> *the key elements that your agreement should contain are the cost or price, services or products provided, what happens if something goes differently than planned, and dates for delivery. An agreement is hammered out so that, ideally, the consequences to be suffered for any possible scenario will be spelled out specifically (para. 4).*

Go to the web resource for an example of a broadcasting contract.

Safety is the number one priority for facilities and the events they host. Security is one of the many services that assist in maintaining a safe environment and one that can be contracted. Risk management and negligence (see chapter 9) are essential considerations when planning an event. Since 9/11, the event industry has had to rethink and rewrite many of its policies and procedures with regard to the safety of all vested parties at an event. Security is the area that has garnered the most attention because facilities will not compromise on the safety of patrons, participants, and their own staff. With heightened security comes not only the expense of offering a safe environment but also the need to negotiate contracts for coverage. You must weigh the cost of not properly securing your event against the cost of contracting with a service provider. In your facility negotiations, you can address whether the facility will provide security or which service provider the facility managers would recommend that you contract.

By reviewing the security services contract for special events at Louisiana State University, you can begin to understand the scope of security and the details that must be contained in such a contract. Areas such as ticket takers, ushers, general security personnel, parking lot personnel, and various supervisors are addressed. This negotiated contract provides the cost of each unit of security requested as well as the facility information and the scope of events to be covered.

Good food is synonymous with a good time at an event. We attend a fair for the corndogs, cotton candy and candy apples; we go to a chili cook-off to taste great chili; and when we are at a sport events we think about burgers, chicken tenders, and pizza. These expectations translate

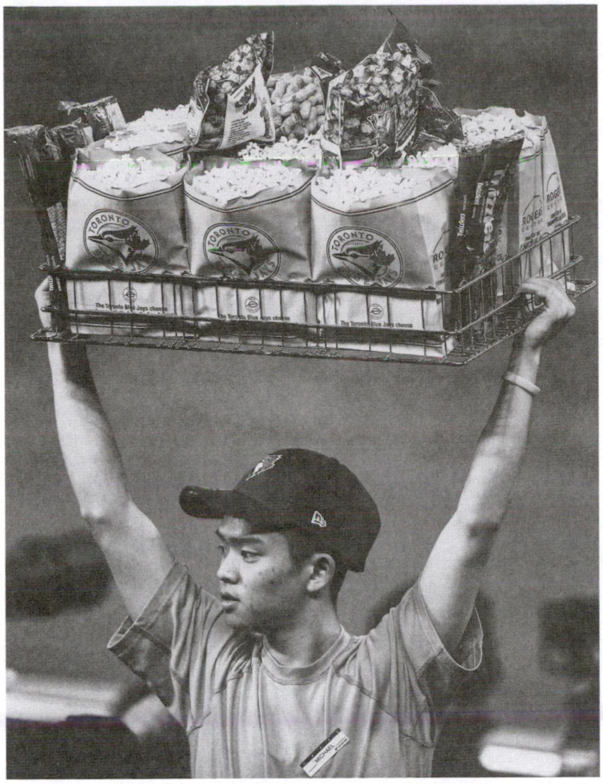

Tom Szczerbowski/Getty Images

Good concessions are a hallmark of any event.

into the need for having quality concessionaires at events. Many people form an opinion of an event around the food and beverages it offers. It is important that you give full consideration to negotiating concession contracts that will enhance your event; it will forever be a part of your event's reputation. Some facilities have standing contracts with food service companies, and you will have to negotiate with them for your concession needs. Steinbach (2008) says that concession agreements can be "sliced and diced" in many ways. It is strongly recommended that you utilize a service provider that is either the current concessionaire with the facility or from a facility-approved list. Because certain requirements and restrictions apply, you need to make sure the utmost care is taken in the preparation of the food. These requirements include food-handling regulations, licenses and permits, health department inspections, and employee hiring requirements. When negotiating with the facility, you can include concessions in that contract, making sure the financial arrangements are detailed, specifically with regard to payments or the percentage of monies you will receive from concession sales (if this is part of your facility contract).

The web resource shows a simple concession stand contract template used by the ConocoPhillips Sports Complex in Ferndale, Washington. This contract represents the expectations that you will provide your own staff and concession food and beverages. It is a great example of a food and beverage contract for a small-scale event.

Go to the web resource to view a simple concession stand contract from ConocoPhillips Sports Complex. WWW

If you host a participatory event such as a sports competition, an athletic event with entries, or a recreational activity, or if members of the crowd are invited to participate in a game promotion, it is important that you utilize waivers and releases. A **waiver**, which a participant signs before an event, releases the organization from liability should the participant become injured during the event (Spengler et al. 2016). Kozlowski (1996) described a waiver as "a valid and enforceable agreement" whereby a "participant waives or releases any future negligence claim he or she may have against the provider of a sport or recreational services in exchange for an opportunity to participate" (para. 1). Waivers do not cover the misconduct of a person or representative of the organization with whom the patron signed the waiver. According to Glover (2009), "the term waiver is sometimes used to refer [to] a document that is signed before any damages actually occur. A release is sometimes used to refer [to] a document that is executed after an injury has occurred" (para. 1). Waivers incorporate an assumption of risk by the participant, whereas a release explains in detail the risks associated with participation in an activity.

Minors are precluded from signing a waiver because it is a contract, and as discussed earlier in this chapter, minors do not have the capacity to sign. Parents of minor athletes are familiar with signing waivers in order for their children to participate in an activity. Even though parents may sign a waiver, Glover (2009) cautions that the "law is unclear as to whether parents who sign waivers on behalf of their children will release a potential defendant from liability to the minor. The trend is to enforce such waiver arrangements signed by parents on behalf of a child" (para. 1). Because state laws apply to waivers, it is important for you to use due diligence in researching them. Figure 8.1 shows a waiver used for a recreation program at Trevecca Nazarene University.

INTRAMURAL SPORTS INDIVIDUAL WAIVER FORM

Trevecca Nazarene University—Student Activities Waiver

The undersigned students, employees, and invitees of Trevecca Nazarene University, being 18 years of age or older, acknowledge that they have signed up for recreational sport, and that this activity is voluntary on their part and for which they will receive no compensation, either directly or indirectly, from Trevecca Nazarene University. The undersigned therefore assume all risk incident to the listed activity, including travel to or from such place of activity and acknowledge that Trevecca Nazarene University, its Intramural Director, its employees and the State of Tennessee assume no liability, including financial responsibility for injuries or losses resulting from or occurring during the activity or travel to and from said activity. The undersigned further indemnify, release, and hold harmless Trevecca Nazarene University, their Intramural Director, their employees, and the State of Tennessee against any loss or injuries resulting or claimed to result from the undersigned students'/employees' training, participation, attendance, travel or other involvement in any and all phases of the activity. The undersigned are aware Trevecca Nazarene University posts team rosters on the intramural sports web site, and therefore give Trevecca Nazarene University permission to post their names and photos on said web site. The undersigned further acknowledge that their signatures hereto evidence that they have read, fully understand, agree with and consent to the contents thereof.

Unsportsmanlike Conduct Policy

Unsportsmanlike conduct will not be tolerated in the Trevecca Nazarene University Intramural Sports Program, and could result in ejection from games and/or leagues. A "bad-temper," "natural-instinct," "self-defense," or similar excuse will not be accepted as a reason for misconduct. Unsportsmanlike conduct includes verbal and/or physical abuse of officials, profanity, fighting, pushing and verbal attacks aimed at opponents. The following disciplinary actions can be expected for offenses. *Verbal Abusive Behavior*: If an individual is ejected from a game by an official or supervisor (whether after a written warning or on a first offense) he/she will be ineligible to participate in further competition until he/she meets with the appropriate staff member. *Physical Abusive Behavior*: physical abuse of an opponent, spectator, teammate or destruction of property will result in ejection from the game and carry a minimum penalty of suspension for the remainder of the season. Physical abuse of an official or supervisor will carry a minimum penalty of suspension from all Trevecca Nazarene University Intramural Sports Programs for the remainder of the academic year. In addition to the aforementioned penalties, individuals who are physically abusive will be placed on permanent probation regarding intramural activities.

Participant Signature:______________________________

Parent Signature (Under 18 Years of Age): ______________________________

* Your name and telephone number will be given to your team captain. If you do not want this information released, you must notify Student Activities.

** Your signature indicates that you have read and agree with the Student Activities Waiver and Unsportsmanlike Conduct Policy. You must present a valid student ID or employee ID card in order to play if asked.

FIGURE 8.1 Sample agreement from Trevecca Nazarene University.

Tips for Negotiating Contracts

Every contract you negotiate requires finesse. DeMarco (2014) suggests you enter negotiations with "a planned approach" that includes knowing the facility goals, doing research on the facility, and writing a strong proposal. Facilities differ, games or entertainment vary, sponsorships may be specific, but the need to formalize a relationship with a contract will remain constant as a means of protecting the parties' interests. The back-and-forth negotiations allow each entity to shape the agreement and get it right. During this process, you will identify your needs, express your wants, and firmly discuss the nonnegotiable items. Mandel (2012) offers the following tips for a successful negotiation:

- Don't be afraid to ask.
- Never negotiate against yourself.
- Get it in writing.
- Prepare.
- Listen to the other side.
- There is no substitute for discussion.
- Avoid form contracts.
- Make sure the decision makers are in the room.

"The ability to negotiate vendor contracts effectively—getting the right products and services at the right price and with the right terms—is a crucial skill" (Ambrose 2010, p. 1). Remember to remain flexible. Don't get stuck on costs, but rather value and prioritize what you want and need; ask questions rather than making demands (Gerber 2011; Stim). The more negotiations you are involved in, the better you will become and the more success you will have.

An Attorney's Perspective on Contracts: Neil Braslow, JD

For a valid sport contract to be formed, there must be an offer, acceptance, consideration, mutual assent, capacity, and legality. A contract in the sport world is no different from a contract in the rest of the legal world. Most sport contracts, and in particular professional services or standard players' contracts, are in boilerplate form. This means the same standard terms and wordings can be used over and over without any modifications. Arenas and teams alike usually have standard contracts that are slightly altered each time.

Athletes will often create addenda to their contracts, which are additions usually found at the end. This is particularly true for elite athletes. For example, a stipulation in a standard team contract may give an average baseball player two tickets to every home game his team plays. A superstar player may add additional terms to the contract to read that he is to receive a luxury box for every home game his team plays. An average player is usually offered the standard team contract and told to take it or leave it. For elite players, in addition to the differences in the amount of salary, deviations from the standard team contract are usually bonuses and the option to renegotiate. Because of the addenda and modifications made to the contract, it is sometimes beneficial during the negotiation process for the player to have an agent who is an attorney. However, not all professional leagues require that agents be lawyers, and many players choose to use agents who are not lawyers.

In addition to agents, leagues and teams have their own set of attorneys working on contracts. Although many leagues and teams have been outsourcing their legal work for years, with the current economic climate many are either bringing in attorneys to work in-house or adding lawyers to already existing teams. Although agents do work on contracts for their clients, the role of an in-house attorney generally requires more contractual work. In-house attorneys must deal with all player contracts in addition to apparel, contest, licensing, media, merchandise, sales, sponsorship, vendor, and facility contracts, to name a few.

In-house attorneys deal with many of the legal issues relating to event or game logistics. For example, let's say the Green Bay Packers are playing at Soldier Field in Chicago. On the day of the game, Aaron Rodgers is nowhere to be found and fails to show up. Can the Chicago

Bears and Soldier Field sue Aaron Rodgers? The answer is no. Aaron Rodgers did not sign an appearance contract with the Bears that would have compensated him for showing up to an event. Aaron Rodgers has a professional services contract with the Green Bay Packers. They are the only party that Aaron owes an obligation to. Although the Chicago Bears may not be able to sue Aaron, the Packers could take action according to the terms of his contract since they are the organization that entered into the agreement.

What if Rodgers had said he assigned his contract to Brett Favre to play in Chicago that day? This would not have worked because personal service contracts cannot be assigned to anyone else. An assignment is a transfer of rights that a party has under contract to another person. A personal service contract cannot be assigned because the talents of an athlete, in this case Aaron Rodgers, are unique. The Packers would not have allowed such an assignment to take place.

What if the next day the Packers decided to trade Aaron Rodgers to the Dolphins? Could Rodgers argue that since he was not allowed to assign his rights to Favre, why should the Packers be allowed to assign his rights to the Dolphins? Any contract, including personal service contracts, may be assigned as long as there is permission from both parties. In almost all player contracts, the right to assign is part of the contract. Some players, however, have what is known as a no-trade clause, which keeps the team from assigning their rights to a team they do not want to play for. Teams have become increasingly less willing to award no-trade clauses because this prevents them from trading a player without the player's approval.

Regardless of the position the attorney has with an employer, all lawyers must pay great attention to detail when drafting a contract. Contracts should not be ambiguous; they should be easily interpreted by a third party. If there is a dispute over a contract, courts will seek to enforce the intent of the parties to the contract. The intent to be enforced is what a reasonable person would have believed that the parties intended. In sport, contracts often involve millions and millions of dollars. Attorneys need to proceed with caution and make sure they are drafting unambiguous contracts where the intent can clearly be inferred. For many contracts, the process of drafting and editing could take weeks before the final edition is signed by the parties to be charged.

Federal Legislation

Events must conform to the rules and restrictions of the facility in which they will operate as well as to local ordinances and laws. In addition, event managers must consider various federal laws when planning an event.

Americans with Disabilities Act (ADA)

The **Americans with Disabilities Act (ADA)** of 1990 was instrumental in mainstreaming people with disabilities into all aspects of society. Facilities (places of public accommodation) are required to provide barrier-free accommodations, which could require modifications to the existing layout (Ammon, Southall, and Nagel 2016). In 2011, a Southern University student filed a lawsuit stating that the university failed to comply with ADA law in that there was a "lack of accessible restrooms, elevators and ramps with adequate slope at athletic facilities" (Crisp 2014). Specific to event management, this lawsuit cited Southern's Mini-Dome and Mumford Stadium as not being **accessible**, thus preventing the student from attending events.

According to the International Association of Exhibitions and Events, event managers and planners should be aware of ADA requirements and make reasonable accommodations for inclusion. In fact, Jacobs (2015) boldly stated, "legally and morally, event planners must make good-faith efforts to accommodate them."

Everything from event forms to hotel accommodations to assisted listening devices and even concession areas need to be addressed by the event planners in conjunction with facility

Catherine Ivill/Getty Images

Event managers should be aware of ADA requirements and make reasonable accommodations for inclusion.

managers. Several resources can be found on the Internet that help event managers with ADA compliance. For a more comprehensive look at the ADA law, design help, and technical specifications, visit the web site of the ADA (www.ada.gov) or that of the ADA National Network (www.adata.org). Event managers and planners can consult the comprehensive Accessible Meetings, Events and Conferences Guide (www.adahospitality.org).

Occupational Safety and Health Administration

Specific directives and policies regarding workplace safety and health are administered through the federally created Occupational Safety and Health Administration. OSHA was created by Congress when they passed the Occupational Health and Safety Act of 1970. The primary focus of OSHA is to reduce the number of job-related illnesses, injuries, and deaths.

Since many of your events may require the constructing of scaffolding or rigging, it is important that you understand and abide by the guidelines issued by OSHA as well as by the OSHA guidelines of the state where the event is held. The tragedy of the Indiana State Fair in August 2011 provides us with validation of the critical nature of OSHA guidelines and why they must be followed explicitly. While fans were gathering and waiting for the band Sugarland to take the Hoosier Lottery Grandstand stage, a line of strong thunderstorms with wind gusts up to 70 miles per hour (110 km/h) made its way to the fairgrounds. As announcements were made regarding a possible evacuation, a strong gust of wind blew through the facility, collapsing the stage and the rigging. The collapse led to seven deaths and more than four dozen injuries (Winick et al. 2011). An ensuing investigation by the Indiana OSHA resulted in fines to three contractors hired to construct the stage. It was determined that key risk-assessment planning and inspections were not performed and that the safety of workers was compromised (one of the persons killed was an employee of the contracted companies cited for violations).

This tragic incident illustrates why, as an event manager, you must perform due diligence in hiring qualified and competent staff and subcontractors. Just as risk management relates to a safe and secure environment, the OSHA guidelines are designed to protect employees and attendees.

Technology and Contracts

With the Internet exploding with e-commerce (which began in the 1970s), the idea that contracts would follow suit was only natural. The transacting of business online allows for immediacy, instant communication, and ease of access to transactions that are stored in digital form (Sympson 2010). Because of the digital opportunities to formulate contracts, the laws pertaining to contracts have also had to be adjusted. Courts have had to address the idea of electronic signatures as legal. In many instances, the courts have found that if a person has to type their name in the signature field, that person knowingly and willingly entered into the agreement. Despite the notion that some contracts have to be physically signed by the engaged parties, a federal statute—the Electronic Signatures in Global and National Commerce Act (ESIGN)—and a state statute—the Uniform Electronic Transactions Act (UETA)—were created to validate the legality of electronic signatures on contracts.

Some contracts are time sensitive and delays could cause undue stress on the parties involved. As we rely on technology more and more, we also know that it can fail us in times of urgency: Internet down, slow delivery of e-mail, items lost in cyberspace. Because of the issues with mail delivery (including snail mail), the term *mailbox rule*, which originated in an 1818 court case, was established to protect the acceptance of an offer (Cornell Law School n.d.). We can see how the term applies to both traditional mail and electronic mail. In essence, the term refers to the acceptance of the offer at the time the response is sent. For electronic purposes the date and time stamp attached to any electronic file is used in determining the origination of the sent message (acceptance).

Summary

Protecting your investment is your first consideration when planning an event. First and foremost, you are to provide a safe and secure environment for the event. From the conception of the event through to its end, measures should be taken to ensure an incident-free experience for all involved. In an effort to offer an entertaining and safe experience for attendees, a second requirement of event managers and planners is to thoughtfully consider the contractual partnerships they will enter into and thoroughly vet all contractors. Contracts exist to form the partnership, to identify the terms of each partner and the services expected, and to offer recourse should there be an infringement of the partnership services. Specific events require specific contractual arrangements and clauses that offer further protection for the partners. Through the formation of these partnerships and the hiring of competent and trained staff, you will put together a team of event workers who will execute your plans as you have devised. An understanding of the local, state, and federal laws that are applicable to your event and should be addressed in your contractual arrangement will help provide the safeguards necessary to host a successful event. Should an incident occur, these detailed contracts should be a hedge of protection for you and your event as well as address any recourse.

Contractual partnerships exist because two or more entities have agreed, through negotiations, on the terms of the contract. Prior to producing an event you must do your homework and generate your wants and needs even before discussion begins, so that you enter negotiations well informed and ready to formalize your agreement. Always keep in mind the old adage of "when in doubt, write it out." Contracts must be written and details outlined so there are no discrepancies that could result in legal action. Be sure to use the resources available on the Internet, such as the ADA and OSHA websites. The advent of technology and its infusion into the area of contract law has not only helped facilitate the negotiation process, but has also created a need for defining what is considered legal in terms of the elements of the contract and the legality of the "written and signed" agreement. As technology continues to reshape our lives, the law too has been subject to adjusting to the idea of e-commerce.

LEARNING ACTIVITIES

Having decided to run a concession stand for a Little League organization, you are now charged with acquiring the requisite permits, licenses, and insurance. Because you have not done this before, you turn to legal counsel for guidance.

1. Create a to-do list so you have all the items covered. Once you do that, answer the following questions.
2. What do you see as the necessary legal concerns of running a concession stand?
3. What permits, licenses, or insurance have you determined you will need to acquire?
4. What types of contracts would you be entering into with a concession stand operation?

CASE STUDY: GUARANTEES, CLAUSES, AND LOSSES—CONTRACTS AND THE BOTTOM LINE

In September 2017, Hurricane Irma was churning in the Atlantic Ocean while schools like the University of Louisiana at Monroe (ULM), the University of Connecticut (UConn), and Northern Colorado were making plans to travel to Florida State, South Florida, and Florida, respectively, for out-of-conference matchups. These teams, not considered football powerhouses, frequently travel to play the more notable teams during September. The driving force behind these *cupcake games*, as they have come to be called, is the **guarantee,** or appearance payment. As the business of college sports continues to grow, guarantees to schools like ULM and UConn have become the norm. These guarantees represent a contractual obligation that the host school agrees to pay the visiting school for traveling and playing. These monies augment the already rigid budgets of traveling teams. For example, in week 1 of the 2017 collegiate football season, more than $70 million in payouts were recorded (Berkowitz, 2017a).

As meteorologists from the Weather Channel and the National Hurricane Center, located in Miami, attempted to project Irma's path and strength, they kept a close eye on the Tropics. Local authorities' decision-making depended on the information shared from these trusted weather authorities. Since football is mainly played outdoors, once the path was projected, plans began unfolding to move, postpone, or cancel many events that were to take place over the weekend, which was the predicted time of Irma's landfall (Chavez 2017; Culpepper 2017).

To set the tone of what was at stake, ULM was to be paid $1.35 million by Florida State (Hunsucker 2017) and Florida promised Northern Colorado $625,000 (Berkowitz 2017b). These figures were negotiated between the schools and put into the game contracts. It is customary for guarantee games to "routinely include a provision saying that if any of a variety of circumstances—including a hurricane—make it impossible to play the game, the contract is voided" (Berkowitz 2017a). In legal terms, this clause is called a **force majeure** clause. Once the force majeure clause is enacted, it releases the payer from financial obligation to the payee.

An interesting caveat to these guarantee games is the coach's employment contract, which may include a bonus clause directly impacted by the loss of the guarantee monies. Many schools offer a bonus to a coach if they travel to the guarantee game and upset the home team or even just schedule a Power Five team. "Wyoming's Craig Bohl gets a $100,000 bonus for each regular-season win the Cowboys record against a Power Five team. Appalachian State coach Scott Satterfield gets a $10,000 bonus if his squad plays a Power Five team at that team's stadium" (Berkowitz 2017b).

Case Study Application

1. In the sport and entertainment industry, contracts are the backbone of every partnership that we form: employment, concessions, games, and vendors. All of these examples can be linked to a single event like a football game. If you were the head coach and athletic director for Bussell University, a Division I school located in the foothills of the Smoky Mountains in Tennessee, what schools would you look to negotiate with for a guarantee game contract? Would you include any bonus for the coach? Why or why not?
2. Develop a spreadsheet that outlines how you would distribute the monies earned from the guarantee among the six men's and eight women's teams in your athletic department.
3. How would you "sell" this cupcake game to your president, your board, your alumni, and your fans? Discuss the benefits and drawbacks to scheduling such a game.
4. Finally, assume you have been guaranteed $1 million to play a game and the force majeure clause is enforced because of a hurricane. Do you attempt to schedule a new game or just play 11 games that season? How do you recoup those anticipated funds?

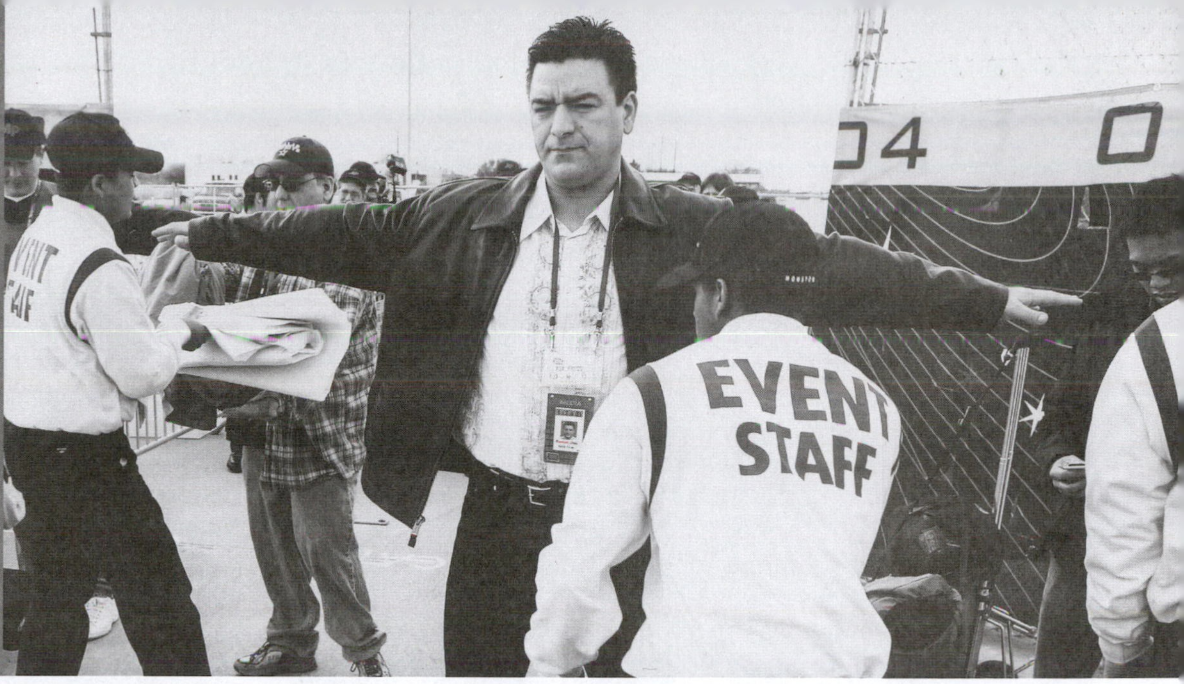

Andy Lyons/Getty Images

CHAPTER 9

Risk Management and Negligence

CHAPTER OBJECTIVES

After completing the chapter, the reader should be able to do the following:

- Describe risk management.
- Identify the risk management process and generate a risk management plan.
- Recognize risks that could hinder an event.
- Understand crowd control.
- Devise an emergency plan.
- Understand that a competent, trained staff is critical for securing a safe environment.

INDUSTRY PROFILE

James A. DeMeo, Unified Sports & Entertainment Security Consulting

James A. DeMeo has nearly 28 years of experience in the security industry and is considered a foremost expert on event security. He is a retired detective from the Nassau County Police Department, Long Island, NY, having served 21 years in law enforcement. He is the founder, president, and CEO of Unified Sports & Entertainment Security Consulting (USESC), based in Raleigh, North Carolina.

With USESC, DeMeo's goal is to create value for stadium ownership groups by raising the level of professionalism for event staff while reducing employee turnover. Making sure that staff can connect with fans on a human level enhances an amazing game-day experience, he says, emphasizing the benefits of de-escalation and verbal communication skills to a cohesive security program.

DeMeo was an integral member of a research team for a poster project presented at the North American Society for Sport Management (NASSM) conference in June 2016, "Professional Sport Security and Marketing Interface: A Delphi Study. Assessing the Influence of Sport Security Operations on the Guest experience: Using the Delphi Method to Understand Practitioner Perspectives." The conference proceedings were later published by the University of Southern Mississippi in its *Journal of Sport Safety and Security*.

DeMeo earned his master of science degree in sport management from Adelphi University in 2012. He is a member of ASIS International. Recognized by *Security Magazine* as one of the most influential people in security 2017, he serves as an online adjunct instructor for Tulane University's School of Professional Advancement & Security Studies Program, teaching graduate students about sport event security. He is the bestselling author of *What's Your Plan? A Step-by-Step Guide to Keep Your Family Safe During Emergency Situations*.

When someone says they need to develop a risk management plan for their event, what are they really talking about?

Safeguarding today's sporting events at stadiums, venues, and arenas has become quite complex and presents numerous challenges for frontline staff entrusted with duty of care responsibilities within the confined space. A thorough and complete risk management program starts with stadium leadership viewing the aspect of security from multiple angles and features a top-down- bottom-up holistic approach with all key stakeholders speaking the same language in the interest of public safety. Crowd control, terroristic threats, errant drones, active shooters, workplace violence, improvised explosive devices (IEDs), weather challenges, and chemical, biological, or radiological agents are just a few examples of what a risk manager's duties and responsibilities might entail for protecting fans, brand, and organization assets.

Integrating technology with physical security measures—ingress screening, hand wanding, metal arches, bag checks, and so on—bodes well for ownership groups in these endeavors. Ask owners what keeps them up at night and they will tell you it's the thought of a security breach at their stadium, venue, or arena. Being proactive in conducting threat and vulnerability assessments, tabletop exercises, computer simulations, fire drills, active shooter training, threat and behavioral analysis, and verbal de-escalation skills training can help the stadium risk manager confront challenges.

Does the size of the event dictate what you would do to create a safe environment?

Yes. Understanding not only the size of the event but also the crowd demographics, based on the featured artist or performer, dictates the type of patrons attracted to the venue. A general rule of thumb is the 1/250 rule, which states that for every 250 patrons you should deploy one highly trained security officer for the event. The challenge of part-time staff versus full-time in-house personnel working the venue is ever present. There tends to be a higher turnover in personnel when third-party part-time contract security staff is used to take advantage of lower wages, benefits, and so on. An organization tends to have more control of in-house staff, who buy into and are more familiar with the organization's mission, culture, goals, and objectives.

Would you say that owner negligence is a big factor in many of the safety concerns that are present at events?

The aspect of duty of care is the legal standard to which organizations are held when safeguarding fans attending events. Preventing slips, trips, and falls is a key risk-mitigation strategy deployed by guest services, security, and housekeeping inside the venue. The accurate and detailed documentation of patron injuries is central in protecting organizations from facing potential litigation and inherent liabilities within the space. EMS documentation and calls for service must be tracked accurately inside a venues command center.

What challenges do event planners face with regard to risk management and security?

Safeguarding today's events is constantly evolving, based upon the numerous threats seen within the space. The smooth, safe, and efficient screening of fans helps prevent potential chokepoints and bottlenecks in densely populated ingress and egress checkpoints. Terrorist organizations as well as the extremely unpredictable lone wolf conduct reconnaissance to see where these potential bottlenecks may occur. The goal of a terrorist organization is to inflict mass casualties in densely populated areas of stadiums, venues, or arenas, which include egress checkpoints that flow into mass transportation hubs and entertainment zones. This was exemplified by the suicide bomber who waited for fans to exit Ariana Grande's Manchester concert. And the unprecedented aerial assault that took place at the Harvest 91 Concert in Las Vegas changed the event security landscape in its aftermath.

How have social media usage impacted risk management?

Responsible social media monitoring is a key risk-mitigation strategy for safeguarding today's events. Information of a threatening nature posted or shared on social media platforms such as Twitter, Facebook, Instagram, and Pinterest can be monitored by stadium command centers in real time. This information can be passed along to security and law enforcement to help mitigate a potential threat. The Joint Terrorism Task Force (JTTF) and Fusion Centers are governmental resources available to the professional stadium risk manager.

Do sporting events create a greater or a different challenge in terms of planning and preparation than, say, a school building? Please explain what those differences require.

Safeguarding events is different from protecting a school building, but the same protocols and procedures can be utilized in both verticals. High school basketball games, football games, and other special events can take place in both high school and higher education learning environments. *Lesson learned* is the prevailing theme from both the Parkland and the Santa Fe school shootings. The sharing of best practices between security leaders and law enforcement agencies helps to prevent future attacks. An After Action Report (AAR) is a useful learning tool that can be utilized by key stakeholders working within the space.

How critical is training staff (paid and volunteers) in creating a viable plan?

The need for proactive event staff training cannot be overemphasized. Reactive measures no longer suffice during these difficult times. Organizations can operate from a position of strength when they are out in front of the curve. This starts with a proactive security mindset where learning is metrically measured for retention and aptitude. Proper vetting, and background checks of all staff, including volunteers, are paramount for today's risk manager. The stakes are way too high for not properly preparing staff to meet these challenges.

> *continued*

James A. DeMeo, Unified Sports & Entertainment Security Consulting > *continued*

In your years of experience, what would you say is the one area of risk management that many people overlook?

Proactive training. Security theater—a window-dressing approach that simply involves checking all the boxes—makes poor business sense. Business continuity and resiliency are the buzzwords in today's industry. You don't want to be known as that one organization that skimped on security and found itself in court six months down the road facing a potential multimillion-dollar lawsuit.

What critical skills allow an event manager to provide a safe and secure environment for patrons, staff, and participants?

Proactive staff training, efficient staff deployment, threat and behavioral analysis, emotional intelligence, thoughtful leadership, and verbal de-escalation skills training.

What advice do you offer to current or future event planners and managers with regard to risk management and safety?

Continuing education and professional career development resources for event staff. Forward-thinking organizations such as the National Center for Spectator Sports Safety and Security (NCS^4) and the International Association of Venue Managers (IAVM) are excellent educational resources for the aspiring venue manager safeguarding today's events.

Furthermore, the ability to empower your staff by tuning in to what motivates them in their respective careers helps to reduce staff turnover. A happy, engaged, and well-trained event staffer is more likely to buy into organizational culture and not leave for greener pastures. Today's sports and entertainment industry is a multibillion-dollar juggernaut. It's all about the fan experience. When fans feel safe and entertained and are treated with dignity and respect by event staff, the likelihood is they will return to the venue time and time again.

Risks are inherent in activity. Copious energy must be afforded this area of concern in event planning. Doing your due diligence in the planning phase will help in identifying, scrutinizing, evaluating, minimizing, or eliminating and controlling any potential risks or threats to your event. Today's event landscape presents an even greater challenge to managers, planners, workers, and fans. Planning a safe and secure experience is a collaborative endeavor that requires all stakeholders to be involved, prepared, and observant. The concerted effort must address any potential hazards and threats to the overall event experience. Two such areas that need specific attention are risk management and negligence. These two concerns are inextricably woven into managerial responsibilities, whether you are a coach, a teacher, a recreation program administrator, or a manager in a high school, college, Olympic, or professional sport organization. Most members of the general public are unaware of the inner workings of producing an event and the countless hours and efforts that go into running it, but they do have the expectation of being in a safe and secure environment and that they will be entertained.

Carefully identifying and addressing the potential risks associated with an event is essential in meeting the expectations of the event and the public. Spengler, Connaughton, and Pittman (2016) define risk management as "reducing or eliminating the risk of injury and death and potential subsequent liability that comes about through involvement with sport and recreation programs and services" (p. 2). Sharp, Moorman, and Claussen (2010) stress the preventive nature, identifying what-if scenarios to determine potential threats and address them in the planning phase. Risk management at its simplest is a "process for managing the risks that you can identify—and insuring those you can't manage" (Ashley and Pearson 1993, p. 1). DeLisle (2009) emphasized the use of common sense and prudent responsibility to minimize threats.

All definitions lead to one conclusion: You must be diligent in identifying potential hazards and craft a plan for managing them. It is very easy to become comfortable with the way things are when you have not been confronted with an incident to challenge your response. According to Trump (2009), "the most challenging obstacle . . . is complacency. Time and distance from a major high-profile tragedy breeds complacency and fuels denial" (para. 7). This complacency and denial could position an event manager on the wrong side of a lawsuit. Taking a cue from the Boy Scouts of America, it is in our best interest to always be prepared.

Risk Management Process

It is virtually impossible to eliminate all potential risks, but you can act to protect your investment. The risk management process is not a one-and-done exercise but rather a dynamic process utilizing everyone involved in the planning and execution of an event. Your risk management plan is a holistic approach that comprises **crisis management plans**, **emergency action plans**, and a **communication plan**. **Risk management planning** best embodies Murphy's Law that if anything bad can happen, it probably will, and you want to be prepared.

Tarlow (2002) outlines the risk management process as identifying risks, projecting potential issues related to the risk, identifying remedies, doing what is necessary to prevent injuries, anticipating the reaction to the crisis, and creating a plan for both the crisis and how it will be communicated to the public. Sharp, Moorman, and Claussen (2010) offer the following elements of risk management:

- *Identification*. Conducting a legal audit identifies the deficiencies that need to be addressed or corrected during the planning process of a risk management plan (discussed later in this chapter).
- *Assessing and classifying*. Documentation of previous incidents is of great use when assessing issues and attempting to classify them. The risk matrix in figure 9.1 is a great tool for helping you with risk identification, defining the levels, classifying the severity, and assessing the probability of occurrence.
- *Treating and managing*. Risk treatment refers to the process of determining the options for addressing potential risks. Once these are determined, there are four possible paths to treating the risk: accept, reduce, avoid, or transfer. Accepting the risk means retaining the risk and working around it. Reducing the risk is accomplished by putting measures in place to lessen the impact of a hazard such as severe weather. Risk avoidance involves deflecting potential threats in hopes of minimizing the effects, such as training and policies. The final treatment involves transferring liability to a third party (e.g., via an insurance policy), thus shifting liability (Cotten and Wolohan 2017).

The management of risks requires the generation of standard operating procedures (SOPs), which provide consistency and uniformity for job performance. Parkhouse (2005) defines an **SOP** as a "strategic plan that will provide the most efficient and effective way to decrease the occurrence of risks" (p. 160). When developing your SOPs, you should take care to involve all vested personnel since they know specifics about each area that needs to be covered and these should be simply stated to reduce the potential for confusion. These SOPs become guiding principles for an event, outlining processes and procedures to be followed for identified risks.

Risk Management Planning

Proactively identifying and classifying potential risks will assist in the development of risk management plans. The **DIM process** is a way to remain proactive rather than reactive during a crisis situation by developing, implementing, and managing the plan.

Severity of Risk / Category	PROBABILITY THAT SOMETHING WILL GO WRONG: **Frequent** Likely to occur immediately or in a short period of time; expected to occur frequently	**Likely** Quite likely to occur in time	**Occasional** May occur in time	**Seldom** Not likely to occur but possible	**Unlikely** Unlikely to occur
CATASTROPHIC May result in death	E	E	H	H	M
CRITICAL May cause severe injury, major property damage, significant financial loss, and/or result in negative publicity for the organization and/or institution	E	H	H	M	L
MARGINAL May cause minor injury, illness, property damage, financial loss, and/or result in negative publicity for the organization and/or institution	E	M	M	L	L
NEGLIGIBLE Hazard presents a minimal threat to safety, health, and well-being of participants; trivial	M	L	L	L	L

RISK DEFINITIONS

Many events, without proper planning, can have unreasonable levels of risk. However, by applying risk management strategies you can reduce the risk to an acceptable level.

E	**Extremely High Risk**	Activities in this category contain unacceptable levels of risk, including catastrophic and critical injuries that are highly likely to occur. Organizations should consider whether they should eliminate or modify activities that still have an "E" rating after applying all reasonable risk management strategies.
H	**High Risk**	Activities in this category contain potentially serious risks that are likely to occur. Application of proactive risk management strategies to reduce the risk is advised. Organizations should consider ways to modify or eliminate unacceptable risks.
M	**Moderate Risk**	Activities in this category contain some level of risk that is unlikely to occur. Organizations should consider what can be done to manage the risk to prevent any negative outcomes.
L	**Low Risk**	Activities in this category contain minimal risk and are unlikely to occur. Organizations can proceed with these activities as planned.

FIGURE 9.1 University of Wisconsin –River Falls risk-assessment matrix.

Reprinted by permission from University of Wisconsin - River Falls.

Developing the Plan

The first step in developing a risk management plan is to identify the potential risks that could be associated with an event (Cotten and Wolohan 2017; Ammon, Southall, and Nagel 2016). Various methods can be utilized to collect this information, from fans reporting potential hazards to a full-fledged walk-through of the host venue. Most venues will already have SOPs in place for addressing potential situations, but anything that has not been previously experienced may require special attention. Involve as many people as necessary to ensure the safety of all involved. This process is also referred to as risk assessment.

Once the venue, whether indoor or outdoor, has been carefully considered, the identified risks must be classified (Ammon, Southall, and Nagel 2016). Classifiying potential risks in a hierarchical order allows their frequency and seriousness to be understood (Spengler, Connaughton, and Pittman 2016). As mentioned earlier in the section on assessing and classifying risks, a risk matrix is a common tool used by event and facility personnel for this purpose. Barringer (2006) summed up a **risk matrix** as a graphic tool that highlights the chance of a risk with the consequence of the risk. Next, event managers need to decide how to manage or treat the identified risks. Various authors have identified the four possible treatments as retaining, reducing, avoiding, or transferring to a third party (Cotten and Wolohan 2017; Ammon, Southall, and Nagel 2016; Spengler, Connaughton, and Pittman 2016).

Implementing the Plan

Implementation of a risk management plan requires that all involved understand the expectations the plan has established and also understand their role in making sure these expectations are met. If properly trained, event staff should be confident and able to do what is expected of them. Buy-in is critical. This can be achieved by involving the staff in the development of the plan or, if utilizing volunteers, asking for suggestions during training (Ammon, Southall, and Nagel 2016). A key ingredient in the facilitation of a risk management plan is the effectiveness of communication. Handbooks, e-mails, posters, fliers, and other forms of conveying information are essential for maintaining open lines of communication and consistency in expectations.

Managing the Plan

All the hard work put into devising the plan is now ready to pay off. You've hired the staff, trained them, and prepared them for potential risks. It is crucial that you have confidence in the person or persons hired to oversee the risk management process. The risk management plan is an evolving document. Over the course of an event, things will happen that may not have been addressed in the plan. The risk manager will document these incidents and develop strategies for addressing them in the future. Each event should end with a formal evaluation. The final step in most processes—evaluation—allows for pinpointing where something went wrong and, more important, where things went right. Do not assume that an incident-free event means the plan is foolproof. Event managers must be constantly considering what can be done to best serve patrons, keeping them safe and secure while at an event. Remember, a satisfied customer is a repeat customer!

Threats to Events

When attending an event, a patron does not plan to become part of the action, but sometimes a foul ball or a broken bat ends up in the stands, or a hockey puck misses the Plexiglas and sails 12 rows up, or a patron spills a drink and it goes unreported or the custodial staff does not respond immediately. All these incidents unrelated to the event itself have the potential to cost the event and facility managers in legal fees. Spengler, Connaughton, and Pittman (2016) outline some of the potential **threats** that require special consideration in risk management planning: medical attention, heat-related illnesses, lightning safety, bloodborne pathogens, equipment and supervision, and insurance. We add to that list all types of weather issues, food safety, drones, natural disasters, and human trafficking. A discussion of some these potential threats follows.

Medical Attention

The medical attention an event manager needs to provide is dictated by the type of event and the governing body. We know that injuries are inherent in sport and that we can prepare for what might happen. At the very least, staff should be certified in first aid, cardiopulmonary resuscitation (CPR), and the use of an automated external defibrillator (AED). Event personnel should carry cell phones in case they need to call 911. In a medical emergency, response time can be the difference between life and death. Establish a clear communication plan for every situation, including who will be the designated caller (Spengler, Connaughton, and Pittman 2016).

Heat-Related Illnesses and Other Weather Issues

According to the National Oceanic and Atmospheric Administration (NOAA) (2018) the most common weather-related killer in the United States on average for the past 30 years is heat. In 2017, heat-related death ranked second to flooding, which ranks second in the 30-year average category. NOAA works diligently with local National Weather Service (NWS) offices to report weather conditions. As the weather becomes warmer, the NWS begins to issue excessive heat outlooks, watches, warnings, and advisories. Identify someone from the event management staff who will be responsible for checking the extended forecast so that alternative plans can be considered if necessary.

Reports of well-conditioned athletes collapsing from heat-related causes are far too common. The death of Minnesota Vikings player Korey Stringer in 2001 sparked the need for increased awareness and education on heat-related illnesses. An estimated 2,100 people sought treatment for exhaustion and dehydration at the 2012 Boston Marathon (Turchi 2018). Summer 2018 workouts in 85-plus-degree weather cost a University of Maryland football player his life. During the summer of 2011, six high school football players died from heat-related injuries in Texas, and in November 2011, a University of Miami football player was found unconscious on the field at an early-morning practice (Siegel 2011; Kercheval 2011). Even one death is too many; you need to make sure that any event you are hosting outdoors during high temperatures has a plan in place to help relieve the heat and replenish nutrients.

Severe Weather and Lightning Safety

NOAA also offers guidelines for other severe weather-related issues such as hail, flooding, tornadoes, and lightning. Weather preparedness needs to start before there is a storm. In their presentation on preparing venues, the NOAA offers four stages of severe weather warning response for keeping attendees safe: planning , practicing and preparing, monitoring, and acting. Each stage should address the actions you should be taking related to various weather issues. It is also important for you to understand the weather-related definitions in the sidebar.

Lightning can strike when least expected. In March 2012, four members of the Seymour (Indiana) High School softball team were injured, one critically, from a lightning strike on what was described as a hot, sunny day (WRTV 2012). NOAA calls this phenomenon a "bolt from the blue," stressing that lead time for lightning strikes varies from minutes to hours and that warnings are not issued for this type of severe weather. A serious concern for event managers, lightning can travel as far as 25 miles (40 km) from its origin before it strikes. Consulting the various organizations that address lightning safety, such as the National Athletic Trainers' Association, National Lightning Safety Institute, National Collegiate Athletic Association, and state high school sports associations, is highly recommended (Spengler, Connaughton, and Pittman 2016).

In 2017, the red carpet walk for the MTV Movie and TV Awards held in Los Angeles was interrupted by a freak rainstorm that quickly turned into an even more rare hailstorm (Reuters 2018). The rain had been predicted but the thought of hail never crossed the organizers' mind. Ultimately, the red carpet was abandoned. NOAA's lead time for predicting a hailstorm is listed as approximately 20 minutes. Regardless of its size, hail can cause damage or injury so you should have a precaution in place to move attendees to a solidly constructed facility (if outdoors) and away from any windows.

Event directors of the 2018 Senior PGA Dick's Sporting Goods Open held in Endicott, NY, found themselves knee deep in water, literally, when a rain and flash flooding paralyzed preparations for the tournament (Houghtailing 2018; Paddock 2018). This was more than just a golf tournament, and organizers and workers

Terms for Predicting the Potential for Severe Weather

Warning

A *warning* is issued when a hazardous weather or hydrologic event is occurring, imminent, or likely. A warning occurs when weather conditions could threaten life or property. People in the path of the storm should take protective action.

Watch

The term *watch* means the risk of a hazardous weather or hydrologic event has increased significantly, but its occurrence, location, or timing is still uncertain. A watch means that hazardous weather is possible. People should have a plan of action and be prepared for a possible storm. They should stay alert and watch for later information and possible warnings, especially when planning travel or outdoor activities.

Advisory

An *advisory* is issued when a hazardous weather or hydrologic event is occurring, imminent, or likely, could cause significant inconvenience, and if caution is not exercised, could lead to situations that may threaten life or property.

Outlook

An *outlook* is issued when a hazardous weather event is possible within the upcoming week. Outlooks are intended to warn affected people of the potential for significant weather that could lead to situations that may threaten life or property.

---

had to work throughout the night pumping water from several holes and erecting hospitality tents and a stage for country music star Blake Shelton to perform on the Friday night of the event. Because weather is unpredictable, having contingency plans and being familiar with weather patterns is a necessity for an event planner.

Sometimes you may have only seconds to react to what the weather brings you. Take for instance the 2008 Southeastern Conference Men's Basketball Tournament. An F1 tornado struck downtown Atlanta during the Mississippi State vs. Alabama game. Videos taken during the event show debris falling from the ceiling while the PA announcer confirms severe weather in the area and instructs attendees to move to the corridors (ESPN 2008).

As has been shown, severe weather can and will have an adverse effect on your event. Rain or snow can lower your attendance numbers; more severe weather could lead to critical injuries or even death. During the planning phases for your event, make sure you include a severe weather plan. NOAA recommends you include the following in your plan:

- Develop it around your hazard assessment
- Address vulnerabilities
- Clearly define who is in charge of making weather-related decisions
- Details on how to obtain weather information
- Weather thresholds that trigger decisions or actions
- *All* staff members must be trained and should practice
- Capabilities and resources available both on- and off-site
- Communication capabilities (back-ups)
- Address crowd control (panic)
- Don't forget about people with special needs
- Work with your local emergency manager or local response officials or with your insurance company

Another recommendation is to find out whether the community or venue in which you are hosting is a StormReady member. StormReady is an NWS program that helps communities proactively prepare for what could happen during severe weather. It brings together multiple entities in an effort to alert and respond to any severe weather events (National Oceanic and Atmospheric Administration n.d.).

Blood-Borne Pathogens

In many sports, injuries are a given. Some injuries involve the muscles and joints, while others involve the loss of blood. Strict precautions regarding handling blood are specified by the Occupational Safety and Health Administration (OSHA). OSHA guidelines exist to prevent the spread of diseases through contact with blood. Using latex gloves and thoroughly washing hands are two preventive measures. Sports such as boxing and the martial arts in particular are scrutinized when it comes to blood-borne illnesses.

Equipment and Supervision

Equipment is essential in sport. For the protection of the participants, safety inspections must be performed to make sure that equipment is maintained and in proper working order. It is critical to make sure that equipment and **supervision** are adequate for the age of the patrons (Cotten and Wolohan 2017). From a legal perspective, both equipment and supervision fall within the realm of liability law. Sharp, Moorman, and Claussen (2010) report concerns of liability with regard to supervision. The quality of the supervision (a competent, trained staff) and the quantity of supervisors (ratio of supervisors to participants or attendees) must be adequate for the activity or event.

Hiring competent staff and conducting a thorough screening process, including background checks, are necessary supervision criteria. Although events rely heavily on volunteers, not every person who applies needs to be hired. According to Van Der Wagen and Carlos (2005), training should address three areas: event objectives, the facility, and each staff member's job duties. Becoming familiar with expectations allows the staff to fully grasp the intent of the event. Touring the facility familiarizes them with exits, evacuation routes, concessions, and any other aspects necessary for them to do their jobs properly. Be sure to let employees and volunteers know the expectations of their specific jobs and how they fit into the overall experience that patrons will have while at the event.

As a shining example of how properly trained staff make for a spectacular event, we need only look at the 2012 Super Bowl in Indianapolis. The Super Bowl Host Committee provided numerous training sessions over the course of a year for its 8,000-plus volunteers. The volunteers were subjected to background checks by Homeland Security and were trained on how to respond to certain issues should they arise. Communication was critical to the success of the Super Bowl volunteer program, and text messages, e-mails, and websites were vital tools for disseminating the necessary information about schedule or venue changes.

Insurance

Insurance needs are determined by the type and location of an event but, at a minimum, event organizers need to secure liability insurance to protect their financial investment and protect against potential legal action related to civil or criminal law (deLisle 2009; Supovitz 2005). Liability insurance is necessary because facility owners will require you to purchase it to protect their interests in your event and because of the duty owed to participants, spectators, and workers (Supovitz 2005). This duty refers to the requirement of the party hosting the event to provide a safe environment for all involved. Due diligence in the planning process should account for potential issues that could result in injury or worse to participants, spectators, or workers. According to Van Der Wagen and Carlos (2005), liability claims "can be reduced by careful risk analysis and prevention strategies" (p. 52). It is especially important that event planners allocate the funds necessary to procure the appropriate amount of liability coverage. Each event is different and will require insurance coverage based on the size, complexity, and location of the impending event (Supovitz 2005).

Food Handling and Safety

For many, the food experience at an event can be even more meaningful than the event itself. Many people rate the quality of the food just as important as the event itself. White (2017) states that stadiums "count on food and beverage sales as a major revenue source; menus now play a more substantial role in these venues" (para. 2). The Center for Disease Control and Prevention (CDC) estimates that 48 million people a year get sick from foodborne illnesses like norovirus, salmonella, clostridium perfringens, and campylobacter (CDC). Since food poisoning leads the list of foodborne illnesses, the CDC has created the simple four-step guide to food safety found in Figure 9.2. If you will be serving food, these steps are mandatory and training all employees is a must. Specific guidelines must be followed to ensure food safety, workplace cleanliness, and proper sanitation. If you contract your concessions, be sure to review the health ratings of the companies you are considering.

Drones

Drone usage is not new in terms of providing a bird's eye view of a location or a game. In October 2014 a drone was witnessed hovering over the student section at a University of Wisconsin football game. Although the drone was determined to be harmless, the university did not have a plan for how to handle such an occurrence. And now, with drones becoming more affordable and the increasing likelihood that someone could use them for harm, this technology has to be addressed in your risk management plans. Many venues have had to create policies and post no-fly-zone signs to thwart the amateur pilots from invading stadium air space. A 2014 triathlon incident in Australia depicts the harm drones can cause, even if they are being used with the best intent. Triathlete Raija Ogden was hit in the face by an event drone that was tracking the racers just shortly after she started the running portion of the event (Taillier 2014). A similar drone spotting happened that same year at PNC Park during a Pittsburgh Pirates game. Authorities quickly responded to the sighting and the operator was ordered to stop flying. He "willingly complied and was not cited or arrested" (Sanserino and Todd 2014). Both of these incidents were harmless uses of drone technology, but many event and facility mangers are concerned about the unauthorized, illegal, and possibly devastating use of drones at events.

BASICS FOR HANDLING FOOD SAFELY

Safe steps in food handling, cooking, and storage are essential to prevent foodborne illness. You can't see, smell, or taste harmful bacteria that may cause illness. In every step of food preparation, follow the four steps of the Food Safe Families campaign to keep food safe:

- Clean—Wash hands and surfaces often.
- Separate—Don't cross-contaminate.
- Cook—Cook to the right temperature.
- Chill—Refrigerate promptly.

FIGURE 9.2 Four Steps to Food Safety as recommended by the CDC.
From the U.S. Food and Drug Administration. www.fda.gov

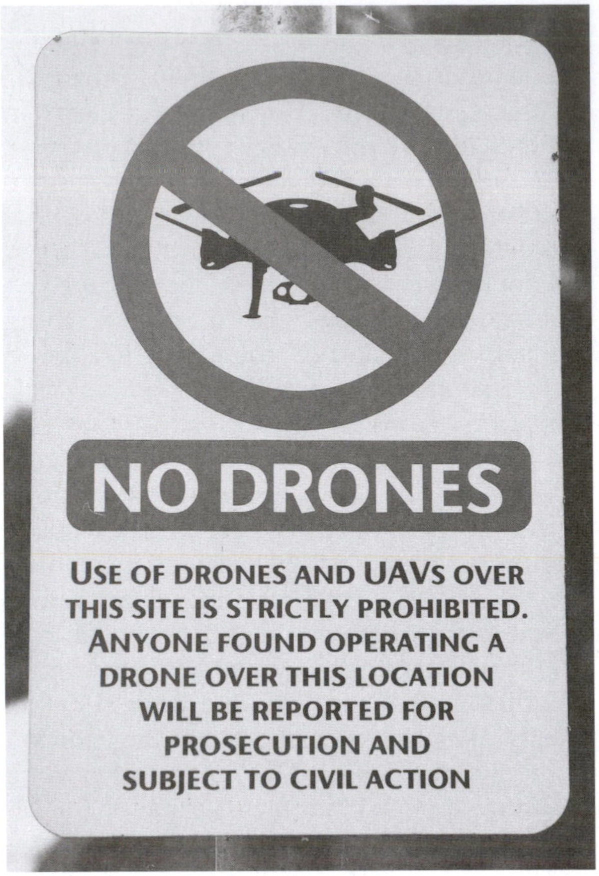

OLI SCARFF/AFP/Getty Images

Drones present a greater threat than many people realize.

The NCS[4] at the University of Southern Mississippi claims that drones present a greater threat than many realize. A 2017 incident at Levi's Stadium in San Francisco shows how a drone can "penetrate the air space above the stadium" dropping "a payload on the more than 65,000 fans in attendance. Fortunately, the drone only dropped fliers" (*Gameday Security* 2018, p.18). This was only another innocent use of a drone, but what if that payload had been a biological weapon? Imagine what the results could have been. This is not to scare you, but to make you aware of how new technology, like drones, can cause a threat to your event.

Natural Disasters

As we saw in chapter 8, natural disasters such as hurricanes can cause the delay, relocation, or cancellation of an event. Game 3 of the 1989 World Series was interrupted when a 6.9-magnitude earthquake rattled the San Francisco Bay area (Bahr 2015). The obvious difference between these two natural disasters is that one of them you know is coming and can prepare for and one other one you do not.

Human Trafficking

Although it is discussed only in relation to mega sporting events in the literature, human trafficking has been listed as the fastest-growing crime in the world (Ochab 2017), ranking second behind illegal drug trafficking (UNANIMA). Everyone in event management needs to be aware of and trained in how to spot a potential issue. As a part of the 2013 NCAA Men's Basketball Championship in Atlanta, Georgia, Dr. Danzey-Bussell (coauthor of this textbook), who volunteered for the event, was required to attend a training hosted by the FBI addressing the issue of human trafficking and its prevalence in the Atlanta area (a major airport hub) and was trained in spotting a trafficking victim. Victims are pressed into what has been termed *modern-day slavery* for various criminal activities and labor exploitation (UNANIMA).

Crowd Control

Among the many skills required of facility managers is an understanding and appreciation of crowd dynamics and the relationship of crowding to facility design and management. Fruin (1984) reported that good crowd planning and management improves the public's enjoyment of events and encourages attendance. It also reduces crowd-related accidents, their associated liability claims, and the possibility of more serious and costly incidents. This management skill is critical for both the patron and the manager. Event planners must understand the difference between crowd management and **crowd control**. Berlonghi (1994) defined crowd management as those measures taken to facilitate the movement and enjoyment of people. He contended that properly managing a crowd reassures people that they will get what they paid for and that they will return home safe and sound.

Crowd Management Plans

Crafting a **crowd management plan** (CMP) that includes the strategies necessary for creating a successful and safe event is one part of the overall risk management plan. A CMP helps provide a safe and enjoyable environment for patrons. An effective plan addresses the following.

- Number of people at the venue
- Behavior of spectators
- Layout of the facility
- Movement and activities of guests
- Emergency response
- Specific concerns of guests visiting the facility

Here are some key terms related to crowd management:

- *Crowd expectations*. Patrons have the expectation that the environment they are entering has been prepared for the event and is safe and secure. They assume that every precaution has been taken to prevent accidental, intentional, or negligent acts that could cause harm. A great example of a proactive effort to put fans at ease can be found on most university websites under "Game Day Information." Like many other campus and professional sporting venues, the University of Alabama has taken a bigger step and installed metal detectors at Bryant-Denny Stadium. The university utilized social media to get the word out.

WWW Go to the web resource to access the FAQ page of the University of Alabama.

- *Crowd dynamics and demographics*. Every crowd has its unique qualities. According to Fell (2003), crowd dynamics refers to "the management and the flow of pedestrians in crowded venues and situations" (p. 1). The demographics of the crowd also play a role in the dynamics.
- *Movement theory*. How people move inside and outside a facility relates to pedestrian traffic flow. In terms of an equation, movement theory considers the flow to be the speed at which a crowd is moving multiplied by the density and the width of the crowd. Hoogendoorn and Bovy (2003) assert that certain factors contribute to walking speeds, such as "personal characteristics of pedestrians (age, gender, size, health, etc.), characteristics of the trip (walking purpose, route familiarity, trip length), properties of the infrastructure (type, grade, attractiveness of environment, shelter), and finally, environmental characteristics (ambient and weather conditions)" (p. 154).
- *Evacuation procedures*. The mass exodus of crowds requires that adequate exits be unlocked and ready for use. Tragedies such as the Rhode Island nightclub disaster of 2003 are preventable if evacuation routes are not blocked or locked, preventing people from exiting the building. Pyrotechnics were set off during a rock concert, catching the nightclub on fire and creating chaos in the crowd. Several exits to the facility were chain-locked from the inside, preventing escape from the burning building and resulting in the death of nearly 100 people (CNN 2003).

Go to the web resource to access the Department of Homeland Security's comprehensive manual on evacuating stadiums. WWW

- *Alcohol policy*. Selling alcohol requires careful consideration. If the decision to sell alcohol is made, an alcohol policy must be in place to manage the sale of alcohol and to address the handling of intoxicated and obnoxious fans. Removing the patron as quickly as possible, without incident and without becoming the main attraction, is the goal.

- *Training*. Ammon, Southall, and Nagel (2016) contend that properly training staff is the first component of an effective CMP. Ticket takers, ushers, and bag-check personnel are the first line of defense in controlling risks and crowds, and these employees should be trained accordingly. Training should also include the scope of their duties and cover the second component of an effective CMP: activation and implementation of an emergency plan. Procedures for dealing with unruly or intoxicated fans should be well thought out and explained. In devising your emergency plan, consider creating a working document that all employees will have access to. The table of contents of Washington & Lee University's emergency plan is a good example of what to include (see the web resource).

- *Crowd control*. Crowd control more directly relates to the actions implemented once a crowd begins to act in a way that was not planned. Examples include engaging in unsafe activities, becoming rowdy, pushing or shoving, and fighting. The 2004 Malice in the Palace fiasco helps us better understand how a situation can turn ugly in a matter of seconds. The Pacers-Pistons brawl originally started on the court but ended up in the stands, with players and fans battling it out Wild West style (Lage 2004; Associated Press 2004).

- *Signage*. A key ingredient of crowd control is adequate signage inside and outside a facility. Signage is one aspect of the communication plan that gives patrons the information they need in order to move to, from, and within an event. Two typical types of signage are as follows:
    - Directional signs, which provide patrons with directions to important locations such as interstates, main roadways, and parking areas. Inside the facility, such signs help patrons navigate the facility.
    - Informational signs, which inform patrons of things such as prohibited items, facility rules, and important locations within the facility.

Go to the web resource to access the table of contents for Washington & Lee University's emergency plan. WWW

Negligence

Generally speaking, events are produced with minimal cause for concern. Most of the issues that arise are behind the scenes and are unknown to participants and spectators. But in the event something happens that places participants and spectators in harm's way, you must have a plan in place to remedy the situation. This can be addressed during the initial planning phase, where it is critical for you to take the initiative and consider the potential hazards that might interfere with hosting a safe and secure event. Specifically, the tort of negligence must be visited. You can decrease your liability with proper planning.

Cotten and Wolohan (2017) define **negligence** as an unintentional wrongdoing that results in injury to a person, property, or reputation. They go on to state that this is the area of law in which the sport industry sees most of its lawsuits. Simply put, negligence is failing to provide a safe environment, resulting in someone or something being injured or harmed.

Establishing negligence is not as simple as it may seem. There is no guarantee that a person injured at an event will be able to recover a monetary reward. In today's litigious society, too many people believe that something as simple as slipping and falling is cause for compensation. But in order to make such a claim and potentially receive restitution, negligence must be proven. To prove negligence, four elements must be present: "duty, breach, cause, and damage" (Owen 2007, p. 1673).

- *Duty*. This term refers to a recognized social norm regarding how you should conduct yourself with others (Cotten and Wolohan 2017). The relationships covered by a duty are those that are viewed as inherent to the situation, such as a facility owner and invitees, coach and athlete, or teacher and student. Bell (1995) highlighted the following six groups as those that must be afforded special relational considerations: (1) students, (2) employees, (3) volunteers, (4) tenants, (5) authorized visitors, and (6) trespassers. Specifically, with regard to your event, you must consider the following duties: "the duty to protect against foreseeable dangers, the duty to provide adequate security and the duty to warn about known dangers" (Bell 2005, pp. 2-3).

- *Breach*. As mentioned earlier, you are expected to provide a safe and secure environment for all involved in the production of your event. If you fail to provide such an environment, you are considered in breach of your duty. A breach can involve either misconduct that occurred or a person's action or oversight (Owen 2007). Breach of duty is centered around two risks: those that are inherent to the activity (audience participation in a halftime game) and those that are negligent behaviors (climbing on a railing at a facility and falling).
- *Cause*. To determine whether a defendant's actions or lack of actions were responsible for the plaintiff's injuries, the plaintiff must prove cause and effect. In other words, if someone claims he was injured while attending your event, he must prove that you (event manager or facility manager) created the situation that caused the injury (negligent behavior), either by not taking the necessary precautions or by failing to warn. It is best that event managers work closely with the facility to ensure that all potential situations are addressed before the event or that a plan is in place to address them as they arise.
- *Damage*. For recovery, there must be damages. The damage is typically either physical or emotional injury. Compensable damage can be financial loss, emotional distress, or impairment.

Because sporting events involve competition, with some being very physical in nature, and spectators who tend to become rowdy, it is no wonder that event managers need to prepare diligently for charges of negligence. Rowdy fans can become verbally violent, which may lead to a physical altercation. On the other end of this spectrum, jubilant fans can also become rowdy as they express unbridled emotion for their teams. Either can develop into a crowd management issue that could turn deadly. From soccer matches in Europe to concertgoers in the United States, it is hard to manage a mobile crowd, so injury or death could occur. Far too often we hear of tragic situations in which people are trampled by out-of-control crowds.

As an event manager, you need to consider all potential areas of liability that are within your purview, including spectators, participants, and event workers. Ultimate liability lies with you. Liability laws vary from state to state, so you need to be aware of your responsibilities if you are managing a mobile event (Cotten and Wolohan 2017). According to Cotten and Wolohan (2017), there are three potentially liable parties to consider: employees, the administrators or supervisors, and the corporate entity (owners). For this reason, it is critical that you hire competent staff who are responsible and trustworthy and then train them for their specific tasks.

Spectators and participants must also share some of the burden for potential problems. Spectators assume the risk of attending an event knowing that some sports have potential dangers, such as a puck clearing the Plexiglas and entering the seats, a baseball or bat flying into the stands, or an errant golf ball finding its way into a gallery. Situations such as this can be addressed through various means such as a disclaimer on the back of a ticket or signage around the event that provides warnings for spectators.

Participants in your event should be required to sign a waiver or release form before competing. Considered contracts, waivers, and releases inform participants of the potential dangers associated with participating. Upon signing these forms, the participant assumes the potential risk for participating and surrenders the right to sue if injured during the activity (Cotten and Wolohan 2017). It is advisable to secure the services of a lawyer to help you create the necessary forms (waiver and releases) and provide counsel for local and state laws.

Summary

Providing a safe and fun experience for patrons is not only expected but also legally required. Risk management strategies help address any potential issues before an event is held. Creating an overarching risk management plan, inclusive of crowd management strategies, emergency responses, and an effective communication plan, will offer protection against potential injuries and lawsuits.

Safety and security are sometimes used synonymously, but they are different. Peter Taylor, former lord chief justice of England and Wales, summed up that difference with the following quote: "You cannot create a safe environment without effective security. If a crowd gets out of control, safety will be compromised." Ultimately, facility management is responsible for maintaining order. Event and facility managers work attentively to create detailed crowd management plans that address crisis situations such as *fandemonium*, the state of crowd chaos. Once a crowd reaches this level, law enforcement officers or security personnel will be called to action.

A popular adage has it that failing to plan is planning to fail. Set an event up for success; be diligent in taking the necessary precautions to prepare for a successful event through proactive planning. Be keenly aware of the various threats mentioned in this chapter that could challenge you and your event, have a plan of action for handling them, and make sure that all staff, paid and volunteer, are aware of the plan.

LEARNING ACTIVITIES

Select a facility of your choice, and attend an event hosted by that facility. During your visit, complete a checklist that will help you evaluate the facility's safety. Once you have assessed the safety of the facility, you are to construct an executive summary of your findings and submit it for grading. The purpose of this exercise is to challenge you to view things from a facility management perspective in order to focus on preventive rather than reactive management. Before your visit, do your homework. Consider the following regarding the facility you have chosen to visit:

- Age of the facility
- Location: rural, urban, inner city
- Renovated or new facility
- How the facility is or was financed
- The facility's competition

Use the following survey to record your observations during your site visit (figure 9.3).

SAMPLE FACILITY INSPECTION CHECKLIST

This form is provided as a sample facility inspection checklist and is designed to help you develop a checklist specific for your facilities. This checklist is incomplete.

Name of inspector: ______________________

Date of inspection: ______________________

Name and location of facility: ______________________

Facility Condition

Circle Y (yes) if the facility is in good condition and N (no) if it needs something done to make it acceptable. Fill in what needs to be done on the line to the right.

Gymnasium

Y N Floor (no water spots, buckling, loose sections) ______________________

Y N Walls (vandalism free) ______________________

Y N Lights (all functioning) ______________________

Y N Windows (secure) ______________________

Y N Roof (no adverse impact of weather) ______________________

Y N Stairs (well lighted) ______________________

Y N Bleachers (support structure sound) ______________________

Y N Exits (lights working) ______________________

Y N Basketball rims (level, securely attached) ______________________

Y N Basketball backboards (no cracks, clean) ______________________

Y N Mats (cleaned, properly stored, no defects) ______________________

Y N Uprights and projections ______________________

Y N Wall plugs (covered) ______________________

Y N Light switches (all functioning) ______________________

Y N Heating and cooling system (temperature control) ______________________

Y N Ducts, radiators, pipes ______________________

Y N Thermostats ______________________

Y N Fire alarms (regularly checked) ______________________

Y N Directions posted for evacuating the gym in case of fire ______________________

Y N Fire extinguishers (regularly checked) ______________________

Other (list) ______________________

Locker Rooms

Y N Floors ______________________

Y N Walls ______________________

Y N Lights ______________________

Y N Windows ______________________

Y N Roof ______________________

Y N Showers ______________________

Y N Drains ______________________

> *continued*

FIGURE 9.3 This form provides a starting point for evaluating facility safety.

Reprinted by permission from ASEP, *Event Management for Sport Directors* (Champaign, IL: Human Kinetics, 1996), 8.

Y N Benches ______________________________

Y N Lockers ______________________________

Y N Exits ______________________________

Y N Water fountains ______________________________

Y N Toilets ______________________________

Y N Trainer's room ______________________________

Other (list) ______________________________

Field(s) or outside playing area

Surface

Y N Not too wet or too dry ______________________________

Y N Grass length ______________________________

Y N Free of debris ______________________________

Y N Free of holes and bumps ______________________________

Y N Free of protruding pipes, wires, lines ______________________________

Y N Line markers ______________________________

Stands

Y N Pitching mound ______________________________

Y N Dugouts ______________________________

Y N Warning tracks and fences ______________________________

Y N Sidelines ______________________________

Y N Sprinklers ______________________________

Y N Garbage ______________________________

Y N Security fences ______________________________

Y N Water fountains ______________________________

Y N Storage sheds ______________________________

Concession area

Y N Electrical ______________________________

Y N Heating and cooling systems ______________________________

Other (list) ______________________________

Pool

Y N Equipment in good repair ______________________________

Y N Sanitary ______________________________

Y N Slipperiness on decks and diving board controlled ______________________________

Y N Chemicals safely stored ______________________________

Y N Regulations and safety rules posted ______________________________

Lighting: adequate visibility

Y N No glare ______________________________

Y N Penetrates to bottom of pool ______________________________

Y N Exit light in good repair ______________________________

Y N Halls and locker rooms meet code requirements ______________________________

Y N Light switches properly grounded ______________________________

Y N Has emergency generator to back up regular power source ______________________________

FIGURE 9.3 > *continued*

Exits: accessible, secure

Y N Adequate size, number ______

Y N Self-closing doors ______

Y N Self-locking doors ______

Y N Striker plates secure ______

Y N No obstacles or debris ______

Y N Office and storage rooms locked ______

Ring buoys

Y N 20-inch diameter ______

Y N 50-foot rope length ______

Reaching poles

Y N One each side ______

Y N 12-foot length ______

Y N Metal stress ______

Y N Good repair ______

Guard chair(s)

Y N Unobstructed view ______

Y N Tall enough to see bottom of pool ______

Safety line at break point in the pool grade (deep end) ______

Y N Bright color floats ______

Y N 3/4-inch rope ______

First-aid kit

Y N Inventoried and replenished regularly ______

Stretcher, two blankets, and spine board

Y N Inventoried and in good repair ______

Emergency telephone lights and public address system

Y N Accessible ______

Y N Directions for use visibly posted ______

Y N Powered by emergency generators as well as regular power system ______

Y N Emergency numbers on telephone cradle or receiver ______

Emergency procedures

Y N Sign posted in highly visible area ______

Track

Surface

Y N Free of debris ______

Y N Free of holes and bumps ______

Y N Throwing circles ______

Y N Fences ______

Y N Water fountains ______

Other (list) ______

Recommendations/observations: ______

______

______

FIGURE 9.3 > *continued*

CASE STUDY: 911, WHAT'S YOUR EMERGENCY?

You are sitting in the stands watching a high school football game and all of a sudden you hear pop-pop-pop, and you know it was gunfire. You pick up your phone and call 911. Not a call that anyone wants to make, especially from a high school football game. I mean, it *is* high school football! Over the past few months, this nightmare has become a reality for more than a dozen schools in several states, and it is becoming far too frequent a headline story. Below are just a few of the incidents that have happened during August and September 2018 either at a game, on campus, or near a school while a football game was underway.

August 18, 2018. Wellington, Florida. Dwyer High School vs. Palm Beach Central High School. Two persons shot.

During the fourth quarter of the Dwyer-Palm Beach Central game, chaos broke out as fans ran for cover when four shots were fired from the end of the bleachers where the band sits. As the investigation ensued, it became apparent to authorities that this was a targeted shooting rather than a school shooting, even though it occurred on school grounds.

August 23, 2018. Montgomery, Alabama. GW Carver vs. Jeff Davis, playing at Alabama State University. Shots fired in stands; no injuries.

During the fourth quarter, multiple gunshots were fired from a walkway on the west side of the stadium. Violence is not new to the opening night football games hosted at ASU stadium. The previous year several students were escorted out of the stadium and off the campus for fighting.

August 24, 2018. Jacksonville, Florida. Lee High School vs. Raines High School. Shots fired; two injured, one dead.

It was a typical hot August Friday night in Florida. An estimated 4,000 fans made their way to Raines High School football stadium in Jacksonville, Florida, for the game against Lee High School. From all indications, it was a good night; minor skirmishes in the stands, but when the game was over the fans exited the stands and headed home. Around 10 p.m., approximately 15 minutes after the game was over, shots were fired, two people were injured and one was pronounced dead at the scene. This was a shocking end to what was considered a successful football event. Superintendent Diana Green commented "it was a great game; it is shocking, I was actually at the game."

August 24, 2018. Fairfield, California. JV football game at Armijo High School. Shots fired; one person dead, one critically injured.

ABC News reported that the shooting took place just outside Armijo High School, where a junior varsity football game was being held. About 500 of the attendees were ushered into the gymnasium and the school was placed on lockdown during the search for two shooters, according to the Fairfield Police Department. One of the suspects made his way into the gymnasium with the fans and was subsequently arrested, while the other suspect was found and arrested a few blocks from the shooting.

August 24, 2018. Rockford, Illinois. Freeport High School vs. Auburn High School. Shots fired; no injuries.

Shots were fired near Auburn's Wyeth Stadium. Although the shooting took place in the parking lot outside the stadium, it was reported that this incident had no connection to the game.

September 7, 2018. Murphy, North Carolina. North Georgia vs. Murphy. Shots fired; game put on hold on account of a shooting at a nearby store.

A shooting in a parking lot of a store located near the stadium where the game was being played forced an end to the game and evacuation of the fans.

September 14, 2018. Everett, Washington. Kamiak High School vs. Mariner High School. Shots fired; no injuries.

Shortly after 911 was called for a fight in the parking lot during the Kamiak-Mariner football game, the PA announcer interrupted the game urging the fans to "hit the deck" after five or six shots were heard coming from the area of the reported fight. No injuries were reported from this incident.

Friday night lights are for cheering your home team, supporting the band, crowning a homecoming king and queen, and hanging out at the local burger joint after the game—all innocent pastimes surrounding high school football. But what happens when that innocence is rocked by gunfire? The innocence is lost, and the ritualistic pastimes now require safety measures that were once thought would never be needed in interscholastic sport. In much the same way as college and professional sports reacted after 9/11, this rash of violence has led interscholastic administrators to rethink their risk management plans and to consider heightened security tactics.

Event managers must constantly scan the environment for information, ideas, and potential issues that could influence their plans and expose a potential hazard for their event. You have studied the importance of risk management planning in this chapter. Now it is your turn to make some key decisions on how to handle a crisis like the ones listed above.

Football stadiums are sitting duck targets for violence. The size of the stadiums, even high school stadiums, presents challenges for administrators.

Case Study Application

1. Create a list of security measures you could implement in subsequent games that would help ease the fears of fans attending games.
2. For a few of these shootings the actual events had nothing to do with the game but only happened near the stadiums. Many of these were not classified as school shootings; rather, they were seen as community issues. You are responsible to those in attendance to keep them safe through any incident. What would be your plan of action (CMP) for an active shooter at or near your stadium? (Note: One of the shooters in an above incident was ushered into the gym along with the fans.)

Mitchell Layton/Getty Images

CHAPTER 10

Event Staffing

CHAPTER OBJECTIVES

After completing the chapter, the reader should be able to do the following:

- Describe organizational structure and explain the use of an organizational chart in event management.
- Analyze the factors taken into account when staffing a sport event.
- Explain various tools used in scheduling staff.
- List reasons why organizations might use outsourcing for their events.
- Present and describe a number of motivational theories.
- Provide suggestions for adopting a personal management and leadership style.
- Discuss the stages of meeting management.
- Define communication and describe various forms of social media.
- Highlight the need for event volunteers.

INDUSTRY PROFILE

Mandy Adkins, San Antonio Sports Commission

Mandy Adkins has been involved in planning numerous events with the San Antonio Sports Commission. She holds both a bachelors and a masters degree in sport and recreation management from James Madison University in Virginia. She has worked as a regional trainer for the Virginia State Police Association and as the recreation director for the Shenandoah Valley United soccer club. In 2014, Adkins moved to San Antonio, Texas, where she has served as the youth programs manager and in her current position as director of youth and community programs.

What are your primary responsibilities in this job? Please describe a typical day.

San Antonio Sports serves as the local sports commission in San Antonio, but our heart beats for kids. The mission of San Antonio Sports is to transform the community through the power of sport. One of the ways we do that is through the youth and community programs that I oversee. My primary responsibilities are overseeing the planning and execution of San Antonio Sports' four youth and community programs: i play! afterschool, Fit Family Challenge, Go!Kids Challenge, and KiDS ROCK. The two largest programs, i play! afterschool and Fit Family Challenge fill the majority of my time. The i play! afterschool program teaches early stage development to third- to fifth-graders in five sports. Each unit is five weeks long and culminates at a program-wide sports tournament every five weeks during the school year. The program is currently offered in 48 elementary schools and serves 1,200 students annually. Fit Family Challenge is a free health and wellness program designed to get families active, eating better, and learning about health and fitness. Fit Family Challenge hosts eight free group fitness classes per week for 12 weeks during the summer and a large community event on a Saturday morning every three weeks. In my line of work, every day is different. Some days are spent in the office proofreading grants, evaluating program data, and event planning. Other days are spent out of the office implementing program events or visiting our i play! afterschool or Fit Family Challenge program sites.

Provide a list of your most recent events and describe some of your job duties that may relate to staffing for the event.

San Antonio Sports has three different types of events: events that bring economic impact (e.g., the 2018 NCAA Men's Final Four), owned events (e.g., the San Antonio Sports High School All Star Football Game), and youth and community program events. The latter take place every three to five weeks year round and are free to participants and their families. At these events, I am the primary event manager and responsible for the planning and execution of the event from start to finish.

San Antonio Sports has a fairly small staff (20 people) and so many of our events are all-hands-on-deck events. At these events our staff serve as ticket takers, game operations staff, program salesmen, and much more! The most recent major event in San Antonio was the 2018 NCAA Men's Final Four. My duties during this event included working in the NCAA office, implementing the memento program and providing staff support at the community and legacy program events throughout Final Four weekend.

How important are volunteers to an event, and what are some ways you motivate them to return?

Volunteers are an integral part to every event, no matter the event size. San Antonio Sports relies on our network of volunteers. We have an incredible group of volunteers who help make all our events a success. We strive to get to know our volunteers and help them have a great experience. Our volunteer manager works to align volunteers' interests and experiences with volunteer positions. In addition, San Antonio Sports hosts regular volunteer appreciation events to thank our volunteers.

What are your biggest challenges in terms of working with volunteers?

The biggest challenge when working with volunteers is attrition rates. Our volunteer manager carefully estimates the number of volunteers needed for an event and then tries to calculate how many of those may not show up on event day, based on different factors such as the day of the week of the event, time of day, weather, and holidays. In preparation for attrition, the volunteer manager recruits more volunteers than needed.

When planning a large event like the NCAA Final Four, how often do you have meetings? Who is involved in the meetings? Can you describe a typical meeting, or is every meeting different?

When planning for a large event like the NCAA Men's Final Four, meetings happen on a regular basis. As the event gets closer, the meetings may take place on a weekly or even daily basis. The San Antonio Local Organizing Committee (SALOC) is made up of San Antonio Sports, the City of San Antonio, and the host institutions (UTSA for 2018 and UTSA and UIW for 2025). Planning for an event like this begins years in advance. The NCAA staff visits San Antonio on a regular basis for meetings in the year leading up to the event. Each meeting leading up to a large event is different.

Planning and implementing a sporting event can be a complex process. Consider, for example, the numerous stakeholders involved (e.g., athletes, coaches, venues, hotels, sponsors, rights holders, sports commissions), the organizations, and the people within each organization. In many cases, multiple technologies are employed, and for those events that travel from place to place, new cultures are explored. In addition, events must adhere to government and environmental regulations. There are a number of reasons why you need an **organizational chart** for a sporting event. The organizational chart defines areas of responsibility and accountability, helps streamline decision-making, and assists in more clearly communicating to those who work within an organization and to key external contacts (Supovitz 2005). Most importantly, the organizational chart helps employees understand levels of authority and responsibility. Although not all organizations involved in developing an event have an organizational chart in document form, the chart is important for letting employees know to whom they report, who reports to them, and what level of responsibility each has at a certain point in time (Goldblatt 2011).

Organizational Chart

The organizational chart displays the structure of an organization (i.e., the way an organization arranges its employees and jobs so that work can be performed and organizational goals met). Organizations may be characterized by a tall or a flat organizational structure. For example, the International Olympic Committee has a **tall organizational structure**. Tall structures have many levels of management, with each supervisor having a narrow span of control, meaning the number of employees each one is responsible for managing. The advantage of a tall organizational structure is this narrow span of control, which allows for close supervision of employees. Tall organizational structures are often referred to as *bureaucratic* in nature, which can be very beneficial in terms of the stability of the organization. Many large organizations, such as governments and educational institutions, have such a long history of survival because of their bureaucratic nature. On the other hand, as an organization grows and becomes a bureaucratic structure with multiple hierarchical layers, communications begin to break down, and it takes too long to exchange information between levels. Thus, **flat organizational structures** (e.g., USA Field Hockey) can be advantageous because of their flexibility and consequent ability to adapt to change. Flat structures have fewer management levels and a broader span of control. This structure gives employees more autonomy, allowing them to be more innovative and flexible in solving problems and making decisions.

Although the traditional organizational chart is helpful for defining relationships within the organization, sporting events are often planned and implemented by networks of multiple organizations. Because of these interorganizational relationships, a good strategy for developing an organizational chart is to break the event into functions. According to Supovitz (2005), typical functional areas for sport event organizations include the following:

- *Operations*: Facility management (e.g., ticket takers, ushers, security, first aid, EMTs), staff and vendor accreditation, transportation, office services, staff uniforms and attire
- *Competition*: Tournament and competition scheduling, athlete scheduling and communications, playing field preparation and maintenance, competitive equipment acquisition and maintenance, officiating and judging, training facilities, equipment, athlete medical services
- *Guest services*: Ticketing, VIP invitation and seating, VIP gifts, VIP hospitality, information guides, hotel room and function space management
- *Marketing*: Sponsorship, creative services (e.g., logo development, style manual, printed materials, marketing artwork, sponsor signage), advertising, promotions, publicity, merchandising
- *Presentation*: Creative services (e.g., rundowns, scripting, music, costumes, and wardrobe), production management (e.g., talent booking of announcers and entertainers, rehearsal scheduling), stage management, scoreboard operations, video production and technical production (e.g., staging and set construction, lighting, sound, special effects such as lasers and pyrotechnics)
- *Other common functional areas*: Hospitality and social events (e.g., receptions, parties), fan festivals and activities, business affairs (e.g., accounts payable, accounts receivable, purchasing, and legal), broadcasting on television, radio, and the Internet

Identifying Necessary Staff

Identifying necessary staff members is key to the success of any sporting event. Perhaps no industry is as dependent as the event industry on the management functions of planning and organizing. *Planning* involves setting organizational goals in order to reach objectives; *organizing* is the process of allocating your human resources in an effort to accomplish the organization's goals. Numerous factors must be taken into account when a sport event manager analyzes staffing needs, including the following:

- *The type of event being planned*. Types of events include action and extreme events, cross-cultural events, events for people with disabilities, family events, fixed and nonfixed events, international events, mega-events, multisport events, multiple-location events, senior events, small-scale events, and youth events. Some events require specialized staffing needs. For example, international or cross-cultural events may require staff to speak multiple languages, mega-events may require a very large staff, and events for people with disabilities may require various health-related specialists, and family events may require personnel who are familiar with working with children.

- *Destination-specific factors*. The location of the event is a major factor, especially in relation to volunteers. Sporting events being hosted by smaller-market destinations may not have the same access to a large database of volunteers. Another destination-specific factor is the level of support and assistance in securing staffing by the host destination. Some sports commissions and convention and visitors bureaus provide better support than others. A third factor may be the demographics of the destination. Depending on the staffing needs of the particular event, certain destinations may have the ability to staff more effectively; for example, Arizona has a large population of elderly citizens who are willing volunteers. A fourth and final destination-specific factor is the current economic environment of the host region. For example, in geographic regions with high levels of unemployment at the time of an event, it seems reasonable to believe that residents would be seeking employment. This is a detriment when the staffing needs are primarily volunteer, because such depressed regions tend to provide fewer corporate volunteers.

- *Duration and time of event*. The longer an event lasts, the more staff you will need. A small-scale sporting event such as a three-hour baseball game played on a Tuesday evening is easier to staff than a mega-event such as the Olympic Games or the Paralympic Games, which occur over the course of a two-week period and entail multiple events lasting multiple hours each.
- *Functional factors*. Some factors are specific to the functional skills of employees. In the section on organizational charts earlier in this chapter, we listed a variety of functional areas such as marketing, operations, guest services, competition, and presentation. Certain staffing positions require greater training and skill than others. For example, ticket takers and ushers require less training and specialized skill than do officials. Generally there are significantly more potential employees to fill a ticket taker position than those employees who have been specially trained to officiate.
- *Relationship with organizational actors within the sporting event network*. As suggested earlier, the planning of a sporting event requires the collaboration of a number of representatives from the multiple organizations that make up a sporting event network. For example, an event may require the staffing of officials from the league office, local government officials, a local hotel, media, sponsors, and many other actors. The relationships that develop between these interorganizational actors are vitally important to the success of the event (Shonk and Bravo 2010). In this respect, a rights holder who has a very strong relationship with an existing sponsor may be able to staff the event with employees who work for the sponsorship organization. For example, since 2005, toymaker Mattel, Inc. has had more than 8,500 employees from 35 countries volunteer at hundreds of local and national sporting events. One of Mattel's strong partnerships is with the Special Olympics, and between 2013 and 2017 the organization had more than 35 percent (amounting to 11,100 employees) of their global workforce volunteer at Special Olympics competitions (Special Olympics 2018).

Scheduling Staff

Scheduling the appropriate number of staff members who are qualified to carry out the objectives of the event is critically important. Some organizations use a project management system to assist with scheduling full-time, part-time, and volunteer staff. According to Goldblatt (2011), in a project management system, tasks are usually divided into two types of scheduling: parallel and serial. *Parallel scheduling* refers to tasks that may be performed at the same time; *serial scheduling* refers to tasks that must be performed in a sequence. An example of parallel scheduling would be the tasks pertaining to merchandising at a baseball game, which may entail operating cash machines at multiple locations or hawking concessions in multiple seating sections. A good example of serial scheduling would be the tasks involved in public address announcements at the same baseball game, which may begin with the starting lineup, followed by the national anthem, and then the first pitch, in this particular order for every game. Similarly, the grounds crew must complete their field maintenance before the players take to the field for the start of the game. Staff scheduling should take into account tasks before, during, and after the event.

Staffing Before the Event

A number of factors must be taken into account when scheduling staff before an event. Perhaps the most important question facing event planners is what must be completed before the event takes place. Goldblatt (2011) suggests that once the event is clearly defined, the work must be carefully analyzed and divided into smaller units of work called tasks. Tasks are singular, independent entities that are individually managed, require clearly assigned resources (e.g., labor, finance), and have specific start and finish times. Certain tasks cannot be completed once the event is under way. For example, most caterers require that food orders be placed before the event. Obviously, print programs cannot be produced while the event is taking place, and tasks such as busing require prior planning to meet the requirements necessary for servicing event attendees.

Once a clear list of tasks has been developed, it is easier to divide the work and schedule staff for specific tasks. Supovitz (2005) recommends using a critical dates calendar, which is distributed to a wide audience. Everyone listed in the responsibility column of the calendar should receive a copy, and confidential or sensitive information should be deleted from widely distributed calendars.

Table 10.1 shows a sample critical dates calendar that outlines necessary tasks such as calling and scheduling busing, ordering equipment, and securing a title sponsor. Maria is responsible for calling and scheduling the busing; she started on January 2 and needs to complete this task by June 1, 2019. Thomas is responsible for ordering equipment and has less than a month to accomplish this task between January 2 and January 30, 2019. Michael and Sara are working on securing a title sponsor for the event; they have a full year to accomplish this task between January 2 and December 31, 2019.

Staffing During the Event

Almost any event planner will tell you that the keys to success are planning and preparation. Once the event begins, planning is over and event maintenance and operations kick in. Now the goal is to implement the plans that were made before the event. One of the key staffing goals during the event is to have enough workers scheduled so that the event runs smoothly. Still, supervisors should monitor staffing issues during the event to make sure that workers are actually needed in various positions. Supovitz (2005) describes a number of tools that can be developed beforehand and used during the event. These tools include the event rundown, scripts, production schedules, and cast lists, all of which are very helpful in the scheduling process.

The **event rundown** is an event presentation tool that outlines the precise details of how the event will unfold, including a description of various activities, the time and duration of activities, and any audiovisual needs. During the event, the host or public address announcer should read from a script that details important components of the event such as player introductions, customer service information, sponsor acknowledgments, game analysis, and the introduction of special performers such as the one who will sing the national anthem. The **production schedule** highlights all the activities at the event facility and is the primary tool for the actual presentation of the event. Some events may also include a **cast list**, which is a roster identifying the various people or groups and listing their roles or functions as defined in the running order.

A sample production schedule for the Dodge National Circuit Finals Rodeo (DNCFR) in 2019 is provided in table 10.2. For example, on Wednesday, March 30, the stall office opened for contestants at 8:00 a.m. and remained open until 6:00 p.m. The barrel stakes needed to be set for the Women's Professional Rodeo Association at 10:30 a.m. The schedule also indicates times and locations for working and running the timed event cattle and the DNCFR kickoff party from 7:00 to 9:30 p.m. at the Renaissance Hotel.

TABLE 10.1 Sample Critical Dates Calendar

Task	Start date	End date	Responsibility
Call and schedule busing	1/2/19	6/1/19	Maria
Order equipment	1/2/19	1/30/19	Thomas
Secure title sponsorship	1/2/19	12/31/19	Michael, Sara

TABLE 10.2 Sample Production Schedule for the Dodge National Circuit Finals Rodeo 2019

Day/date/time	Activity	Location
Wednesday, March 30		
8:00 a.m. to 6:00 p.m.	Stall office open for contestants	HP / KI
10:30 a.m.	Set barrel stakes for WPRA	TG / WPRA
1:00 p.m. to 2:00 p.m.	Work and run timed event cattle: SW	Ted / FT / JG / TC
2:00 p.m. to 3:00 p.m.	Work and run timed event cattle: CR	Ted / FT / JG / TC
3:00 p.m. to 4:00 p.m.	Work and run timed event cattle: TR	Ted / FT / JG / TC
7:00 p.m. to 9:30 p.m.	DNCFR kickoff party at Renaissance Hotel	ML / All

Staffing After the Event

The staffing plan should be evaluated at the conclusion of a sporting event. Both supervisors and all staff who worked the event, including volunteers, should be included in the evaluation process. Critical areas of evaluation include identifying tasks or activities that were either overstaffed or understaffed. In addition, supervisors should conduct exit interviews with volunteers as well as a brief performance appraisal of staff members. Key staff should also provide feedback concerning the strengths and weaknesses of the event, along with identifying additional human and material resource needs that would improve the event.

Considering Outsourcing Staff

The global outsourcing market grew steadily each year between 2000 and 2012, but has been unsteady more recently with revenues of global outsourced services amounting to $82.9 billion in 2013, $104.6 billion in 2014, $88.9 billion in 2015, $76.9 billion in 2016, and $88.9 billion in 2017 (Statista 2018). Mol (2007) defines **outsourcing** as the state or process of procuring goods and services from external suppliers. According to Burden and Li (2009), "outsourcing is a means of providing the organization access to highly skilled and knowledgeable personnel often not available in-house and increased flexibility in conducting business" (p. 139). Many examples of outsourcing across multiple segments of the sport industry can be cited. Most notably, athletic programs at colleges and universities throughout North America have focused on outsourcing such items as merchandise, tickets, and advertising, radio, and broadcast rights. Georgia Tech's outsourcing to Aspire Group to handle ticket sales for football and men's basketball was the first case of a university outsourcing its ticket operations (Lombardo and Smith 2009). In 2009, Ohio State outsourced their marketing and media rights to IMG College for a guaranteed $110 million over 10 years, making it the richest annual rights fee ever given to a university (Smith 2009). Not to be outdone, the University of Texas is now paid $12.7 million annually for their multimedia rights; the University of Georgia is paid $10.6 million; and in 2017, Ohio State University received $10.2 million to sell advertisements and sponsorships at athletic events (Knox 2017).

The reasons companies outsource may vary depending on the circumstances. Burden and Li (2009) suggest that companies generally outsource for one of the following four reasons:

1. Outsourcing helps companies operate in a more efficient manner by focusing in-house resources on core competencies while outsourcing peripheral functions.
2. Outsourcing provides the company with economies of scale because the unit cost charged by the service providers is generally reduced because they are dealing with multiple organizations at one time.

3. Companies that outsource eliminate personnel costs such as recruitment, retention, and employee relations. The company gains access to highly skilled and knowledgeable personnel who may not be available in-house.
4. Companies outsource because they do not have the technical expertise in-house, the resources to invest in new technology, or the ability to train staff.

A wide variety of functional areas are outsourced in the sport industry. For example, concession operations are often outsourced to companies such as Aramark, Levy Restaurants, and Centerplate. These companies operate concessions in major professional leagues, such as the NFL, the NBA, and the NHL as well as Major League Baseball and Major League Soccer, and in minor league venues, convention centers, and entertainment centers. Ticketing is another functional area that is often outsourced. Ticketmaster is the largest company in this market, serving thousands of events; in 2009 it was appointed the official ticketing services provider for the London 2012 Olympic Games and Paralympic Games (Ticketmaster 2012). The sale of marketing and media rights along with scoreboard operations are also often outsourced, and some organizations choose to outsource the maintenance of their athletic fields. For example, Lakes Community High School, located in a Chicago suburb, outsources field maintenance requirements such as aeration to Lohmann Sports Fields, a company from Marengo, Illinois, that renovates, constructs, and maintains athletic fields (Phillips 2011). Similar companies, such as ABM Industries, provide services such as mowing, fertilization, pest control, aeration, overseeing, irrigation, field design, construction, and renovations for athletic fields and venues (ABM 2018).

The practice of outsourcing is becoming a larger part of the industry from a human resource perspective. Because of the transient nature of some sporting events that travel from market to market, the challenge of staffing is often solved by outsourcing. For these types of events, volunteers play a vital factor in staffing everything from concessions, merchandise booths, ticket booths, registration tables, welcome centers, hospitality tents, and shuttle services for players and coaches, along with performing other duties such as officiating, scorekeeping, and timing. In many instances, destination marketing organizations (DMOs) such as the regional convention and visitors bureau or **sports commission** can be very helpful in assisting event planners with the recruitment of volunteers and other paid part-time employees. As noted by Mandy Adkins in the industry profile at the beginning of this chapter, a **sports commission** will help gather volunteers, which is a big component of what the commission is able to offer to the event rights holder. Upon booking an event, some DMOs will state in the contract the number of part-time employees they will provide for the event. In some cases, the staffing is outsourced to temporary employment agencies such as Manpower or Kelly Services. According to the American Staffing Association (2012), U.S. staffing companies such as these hired 15.49 million temporary and contract employees in 2017 with an average length of employment of 10.7 weeks. Using a temporary employment agency can be an excellent way to make sure that the functional needs of a sporting event are fully staffed. Some temporary agencies are more reputable than others; event planners should do some research before choosing a company.

Managing and Motivating Staff

Managing and motivating an event staff can be a challenge at times, but these tasks are vitally important to the success of the event. The primary challenge may be that the event planner is managing a staff of both full-time and part-time employees as well as volunteers. A one-off event may be happening so soon that it leaves little time for the event planner not only to train employees but also to build any type of cohesion among them. Job performance is considered a function of one's ability multiplied by motivation multiplied by resources

(Lussier and Kimball 2009). Although many management scholars agree on the importance of hiring talented people who are highly skilled and knowledgeable, there is no consensus as to how to motivate employees. A number of theories have emerged throughout the years regarding employee motivation, including those offered by Taylor and colleagues.

Frederick Taylor's Scientific Theory

In the late 1800s, Frederick Taylor argued that employees are primarily motivated by pay. Taylor's scientific theory of management suggests that employees do not naturally like work and therefore need close supervision. Scientific management theorized that how tasks were performed could be optimized by simplifying the jobs in order to train workers to perform a specialized sequence of motions in the one "best" way. Thus, workers were focused on one set task and encouraged to work hard in an effort to maximize productivity. But the routine nature of these tasks soon became boring for many employees, and it became apparent that this approach to motivation treated employees more like machines than like human beings.

Elton Mayo's Human Relations School

Between 1927 and 1932, Elton Mayo conducted a series of experiments at the Hawthorne factory of the Western Electric Company in Chicago, Illinois. Coming from the Taylor school, Mayo soon learned that workers were motivated not only by money but also by having their social needs met. In essence, Mayo found that scientific management was unable to explain certain aspects of employee behavior in the workplace. Workers were best motivated when managers and employees had better communication, when there was greater management involvement with the employees, and when employees worked in teams. Mayo's research suggested that recognition, a sense of belonging, and job security were important factors for employees.

Maslow's Hierarchy of Needs Theory

In the 1940s and 1950s, Abraham Maslow developed his hierarchy of needs theory, which highlighted the responsibility of employers to provide an environment that encourages their employees to reach self-actualization. The thrust of Maslow's theory is that human beings are motivated by unsatisfied needs and that certain lower-level needs must be addressed before a person can meet the next level of needs. The first level is physiological needs such as hunger and thirst. Safety needs such as security and protection are the second level of needs. Third, people need to be loved and feel a sense of belonging, which Maslow referred to as social needs. Only when these lower-level needs are met can a person progress to higher-level needs such as esteem and self-actualization. Esteem includes such needs as self-esteem, recognition, and status. Self-actualization is the summit of Maslow's needs and can never be fully satisfied.

Herzberg's Two-Factor Theory

Closely linked to Maslow, Frederick Herzberg developed a two-factor theory consisting of hygiene factors and motivational factors. Hygiene factors are those that surround the job rather than the job itself. They are essential for the existence of motivation in the workplace and when absent lead to dissatisfaction in the workplace. Hygiene factors may include pay, safe working conditions, company policies, fringe benefits, job security, status in the workplace, and interpersonal relationships. Motivational factors are more concerned with the job itself, yield positive satisfaction, and motivate employees to strive for superior performance. Herzberg referred to motivational factors as satisfiers, and employees are intrinsically motivated by these factors. Motivational factors may include recognition, job enlargement, job enrichment, sense of achievement, responsibility, and meaningfulness of an employee's work.

Other Studies on Motivation

Some studies suggest that various motivational tactics can lead to desirable behaviors and thus greater performance. For example, Perry, Mesch, and Paarlberg (2006) suggest that financial incentives and challenging and specific goals improve an employee's task performance. Numerous studies have shown that employees become more loyal when they receive praise and recognition from supervisors. Nelson (1999) provides the following low-cost suggestions for developing a loyal and committed group of employees.

- *Interesting work*. The duties of employees working in the event industry may change on a daily basis. For example, one day an employee may need to travel to conduct a site visit, while the next day she may be on the computer developing a proposal for a client. Although the work for an event planner never gets boring, this may not be true for part-time and volunteer employees involved in game-day operations such as ticket takers or parking attendants. The key to keeping such employees motivated may be to provide training for multiple jobs and to rotate them between jobs.
- *Information*. Employees want and need to have the information required to do their jobs effectively. Volunteer and part-time workers often believe they are not provided with adequate information. A study by Taylor and colleagues (2006) found that volunteers expect management to consult them regarding their positions and tasks, but this rarely happened. Employees also desire feedback as to how they are doing in their jobs. *Inc.* magazine suggests that employers open the channels of communication, allowing employees to be informed, ask questions, and share information.
- *Involvement*. Employees appreciate being involved in decision-making, and as you involve others, you increase their commitment and facilitate the implementation of new ideas. There are a number of ways to get employees involved in various aspects of an event. You can assign them various leadership roles, ask for feedback, empower them to make certain decisions, and generally let them know on a regular basis that you value their involvement.
- *Independence*. Most employees appreciate the autonomy of not having someone looking over their shoulder so they can do their jobs as they see fit. With any job, but especially with volunteers and short-term labor, it is always a good idea to set guidelines and highlight your expectations, but once you have done so, it is best not to micromanage your employees.
- *Increased visibility*. Most people need a pat on the back or a compliment every once in a while. Managers who do this and provide their employees with new opportunities to learn and grow as a form of recognition are highly prized.

Personal Management Style and Effective Leadership

Leadership is critically important to the success of a sporting event. Although early leadership studies focused on the individual leader, today the study of leadership also focuses on additional factors such as followers, peers, work setting, supervisors, and culture (Avolio, Walumbwa, and Weber 2009). Scholars have set forth numerous definitions of leadership. Chelladurai (2005) suggests that most definitions of leadership contain the following three significant elements: (1) Leadership is a behavioral process, (2) leadership is interpersonal in nature, and (3) leadership is aimed at influencing and motivating members toward group or organizational goals. Bass (1990) defined leadership as an "interaction between two or more members of a group that often involves a structuring or restructuring of the situation and the perceptions and expectations of the members" (p. 19). Tosi and Mero (2003) defined leadership as a "form of organizationally based problem-solving that attempts to achieve organizational goals by influencing the action of others" (p. 248).

The successful planning and implementation of a sporting event is critically dependent on strong leadership. A leader in the sport event industry must be capable of influencing people within multiple organizations and representatives of various stakeholder groups to achieve common goals for the advancement and successful implementation of the event. Regardless of your job title, if you work in the sport event industry, you will be asked to take on a leadership role. Some questions to consider include the following: What leadership traits do I possess? What steps can I take to become a more effective leader? What is my role in the leadership process? What style of leadership describes me?

According to Chelladurai (2005), leadership theories fall into three categories: trait theories, behavioral theories, and situational theories:

1. *Trait theories*. This approach assumes that people inherit certain traits that make them better suited for leadership. The early research on leadership tried to identify specific traits such as height, weight, age, intelligence, personality, dominance, aggression, self-esteem, and achievement.

2. *Behavioral theories*. Contrary to the trait approach, the behavioral approach to leadership assumes that leaders are made and not born. Research studies at Ohio State University and the University of Michigan supported the thought that leader behavior was a significant factor.

    - The Ohio State studies indicated that nine behaviors were indicative of leader activity. Later research condensed these nine behaviors into two broad categories: consideration and initiating structure. **Consideration** is defined as the leader's concern for member well-being and warm and friendly relations within the group. **Initiating structure** is defined as the leader's concern for the effective performance of the group's tasks.
    - The Michigan studies also identified two styles of leadership behavior, employee orientation and production orientation. **Employee orientation** is defined as the degree to which a leader is concerned about human relations on the job, while **production orientation** highlights the degree to which the leader is concerned about the technical aspects of the job and about productivity.

3. *Situational theories*. Different styles of leadership may be most appropriate for making specific decisions, therefore leaders must take situational variables into account. Three common situational theories include Fiedler's (1967) contingency model of leadership, House's (1971) path-goal theory, and Osborn and Hunt's (1975) adaptive-reactive theory of leadership.

    - Fiedler's (1967) contingency model of leadership: Fiedler sought to determine the orientation of the leader (relationship or task); the elements of the situation (leader-member relations, task structure, and the leader's position power); and the leader orientation found to be most effective as the situation changed from low to moderate to high control. Fiedler found task-oriented leaders to be more effective in low- and moderate-control situations and relationship-oriented managers more effective in moderate-control situations.
    - House's (1971) path-goal theory of leadership: The path-goal theory focuses on members' personal goals, their perception of organizational goals, and the most effective paths to these goals. This theory suggests that a leader should motivate subordinates by emphasizing the relationship between the subordinates' own needs and the organizational goals as well as clarifying and facilitating the path subordinates must take to fulfill their needs and the organization's needs.
    - Osborn and Hunt's (1975) adaptive-reactive theory: Osborn and Hunt conceptualized leader behavior as a dichotomy consisting of adaptive and reactive behavior. Adaptive behavior is concerned with how much the leader adapts to the requirements of the organizational system. Reactive

behavior considers the leader's behavior in reaction to member preferences and the various differences among the tasks performed by members.

Environmental factors and the changing and evolving nature of organizations have had an impact on leadership. An environmental factor such as the economy can impact leadership and how a leader allocates resources. The complexity of planning and implementing a sporting event is evident when we consider that multiple organizations, people, and stakeholder groups are attempting to deliver a carefully crafted experience that is so polished that the mechanics are imperceptible to the consumer. This goal becomes increasingly complex when you consider that each of these organizations, people, and stakeholder groups has diverse goals and objectives. A strong leader can take these diverse goals and focus on the primary goals of the event. The changing climate of business requires leaders who can also transform organizations. Transactional and transformational leadership are two popular styles of leading.

Transactional Leadership Style

According to Yukl (1981), **transactional leadership** involves exchanges in which both the leader and the subordinate influence one another reciprocally, each deriving something of value. Both the leader and the followers receive something they want (Kuhnert and Lewis 1987). Chelladurai (2005) suggests that transactional leadership is a very fruitful approach when the environment of the work group is stable and when both the leader and the followers are satisfied with the work group's purposes and processes. To be effective, transactional leaders must regularly meet the expectations of their followers; effective transactional leadership depends on the leader's ability to meet and respond to the reactions and changing expectations of the followers. Most sporting events are planned between representatives from multiple organizations, therefore leadership is often transactional because of the expectation that various organizations will exchange resources in an effort to create a successful event.

Transformational Leadership

The critical focus of transformational leadership is the vision and a general discontent with the status quo. Transformational leaders are often described as charismatic. **Transformational leadership** originates in personal values and beliefs and can be defined as "the process of influencing major changes in the attitudes and assumptions of organization members (organizational culture) and building commitment for major changes in the organization's objectives and strategies" (Yukl and Van Fleet 1992, p. 174). According to this definition, Chelladurai (2005) suggests that transformation occurs at three levels: (1) an organization's objectives and strategies, (2) a member's commitment to goals and strategies, and (3) a member's assumptions and attitudes. Through their personal values and beliefs, transformational leaders are able to both change follower goals and beliefs and unite them (Kuhnert and Lewis 1987). The end result of transformational leadership is higher levels of performance by followers (Bass 1985).

Management Meetings

In the event industry, it is not unusual for an event planner's entire day to be consumed by meetings. Endless meetings can be both boring and tiring, but meetings do not have to be this way. It is important for event planners to become proficient at meeting management. Depending on your role within the organization and in planning the event, you may be required either to call meetings or to attend them. Meeting attendees may include employees within your organization and representatives of network organizations involved in planning the event. Each of these network organizations probably has a stake in the event. Numerous stakeholders may attend the meeting, including government officials, sponsors, governing and sanctioning bodies, sport venue personnel, representatives from the organization that owns the rights to the events, local businesses, sports commissions, convention and visitors bureaus, chambers of commerce, local hoteliers, representatives from local attractions and rental car companies, and security personnel.

Poorly planned meetings can influence a sporting event. Streibel (2007) suggests that bad meetings waste time, talent, and resources and can negatively affect the climate, culture, and image of an organization, whereas good meetings help answer questions, assist in the discovery of new questions, and allow for discussing important issues and reaching decisions as a group. Francisco (2007) provides guidance for planning and running a successful meeting using crucial checklists. She claims that creating and facilitating effective meetings requires (1) preparation, (2) conducting and documenting the meeting, and (3) following up after the meeting. The following section discusses each of these stages.

Stage 1: Preparing for the Meeting

One of the first questions to consider is whether or not you actually need to call a meeting. Francisco suggests that meetings are needed for the following reasons:

- To present information that is better delivered in person
- To get input from others
- To gain buy-in on an issue
- To motivate and energize a team or individuals
- To solve problems

When considering whether you should meet, Francisco suggests taking the following important questions into account:

- Can you state the purpose of the meeting?
- Is the purpose of the meeting worth the participants' time?
- Would an e-mail or phone call produce a more efficient result than calling a meeting?
- Do you truly want or need participant input?
- Will you truly act on participant input?
- Do you have all the information you need to meet productively?
- Have you given yourself and the participants enough time to prepare for the meeting?
- Are the participants able to work together on the issues necessitating the meeting?

If you do call a meeting, it is important to set a purpose for the meeting and to develop objectives that will be accomplished during the meeting. You also need to develop and distribute an agenda, secure a meeting location, and inform attendees of the meeting date, purpose, and location.

Stage 2: Conducting and Documenting the Meeting

Because everyone is so busy, some staff will enter a meeting without adequately preparing for it. Francisco suggests that meeting facilitators attempt to get everyone on the same page by leading an exercise that highlights the purpose and objectives of the meeting and by having the group identify norms for behavior. During the meeting, the facilitator needs to strike a balance in how the group approaches critical and creative thinking. The group can become overwhelmed with too much creative thinking; alternatively, excessive critical thinking can lead to situations where ideas are not given enough time to come to life. Another component of this stage is documenting the discussion, decisions, and actions that take place in the meeting. Facilitators should delegate the responsibility of taking meeting minutes to another staff member involved in the meeting.

Stage 3: Following Up After the Meeting

Particularly in the sport event industry, the real work begins at the conclusion of a meeting. Follow-up and follow-through are critical components of the successful implementation of an event. Meeting minutes will need to be distributed, and action items from the meeting will need to be carried out. In particular, specific action items in the minutes should be documented for further follow-up along with listing the staff member responsible for each item.

Communicating With Staff

Communication is defined as "the process of transmitting or interchanging information thoughts, or ideas through speech, writing, images or signs" (Irwin, Sutton, and McCarthy 2008). Communicating with staff members is vital for success, especially before and during the implementation of a sporting event. Staff communication can take place in a number of ways, including direct interpersonal communication, social media, and on-site event communications.

Direct Interpersonal Communication

Although we live in a society where direct human interactions have largely been replaced by the newest and trendiest forms of technology, employees still need and want strong interpersonal relationships with their coworkers. This involves face-to-face interactions between a sender and a receiver of a message. Interpersonal communication is so important because it provides that human link we all need.

The key to effective communication is listening to staff and conveying a sense that you understand their issues and concerns (deLisle 2009). But it also involves clear and consistent communication with employees. Employees develop a sense of direction and focus and exhibit a higher level of satisfaction when communication is clear and simple (Green 2009). Providing feedback is also an important element of building a relationship because it closes the circle of communication that links the listener and speaker. The people involved in the communication are either speakers or listeners until feedback is provided. Once the speaker receives feedback, the roles switch and both parties are equally involved in the conversation (Axzo Press 2002).

Social Media

Social media is a vital part of the sport event management industry, especially when event planning involves a wide variety of stakeholders. At a rapidly increasing pace, organizations are using social media as a way to communicate with each other. Some of the types of social media used in the planning and implementation of sporting events are listed here.

- *Social networks*. Websites that connect people. Facebook is a popular social networking site that allows users to connect with friends, share photos, and send messages. It allows users to create a profile and a timeline that chronicle their lives. Event planners use this site to cultivate relationships with attendees, families, friends, colleagues, and clients.
- *Blogs*. Websites that allow authors and readers to engage in conversation. Authors write and record their information in the format of a diary. When writing a blog, authors should do the following:
    - Use plain language.
    - Organize content so it is easy to read.
    - Include bullets, bold letters, and key words.
    - Develop connections with the reader by sharing how work and personal life connect.
    - Use audio, video, photos, and images to enhance interest.
    - Provide links to supporting information.
    - Show readers where to find additional information (HowTo.gov 2012).

  Many websites provide free blogs; one of the most popular is WordPress. For example, *SportsEvents* magazine hosts a WordPress blog.
- *Microblogs*. Similar to a text message, microblogs allow the writer to post short messages. With more than 175 million users, Twitter is the most popular microblog. Twitter allows users and senders to receive and send photos, videos, and text-based posts of up to 280 characters. Event planners use Twitter to send out photos and videos along with short messages

to announce, promote, or provide information about an event or to provide recognition to an organization or a person.

- *Videos*. Videos can communicate a variety of types of information. A common website for videos is YouTube, which allows people to upload and watch originally created videos. Destination marketers use YouTube as a tool for selling a destination. For example, you can learn about the city of Louisville, Kentucky, if you type "Louisville, It's Possible Here" into the YouTube search bar. Event planners also use YouTube to promote and chronicle events. If you type in the name of the organization, you can learn more about the National Senior Games Association by watching its promotional video.
- *Discussion forums*. Also known as discussion boards, these are online communities that allow for discussions by groups with a common interest. Posts to the site are organized into related threads around questions and answers or by community discussions. Rivals is a popular website that provides discussion forums for high school and college sports. According to its website, Rivals (2012) drives what it calls the "ultimate fan experience" by integrating exclusive expert content into a network of team-based sites with message boards and various community tools.
- *Photo sharing*. Sites such as Flickr allow users to share their photos to a large audience via the Internet. Event planners may use photo sharing as a customer service and relationship marketing tool by posting event photos after the conclusion of the event. These photos can then be used by multiple parties for various purposes.

On-Site Event Communications

In many cases, the social media forms just described are used predominantly before and after a sporting event. However, on-site communication during the event is also critically important. Key staff personnel should be readily available during the course of an event. Staff members can communicate with each other and with other key stakeholders during the course of a sporting event in a number of ways. One way is via handheld two-way radio devices. Perhaps most often used is mobile technology, including cell phones, texting, and various mobile applications. A number of professional teams (e.g., the San Francisco 49ers) are using state-of-the art mobile applications that helps fans find parking spots, purchase premium seat upgrades, check in and locate their seats, order food and beverages to be delivered to their seats, find the closest restroom with the shortest line, watch high-definition instant replay videos and close-up videos, view exclusive content, promotions, coupons, and statistics, and get traffic information and the fastest route home after the game (Reddy 2015).

Volunteers

Volunteers are the lifeblood of most sporting events, especially for youth and amateur events that travel between markets. According to the U.S. Department of Labor Bureau of Labor Statistics (2016), 62.6 million people volunteered through or for an organization at least once between September 2014 and September 2015. Volunteering is "an activity which takes place through not for profit organizations or projects and is undertaken to be of benefit to the community and the volunteer; of the volunteer's own free will and without coercion; for no financial payment; and in designated volunteer positions only" (Cuskelly, Hoye, and Auld 2006, p. 5). According to Volunteer Canada (2017), approximately 30 percent of Canadians volunteer their time and 50 percent volunteer their money. In 2002, 14.8 percent of adults in England volunteered in sport programs (Sport England 2012).

Finding Volunteers

The quality of volunteers for a sporting event is directly related to the efforts by event planners to attract people who will make a positive contribution to the success of the event (deLisle 2009). According to Kim and Bang (2012), several factors are important in recruiting and

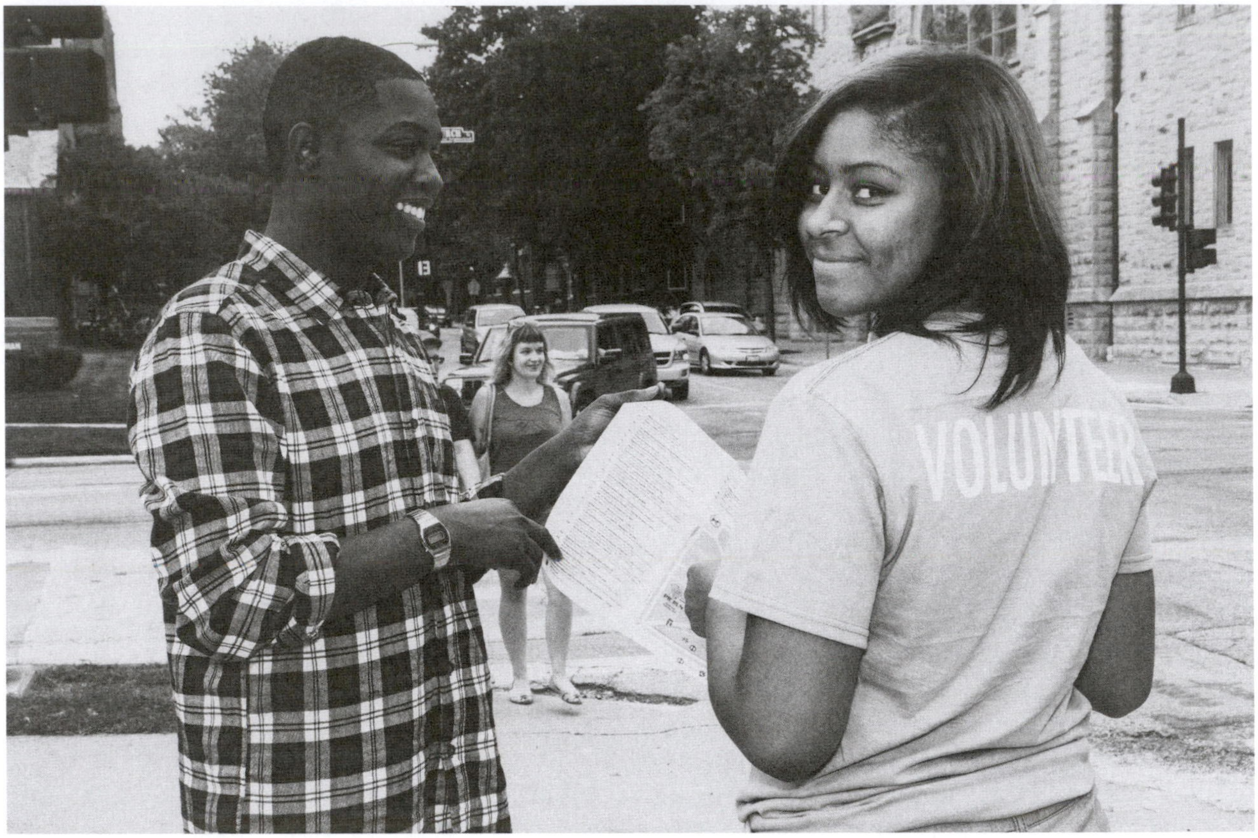

It is important to engage quality volunteers who will have a positive impact on the event.

hiring volunteers. First, it is important that managers understand the demographics and the motivation of volunteers. For example, the demographic makeup of volunteers for a marathon may be middle-aged males, while another event involving extreme sports may consist of younger volunteers. People's motivations may also differ. A volunteer may be motivated for egoistic, humanitarian, leisure, or career-related reasons. But most people volunteer because they want to be involved with something worthwhile, make the event a success, contribute to a better society, and give back to the community. Second, event managers should seek to identify individual fans and participants who may have an interest in volunteering. For example, avid golf fans may be willing to volunteer for an event such as the U.S. Open because they are rewarded with free tickets in exchange for their work. Third, it is important for event planners to place volunteers in positions that match their skill and aptitudes.

Working With Volunteers

Although the event industry is highly dependent on volunteers, utilizing them properly is one of the biggest challenges of many organizations. There are many reasons why volunteers are not effectively utilized; deLisle (2009) offers a number of strategies for enhancing the volunteer experience.

Organizations should interview volunteers and be prepared to answer questions related to the job such as the necessary responsibilities and qualifications. The sport organization should gain an understanding of the motivation of each volunteer and try to satisfy the volunteer's needs in terms of her motivations. As suggested by deLisle, some volunteers want to feel important as they carry around a two-way radio, and others simply want a free T-shirt. The interviewer should provide a volunteer with information about the organization and should start the process of developing a positive rapport with the candidate. The interviewer should also assist with placing the volunteer in a position in which he will succeed because of his qualifications and motivations.

Volunteer training is critical to the success of the event. Organizations spend months and years planning for a successful event that will be delivered both to participants and to spectators. Unfortunately, many of these same organizations do not train those persons who will be interacting with the event participants and spectators. Volunteer training should not happen on the job; rather, an orientation meeting should occur before the start of the event. According to deLisle, the orientation meeting should cover the following topics:

- Introduction to the organization and the staff
- Goals and objectives of the event
- Rights and responsibilities of volunteers
- Discussion and distribution of the volunteer manual
- Accident procedures
- Scheduling, attendance, and absenteeism
- Dress code
- Performance evaluation procedures
- Progressive discipline policies
- Parking and access to the site

Team Building

A **team** is a group of people who unite to accomplish a common mission or objective. Organizations develop teams in an effort to empower employees to contribute more fully and in order to increase productivity (Shonk 1992). In the case of a sporting event, a number of teams may be involved. For example, in a basketball game there are two teams contesting against each other, with the common objective of winning the game. Because event planners have no control over the outcome of the actual contest, they must have a much wider and holistic perspective on the sporting event. Healthy teams that regularly contribute and are committed to planning and resource funding are vital to the success of any sporting event.

According to Shonk (1982), teams function more effectively when they are able to meet regularly because they are in close physical proximity and have the appropriate skills and the levels of organizational authority present on the team. In contrast, poorly functioning teams are often characterized by a physical separation, which prevents them from meeting regularly. In addition, poorly functioning teams are often not given adequate resources to do the job, there is no recognition of team effort, and the leadership often does not even recognize that a team exists. One of the most important elements of a team is the trust between members. Lees (2011) provides the following suggestions for building trust on the team.

- When a team is new or changing, get everyone together to agree on how you will work together.
- Encourage and model honest and direct communication.
- Clearly support team members when they raise contentious and challenging issues.
- Be willing to admit weaknesses and mistakes and ask for help.
- Give others the benefit of the doubt before arriving at a negative conclusion.
- Focus time and energy on important issues, not politics.
- Offer and accept apologies without hesitation.

Summary

The planning and implementation of a sporting event can be a complex process because of the numerous stakeholders involved. Staffing the event is a key component of the planning process, and a number of tools such as organizational charts, event rundowns, scripts, production schedules, and cast lists can be helpful to event planners. Understanding the functional areas of event management such as operations, competition, guest services, marketing, and presentation is also a key component of effectively staffing the event. In addition to full-time staff, key personnel for a sporting event often include volunteers and part-time workers. One of the central components of an effective staffing plan is to align the qualifications, motivations, and abilities of these personnel with your needs in terms of the job descriptions.

Event planners have a wide variety of responsibilities in relation to staffing an event. In some cases the event planner must outsource staffing for such components of the event as concessions, merchandising, scoreboard operation, and hospitality. Event planners are often required to attend meetings and must serve in leadership roles. During these times, the event planner may assume either a transactional or a transformational leadership style. Event planners are always working toward developing a highly functional team that will effectively plan and implement the event. Communication with staff during the process may entail direct interpersonal communications along with the use of social media and on-site communications such as two-way radios. As you can see, meeting all these roles within the context of staffing a sporting event is a challenging proposition for an event planner. Therefore, she must be willing and able to adapt to change and to work with a wide variety of people, groups, and organizations staffing the event.

LEARNING ACTIVITIES

1. Volunteers are an excellent labor force for event managers, and the fact that they are not paid is helpful to the budget. Still, volunteers may need to be motivated and inspired to participate. Write a 7- to 10-sentence paragraph that outlines the reasons why someone should volunteer even though they will not be paid.
2. Imagine you are responsible for planning a 5K run on the campus of your college or university. Create an event run-down for how you would organize this event.
3. Have you volunteered with a nonprofit organization within the last year? If not, before the semester ends, please volunteer with one nonprofit organization (preferably a sport organization) for at least a portion of one day. What did you learn from volunteering? Other than completing this assignment, what other factors motivated you to volunteer? Finally, list this volunteer experience on your resume. It will be helpful as you move forward in your career.
4. Interview someone within the athletics department at your college or university and ask them the following questions: What services are outsourced within the athletics department? Why are these services outsourced? What are the advantages of outsourcing? The challenges?

CASE STUDY: STAFFING AT RHINO SPORTS & ENTERTAINMENT SERVICES

Rhino Sports & Entertainment Services is an event management company that provides game-day customer service to a variety of intercollegiate athletics programs. Their clients include athletics programs at Clemson University, Duke University, Liberty University, North Carolina A&T, Virginia Tech, and Wake Forest University. Established in 2012, the company is based in Winston-Salem, North Carolina, and was formed as an outgrowth of the Winston-Salem Dash Minor League Baseball Team. The company prides itself on providing superior customer service, and its employees seek to create a positive experience both for fans and for customers at each of these venues.

While it is not a large company, Rhino prides itself on recruiting high-quality people who are dedicated to enhancing the brand of the clients they represent, and focuses on training them to be even better. The company's training incorporates team-building activities that not only helps their leadership team but also helps to develop staff relationships so they will inform each other about their strengths, weaknesses, personalities, and unique skills. Rhino also believes in setting aside time for employees to be engaged in staff picnics and other informal staff gatherings that helps to create a more unified organization.

At the Virginia Tech property in Blacksburg, Virginia, Rhino employs approximately 300 part-time and five full-time employees. Rhino is responsible for all event staffing on the Virginia Tech campus, which includes everything from athletic to concert events, parking for events, and even security for a psychology exam on campus. The full time-staff at Rhino hire primarily two types of part-time employees: (1) security licensed personnel and (2) customer service personnel who are not licensed in security. Employees may be employed as ushers, security personnel, ticket scanners, bag checkers, field security (protecting players), or access control.

Licensed security personnel work in various locations around the sport facility on game days, and work front- and back-of-stage during security for concerts. Security personnel are responsible for checking bags, and generally speaking, for keeping all customers safe while they are in the venue. Virginia Tech has a clear-bag policy by which only items in a clear bag are allowed through the gate. All security personnel at Virginia Tech must adhere to a hands-off policy; they may not make any physical contact with customers. In the event of a serious security threat, these personnel are trained to contact the appropriate police jurisdiction.

The second type of part-time employee is not licensed in security, but must have excellent customer service skills. These employees work in various capacities around campus. Some of them are employed as house management personnel, required at any event with over 1,000 attendees on the Virginia Tech campus where there may be a need for attendees to evacuate. This requires an employee who can clearly communicate appropriate evacuation procedures and who possesses excellent customer service skills. Parking areas are another point of contact for these employees. There are 20 permit lots, public paid parking, and RV parking lots on campus. Training for parking personnel includes customer service and parking training. These people are trained as to know what types of tags to look for in various parking areas on campus, including recognizing hanging tags, year number, and game number. It is very important for these people to be detailed oriented to ensure that customers are displaying the appropriate tags. Their knowledge of campus has to be very good. Finally, some of these employees are positioned in premium areas such as the stadium suites, where they work as greeters or elevator attendants. Employees who are positioned in the suites must confirm that customers on their floor hold the appropriate credentials, only allowing those with appropriate credentials to access certain parts of the facility.

A good employee at Rhino is normally someone who is outgoing, smiles, and is approachable by attendees. This is emphasized during the two-and-a-half-hour customer service training that takes place on campus. During this time, Rhino staff learn the Rhino mission statement: "Unsurpassed customer service to every customer every time." Part of this training focuses on proper interactions with people, forming relationships with customers, building bonds, and taking care of customer needs while they are in the facility. Another aspect is positional training, which is unique based on where an employee works on campus (e.g., basketball arena, football stadium, parking area). During this time, employees learn more about the facility, where to park when arriving to work, checking in, and getting their uniform, and overall job expectations.

Case Study Application

1. Virginia Tech outsources their events to Rhino Sports & Entertainment. List three or four of the primary reasons why you think Virginia Tech would outsource and not run their athletic events in-house.
2. The case describes two types of part-time employees (licensed security personnel, and those who are not licensed in security) who work for Rhino at Virginia Tech. This chapter discusses a number of theories concerning motivation of employees. Using these theories, compare and contrast how a full-time Rhino employee might motivate these two types of employees.
3. The chapter suggests that volunteer training is critical to the success of an event. Based on what you have read in the case study, what areas of training does Rhino do best? Are there areas of training where Rhino could improve? Write a two-paragraph essay describing their areas of strength and weaknesses.
4. The case describes some team-building activities employed at Rhino. Outline two or three other strategies that Rhino might employ in an effort to build a stronger team of employees at Virginia Tech.

CHAPTER 11

Event Services and Logistics

CHAPTER OBJECTIVES

After completing the chapter, the reader should be able to do the following:

- Describe the logistical planning process and the timeline for a sporting event.
- Explain various logistical operations areas in the event process.
- Compare and contrast how logistics differ based on the type of sporting event.
- Be prepared to think critically about the numerous logistical activities that occur in a sporting event.
- Apply theoretical concepts that are important to event services and logistics.

INDUSTRY PROFILE

Dennis Robarge, Virginia Tech for Rhino Sports

Dennis Robarge is the account manager at Virginia Tech for Rhino Sports. Rhino Sports & Entertainment Services is an event management company that provides game-day customer service to a variety of intercollegiate athletics programs. At Virginia Tech, Rhino provides event staffing for all campus events, including athletics, concerts, and fraternity events. Robarge has a wealth of experience in sport management and in the managing of events. He started his career in radio and during his early career was as an assistant general manager in baseball in the New York-Penn League and the Carolina League. He has held top-level management positions as either president or general manager with teams in the East Coast Hockey League, the National Basketball Development League, and the Atlanta Dragway in the NHRA. He also ran a successful consulting company with clients ranging from sports teams to small businesses to nonprofit organizations.

How do you see your role as an event manager?

My role is somewhat dependent upon the size of the event. For larger events, I act as event manager, working closely with my staff to ensure the event is successful. For some of the smaller events, I have one of our supervisors serve as the event manager on the day of the event. My role is to do a lot of the preliminary work such as talking to the client, booking dates, and handling various background logistics. For example, some events have diagrams with very specific layouts and specifications. I prepare a briefing sheet and coordinate with my supervisor as to where our employees will be stationed throughout the entire event. We also discuss the primary purpose of the event and how this impacts our responsibilities and interactions on the day of the event. The briefing sheet normally includes the name of the event, the name and mobile phone number of a key Virginia Tech contact person, and a schedule of activities.

What is the thinking behind placing employees in certain areas throughout an event venue?

Once again, this is dependent upon the type of event. If the event involves alcohol, employees are positioned at all points of entry and exit to make sure the alcohol stays contained in areas licensed for alcohol consumption. For a concert, employees do both back- and front-of-stage security to make sure nobody jumps onstage. Employees are also positioned at points of entry and serve as bag-checkers. All of the bigger events on the Virginia Tech campus adhere to a clear bag policy. For athletic events, employees are positioned at points of entry, restricted access areas, and in parking areas.

What are some of the challenges related to managing an event on a large college campus?

Probably the biggest challenge in a lot of cases is staffing: making sure we have enough employees, and stressing that they were hired to work the larger events. At Virginia Tech, we emphasize that all hands are needed on deck at football games. Another challenge is managing any last-minute changes by the client. After an event, we are also managing any complaints or concerns that our client may have received from fans or attendees. In some cases we have to justify what we did and remind the client of policies we were enforcing at their request. In terms of space, it is a challenge when we have multiple events that are spread out without a natural perimeter. Not having a perimeter to control becomes particularly challenging when people are consuming alcohol. Finally, from a logistical standpoint, we are always having to manage the transport of material and equipment from place to place. For example, during football games, employees must wear matching uniform shirts and hats, and we are always prepared with rain ponchos. Other items include sticks for bag-checkers, flashlights, reflective vests, radios, coolers for bottled water, and clipboards for supervisors.

What are some tips for effectively planning the logistical aspects of an event?

First and foremost, representatives of the event management company must have a firm understanding of their area of expertise and their standards. There are many companies that provide security, but not all have the same standards. If you understand your expertise and standards, it is easier to back into what you need. For us, we strive to improve the fan experience; that is why investing in uniforms so that everyone looks similar is important. Also important is investing in the tools needed in order to effectively communicate. Prior to an event, I do a site survey and visual walk-through in addition to talking with the client to better understand their expectations. After speaking with the client, I make sure that my employees have as much information as they need in order to work the event and meet these expectations.

Early on in the relationship with a client there is a period when you are perceived as an outsider, even though you are helping them to meet their goal. Over the course of our four years at VT, I feel like we are now in the loop, which was not always the case. We want to be a part of the feedback and decision-making as to what needs to happen at an event. Also, there are occasional communication issues where you don't have information because the client has not told you. For example, weather situations can cause issues on a game day when suddenly EMT, police, fire and rescue, the university meteorologist, and the athletics department become involved. It is vital that we are also at the table during any discussions with these departments. If we are going to evacuate or shelter in place, I need to know as soon as possible so that I can share this information with my supervisors.

How do you provide quality service for your client?

My employees must understand expectations, particularly client expectations; and I need to provide each employee with as much information as possible. We have a handbook called the "Hokie Standard" that slips into the back of each employee name badge. This little sheet provides employees with football-specific information and gives them everything they need to know about the stadium. In addition, parking attendants have parking maps so they can provide information about all lots on campus. We want to be able to answer any and all questions. Finally, it is important that each supervisor is invested in providing high quality service. I don't want them just to clock in but to understand the responsibilities of managing people in their area and to take ownership of their position.

Event planners are responsible for coordinating the logistics of a sporting event, which entails making sure the right people, equipment, and services are available in the right place at the right time. Some important logistical components of any sporting event include financial resources, equipment, ticketing, human resources, site selection, information, and sponsorship. But a lot more is involved in planning an event beyond these logistical components. For example, Allen (2009) suggests the following factors are important when considering where to hold an event: location (local, out of state, out of country), date (taking into account national or religious holidays), season (spring, summer, fall, winter), time of day, indoor or outdoor (how bad weather will affect your event), single or multiple locations, and budget considerations.

Event Timeline

A timeline is an important tool for successfully implementing a sporting event. According to Goldblatt (2014), an **event timeline** is a sequential listing of all the tasks and duties associated with an event; it is divided into various phases consisting of event research, planning, coordination, and evaluation (figure 11.1). The timeline provides all stakeholders with a tool for managing the event. It is important that the

FIGURE 11.1 Phases of an event timeline.

primary event planner receive a timeline from each vendor and stakeholder and that these be incorporated into a master timeline. One of the reasons events fail is insufficient time to research, plan, and coordinate.

Research Phase

The **research phase** is important because it provides information about previous events and assists in outlining the needs and resources of the current event. During this phase of the event timeline, the event planner is primarily gathering data that will help in planning the event. For example, the event manager may collect data from the last two years the event was held. Research before the event may be either quantitative or qualitative. Quantitative data is gathered from prospective attendees by means of a questionnaire or survey, which is then analyzed using some form of statistical analysis. Quantitative research provides the event planner with demographic information (e.g., age, gender, household income) and participation rates, which is helpful in appealing to these groups when they arrive at the event venue. Qualitative research—in the form of focus groups, case studies, content analysis, or participant observation—is useful in event planning as a way to get deeper information from respondents.

Event Planning Phase

The planning phase should take into account the previous research conducted in relation to the event. It should also specify the objectives of your event, and a good plan should help those involved reach these objectives. A strategic plan outlines the key stakeholders, the necessary steps for hosting a successful event, and the event's time frame. The planning process starts with a meeting involving all key stakeholders in the sporting event network. It is important to include those people who have responsibilities and the authority to make decisions.

Coordination Phase

In the **coordination phase**, the event planner synchronizes and integrates activities, responsibilities, and organizational structures to make sure that resources are used efficiently to achieve organizational objectives. Some activities that may transpire during the coordination phase are identifying prospective vendors, contracting vendors, and developing and implementing production schedules. Goldblatt (2014) suggests that event planners use critical analysis along with professional training during this phase to make correct decisions. He recommends the following six steps as simple but effective ways to make decisions.

1. Collect all the information, because many problems have multiple sides to review.
2. Consider the pros and cons of decisions, especially in terms of who will be affected.
3. Consider the financial implications of your decisions.
4. Consider the moral and ethical implications of your decisions.
5. If possible, do no harm to others or yourself.
6. Make your decision and move forward.

Evaluation Phase

According to Myhill and Phillips (2006), evaluating an event helps the event planner determine whether the event objectives were met, and also provides guidance for planning future events. Some of the tasks during the **evaluation**

phase include preparing and distributing surveys or questionnaires; collecting, tabulating, and analyzing data; preparing reports of findings and recommendations; and submitting a final report (Goldblatt 2014). Myhill and Phillips (2006) provide the following purposes of evaluation:

- To determine success in accomplishing event objectives
- To identify the strengths and weaknesses in the event management process
- To compare the event costs to the benefits
- To decide who should participate in future events
- To identify which participants were the most successful
- To reinforce major points to event participants
- To gather data to assist in marketing future events

Event Registration

The need for event registration varies depending on the type of event being planned. For example, a marathon runner or a participant in a youth volleyball tournament may register at the event site at a participant check-in. In contrast, a professional baseball game would not have a registration area for participants. It is also common for registration to be done online or through a kiosk on-site. Generally speaking, events catering to active participants are more likely to have some type of registration process in comparison to a regular-season contest attracting passive spectators. Registration is an important component of these types of events because it is the first interactive experience the participant has with the event. Many events offer the participant the opportunity to register in advance. Advance registration requires database software along with careful planning and skilled organization to prevent problems such as misplaced checks or incorrect paperwork, which ultimately results in angry customers (Carlisle 2006).

Ticket Sales

Ticketing is an important element of a sporting event, and the event manager must be concerned both with the raw material (i.e., the tangible tickets) and with the distribution and human resource systems needed to sell them (Shonk 2011). As Fried (2015) suggests, ticket sales have changed over the years with new marketing techniques. Sports fans and spectators now have a variety of choices in terms of ticketing inventory from general admission, reserved seating, and box seating to more luxurious seating inventory such as club seats and luxury suites. In some cases, a customer must purchase a **personal seat license** (PSL) in order to buy a season ticket. PSLs refer to "a contractual right a person acquires for a fee that allows the person to purchase tickets for a specific seat; others cannot acquire tickets for that seat as long as the PSL contract is in effect" (Fried 2015, p. 405). Purchasing tickets has also become more convenient for consumers. The secondary ticket market and websites such as StubHub and Live Nation provide consumers with easy accessibility to tickets for numerous events. In addition, many teams now allow season ticket holders to sell unused tickets via their websites.

It is important for event managers to research the various ticket options that will be used to sell the event. A spectator can walk into many sport venues today and use mobile technology to gain entry. However, for some events the physical ticket is still an important part of the experience because it represents the patron's first tangible contact with the sporting event. A ticket on cheap paper stock, one that is poorly designed, or one that has spelling or grammatical errors portrays the event in a negative light. A number of automated ticketing systems are now available that make the distribution of tickets much easier for event managers. Ticketmaster, Live Nation, and TicketCity are examples of companies that compete in the ticketing and live entertainment industry. Because of bar-coding technology, tickets can now be printed on letter-size paper by the consumer and scanned at entry into the event.

Tickets can also be purchased on the secondary market from websites such as StubHub, SeatGeak, Vivid Seats, Gametime, and others.

Food and Beverage Operations

It is rare to find any large events that do not have some type of meal offering. Even youth events often include a postgame snack or beverage provided by a parent or coach. Food and beverage operations at an event are vitally important and can be a significant source of revenue. An event planner has a number of considerations in terms of food and beverage services. Most events require a meal for active participants and concession operations for spectators. Hospitality suites are also common at many sporting events. Corporate hospitality has grown tremendously over the last 30 years, and companies such as THG Sports Hospitality and VIP Sports Marketing Inc. now specialize in providing clients with unique experiences. Shock (2006) outlines the following types of food and beverage services:

- *American service*: Food is portioned and plated in the kitchen and served by attendants. This is the most common, economical, functional, and efficient type of service.
- *Buffet*: Food is arranged on tables, and guests serve themselves and then move to a dining table to eat.
- *Butler service*: Usually offered at receptions; servers offer a variety of both hot and cold hors d'oeuvres on platters or trays to guests.
- *Cafeteria service*: Similar to a buffet, except that attendants serve the food and the guests carry the food to their tables on trays.
- *English service*: A tray of food is brought to the table.
- *French banquet service*: Platters of food are prepared in the kitchen and the servers take the platters to the dining tables and place the food onto the guests' plates.
- *French cart service*: Involves the use of silverware, the heating and garnishing of food table-side by a captain, and the placement of food on a heated plate, which is then served to the guest by a server; plated entrees and beverages are usually served from the right, and bread and butter and salad from the left.
- *Preset service*: Some food is already on the table when guests arrive; foods may include bread and butter, water, salad, and cold appetizers.
- *Russian banquet service*: Food is fully prepared in the kitchen, and all courses are served either from silver platters or from an Escoffier dish (a platter named after Georges-Auguste Escoffier who was a French chef, restaurateur and culinary writer). The server places a plate in front of each guest; after the plates are placed, the server returns with a tray of food and, moving counterclockwise around the table, allows guests to help themselves from a platter presented from their left.

Meals for Participants

Many sporting events have meal functions for the participants that take place at the host hotel, the sport venue, a local restaurant, or a banquet area. Meals may include breakfast, luncheon, refreshment breaks, receptions, seated served dinner, seated buffet dinner, and even theme parties.

According to Shock (2006), breakfast may be served in various ways.

- *Continental*: A fast breakfast that may include coffee, tea, juice, bread, pastries, bagels, and muffins. This style of breakfast is good for participants because it is quick and encourages prompt attendance before daily events.
- *Full breakfast buffet*: Two or three types of meat, two or three styles of eggs, one potato dish, three to six types of bread or pastry, hot and cold cereals, fresh fruit, yogurt, juices, coffee, and tea. This style usually runs about an hour and tends

to be more filling for event participants than the continental style breakfast.

- *English breakfast*: The same foods as the full breakfast buffet, plus action stations with attendants serving foods such as waffles, omelets, or crepes made to order. Once again, this type of breakfast lasts about an hour, and participants must have enough time to truly enjoy.
- *Full served breakfast*: A full-service breakfast where participants order off the menu and servers deliver the meal. This style of breakfast may be best suited at the beginning or the conclusion of an event when participants are more relaxed and not running from one place to another. Some events have a full served breakfast that also includes an awards presentation or a special speaker.

Refreshment breaks vary depending on the type of event. Refreshment breaks for participants in less strenuous events may include beverages such as coffee, tea, bottled waters, and soft drinks. For sports teams, refreshment breaks between games or after a game may include sport drinks and water and may also include some type of fruit such as oranges to provide energy to the players. A successful luncheon can be served in a variety of formats, including box lunch, seated lunch, luncheon buffet, and deli buffet. Many sporting events have some type of reception either before or at the conclusion of the event. Receptions often include entertainment along with hors d'oeuvres, and some events have an open bar. Although the reception can be catered to the needs of your event, guests are usually not encouraged to sit and eat during the reception.

Seated served dinners are normally planned for a time when there are no other imminent events (e.g., workout, press conference, team meeting) so that the guests can enjoy the experience. They normally last about two hours but can run as long as four hours if entertainment, dancing, awards, or other activities are included. A seated buffet dinner may be more appropriate if the participants have activities scheduled later in the evening such as a program, a meeting, or a press conference. If the event has a particular theme, or if it is taking place in a certain geographic region, you may consider having a theme party. For example, when the National Football League Pro Bowl is held in Hawaii, there is often an official Pro Bowl Welcome Luau. Theme parties in New Orleans during the Super Bowl may reflect the laid-back and relaxed culture of the area.

Concession Operations

Concession operations over the years have changed dramatically. Sport venues in the twentieth century ran a concession operation that included such fare as hot dogs, hamburgers, french fries, popcorn, and other snacks and beverages, including alcohol. Today's sport venues offer more upscale amenities including sit-down restaurants, bars, and themed concession stands that offer meals such as Mexican, Chinese, Italian, or local favorites. For example, Oriole Park at Camden Yards in Baltimore offers Maryland crab cakes and a specialty concession called Boog's BBQ, named for Oriole great Boog Powell. In 2018, the Orioles announced a number of new food options at the ballpark, including Attman's Deli, Boardwalk Fries, Pinch Dumplings, Pizza John's, Pollock Johnny's sausage, Stuggy's gourmet hot dogs, and a new Lobster Hut behind home plate on the lower concourse (Case and Welsh 2018). In 2015, food and beverage generated revenues of $59 million at Dodger Stadium in Los Angeles, $53 million at San Francisco's AT&T Park, and $49 million at Chicago's Wrigley Field (White 2017). The need for and sophistication of concession operations will vary based on the type of event being planned. Youth sporting events may run a fairly simple concession setup operated by volunteers such as players' parents, whereas larger professional events will include all the amenities of the concessions at some of the newer professional sport venues. Local, state, and federal health and safety regulations should be consulted when food is served at any event, and vendors should have the proper licensing (Fried 2015). Event planners should take into account the following factors regarding concession operations during the initial site visit to the sport venue.

- How many spectators are expected to attend the event?
- How sophisticated a concession operation does your event require?
- How many points of purchase are there in the sport venue?
- Is the concession operation outsourced to a vendor or does the sport venue operate concessions in-house?
- What are the policies as regards participants bringing food into the sport venue?
- As the event organizer, what is your role in concessions?
- Will you need to train concession workers?
- Will alcohol be served at the event? If so, do you have the necessary permits for the sale of alcohol? Based on the age of the attendees, is it appropriate to sell alcohol at the event? Is security necessary to monitor and control where alcohol is consumed?
- Are concessions a considerable source of revenue for your event, or are they simply an added service for participants and spectators?

It is important to understand the role that food will play at your event (deLisle 2014). If the sporting event is an all-day affair with many spectators, food may be a primary attraction during certain periods of the day. In contrast, an event with few spectators may receive little to no traffic at the concession stands.

Stuart Franklin/Getty Images

Golf tournaments often have hospitality tents that are sold to corporate sponsors.

Hospitality Services

Hospitality entails a relationship between a host and a guest. Because of the integration of sport and tourism, hospitality is an important component of event management. Since many events travel from market to market, the relationship between the host organization and the guest becomes increasingly important. Using hospitality as a means, destination marketing organizations (DMOs) such as sports commissions and convention and visitors bureaus (CVBs) spend considerable time cultivating relationships with event rights holders. For example, upon arriving at the host destination, event planners often find a gift provided by the DMO in their hotel room. During the site visit to the host destination, event planners are often wined and dined by the sports commission or the CVB.

Sporting events such as golf tournaments often have hospitality tents that are sold to corporate sponsors such as Coca-Cola or Budweiser. Since 1993, MSG Promotions has been the exclusive corporate hospitality marketing and management company for the United States Golf Association's U.S. Open Championship (MSG Promotions 2012). In 2017, the U.S. Open was held at Erin Hills in Wisconsin. Because the U.S. Open cuisine reflects the cuisine native to the year's local venue, the 2017 cuisine included a lot of cheese, sausage, beer, cranberries, and baked goods (Jagler 2016). Many sport venues sell hospitality suites as part of their luxury ticketing inventory. As an example, for approximately $300 per game you can sit in the Lexus Presidents Club Suite at Nationals Park in Washington, D.C., home to Major League Baseball's Washington Nationals. The Presidents Club is an exclusive members-only club featuring all-inclusive food and beverages, MVP parking, and access to the closest seats to home plate. The benefits of purchasing include a complimentary chef's table buffet, a complimentary draft beer and house wine, a red-carpet rewards program, VIP parking, an invitation to view batting practice from the field, exclusive club programming, and autograph sessions with the players (Washington Nationals 2012).

Waste Management Services

A key factor of servicing an event is a sustainable program for waste management. One of the largest waste management providers is Waste Management, Inc., a $13-million Houston-based company that provides waste collection, transfer, recycling, resource recovery, and disposal services. The bid requirements for many events require host organizations to submit an environmental plan at the time of their bid submission. The International Olympic Committee (IOC) requires all host organizations to submit a candidature file as early as seven years before the event that highlights their plans for sustainability in terms of waste and other environmental issues such as conservation of carbon emissions, energy, water, materials, biodiversity, and overall environmental impact. The issue of managing waste systems is an important factor not only from an environmental perspective but also in terms of service quality at the venue. The proper placement of waste removal systems and a comprehensive plan for servicing these sites are imperative. For events such as the Olympic Games, environmental issues such as waste management are important because they influence the legacy of the Games.

Custodial Services

Cleaning before and after a sporting event is a critical service factor. Depending on the type of event, custodial services may either be outsourced or make use of staff or volunteers. Most of the time when an event planner contracts with a sport venue, the terms of the contract specify the requirements for keeping the venue clean. Some areas of a venue that may require cleaning include the following:

A key factor of servicing an event is a sustainable program for waste management.

- Stadium and arena seating areas
- Stadium and arena concourses
- Concession areas
- Luxury seating areas
- Bathrooms and portable toilets
- Press box
- Parking lots, especially if the event includes tailgating
- Event field surfaces, especially after mega-events that allow confetti

Transportation Services

Events that involve moving guests from one location to another can be a major challenge and may require various modes of transportation, including transit via air (e.g., private charters, commercial airplanes, helicopter), land (e.g., motor coaches, school buses, private cars, vans, limousines), water (barges, private boat charters, cruise ships), and trains. Allen (2009) suggests that event planners extend the same care and detail to guest enjoyment in the transfer phase as during the actual event. Transportation should be taken into account when budgeting for the event, because there can be a number of hidden costs.

A key factor to consider is that transportation modes can be the first point of contact with the event for many attendees. Most events will employ some form of outsourcing. For example, many events require charter buses from companies such as Trailways, Mears, and local motor-coach fleets. Parking is another service that is often outsourced. For example, parking for golf tournaments such as the Masters and U.S. Open is outsourced to Country Club Services, a New Jersey company that offers a broad range of services, including valet parking, parking directing, shuttle and van operations, traffic control, and parking lot organization and security (Country Club Services 2018).

Allen (2009) suggests that event managers consider the following questions in regard to transportation for an event.

- When and where will transportation be required for each event element?
- What are the various transfer options? Event planners should look at conventional and convenience modes and consider creative transfer options as well.
- What are the choices for various routes?
- How can the transfer experience be enhanced? For example, can you include food and beverages or some form of entertainment during the transfer?
- How can you reduce stress and confusion for passengers, such as parking congestion and overnight airport stays?
- Where will the majority of your guests be departing from, and how can this affect their arrival time at the event destination?
- What is the estimated number of cars or arriving vehicles?
- Will factors such as rush hour traffic or other major events taking place at the same time have an impact on the event start time?
- Where is the closest parking to the event venue?

Goldblatt (2014) provides the following suggestions for considering transportation and parking factors.

- Parking attendants help alleviate the problem of hazardous drivers who don't follow parking lot rules.
- Parking attendants can help safeguard unaware pedestrians from unsafe drivers.
- Signs should be posted in the parking lot requesting drivers to note the location of their vehicles. Event attendees often forget where they parked.
- Shuttle buses should be enclosed in the event of inclement weather.
- Make sure the parking area has sufficient lighting; dimly lit parking lots tend to promote criminal activity.
- Have a drop-off area for children where they can be safely secured so they do not run off while parents are loading or unloading the car.

Lighting

Lighting for sporting events is a critical component of safety and can even contribute to revenue generation (Sawyer 2013). For example, the addition of lights at Wrigley Field in Chicago in 1988 allowed the team to sell tickets and generate additional revenues from fans who could not make day games. Melbourne Cricket Ground, the largest stadium in Australia, holds the world record for the highest light towers at any sporting venue (Tabi 2010). The stadium has six light towers that stand approximately 75 meters high (equivalent to a 24-story building), and the power to the light towers is supplied off an 11-kilovolt electrical ring main into a transformer inside the base of each tower (MCG 2012).

Lighting needs for televised events are also important. According to Jeroen Jansen, Philips Lighting's general manager for Southern Africa, light represents less than 1 percent of many stadium and arena budgets, but it determines 99 percent of the effect seen on TV (van Mierlo and van der Laarse 2010). Illumination levels for baseball and softball fields are 20 foot-candles for the outfield and 30 foot-candles for the infield. The lighting requirements for other team sport fields such as field hockey, football, lacrosse, rugby, and soccer are at a minimum 30-foot candles (Sawyer 2013).

Vendor Relationships

Developing strong relationships with vendors is an important factor in event management. Event managers may interact with a number of different vendors depending on the type of event. Vendors that event planners may form relationships with include the following:

- Concession vendors
- Marketing and advertising vendors
- Media vendors
- Ticketing vendors
- Office supply vendors

- Industrial supply vendors (e.g., companies selling bathroom and cleaning supplies)
- Transportation vendors (e.g., rental car agencies, airlines, and charter bus companies)
- Accommodation vendors (e.g., hotels and motels)

Using outside vendors can reduce, but not totally eliminate, an organization's legal responsibility for safety and quality (deLisle 2014). However, event planners should be careful when selecting vendors because the reputation of the event will be affected by the products and services provided by the vendor. As some marketing studies suggest, often the relationship with the vendor firm's key contact employees is stronger than the relationship with the firm itself (Bendapudi & Leone 2002; Gwinner, Gremler, & Bitner 1998).

Event planners should continually work to cultivate the relationship with their vendors. In cases where the sporting event moves from place to place, the event planner should utilize the resources provided by the local sports commission and convention and visitors bureau. Often, these organizations are helpful in connecting the event planner with local vendors such as transportation providers or airlines that frequently fly into the local airport. If vendors change frequently, one of the challenges facing the event planner is the need to constantly educate the vendor about the needs for the event, but when the event planner has cultivated a strong and lasting relationship, the vendor is able to provide a higher quality of service.

Event Facility Selection

Although event managers are not required to be experts, they absolutely need to understand certain components of sport facilities. This is especially true during the bidding process. During this time, the event manager may need to interact with the venue's facility manager regarding any necessary requirements and specifications for the event. For example, issues such as setup and teardown, equipment needs, temperature controls, field and crowd safety, dressing rooms, and field surfaces may require discussion. Fried (2015) suggests that facility managers must consider the following factors when selecting a site for a sport event:

- A review of feasibility studies (economic and political impact) for the site
- Permits (lease, license, or letter) and whether they can be obtained
- Site information (from environmental issues to historical concerns)
- Regulations (e.g., building codes and health ordinances)
- Community involvement
- Affordability and decision to lease or to purchase the facility
- Easements (will the neighbors have the right to cross the property?)
- Zoning (e.g., cluster, flood plain, open space) issues
- Restrictive covenants that may limit who can purchase the land or how it can be used
- Aesthetic value of the site and whether there are beautiful views; many of the professional stadiums built today are designed for aesthetic beauty and face the skyline of the respective city
- Recreational opportunities; a criticism of some new football stadiums is that they do not benefit the community because they are used only for a handful of home games

Most likely the event planner will have one primary contact for each sport venue but there may be times when she interacts with a wide variety of people. In the case of large sport facilities, several crews are responsible for functions ranging from ticketing, marketing, game operations, and mechanical and janitorial services (Fried 2015). Every event should have a facility manager on call for situations that require maintenance or facility operations. The facility manager should also be readily available in the case of an emergency, security issue, or life-threatening illness.

One of the key issues for the event manager is determining the physical requirements of the event. An important question is how many venues will be needed for the sporting event. In addition, the event planner must interact with the facility manager of the venue or venues to specify issues related to the field surface, seating requirements, sponsor signage, broadcasting facilities and equipment, and concession needs. In addition, many events also require food and beverage functions such as sit-down dinners, exhibit space, meeting space, and registration booths. The event planner will need to specify how much food is required for the sit-down dinner, the number of exhibits, the number of rooms for meetings, and the number of registration booths. These types of physical requirements should be written in the request for proposal (RFP) submitted to the sport venue during or before the initial site visit.

Restroom Facilities

The number of restrooms and hand-washing stations required for an event varies according to local and state sanitary codes based on attendance levels (deLisle 2014). Some events may require additional portable restrooms to meet these requirements. Event planners should pay particular attention to several factors concerning restrooms during the initial site visit. First, is there a regular plan for cleaning restrooms? Cleanliness of the physical environment of the facility is an important factor for consumers. Are the restrooms well lit for evening events? The safety of event attendees should be of primary concern, and restrooms in dimly lit locations can be troublesome. Do restrooms meet ADA requirements for accessibility, and how far do attendees need to walk to find the nearest restroom? Is there signage that points attendees to the nearest restroom? Events that attract families will need changing tables or separate family restrooms.

Traffic Flow Considerations

The flow of traffic can be considered from two standpoints. First, as attendees enter the event in passenger cars, how will traffic flow into and out of the sport venue? Second, traffic flow refers to how you will set up the sport venue or points of purchase within the venue for the flow of spectators or participants. A number of factors must be considered in terms of passenger traffic. Some events outsource parking services to help with the influx of traffic to the sport venue. In cases where parking is paid, the event planner should have a plan for moving traffic in and out smoothly with little interruption. Parking attendants should wear brightly colored uniforms so they are easily identifiable, and attendants should wear an apron with pockets or be housed in a booth for managing cash payments. Parking attendants should be provided with colored cones so they can reroute traffic before and after the event. Signage is also an important safety tool and should be readily visible and easy to read. Parking attendants should have two-way radio communication and be available to assist patrons with disabilities. Depending on the size of the event, local law enforcement can be contracted to assist with traffic flow. In some cases, major highway ramps may need to be blocked, and certain intersections will require police officers to assist with directing traffic.

There are many strategies for dealing with the flow of spectator traffic in the sport venue. Major intersections within the sport venue should be identified during the initial site inspection. Security should be in place to assist with intersections where sport participants come into contact with spectators. For example, before the race, jockeys riding in the Kentucky Derby at Churchill Downs walk from the dressing room to the paddock and must cross through spectator traffic along the way. Popular golfers on the PGA Tour also intermingle with spectators and often require security as they walk from one hole to the next.

Event planners should develop a plan for dealing with pedestrian traffic and crowd control. Crowd control is especially important during mega-events, championships, and rivalry games where spectators may rush onto the playing surface. The pedestrian traffic plan should outline specific areas within the sport venue that may require signage, cones, or stanchions as well as areas that may need to be roped off. Concession and ticketing lines often use stanchions to assist with traffic flow.

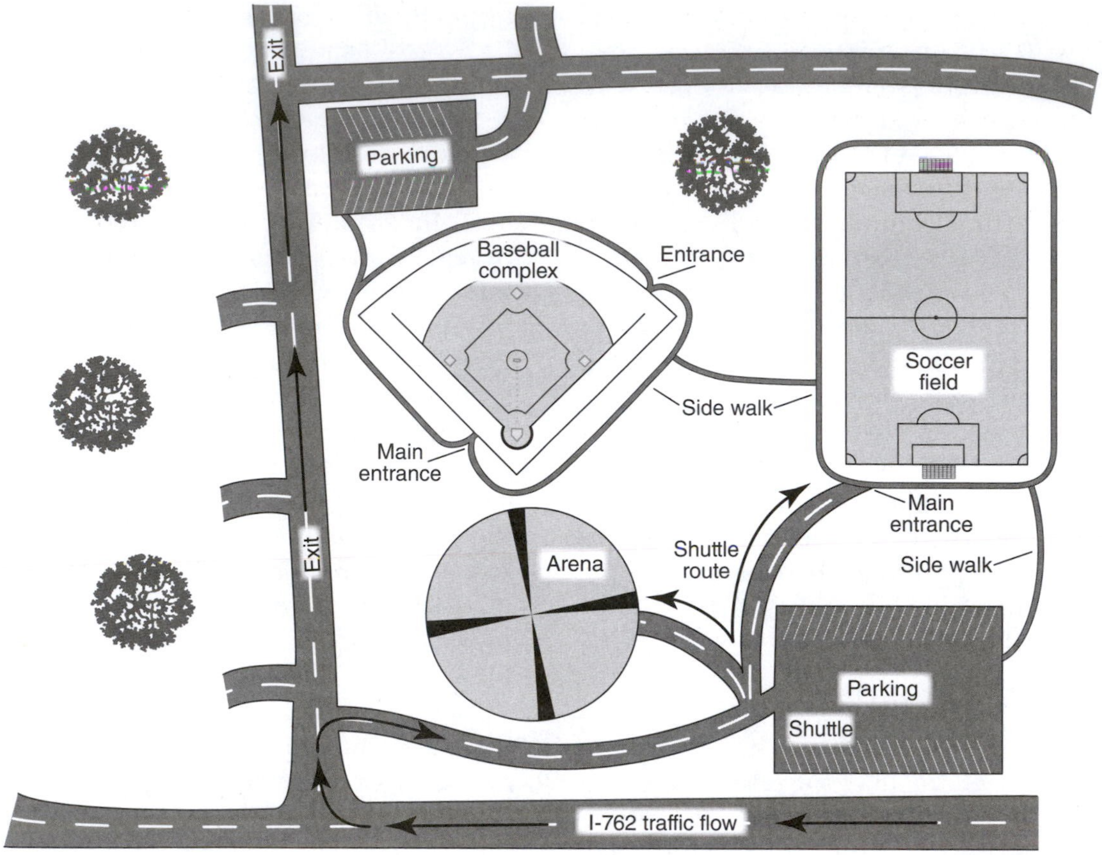

FIGURE 11.2 Sample parking and traffic flow map for sporting events.

Figure 11.2 shows a sample parking and traffic flow map for sporting events.

Seating

The average sporting event lasts somewhere between one and three hours, and some sporting events, such as all-day youth tournaments, last longer. Therefore, event planners should take the comfort of consumers into consideration. Of course, representatives of professional sport venues recognize the importance of seating, and many professional teams in the United States now have sport-specific stadiums. Between 1990 and 2008, Coates (2008) reported that Major League Baseball had 19 new stadiums, the National Football League had 17 new stadiums, and the National Basketball Association opened more than two-thirds of its 30 arenas. Teams in the National Football League alone opened six new stadiums between 2008 and 2017 (Reichard 2017). In addition, a total of 16 of the 23 teams in Major League Soccer now play in a soccer-specific stadium. Many colleges, universities, and high schools have also upgraded their facilities and built new sport venues.

Seating is an important component of many new stadiums. For spectator comfort, almost all the seats at these new professional sport venues are wider and have chairbacks and drink holders. Beyond general admission and reserved seating options, most stadiums and arenas also offer luxury and club seating with upscale amenities such as bars, bathrooms, televisions, upscale furniture, and full-service food and beverage menus with servers. Many of these luxury suites offer excellent sight lines for watching all the action on the field. The Dallas Cowboys Stadium has 300 suites over five levels. All the seats are on rails rather than bolted into the concrete. During the regular season, the seats are 22 inches (56 cm) wide; when more seats are required, those seats are removed and 18-inch (46 cm) seats are installed. In addition, the stadium has six party decks on each level of the end zones for standing-room-only crowds to gather (Barron 2009).

All new stadiums are required to comply with the Americans with Disabilities Act (ADA). The ADA requires new stadiums to be accessible to people with disabilities so that they, their families, and their friends can enjoy equal access to entertainment, recreation, and leisure (U.S. Department of Justice 2012). Most stadiums and arenas also hire ushers who help spectators find their seats, answer questions, enforce seating policies, make sure people are sitting in the correct seats, wipe down dirty and wet seats, transport people in wheelchairs, and generally serve as friendly hosts. Of course, not all sporting events are held at new stadiums and arenas. For example, a beach volleyball tournament does not offer the amenities of new facilities. Transportable or temporary seating may be needed for such events. In addition, event planners should take into account the following factors.

- Will you offer tiered seating (e.g., general admission, reserved, box seats) with different price points, or are all seats the same with one general price?
- Where is a safe place for ADA seating that still allows people sitting in these areas to be close to the action on the field or court?
- Where can you place signage to help spectators find their seats?
- What are some ways to make the seating more comfortable?
- What safety considerations need to be taken into account? For example, spectators, especially children or the elderly, could fall from older mobile bleacher seats.

Sound Considerations

Sound-related factors should be considered throughout the entire event planning process and specifically evaluated during meetings with event facility managers. Although some sounds can be controlled by the facility manager, others cannot. According to Fried (2015), recreational activity sounds are caused by normal facility use and cannot be controlled. One type of recreational activity sound is airborne sound, which is caused by facility users and may include whistles, voices, music, and cheers. Structure-borne sounds are those caused by direct impact with some part of the facility's structure, such as a bouncing basketball's vibration that is then transmitted into the air. Mechanical sounds are produced by the machinery used to operate the facility and can be controlled by a facility manager. It is important that event planners meet with facility managers during the initial planning stages and provide details concerning their needs for each facility space. For example, if the event requires space for a quiet and focused board meeting, this should be mentioned in the initial meeting so that a quiet room can be scheduled.

There are a number of factors event planners should consider in terms of managing the sounds of a sporting event.

- What are some potential recreational sounds that may occur at the event, and what is the most appropriate course of action for dealing with them? For example, consider an event being planned at a venue next to a train track or an outdoor event next to a busy highway. What can be done to reduce the impact of the sound of a train whistle, passing trucks, or car horns? Some options include asking the train company whether the trains can run during off-event times, and not scheduling events during rush hour traffic.
- What are the needs in terms of a sound system for the sporting event, and does the venue have an appropriate system already in place?
- Does the venue provide all the necessary sound equipment needed for your event?
- Do some venues for your sporting event require portable sound systems? For example, some outdoor events require bullhorns or portable speakers and wireless microphones.
- What is the quality of the sound system at each sport venue in which your event will take place?

- What is the compatibility of your sound equipment with that of the venue?
- Who will be responsible for playing music and making any necessary public address announcements during the course of the event?

Sport marketers commonly use music to enhance the atmosphere of the stadium or arena and to excite crowd emotion. Spectators often sing and dance in their seats when music is played. The public address system is used to announce event action and to make other types of announcements. Most sporting events in the United States begin with the national anthem and often include school or team alma mater or fight songs. The music at some events arises from crowds singing songs, anthems, and chants. Many cities have a noise ordinance that takes into account decibel levels and times for general "reasonableness" when it comes to loud music and sound (Manning 2012). These ordinances vary from locality to locality and can be a challenge for late-evening games that go on well into the night.

Hotel Availability

As already discussed, the merger of sport and tourism is a considerable factor in the sport event industry. As more events travel from one destination to another, the participants and spectators who follow along are in need of a place to stay. Event tourism continues to be one of the fastest-growing sectors of the leisure-travel market, and sporting events create a demand for room nights in most cities (Chalip 2004). Research by the World Travel and Tourism Council (2018) reports that travel and tourism contributes to 10.4 percent of global GDP and 313 million jobs, or 9.9 percent of total employment. A study by *SportsEvents* magazine of event rights holders who participate in events that move from one destination to another reports that athletes spent $932 per competition in 2017 (O'Connor 2018).

Negotiating hotel contracts and room blocks is an important duty for sport event planners during site selection. Foster (2006) provides the following guidelines for negotiating hotel contracts.

- Make sure the room block is adequate to cover the needs for the event but not so large as to trigger attrition charges if attendees do not use all the guest rooms reserved in the block.
- Calculate as best as possible how many participants will stay the entirety of the event, how many local attendees will not need guest rooms, and whether attendees may stay at other hotels.
- The contract should specify the guaranteed room rates if the contract is signed one or two years before the event.
- Include a clause in the contract specifying that all rooms occupied by event attendees will count toward performance clauses based on room pick-up, regardless of the rate paid.
- Specify how reservations will be made by attendees (e.g., individual reservations, housing bureau, rooming list) and individual deposit requirements.
- Find out whether there is an early check-out fee.
- Make sure the hotel will honor all reservations guaranteed by event attendees. You may have a public relations fiasco if the hotel decides not to honor the reservation of one or more of your attendees.
- Include a cutoff date in the hotel contract. The cutoff date specifies the last date the hotel will hold out of its inventory the guest rooms blocked for your event.
- Include an overbooking clause in the contract to protect you from the hotel's selling any of your room block before the cutoff date.
- Carefully read the wording for the attrition clause that many hotels include in a contract. Attrition is the difference between the actual number of guest rooms picked up and the number of guest rooms or minimum amount of revenue guaranteed by the event rights holder in the contract.

Many factors related to hotel accommodation must be taken into account during the planning stages of the event. One of the toughest challenges is estimating the number of hotel rooms required. It is helpful when you have a history of conducting the event at a certain destination because you can look at prior room pick-ups, but this information is not available when the event is being held at a new destination. Depending on your room block requirements for the event, you may be able to use just one host hotel. The advantage of using one host hotel is that all your event attendees are at the same location, making it much easier to manage the event and to convey information. If the room block exceeds the capacity of one hotel, you will need to include additional hotels. The following are considerations when using multiple hotels:

- The distance between the hotels and the convenience and cost of transporting attendees
- The difference in cost between the hotels (the cost to event attendees may rise or fall depending on the types of hotel property you choose)
- The level of service and amenities provided by each hotel

Customer Service

A **service** is an act, deed, performance, or effort (Berry 1980). Event managers work in a service-related industry, and the quality of service provided during the event can be a competitive advantage. A sporting event can be described as an intangible experience that must be carefully crafted by event planners, and every interaction with the customer must be analyzed. The service experience for active participants and spectators begins the moment they depart from their home residence and lasts until they arrive back home. The participants and the spectators will judge the quality of the experience based on the difference between their expectations of what will be delivered at the event and the actual service. If their overall experience at the sporting event exceeds their expectations, then it means that a high-quality experience was delivered. On the other hand, service failures, or breakdowns in service delivery, can cast the event in a negative light. At the October 2007 Chicago Marathon, one runner died, 49 were hospitalized, and many others were denied the opportunity to cross the finish line because of 88-degree (31-degree C) heat and a lack of sufficient water and sport drinks. During the planning stages, it is vitally important to consider every area where the event process may break down and suffer such a service failure.

The service quality delivered at an event is important because higher-quality service produces more satisfied customers who return to the event in subsequent years. Shonk and Chelladurai (2008) suggest that quality in event sport tourism is measured in terms of access, accommodation, venue, and outcome. Access quality refers to the accessibility of the destination, the sport venue, and the hotel. Accommodation quality refers to such service factors as customers' perceptions of the physical environment of the hotel, their contact with hotel employees, and the value the hotel provides. The physical environment at the sport venue, interactions with employees such as ushers and ticket takers, and the value of various pricing options are important components of venue quality. Outcome quality refers to the process of the contest (e.g., quality of officiating and public address announcements) and the actual outcome in terms of wins and losses.

Customer service must be a primary concern of everyone involved in hosting a sporting event. Many events have customer service areas where attendees can ask questions and have their problems solved. Event planners should develop a comprehensive plan for delivering high-quality service before the event and then communicate their expectations of what constitutes superior service to all event employees and volunteers. One of the challenges event planners face is controlling the level of service. For example, an event planner may have little control over the service delivered by a vendor who has been outsourced to serve concessions at the sport venue. However, human resource initiatives such as volunteer training along with clearly communicating service expectations can help solve some of these issues. One way to approach customer service is to focus on the various touchpoints for customers. A touchpoint at a sporting event may be a consumer's interaction with a parking attendant, an usher, a ticket taker, or security personnel. A touchpoint may also be a message the consumer receives from the organization in the form of an e-mail, or interacting with the online ticketing portal. In sum, a **touchpoint** is any interaction between the consumer and the event or the organization running the event.

Awards Ceremonies

Awards ceremonies are usually celebrated at the conclusion of an event. Championship events are notorious for having awards ceremonies. For example, almost 40,000 fans came out to the 2018 NCAA college football championship celebration of the University of Alabama's win against the University of Georgia. Awards ceremonies may take place after a game or may be incorporated into a more formal event held at a hotel or other venue that includes dinner, entertainment, and plaques, trophies, scholarships, gifts, or cash awards for honorees. Event planners should consider the following factors when planning an awards ceremony.

- Do you have a fair and organized process for determining award winners?
- What technical equipment (e.g., wireless microphone, video) will you need for the awards ceremony?
- Are invitations necessary, and if so, to whom do you send them?
- Will you invite the media to the awards ceremony? If so, what arrangements must be made to accommodate the media?
- What award (e.g., trophy, certificate, gift) will recipients receive during the ceremony?
- Who will serve as the master of ceremonies?
- How will you honor past award winners?

Summary

Event planners are responsible for coordinating the logistics of a sporting event, which entails making sure the right people, equipment, and services are available in the right place and at the right time. An event timeline, starting with a research phase and followed by event planning, coordination, and evaluation phases, is a helpful tool for coordinating the logistics. Some of the logistical considerations that event planners must take into account include facilities, ticket sales, food and beverage operations, hospitality, waste management, transportation, custodial services, working with vendors, restrooms, traffic flow, seating, customer service, hotels, sound, and awards ceremonies.

LEARNING ACTIVITIES

1. Using the research and event planning phases as described in this chapter, please design a new and creative sporting event. The event might include the introduction of a new sport. Give the event a name, and describe the various activities that make up the event.
2. You are responsible for organizing a marathon at your college or university. Imagine that you will be running in the marathon. From the beginning of learning about and registering for the event until its conclusion, make a list of all of the touchpoints you may encounter.
3. This chapter describes the logistical considerations of a sporting event, including facilities, ticket sales, food and beverage operations, hospitality, waste management, transportation, custodial services, working with vendors, restrooms, traffic flow, seating, customer service, hotels, sound, and awards ceremonies. Search the Internet for an article about one of these logistical operations, and summarize the article in one double-spaced page.

CASE STUDY: D.C. UNITED AND AUDI FIELD IN WASHINGTON D.C.

D.C. United is one of 16 of the 23 Major League Soccer (MLS) teams that now have a soccer-specific stadium. The ribbon cutting ceremony for the new stadium took place on July 9, 2018, and on July 14, D.C. United had their first match in the newly built Audi Field. Since their formation in 1995, the team had played in RFK Stadium. Opened in 1961, and the former home of the Washington Redskins (NFL) and the Washington Senators (MLB), RFK simply did not offer the team the amenities or service options that fans have come to expect. Soccer-specific stadiums, averaging about 25,000 seats per stadium, are the trend in the MLS. They are designed to get the fans, and fan noise, as close as possible to the players.

Situated in Buzzard Point in Southeast D.C., Audi Field is part of a gentrification strategy in this part of the city to attract people and businesses to the area. With a capacity of 20,000, Audi Field is state-of-the art and offers 31 luxury suites, a 10,000-square-foot indoor lounge, a rooftop patio with a view of the city and monuments (e.g. the Capitol dome and the Washington Monument), club areas, valet parking, a supporter section, and seats very close to all of the action on the field. The stadium is just two blocks from the Nationals Park, home of the Washington Nationals (MLB). Parking for Audi Field is very limited. To deal with this problem, the team has partnered with SpotHero to provide 3,700 spots in nearby lots and offer reservations for about 1,000 parking spaces. Valet service is also available. However, most fans are encouraged to bike, walk, or ride the Metro. The closest Metro station is at Navy Yard, which is just .7 miles from the stadium. Up to 190 bicycles can also be dropped with a bike valet on game days. The Potomac Riverboat Company also offers round-trip soccer-boat rides from a dock in Old Town Alexandria to Nationals Park.

Audi Field was designed to be eco-friendly and the team has earned LEED Gold certification for environmentally friendly buildings. More than 300 sports lights come on instantly, can do colored light shows, and are longer-lasting than traditional lights. The turf, cut to three-quarters of an inch tall, is classified as Northbridge Bermuda grass. The field is bowed for proper drainage, and water filtration systems below the field collect water and pump it into the city's storm sewer system.

A total of 1,500 seats are allocated for three D.C. United supporter groups: the Screaming Eagles, La Barra Brava, and the District Ultras. Supporter group members add to the fan experience with their chanting and drumming, and are consistently in the stadium, come rain or shine. These supporter groups also help D.C. United differentiate themselves from any other team in the market because this experience is not available at any other stadium. The supporters are positioned close to the pitch on the North Stand, the only area in the stadium that is the lowest price point (general admission seating) and is first-come, first-served seating.

D.C. United also offers some other unique opportunities to enhance the fan experience for those attending the match. For example, groups with youth 12 years of age and under can walk out hand-in-hand with the home and away teams; both adults and kids can be home-team bench warmers for the first 30 minutes of warmups, youth 14 years of age and up can serve as ball-kids; and youth and adults can participate in a fan-tunnel experience.

Food services are another important factor at Audi Field. Specific areas in the stadium offer in-seat concession service. Concessions are outsourced to Levy Restaurants and in collaboration with famed D.C. chef José Andrés, who serves as culinary curator. Concessions include items like shredded beef and chicken from Arepa Zone, and burgers, hot dogs, chicken tenders, crab pretzels, and fries from the Black and Red Grill. Suiteholders can enjoy their own separate dining experience that features Spanish dishes such as ibérico de bellota, mini hamburguesas, gambas al ajillo, flan al estilo tradicional and other delights.

The guest experience staff at Audi Field comprises about 350 to 400 individuals who are trained to provide the best experience on match day. D.C. United ticketing is fully digital and mobile. While RFK Stadium did not have Wi-Fi capabilities, Audi Field provides easy access to Wi-Fi for fans. The experience platform integrates with the D.C. United mobile app and allows fans the ultimate flexibility by giving them the option to use virtual currency for seat upgrades, additional seats and experiences, and in-seat ordering from a specific concession stand. Fans are asked to create an account, which provides D.C. United with access to a large database of customers.

Case Study Application

1. Based on the case study, list some of the touchpoints at Audi Field.
2. Describe some elements of the physical environment at Audi Field.
3. Based on what you have read about the case, are there any services that you deem important but that are not mentioned?

© Chris Greenwell

CHAPTER 12

Event Day Management

CHAPTER OBJECTIVES

After completing the chapter, the reader should be able to do the following:

- Understand the process of managing an event and what needs to take place to ensure a good event day.
- Appreciate the importance of communication in staging sporting events.
- Understand the challenges related to managing staff, participants, spectators, and sponsors.
- Develop a plan for managing staff, participants, spectators, and sponsors.
- Understand the benefits and challenges related to providing good customer service.

INDUSTRY PROFILE

Daron Jones, University of Wisconsin

As director of external engagement, Daron Jones is responsible for staffing, planning, and implementation of nearly 500 athletic events per year. He has also served as game production coordinator for the Rose Bowl Game and as assistant in operations for the NCAA Men's Basketball Final Four.

What do you want to accomplish on event day?

When it's game day, we want the majority of the communications as far as the prep and the planning to be out of the way. Game day should be the easiest part if we've prepared properly leading up to it. It's more that you're putting yourself in a position to be able to react to the things that come up. There are items that you plan out leading up to game day or event date when you're checking the different boxes and making sure things are staying on the timelines so that all the things you had planned for are happening the way they're supposed to. But in a lot of respects, you're also just being prepared to tackle the challenges that come up outside the realm of the things that you've planned for, or maybe they don't go exactly as planned.

How do your duties change throughout the day?

Typically, we plan to get event day meetings out of the way, quickly get staff checked in, and get with our groups who will have a significant role in how the different parts of the event will play out. That includes our security, our guest services staff, our event management staff, our police and other administrators helping with that event. As you get closer to welcoming the public into your building, that's the time where you really have to do your final check and be diligent, making sure that you're prepared to open this facility to a lot of people and that it's going to be a safe, welcoming environment for them to come into. Once the public is in the building and the teams and the officials are in, you have to trust that you've done what you can leading up to it and take care of things that come up from there.

How do you make sure everybody's coordinated and on the same page?

Quick communication not only with the right people but also in a timely fashion is very important. Part of the communication process is the postevent wrap-up as well: taking good information and good notes from the day and sharing them as a follow-up to that event.

What are your tips for success on event day?

Communication is obviously incredibly important, but I would also say building a strong knowledge base of the different areas around us. We really have to have at least some level of understanding of all of those different departments and their interests and what they're trying to accomplish on game day in order to make sure we're acting in the best interest of our overall goals for that event.

What's your approach to customer service?

We really try to do what we believe is in the best interest of the patrons, and we spend time trying to make sure that we're cognizant of what their game day experiences are, what challenges they face, and how we can use those things. We try to listen as much as possible and work through things that come up. We have a fan advisory committee and we've built some trust with those folks and they are very honest with us in return.

What is the most common mistake people in event management make?

The most common mistake is just forgetting to include key groups in the communication process. If you don't include all of the different departments in the process early on, it can really cost you on event day.

Event day is often the culmination of extensive planning and anticipation. For the event manager, event day typically starts early and ends very late because a number of significant tasks have to be managed in order to stage a successful sporting event. The manager has to consider the timing and coordination of event setup, the event itself, and the event takedown. In addition to dealing with participants, officials, spectators, and sponsors, managers also have to work with event staff, facility staff, and event organizers or sanctioning bodies.

Managing Event Day

The number of tasks that need to be accomplished can be overwhelming, but good event managers can make event day run more smoothly if they plan, anticipate, delegate, train and rehearse, and communicate.

Plan

Detailed plans of action need to be in place for how everything will be accomplished throughout the event day. Address each activity, and make sure everyone knows how to handle their tasks.

Managers also need to prepare for how activities will progress throughout the event. Consider a college football game. To the typical sports fan, it may appear that not much happens before the gates open. However, event managers have probably spent many hours orchestrating the flow of materials and personnel into the facility and to their appropriate locations within the facility. Food and drink supplies, television equipment, and staging equipment all have to be delivered to the site and positioned. Police, security, and medical staff need access to the facility. Game staff such as ushers, concessionaires, and event staff all need to be checked in and situated. Closer to game time, media and game officials arrive and need access to special areas of the facility. Then players, coaches, and other team personnel have to be transported to the stadium. Once at the stadium, the logistical issue shifts to getting players from the locker areas to the field. On top of this, spectators entering the facility must be managed.

Anticipate

Event managers need to put substantial thought into what could happen during the course of an event and have a realistic understanding of what it will take to execute the event. Also, things typically take longer and consume more resources than expected. Make sure you anticipate any delays or overruns, and schedule buffers into the event so that subsequent activities will not be delayed.

The importance of developing contingency plans was discussed in chapter 2. This also applies to the day of the event. Contingency plans should be in place to deal with anything that could disrupt the event or place participants, spectators, or personnel in harm's way. No matter how much you may plan and prepare, things can still go wrong, necessitating courses of action different from what you had planned. In these situations, it is the job of the event manager to assess the situation swiftly and be adaptable enough to implement alternative plans. A cool head and a flexible attitude are essential to make sure people and property are protected and to proceed with the event with the smallest possible interruption.

Delegate

Good event managers understand that although they may be responsible for everything, they cannot do everything themselves. They need to entrust staff to accomplish certain tasks. For larger events, managers create smaller teams supervised by a team leader. By delegating tasks and responsibilities to team leaders, management is free to address other issues. Further, trusted team leaders are empowered to make good decisions on the spot.

Train and Rehearse

The manager's job is to make sure the staff have a clear understanding of what their responsibilities are and to guide them through their tasks. When possible, do dry runs of various activities to be sure they can be run smoothly. Managers should put themselves in the place of spectators, participants, staff, emergency personnel, and vendors, and walk through all the situations they may face, such as arrival, parking, check-in, setup, and so on. By this process, managers should be able to develop a natural progression from start to finish.

Communicate

The event manager must be able to coordinate with multiple staff to make sure everyone knows what is happening and when things need to happen. Changes occur constantly throughout the day, so event managers need to continually update staff, participants, and spectators about any modifications or adjustments. To be effective, managers need to understand what needs to be communicated, who needs to be informed, and by what means they should be informed.

Easily Missed Details

Experienced event managers learn that missed details can cause big problems for an event. Double-check everything on your lists. Think of everything that could go wrong and try to plan for even the most unlikely event. Here are some examples of how minor details could affect how the event is perceived by participants, spectators, sponsors, and staff.

- You begin the event with the singing of the national anthem, but there is no flag in the arena, or you play the wrong music.
- You set up a great buffet for your VIPs but forgot eating utensils.
- You are running a volleyball tournament, but the equipment manager forgot to bring game balls.
- Sponsor's or VIP's names are mispronounced (or you misspell one of their names on a sign) because you did not rehearse the script with the PA announcer.
- The halftime show is ready to begin, but the sound engineer cannot cue the music (dancers without music tend to be very awkward).
- There are no towels in the locker rooms for the teams because someone forgot to stock player areas properly.
- Important people cannot get into the arena because the guest list, pass list, or credential list was not double-checked and key names were left off.

As you can imagine, these details can cause quite a headache in addition to creating a bad image for your event.

Event Day Tools

Fortunately, event managers have a number of tools they can use to ensure everything happens as it is supposed to happen and when it is supposed to happen.

- *Schedules and checklists*. Organized lists of everything that needs to happen before, during, and after the event are an important planning tool. Checklists often include the task, location, and person responsible (table 12.1).
- *Contact lists*. Contact lists ensure your ability to communicate with the right person at the right time. Keep lists of performers, staff, or groups taking part in the event, along with key contacts (table 12.2).
- *Event rundown*. This document, outlining what has to happen during each stage of the event (table 12.3), shows specific times next to every activity that will occur during the event. Delays and disorder can be disastrous when athletes and spectators are on-site. Athletes don't like waiting around. Spectators don't like staring at an empty field. Although many of these delays may be short, audiences notice them and can quickly lose their enthusiasm (Supovitz and Goldwater 2014). For this reason, many professional teams hire directors of entertainment to coordinate music, video, mascots, and various other activities to make sure spectators are entertained throughout the event. Timing and coordination are critical elements for running an event smoothly. To make sure everything happens on time, event managers often create additional documents that specify

TABLE 12.1 Sample Event Day Checklist

	Person responsible	Completion date and time
Preevent		
Event schedules		
Contact lists		
Event rundown		
Event script		
Contingency plans		
Risk management plans		
Facility and equipment inspections		
Accessibility		
Spectator parking controls		
Mass transportation drop-off and pick-up zones		
Access and parking for staff, officials, vendors, and VIP guests		
Disabled access and facilities		
Staff management		
Check-in and assignments		
Preevent briefing		
Communications plan and communications equipment		
Staff uniforms and clothing		
Postevent debriefing		
Volunteer management		
Volunteer check-in and assignments		
Volunteer briefing		
Volunteer contact assignments		
Spectator management		
Adequate facility entrances and exits		
Ticketing policies and procedures		
Appropriate directional signage		
Crowd control procedures		
First aid facilities and personnel		
VIP entrances and arrival arrangements		
VIP seating and accommodations		
Participant management		
Arrival arrangements for participants and officials		
Participant liaison		
Locker facilities		
Training facilities		
Postevent evaluation		
Sponsor management		
Sponsor hospitality		
Fulfillment plan		
Sponsor liaison		
Sponsor evaluation		

> *continued*

TABLE 12.1 > continued

	Person responsible	Completion date and time
Media Credentials and check-in Media work room Interview area Press kits Media seating and accommodations		

TABLE 12.2 Sample Contact List

Event	Group or performer	Contact
Honorary captain presentation	John Hughes	Bill Slatts
National anthem singer	University choir	Bill Smith
Color guard	City high school ROTC	Col. Sharp
Halftime show	Slam Dunk Demons	Christine Cobb
Band	University band	Mike Bezcal
Cheerleaders	Home team cheerleaders	Randy Edgar
Dance team	Superstars dance team	Suzy Sunshine

TABLE 12.3 Sample Event Rundown for a Basketball Game

Time	Scoreboard	Event	Audio and visual	
11:00 a.m.		Event staff arrive		
11:30 a.m.		Game management meeting		
1:00 p.m.		Doors open	Highlight videos	
1:18 p.m.	45:00	Court available for warm-ups	Pre-recorded music	
1:30 p.m.		Band begins playing	Band with live video	
1:43 p.m.	20:00	Start 20-minute clock (TV)		
1:51 p.m.	12:00	Teams to locker rooms	Band with live video	
1:52 p.m.		U.S. national anthem Honorary captain presentation	Singer PA announcer with live video	
1:58 p.m.	5:00	Teams return	Band with live video	
2:03 p.m.	0:00	Horn: teams to benches Visiting team intros Crowd build continues Home team intros Crowd build continues	PA announcer with live video Intro video PA announcer with live video Band with live video	
2:06:30 p.m.		Horn: teams return to court	Tip-off video	
2:07 p.m.	20:00	Tip-off		
First half	1st TO	Cheerleaders Sponsor announcements	Band with live video PA announcer with logos	

what has to happen at various points during the event.

- *Event script*. This document outlines the information the PA announcer, host, or emcee will need to convey throughout the event. A script ensures that no details are missed.

Managing Staff

Given that the event manager cannot be everywhere and do everything, many responsibilities fall to the event staff. Your staff will be responsible for executing the event and will most likely have the most contact with participants, spectators, and sponsors; therefore, it is necessary to have a plan for how to manage staff on event day. Your goal should be to have knowledgeable and motivated staff dedicated to giving all your stakeholders the best experience possible.

Arrival and Check-In

Staff arrival should be scheduled to allow plenty of time for staff to receive duties, prepare for work, and acclimate themselves to the environment. Check-in serves to identify who is present and when they arrived, allowing time to adjust for missing staff. Further, it provides an initial contact point for informing staff of their respective responsibilities and tasks. It is important to be specific as to where staff should report (exact locations), to whom they should report (team leader), and time (call time).

Staff Briefing

Staff briefings are meetings with staff before each shift. During the staff briefing, management reviews organizational or operational issues. In addition, management updates staff with any last-minute information or recent

Time	Scoreboard	Event	Audio and visual
	2nd TO	Shootout promotion	PA announcer with live video
	3rd TO	Sponsored trivia question Facility commercial	PA announcer with logos Facility commercial
	4th TO	Cheerleaders Sponsor announcements	Band with live video PA announcer with logos
	5th TO	Cheerleaders	Band with live video
Halftime	15:00	Institution admissions video	Institution admissions video
	14:30	Dance routine	Recorded music with live shots
	11:00	Halftime contest	PA announcer with live clear floor video
	6:00	Teams return	Band with live video
	2:00	Warm-ups	Band with halftime stats
Second half	1st TO	Cheerleaders Sponsor announcements	Band with live video PA announcer with logos
	2nd TO	Student promotion	PA announcer with live video
	3rd TO	Attendance quiz Sponsor announcements	PA announcer with logos PA announcer with logos
	4th TO	Cheerleaders Sponsor announcements	Band with live video PA announcer with logos
	5th TO	Cheerleaders	Band with live video

changes in operations. The staff briefing may include information pertaining to the following:

• *Team introductions*. At this point, event day staff get to know who they will be working with and put a personal touch on the event.

• *Event considerations*. Staff should be briefed on what will be happening during the event. An emphasis may be placed on activities that are outside normal operations, such as pregame festivities, halftime events, and special guests. It may be helpful (especially for staff who interact with the public) to develop a fact sheet including basic details of the event, such as event schedules, ticket policies, emergency information, relevant statistics or facts about the event, VIP biographies, directions, policies, and facility maps.

• *Facility considerations*. Staff may be briefed on issues concerning the facility, such as when gates open, areas that need to be avoided, and facility contacts.

• *Chain of command*. It is important for staff to identify supervisors and management and to understand authority. Everyone should know who to notify in case of questions or problems. Each level of staff should know their immediate supervisor and understand their reporting responsibilities.

• *Responsibility overview*. Specific duties and expectations may be reviewed at this time. This information is much more important for events involving inexperienced or volunteer staff than it is for experienced, trained staff.

Positional Assignments

Whether you are using paid staff or volunteers, each staff member has unique abilities, knowledge, and skills. The goal of the event manager is to find the ideal person for the specific job.

JUAN BARRETO/AFP/Getty Images

Trash collection at the Russia 2018 World Cup

Depending on the position, significant problems can arise when people are put in positions requiring abilities beyond their skill sets. On the other hand, when people have abilities well beyond the position they are assigned, you risk underutilizing their talents, and they may feel undervalued.

Breaks and Rotation

Breaks, and meals if necessary, are important in keeping your staff fresh, considering that many events last several hours and staff may be on their feet for long periods of time. It is important to communicate the break schedule so that staff know when breaks are required and to make sure positions are covered during breaks. In addition, it is good to schedule floaters (people who can fill in at different spots as needed).

Problem Resolution

During any event, problems or issues are likely to arise. Staff should be briefed on typical problems they may encounter and educated on how to deal with these situations. Further, staff should be informed of whom to contact in the case of unusual problems.

Staff Communication

To facilitate efficient lines of communication, each person has to know her contact person and how to reach that person (e.g., personal contact, two-way radio, cell phone, app). Multiple lines of communication need to be considered.

- *Within units.* Each unit (e.g., maintenance, concessions, security) needs to have a plan for how workers will communicate within that unit. For example, the guest services director needs to have contact with the usher supervisors, who then communicate with the ushers.
- *Between units.* There needs to be a plan for how units can communicate with each other (e.g., guest services and maintenance) when issues arise outside their units.Consider an usher who notices a leaking pipe in the concourse. In this case, the guest services staff would need to communicate with maintenance to fix the problem.
- *Emergency reporting.* Staff needs to understand communication procedures for emergency issues and to whom such issues need to be communicated.

Postevent Debriefing

After the event, management and staff review the event, recognize what worked well, and identify areas of improvement for future events. Given that staff are often on the front lines of the event, they have a unique ability to identify problems. Ushers have the most direct contact with customers and are therefore likely to understand customer concerns. Ticket takers

Tips for Managing Event Day Staff

- *Recognize differences in staff members*: Event day staff is often made up of people who are only there for that day, so they are going to be different from people who are working for your organization.
- *Share your vision for the event*: Don't just illustrate what you want done; try to focus on why it is necessary and what you hope to accomplish. By sharing this information, you can help staff to see the big picture and be able to adapt to situations.
- *Incentivize and reward staff*: By making your staff feel valued, you can make sure they work harder to provide a better experience for your spectators and participants. Staff rewards (swag, food, exclusive experiences) make an impression on the people working for you.

are most likely to understand customer ingress and bottlenecks. This type of evaluation is also beneficial when developing a risk management plan because staff working with customers or on the event floor are more likely to encounter facility issues or operational issues needing attention.

Managing Spectators

A common mistake that inexperienced event managers make is to assume that once a spectator buys a ticket and the money has been received, the job is finished. Good event managers, on the other hand, realize that spectators require care throughout their experience. Your goal should be to give your spectators a satisfying and memorable time. You want your spectators to leave the event wanting to attend again and telling others to attend.

Admission Policy

There are many different ways to structure your admissions policy in order to provide the best experience for your spectators. These decisions will depend on the type, size, and location of your event. Some of the issues that need to be addressed include:

- *Ticket type*: Will you offer reserved seating (each ticket is assigned a specific location) or will there be general admission (spectators can sit in any location)?
- *Passes*: Will spectators be allowed to leave and return?
- *Conflict seats*: Will you have seats available for spectators who have issues with their tickets (e.g., obstructed views, duplicate tickets, unruly fans)
- *ADA (Americans with Disabilities Act) seating*: How will you accommodate spectators with impairments? These impairments may require accessible seating, seating for personal care attendants, access for service animals, or auxiliary services for people with a visual or hearing impairment.
- *Security protections*: How will you protect your consumers from fraudulent tickets?

Technology is increasing the efficiency of event operations through specialized software and applications that assist in ticketing, online registration, league management, tournament management, and volunteer tracking. Print-at-home technology creates conveniences for consumers while reducing mail and box office costs. Mobile ticketing not only provides access to the facility but can be used to enhance consumers' experience by allowing them to make purchases via their phones, find seats with interactive maps, order food and drink, and access other facility features. Mobile ticketing can also be used to increase ticket security and to track spectators' purchase behaviors.

Ingress and Egress

Ingress refers to how customers enter the facility. Although it may seem simple, collecting tickets and moving customers into a facility can be problematic without careful planning. Event organizers have to consider how and when tickets will be collected. If it's expected that spectators will arrive over an extended period of time, a relatively small number of entrances and ticket takers may be sufficient. However, if spectators tend to arrive within a narrow time period, more personnel are needed to make sure there are no long lines of angry spectators eager to get into the facility.

There are also several security issues at this point. You need to address gate security and how you will prevent individuals without tickets from entering. In addition, you may be handling large amounts of money, so you will need to address box office security.

Egress refers to how consumers exit the facility. Egress tends to be more concentrated than ingress because spectators generally leave events in a tighter period of time. Issues related to the number of exits, size of exits, locations of pinch points, and space outside the venue need to be addressed in order to make sure spectators can leave quickly and safely.

VIP Entrances and Seating

Many events are attended by spectators who warrant special treatment. These guests may be people important to the community, such as government officials, celebrities, or other dignitaries. In addition, events may provide special treatment to key business partners, such as sponsors, broadcasters, vendors, donors, or other notable contributors. These very important people (VIPs) are often granted complimentary tickets, private entrances, premium seating, and other perks such as preferred parking or personal wait-service to express gratitude for their support or to lay the foundation for future support.

VIPs may have higher expectations for their experience at the event than other guests. Failure to meet VIPs' needs can be disastrous, so special care should be taken to make sure everything goes well for your VIPs. Check to make sure that every benefit promised has been delivered, and be prepared to deliver service above and beyond what has been promised. It is always a good idea to think *extra* with this group (e.g., extra staff to meet needs, extra tickets for last-minute requests, extra perks available only to VIPs).

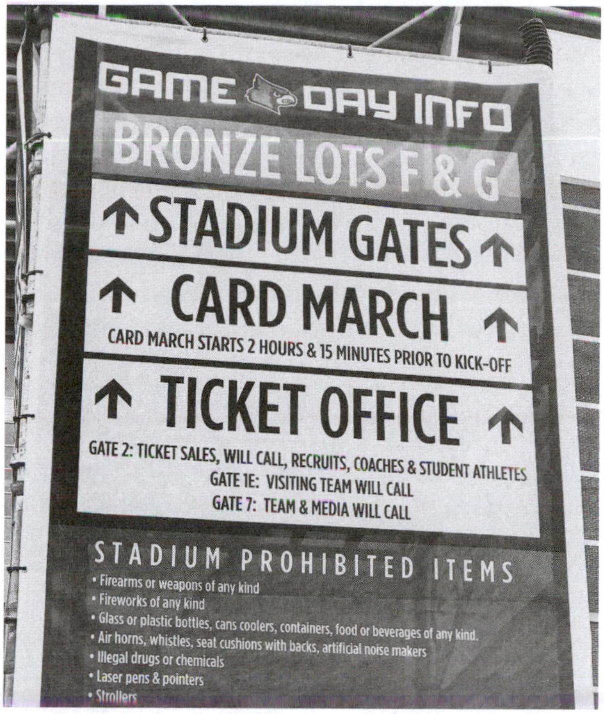

© Chris Greenwell

Informed spectators are more likely to enjoy their experiences and less likely to encounter frustration.

Will Call

Will call is a delivery method in which spectators who have already purchased tickets can pick them up at a designated location before the event. This option is commonly used for spectators who have purchased tickets close to the event date and for spectators who wish to leave tickets for others. With the growth of telephone and Internet sales, will call has become a much more popular option.

Signage

Making signage easily visible is extremely important because spectators are not likely to be as familiar with the facility as you are. Proper signage at entry points reduces backups at ticket lines, directs spectators to the correct entry points, and reduces spectator confusion. Signage should also direct spectators to basic amenities such as restrooms, concessions, merchandise, and customer service locations. Effective signage also plays an important role in spectator safety because it directs them to medical facilities and exits in case of emergency.

Communicating With Spectators

Informed spectators are more likely to enjoy their experiences and less likely to encounter frustration. Use tools such as PA systems, scoreboards and message boards, printed materials, and the media as well as face-to-face communication to convey important information. Consider issues spectators may have with access, parking, ticketing, or changes in event schedules, and devise methods for communicating to spectators any rules, policies, procedures, and changes. You must also develop plans for how organizers can communicate with spectators during a crisis or an emergency. Identify how you can speak directly to your spectators (alarms, public address messages, video) and how you can get vital information to staff that can be relayed to spectators.

Spectator Evaluation of the Event

Spectator evaluations allow organizations to learn about spectators' experiences and identify pressing concerns needing management's attention. Collecting this information allows management to prioritize initiatives to increase satisfaction or decrease dissatisfaction (Greenwell, Lee, and Naeger 2007). Management may solicit spectator input through formal methods such as surveys, depth interviews, or focus groups. Figure 12.1 illustrates a sample spectator survey. Informal methods can also be effective. For example, many organizations provide comment cards to their customers or publicize e-mail addresses spectators can use to pass along comments, concerns, or complaints. Other organizations may encourage their ushers or event staff to converse with spectators to learn important information first-hand.

Managing Participants

The athletes are the core of a sporting event and require different care than spectators. Athletes, as well as their coaches and families, will have special needs throughout the event that must be addressed so they can concentrate on their performances. The event manager's goal is to create an atmosphere where participants don't have to worry about the little things, so that athletes can focus on being their best when they compete. Athletes remember great experiences and let everyone know when an event has exceeded their expectations. They also remember terrible experiences, and let even more people know.

Participant Arrival

Participant arrival is often the first contact point between participants and event organizers, offering the first opportunity to create an impression—positive or negative—of the event. It is important to greet participants when they arrive at the venue. For small events a simple greeting from the event manager may be enough to welcome participants and orient them to the facility and event. For large events, participant arrival can be a complex process involving transportation to the host city, accommodations, and transportation from hotels to event sites. At the event site, movement of people and equipment to locker rooms, warm-up rooms, and the event floor; security; and special requests become the main concerns.

One way to improve the probability of a smooth arrival is to communicate important information to your participants before the event. Send information packages with arrival instructions, hotel and transportation information, local maps, facility maps, restaurant and entertainment options, and contact information for additional questions. A website can also be used to provide up-to-date information that will help smooth your participants' arrival.

Area Logistics

Depending on the event, participants may have different needs ranging from locker and

How did you learn about our event? ____________________

Would you attend again? ☐ Yes ☐ No Why? ____________________

Would you recommend this event to others? ☐ Yes ☐ No Why? ____________________

How would you rate ticketing? (1 = poor, 5 = excellent)	1	2	3	4	5
How would you rate the ushers? (1 = poor, 5 = excellent)	1	2	3	4	5
How would you rate the facility? (1 = poor, 5 = excellent)	1	2	3	4	5
How would you rate parking? (1 = poor, 5 = excellent)	1	2	3	4	5
How would you rate the souvenir stands? (1 = poor, 5 = excellent)	1	2	3	4	5
How would you rate concessions? (1 = poor, 5 = excellent)	1	2	3	4	5
How would you rate your overall experience? (1 = poor, 5 = excellent)	1	2	3	4	5

What can we do to improve this event next year? ____________________

FIGURE 12.1 Sample spectator survey.

shower facilities, meeting rooms, hospitality areas, equipment storage, and warm-up areas. The type of event may dictate the number of security personnel or staff needed. To prepare for these logistics, event managers should meet with team liaisons to understand the entire traveling party's needs and expectations.

Access to these areas as well as sideline, dugout, and bench areas is often controlled by issuing credentials to participants and the traveling party. As well as identifying the bearer, credentials should identify to which areas the bearer has access.

Communicating With Participants

It is important to keep participants and coaches up to date on key information. Specifically, organizers should make sure participants have been given the schedule of events and locations, registration or check-in information, facility diagrams, and contact numbers. In addition, it is important to note that participants may not be familiar with the area or the format of the event. Therefore, communication should be specific and detailed. Table 12.4 gives a sample

TABLE 12.4 Sample Participant Information Sheet: Basketball Game

Equipment delivery	Thursday: delivery of sideline signage, 24 chairs, ball racks, and balls. Return to practice facility on Monday.
Band	Home and visiting bands can deliver equipment at 10:00 a.m. on game day. Delivery must be made at Cole Street Docks.
Training staff	Trainer will deliver equipment at 10:00 a.m. on game day. Equipment will be stored in locker room.
Will-call tickets	General public: Broadway ticket window Players: Broadway ticket window (tickets must be delivered no later than 90 min. before game time)
Parking	Visiting team bus: park at North Cole Street Docks. Student buses: drop off at entrance B. Game officials: park at Cole Street Docks. Band and cheer: buses park at Cole Street Docks.
Entrances	Public: Entrances A and B Booster club: Entrance B Home players: Broadway Central Entrance Visiting players: Cole Street Dock Media: Broadway Central Entrance Staff: Broadway Central Entrance Band: Cole Street Dock Cheer: Cole Street Dock
Locker rooms	Home team: visitor's locker room South Visiting team: visitor's locker room North Officials: officials locker room B Home cheerleaders: auxiliary locker room A Visiting cheerleaders: auxiliary locker room B
Media	Interviews: interview room Media work room: Room 150
Booster club	Hospitality room: Room 140 (floor level)
Gates open	12:30 p.m. Central
Game time	2:05 p.m. Central

of information you might provide to a team arriving for a basketball game.

Communication with coaches and participants comes in multiple formats. Key information may be provided in an information packet or posted in locker facilities. Signage throughout the facility provides information on locations, policies, and timing of events. Public address announcements are utilized to inform participants about upcoming events or schedule changes. Event managers should also assign a participant liaison to each team or entity. This person becomes the key point of communication when questions or special needs arise. Larger events may set up a command center to centralize and integrate communications.

Participant Liaisons

Participant liaisons are key communications tools that are integral to the satisfaction of participants. Liaisons should be educated about event activities and prepared for questions or special requests. Events will often appoint a facility liaison. This person is responsible for assisting participants and event organizers with any issues with the facility or event.

Traveling Parties

Sporting events often have official traveling parties including coaches, administrators, and staff that may be as large as, or larger than, the number of participants. The needs of these people also have to be considered in order to create a memorable experience for all involved. Since team officials are often the ones who make the decision whether or not to return to an event, their satisfaction is vitally important.

Locker Facilities

Changing rooms may be required for each team and its officials. Additional changing rooms may be needed for support groups such as cheerleaders, dance teams, in-game entertainment, other performers, and family. A separate room may also be requested for use as a meeting room or office area. Typical changing rooms include lockers and showers, but participants may also require additional amenities such as laundry services, athletic training equipment, or multimedia devices. Event organizers also have to consider personnel needs related to locker facilities. It may be necessary to provide security, custodial, or laundry staff depending on the event and the needs of the participants.

To ensure this aspect of the event moves smoothly, it is imperative that organizers specify what will or will not be provided and communicate those specifications to participants. A lack of communication is likely to cause confusion and dissatisfaction. Be specific so that teams know exactly what to expect and can prepare accordingly. For example, you might provide the following information to participating teams before an event:

- Locker facilities will be open two hours before game time and one hour after the event.
- Each locker room has an attached training room that is available to teams.
- Ice and water are available in each training room.
- No towels or locks will be provided.
- Locker rooms will be available to team members and the traveling party only.

Participant Departure

There should be a plan for participant departure that covers exits, transportation, and safety. The departure plan should also account for participants' equipment and traveling parties.

Participant Evaluation

A participant's final evaluation of the event is often the determining factor as to whether or not she intends to participate in future events. Considering that many events depend on attracting top competition, incentive programs events are often created to make sure participants enjoy their stay and want to return. Some of the perks that could be included are the following:

- Specialized food service ranging from healthy snacks to gourmet meals
- Athlete lounges with games and activities to fill down time
- Participant gifts ranging from tournament merchandise to high-end products from event sponsors
- Training and massage services
- Social events and exclusive entertainment
- Activities for athletes' children and significant others

To gather information about what participants think of an event and to collect ideas about how the event can be improved, many event organizers create a postevent participant survey. Figure 12.2 shows a sample survey for examining runners' perceptions of a marathon. Results from such a survey can be used to identify strengths and weaknesses of your event in order to suggest changes for future events. In addition, participant evaluations can help planners determine how participants will respond to proposed changes to an event, estimate the economic impact of an event, or gather information to share with sponsors.

Managing Sponsors

Selling a sponsorship is just the first part of the process. Events and sponsors have to work together to ensure sponsors' maximum benefits from their association with the event. Special care must be taken to make sure sponsors are satisfied; the best way to recruit a sponsor is to retain an existing one. To accomplish this, events should strive to deliver all promised benefits, protect sponsors' rights, and develop relationships with sponsors. It is much better to exceed sponsors' expectations by delivering more than what was promised than to fall short on promises. In other words, you should underpromise and overdeliver.

Signage

Signage is a benefit sponsors commonly seek from sponsorship programs. The facility should be carefully evaluated to find the best locations for sponsors' signage. Look for spots that provide the best exposure to participants, spectators, and the media. Identify locations such as sidelines, backdrops, and finish lines that will maximize exposure.

How did you learn about our marathon?______________________________

Would you participate again? ☐ Yes ☐ No Why?______________

Would you recommend this marathon to others? ☐ Yes ☐ No Why?______________

How would you rate registration? (1 = poor, 5 = excellent)	1	2	3	4	5
How would you rate the course? (1 = poor, 5 = excellent)	1	2	3	4	5
How would you rate the staff? (1 = poor, 5 = excellent)	1	2	3	4	5
How would you rate the water stations? (1 = poor, 5 = excellent)	1	2	3	4	5
How would you rate the postrace awards ceremony? (1 = poor, 5 = excellent)	1	2	3	4	5
How would you rate the participant gifts? (1 = poor, 5 = excellent)	1	2	3	4	5
How would you rate your overall experience? (1 = poor, 5 = excellent)	1	2	3	4	5

How far did you travel to get here?______________________________

How many nights did you stay in town? ______________________________

What can we do to improve this event next year?______________________________

FIGURE 12.2 Sample participant survey for a marathon.

© Chris Greenwell

Sponsor integration for a 5K race.

Promotions

Many event sponsorships involve sales promotions that may include premium giveaways, contests or sweepstakes, product sampling, point-of-purchase displays, or other special events. Timing and execution are important to make sure all activities meet sponsors' expectations.

Hospitality

Hospitality for corporate clients is a big part of major sporting events because major sponsors often seek opportunities to entertain their own VIP guests. Look for ways to help your sponsors create exclusive access, experiences, and opportunities to pamper their guests.

Deliverables

Organizers should develop a fulfillment plan for each sponsor that makes sure the event is honoring each contractually obligated component of the contract. Summary sheets outlining the specific deliverables promised to a sponsor can list activities that need to take place, people responsible for these activities, and deadlines for completion.

Sponsor Liaisons

One person from the organization should be appointed as the sponsor liaison; for a large event you may have multiple sponsor liaisons in order to cover all responsibilities. This individual is the main point of contact for the sponsor and manages communication between the sponsor and the event.

Sponsor Evaluation

In contrast to philanthropy, sponsors are typically looking for a return on their investment or a return on their objectives. Event organizers should identify sponsors' objectives before the event and show a commitment to delivering on those objectives. After the event, sponsors should be provided with reports detailing how the sponsorship was fulfilled (e.g., attendance figures, media coverage, advertising value, public relations value, direct sales). Care should be taken to illustrate the value the sponsors received in exchange for their investment.

Customer Service

Regardless of whether you are working with spectators, participants, or sponsors, strong customer service practices and policies can deliver numerous benefits to the organization. Some of the benefits include the following.

- *Retain customers*: Good service keeps customers coming back. It is much easier and more cost-effective to retain current customers than to acquire new customers.
- *Increase positive word of mouth*: Individuals who receive good service are more likely to recommend your event to others (potential customers). Similarly, individ-

uals receiving poor service are likely to tell others of their experiences.

- *Differentiate your event from that of your competition*: Strong customer service is a good way to create a competitive advantage over other competing events.
- *Improve employee morale*: Positive relationships between consumers and employees create a better working environment.

Proactive Customer Service

Being proactive involves taking steps to identify and solve problems before they occur. A proactive approach allows an organization to either avoid or reduce the impact of customer issues, saving the organization time and saving the consumer from aggravation. Some ways to be proactive include:

- *Making service part of your mission*: This involves prioritizing customer service and making a commitment to customer service across all levels of the organization.
- *Taking the time to understand customers' needs*: By understanding your customers' needs you can anticipate and prepare to avoid any issues they may face. Collect customer feedback to identify areas of weakness or concern.
- *Training staff*: Frontline staff, who are more likely to come in contact with customers, should be trained in how to identify problems before they occur.
- *Rewarding staff*: Rewarding staff for providing good customer service helps strengthen the organization's commitment to customer service across the organization.

Reactive Customer Service

Despite your best efforts to be proactive, some problems are unavoidable. These situations are problematic because dissatisfied customers not only are less likely to return to the event but also are likely to tell others of their problems. Responding to problems after they happen is referred to as reactive customer service. Therefore, events should have policies for resolving customer complaints. Some tips for reactive customer service follow.

- *Be accessible*: You would rather hear the customer's issues and have a chance to address them than have the consumer leave angry or complain to other customers.
- *Actively listen*: You can often appease consumers by merely listening to their problems and showing you care. Allow the customer to explain without interruption. It is often helpful to restate the customer's complaint to show you understand.
- *Apologize and thank*: Apologies are not necessarily admissions of fault; they are a way to communicate that you are listening and are concerned. Show them you appreciate them by sharing their concerns.
- *Offer solutions*: Illustrate how you plan to follow up on the complaint and offer solutions to resolve the problem. Be prepared to offer alternative solutions if necessary.
- *Follow up*: Check in to find out how the customer is doing and to see whether he has any other concerns.

Moment of Truth

A popular method of enhancing customer service is to identify moments of truth. Carlzon and Peters (1987) defined a **moment of truth** as any time a customer comes into contact with the company and has the opportunity to make an evaluation. Over the course of a sporting event, customers have numerous opportunities to interact with the facility, staff, and the event itself. The challenge is to identify each of these interactions and formulate strategies to make sure these interactions go well. One way to do so is by mapping the customer's experience from beginning to end. We often spend most of our time thinking about the event itself, but as you can see below, there are ample opportunities to impact the customer (positively and negatively) before and after the competition. The following are just some of the key touchpoints your event may have with consumers.

Participant event

- Registration
- Travel to host location
- Accommodations
- Preevent activities
- On-site parking
- Team check-in
- Changing rooms
- Warm-up facilities
- Competition
- Score and statistics tracking
- Awards ceremonies

Spectator event

- Ticket purchase
- Traffic flow to the facility
- Parking
- Preevent entertainment
- Facility entry
- Security
- Seating access
- Concessions
- Restrooms
- In-game entertainment
- The game itself
- Facility exit
- Traffic flow away from the facility

The following are some examples of innovations sport organizations are using to deliver better service to their consumers.

- The NFL's Houston Texans are offering an artificial intelligence service to answer a wide variety of fan questions. The software can handle thousands of inquiries at once to provide fast and accurate responses to fans' questions (Witthaus 2018).
- Minor League Baseball incorporates chatbots that can provide real-time customer service in both English and Spanish. This technology offers a way to be more responsive to fans and provide them with personalized experiences (Fisher 2018).
- The New Orleans Pelicans were named the NBA's best customer service team in 2016. They provide Disney-style training to their arena employees and employ a staff of data analysts tracking customer satisfaction and purchasing trends (Kushner 2017).
- Churchill Downs, home of the Kentucky Derby, renovated the second floor of the clubhouse facility, putting in additional food locations, restrooms, and betting windows. These renovations were driven by feedback from consumers who desired more options and less time waiting in line (Finley 2016).

Event Day Technologies

Managing event day can be made easier with various technologies. Types of technologies include

- *Staff communication tools*: Various apps have been created to allow communication with staff through text or group messaging. These apps help disseminate important information quickly and efficiently.
- *E-ticketing*: E-ticketing software is convenient for consumers and reduces the risk of lost tickets. Additional advantages for organizers include lower printing costs and the ability to track purchases better.
- *Mobile point-of-service (POS)*: These systems allow consumers to connect with food, beverage, or merchandise vendors in their seats and pay online, reducing time spent waiting in line and allowing vendors to spend less time taking orders and counting cash.
- *Touch-screen kiosks*: Many venues now utilize self-service kiosks around their

facilities to give consumers access to a variety of services and information.

- *Data management systems*: These systems can collect data on everything from purchase behaviors to social media interaction, giving managers better insight into the customer experience.
- *Participant tracking systems*: Most often used for running events, this technology utilizes GPS to track runners' times and locations, creating a better race experience for the runners and enhancing race management.

Technologies such as event-specific apps can also be used to engage with consumers in order to make their experience safer and more enjoyable. For example, individuals attending Super Bowl LII had access to two apps designed to make their experience at the event stress free, fun, and safe.

1. US Bank Stadium app
    - Guest services information with links to ask questions or report concerns
    - Stadium maps highlighting restrooms, first aid stations, concession and merchandise stands, escalators, and exits
    - Directions to the stadium for multiple transportation options
    - Public transportation information with customizable route planning
    - Parking information with options to prepurchase parking
    - Turn-by-turn directions to find seats
2. Super Bowl LII app
    - Venue and area maps for the stadium, Super Bowl LII Experience, and Super Bowl Live.
    - Event schedules for all events leading up to the big game
    - Lists of prohibited items and security procedures
    - Customer service contacts
    - Weather forecasts
    - Game day FAQs
    - Access to instant replays
    - Social media portals

Summary

All the planning and preparation comes together on the day of the event. Numerous tasks must be accomplished throughout game day, therefore managers need to anticipate, plan, delegate, and communicate so that everything gets done in a timely manner. Event managers should make use of various tools such as checklists, contact lists, event rundowns, and event scripts to help coordinate activities.

Event managers need to coordinate with the staff entrusted to accomplish all these tasks. They also have to deal with the needs of spectators, participants, and sponsors. For each group, the manager's goal is to leave them satisfied and wanting to return to future events. This undertaking is made easier if event managers understand each party's needs and commit to delivering experiences beyond expectations.

LEARNING ACTIVITIES

Identify an event and imagine yourself in the position of being responsible for event day.

1. Create a list of things that need to happen, from an operations perspective, for the event to be a success.
2. Create a checklist of necessary activities for each functional area, and identify when those activities need to be completed.
3. Prepare an event rundown for this event. Think of the coordination necessary to make everything run smoothly.
4. Prepare a PA script for one segment of the event (e.g., pregame, halftime).

CASE STUDY: LEADOFF CLASSIC

The National Fastpitch Coaches Association (NFCA) is an organization that was established in 1983 to promote professional growth of fastpitch softball coaches and advance the sport of fastpitch softball. It is an international organization with members from Canada, the Czech Republic, Germany, Great Britain, Ireland, the Netherlands, New Zealand, Singapore, Sweden, and the United States. The organization provides many services to its members, such as education programs, coaches' clinics, awards programs, camps, and tournaments.

One of the tournaments the organization hosts is the Leadoff Classic for collegiate softball teams. Tournaments are arranged by division membership (there are separate tournaments for NCAA Division II, NCAA Division III, Junior Colleges, and teams from the National Association of Intercollegiate Athletics). These events attract some of the top teams from around the country for three days of high-level competition. One participant described it as being "like playing a national championship tournament right out of the gate."

An example of one of these events was the 2018 Division III Leadoff Classic. Thirty-two teams participated over three days in March at Lincoln Park in Tucson, Arizona. In order to accommodate so many teams, games were played on eight fields with each field hosting four games per day (10 a.m., 12:30 p.m., 3 p.m., and 5:30 p.m.). Each team played two games per day for a total of six games over the three days. Awards were provided to the championship team, runner-up, and all-tournament team.

Case Study Application

Considering the number of athletes participating and the number of games played over the three days, making sure an event like this goes smoothly can be a daunting task. If you were running one of these events, you would want to deliver an excellent event so that participants, spectators, and sponsors would have a good impression of the NFCA and want to return to future Leadoff Classic Events. To this end, you would have to put in a lot of planning to make event day successful.

1. Regarding participants' experiences at the event, what would be specific examples of moments of truth? Based on these moments of truth, what services would you need to provide the teams in order to ensure a good experience for them? What information would it be necessary to provide participating teams?
2. It would be impossible for one person to manage all of the games and activities that need to take place, which means you would have to rely heavily on your staff. How would you make sure your staff provides a good experience for everyone involved?
3. The event also draws spectators. What would be your admissions policies? How can you effectively communicate with spectators at the event to make certain they enjoy their experience?
4. Events like these often rely on sponsors to cover costs and provide needed goods and services. How can you make sure sponsors are satisfied with their partnership with you and would want to renew for future events?

Patrick McDermott/NHLI via Getty Images

CHAPTER 13

Postevent Details and Evaluation

CHAPTER OBJECTIVES

After completing the chapter, the reader should be able to do the following:

- Describe activities of importance after the conclusion of the event.
- Provide techniques for securing postevent media coverage.
- List ways to follow up with sponsors after the event.
- Explain various ways of evaluating the sport event and its effectiveness.
- Understand the concept of return on objectives.
- Describe how to measure economic impact.

INDUSTRY PROFILE

Charity Waldron, Virginia Amateur Sports

Charity Waldron is the operations and media relations director for Virginia Amateur Sports (VAS), which is a 501(c)(3) nonprofit that promotes awareness and benefits of physical fitness and healthy lifestyles through sports education, training, and competition. VAS directs more than 10 events throughout the year, including the Virginia Commonwealth Games, the largest multisport festival held in Virginia each year. Waldron is a 2011 graduate of Lynchburg College with a bachelor's in sport management, and a 2013 graduate of East Tennessee State University with a master's in sport management. She joined Virginia Amateur Sports in April 2013 to organize the Virginia Commonwealth Games and the 13 other events that VAS coordinates annually. Waldron is passionate about creative marketing strategies for events and developing interns to be the next generation of leaders in the industry. She is also very active on the national level with the National Congress of State Games, helping to grow new events throughout the country and assisting in developing or kickstarting some of the current ones.

What are some ways in which you evaluate the success of an event?

We evaluate the success of our events a number of ways. We assess athlete participation numbers and spectator ticket sales, compare them to previous years, and evaluate them as to how they align with our goals. We retrieve information concerning room nights to find out how many participants are staying in local hotels and where they are coming from. We get economic impact figures to determine whether the event is continuing to grow every year. We partner with the city of Lynchburg and their tourism department and use the DMAI economic impact calculator. Finally, it is important for us to be around our participants to determine whether they are having a good time. We know that when participants are having a good time they are more likely to spread positive word-of-mouth messages to other potential participants.

How does social media factor into how you evaluate the success of the event?

We use social media a lot in promoting our events through advertising and organic posts and engagement between participants. We encourage participants to post pictures and use hashtags. The engagement back and forth between participants, families, and even our sponsors is a good indicator of the success of the event. Social media like Facebook, Twitter, and Instagram are powerful tools for us. Our participants have a wide age range; younger athletes tend to be more active on Instagram, whereas the preferred platform for parents and older athletes is Facebook. We try to target each platform for a specific audience. During the event, we have Snapchat filters that we encourage participants to use. Finally, we have noticed over the past couple of years that during the event you need to respond constantly to questions and posts on social media. The greatest success with social media has been during times when we as a team were highly engaged by being active, responding to posts, and tracking hashtags. Hashtags often provide us with quotes to use when we do sponsorship follow-up.

What specifically is involved in terms of postevent follow-up?

After the event is complete, we send out surveys to all of our participants. We ask them how they heard about the event, to describe their experience, and to rate various activities like the opening ceremonies and the athlete tailgate. We also ask whether they intend to come back and participate in the event. We often receive e-mails from participants and try to implement those suggestions that are feasible. For each of our races, we conduct a postevent survey and sometimes use focus groups. After the event, we meet as team for a postevent evaluation. Finally, we meet with each of our sponsors individually and provide them with statistics on participation numbers, demographics, and impressions. We meet face to face with each sponsor to make sure we are meeting their goals and reaching their audience.

After any event, some type of cleanup is generally needed to restore the facility to working order. Events that require meeting space and food and beverage breaks need services such as vacuuming of the meeting room, washing the dishes, and resetting the tables and chairs. Sporting events such as a baseball game require field maintenance such as raking and covering the mound. In addition, the seating, concession, and ticketing areas must be swept and cleaned thoroughly. In cases where a vendor is allowed to operate in the sport facility, standards of cleanliness should be set and clearly communicated along with a deposit taken in the event you need to pay a third party to clean the area (deLisle 2014).

Many other factors besides cleaning must be considered during breakdown. Some events rent equipment such as computers, printers, two-way radios, sporting equipment, telephones, food and beverage equipment, and audiovisual equipment. These items must be inspected and returned to the rental agency before the end of the contract date. It is important that this equipment be inventoried before the event and secured in a safe location after the event. The setup and breakdown portion of any event can be chaotic, and valuable items are susceptible to being stolen or easily misplaced.

Once an event is over, it can be difficult to find staff to help with breakdown and cleanup. Many facilities employ a housekeeping team or event staff members who are responsible for cleanup. If vendors are involved, event planners should include specific language in the contracts negotiated with them in terms of the requirements for cleanup. Some jobs in the sport industry require a large amount of work during the cleanup phase at the conclusion of the event. For example, an equipment manager is responsible for postevent duties such as laundry, equipment maintenance, and inventorying, along with the transport and storage of equipment.

Postevent Promotions

Communicating with the audience is important even after the sport event is over. **Promotion** is defined as communicating with and persuading defined user groups (Irwin, Sutton, and McCarthy 2008). By reaching out to these defined user groups through postevent promotions, the event planner stays in touch with the primary consumers of the event. Postevent promotion can take many forms, such as sending out newsletters, following up on contests or sweepstakes that occurred during the event, posting photos or videos on social media sites, sending certificates and awards, implementing customer service surveys, and sending out promotional information about next year's event while the consumer is still thinking about this year's. Event planners should remember the importance of **aftermarketing**—providing continuing satisfaction and reinforcement to past or current customers in order to create lasting relationships (Irwin, Sutton, and McCarthy 2008).

Postevent Media Coverage

Sport is widely popular in North America, and there is strong demand from the general public for information. Fans of a sports team who just won a championship game want to continue the celebration and demand immediate media coverage with analysis by players and coaches. Media coverage is often built into the estimated economic impact of a sport event (Dwyer et al. 2000). Depending on the type and impact of the event, securing some form of postevent media coverage may or may not be necessary. For example, avid fans not only expect but also eagerly anticipate postevent media coverage after mega-events such as the Kentucky Derby, the NCAA Division I championships, the NFL Super Bowl, the NBA Finals, the MLB World Series, and the Olympic and Paralympic Games.

Although most event planners do not have to deal with the media scrutiny that accompanies mega-events, every event should capitalize on some form of public or media relations. Media relations programs maximize favorable publicity and minimize unfavorable publicity for the sport organization. For smaller events, it is not difficult to invite a local newspaper or television station to carry a human interest story about an event participant. Statistical information about the event can easily be reported to the media. Postevent media coverage can take the form of short, spontaneous interviews of players and coaches or of more widely planned postgame press conferences. Isenberg (2018) offers the following tips to athletes and coaches when talking to the media.

- Be personal by making eye contact, calling reporters by their first name, and being friendly even when they're not interviewing you.
- Be prepared by thinking about what you want to say beforehand.
- Be professional and respectful by showing up on time for scheduled interviews, understanding the media will report both good and bad, and not taking what they say personally.
- Be engaging by providing thoughtful answers, appropriate humor, concise answers, and no ethnic, gender, or religious slurs or insults.
- Be accommodating by befriending the media.
- Live by the locker room code that claims that what happens in the locker room should stay in the locker room.
- Know how and when to say No comment.
- Do not lie or mislead.
- Avoid off-the–record comments.
- Act like this is fun.

News Conferences

Stoldt, Dittmore, and Branvold (2012) suggest the goal of a news conference is to "disseminate noteworthy information from an organization to its targeted publics" (p. 181). One of the key components of sport events is the emotion that emanates from the competition. This emotional component has led more than one athlete and coach to mutter words immediately after the contest that they would later regret. Event planners should factor in a time period, after the event and before the news conference, in which coaches and players can decompress and cool down from an emotional standpoint. The event planner may need to serve as the liaison between the media and the teams during this cool-down period. Irwin, Sutton, and McCarthy (2002) suggest setting up the press conference facilities at least one hour in advance, and they provide the following checklist to ensure success:

- Blackboard, easel, screen, and projector
- Chairs and tables for principals
- Designated place for video cameras
- Floor microphones for questions if the room is large
- Full staff at entry door to greet media
- Lectern brackets for press microphones
- Organization logo displayed (normally projected in the background)
- Outside directional signage indicating room location
- Podium height and lighting
- Posters, graphics, and other artwork
- Press kit or handouts at registration desk
- Public address system, including microphone and speaker
- Registration desk or book
- Schedule of photos for house photographer
- Sufficient chairs for reporters
- Technical service operator for all equipment
- Water glasses for speakers

Impact of Social Media on Postgame Media Coverage

It is important to understand the impact of social media on sport events. Many professional and collegiate athletes use Twitter to reach their followers, bypassing more traditional media routes. Both sports participants and spectators can deliver newsworthy information at the click of a button via various social media sites. Photos can be taken using mobile telephone technology and immediately uploaded. One of the strangest examples of the instantaneous nature of these social media sites was a live tweet in April 2012 by former NFL great Deion

Sanders alleging he was being assaulted by his wife. He posted photos of himself and his kids filling out police reports; the photos were later removed. Trolling is another disturbing trend in social media to which athletes, coaches, officials, and management are susceptible. **Trolling** is the "anonymous sending of threats, insults or other harassment, usually online, from a distant remove" (McKnight and Bishop 2018). Niche social media sites, such as MLB's Infield Chatter, do not allow trolling. Infield Chatter is a space where MLB players can connect with fans.

The Mashable Entertainment (2012) website reports that more than 80 percent of sport fans monitor social media sites such as Twitter and Facebook while watching games on TV, and more than 60 percent do so while watching live events. In fact, certain players may be trending on Twitter, which suggests they are the most popular topic being discussed on Twitter. Twitter revealed that the most tweeted-about sporting event was the FIFA European Championship of 2016. The New England Patriots comeback victory over the Atlanta Falcons in the 2017 Super Bowl also received much attention on social media.

Sponsor Follow-Up

The relationship with corporate sponsors does not end once the event is complete. In fact, all sponsorships should be evaluated throughout the entire process, and a postevent **sponsor follow-up** is both expected and imperative. The follow-up procedure is important because it not only helps the sponsor fulfill goals and objectives but also allows the rights holder to identify problem areas or points of dissatisfaction. According to Irwin, Sutton, and McCarthy (2008), an entire audit of the event sponsorship should be conducted at the end of the campaign to determine how well the goals and objectives were met. If the sponsorship was conducted effectively, it is more likely the

Keyur Khamar/PGA TOUR

The relationship with corporate sponsors does not end once the event is complete.

sponsor will reactivate or renew during the follow-up meeting.

Shortly after the conclusion of the event, contact the sponsor and schedule a meeting. During this meeting, the sponsor representative should be given a number of metrics that are helpful in measuring the success of the sponsorship. Lynde (2007) suggests that some elements of a sponsorship package such as media rights, signage, and tickets are easier to quantify because a market rate has been developed over time. Other elements, such as category exclusivity, use of intellectual property, and pass-through rights, are more difficult to quantify. As Lynde states, it is easier to evaluate a sponsorship package when the true value of the sponsorship assets can be quantified and emotion is not involved in decision-making. With some sporting events, emotion plays a big part when sponsorship decision makers are fans of a certain team.

Postevent Debriefing

A postevent meeting or debriefing with the most important stakeholders involved in planning the event is an important opportunity for event planners to gain feedback about the event. Key personnel who might attend this meeting include facility managers, security personnel, event organizers, hotel managers, and representatives from destination marketing organizations along with other people involved in planning the event. It is also advisable to invite members of traffic and safety agencies because they can provide feedback that will help improve future traffic management plans (deLisle 2014). The debriefing may take place at the sport venue, the host hotel, or any other location convenient for all stakeholders. Depending on the schedule of the various people involved, as well as facility availability, the debriefing may include a food and beverage function such as a luncheon.

Event planners may ask the various stakeholders to complete a report that highlights findings from the event and provides recommendations for improving future events. For example, a report from traffic coordinators may highlight key times when traffic congestion detracted from the event and offer suggestions for better handling the flow of traffic filing into the sport venue and the corresponding departure. Event planners may also use some form of survey research during this phase. Online or paper-and-pencil surveys may be distributed to stakeholders requesting their feedback for improving the event. Both open-ended and yes-or-no questions may be included on the surveys, which can be administered before, during, or after the debriefing.

The debriefing can take many forms. At one extreme, Masterman (2014) suggests that the debriefing is a celebration of the event and a postevent party. In contrast, the debriefing can be simply one meeting, submeetings, or a series of meetings, and the agenda should address all aspects of the event. Another question to consider is when the debriefing takes place. Final evaluative reports for some events are not completed until many months or years after the conclusion of the event. Masterman recommends holding the debriefing within a week of the event so that memory does not detract from the process. When conducting the debriefing, all stakeholders should be given an opportunity to report their findings. It is important that the tone of the debriefing not be too celebratory, but attendees should also avoid highly critical personal attacks. The primary purpose of the debriefing is to record important institutional knowledge that was gained from the event and to use it in future planning.

Event Evaluation

One of the weaknesses in the sport event industry is the lack of evaluation by event planners. An evaluation of a sport event allows the planner to better understand whether the objectives of the event were accomplished. It also shows the various areas within the event that need to be improved. This section discusses the various levels of evaluation as well as several evaluation methods.

Levels of Evaluation

Myhill and Phillips (2010) outline up to six levels for evaluating objectives for a meeting or convention throughout the meeting industry, which are listed here. These levels can also be applied in the sport event industry.

- *Level 0*: Statistics, scope, and volume; this level collects data such as the scope and volume of attendance, press coverage, website traffic, and similar statistics.
- *Level 1*: Reaction, satisfaction, and planned action; this level gathers information on what stakeholders thought of the planning process, marketing efforts, facilities, and so forth.
- *Level 2*: Learning evaluation measures the extent to which principles, facts, techniques, skills, and professional contact have been acquired during the meeting. Similar types of learning take place at a sport event and can be applied in a similar manner.
- *Level 3*: Application measures the extent to which skills, knowledge, and professional contacts learned at the meeting were applied on the job or in the personal life of attendees.
- *Level 4*: Business impact monitors organizational improvement of business measures such as sales, cost savings, work output, and quality changes. Within the context of sport event management, business impacts would refer to sponsor impacts.
- *Level 5*: Return on investment (ROI) for the various stakeholders of the meeting, calculated as the ratio of benefits to costs.

As in the meeting industry generally, the sport event industry can use these levels of evaluation to determine ROI. Sport event planners can also use methods such as in-game evaluations, staff and management evaluations, budgeting, and attendance as evaluative measures.

In-Game Evaluations

There are a number of ways to evaluate an event during the contest itself. Participants and spectators can provide feedback using a street-intercept methodology, whereby people are surveyed as they enter or exit a sport venue. Street intercepts are useful in cases where you want feedback from hard-to-reach people in a real-life situation. One of the key factors to keep in mind when conducting any type of survey research for evaluative purposes during an event is to be brief because participants and spectators are not there for the purpose of completing your survey but rather to participate in or watch the event.

Both qualitative and quantitative types of research can be used for evaluation. Quantitative methods include short questionnaires or surveys distributed during the event. If you conduct a quantitative survey, here are some key factors to consider:

- Where will you distribute the questionnaire or survey? Will it be at an entrance or an exit? If you distribute at an entrance you should consider timing, because people arriving early are more likely to respond than those running late. If you are distributing the questionnaire at the end of an event, keep in mind what time the event ends. Will people leave the event early?
- You should provide pens or pencils for completing the questionnaire.
- Will you offer an incentive for completing the questionnaire (e.g., future tickets to an event, souvenir merchandise)?
- Who will help you distribute the questionnaire, and how many helpers will you need in order to get a good response rate?

One form of qualitative evaluation is participant observation. This unobtrusive form of evaluation allows you to learn more about active event participants or spectators within the real setting of the event. The disadvantages of using participant observation to evaluate an event include the following:

- It is time-consuming for the observer.
- The observer cannot be everywhere at once.
- The observer can affect the behavior of the person being observed.

Individual interviews and small focus groups can also be used to evaluate various aspects of an event. Interviews ask for individual opinions, perceptions, beliefs, and attitudes about the event. Focus groups do the same, but the interview is conducted with a small group of people rather than a single individual. Timing is critical for both these forms of qualitative evaluation because participants do not want to be interrupted at key times during the event. You should consider this form of evaluation at points when your subjects have discretionary time, such as between innings at a baseball game, during intermissions, or before or after the event.

Staff Evaluations

Evaluation of staff members is a good way to maintain control over the success of the event and is helpful for professional development. Observation during the course of the event can be more useful if staff members are trained beforehand (Masterman 2014). Benchmarking is advocated as a way to achieve a level of standardization in the evaluation process (Allen et al. 2002). Attiany (2009) defines **benchmarking** as "a systematic approach through which organizations can measure their performances against the best-in-class organizations and it is a powerful and effective tool to learn from others in order to get the excellence." A number of event management areas may be benchmarked in terms of staffing. For example, an event planner may benchmark event staffing in relation to the following:

- Uniforms for staff members
- Number of staff members placed at each point of purchase
- Salaries or pay rates for part-time and full-time staff members
- Shift hours for staff members
- New and creative types of staff positions

A second way for event planners to evaluate staff members is to engage in a technique called management by wandering around (MBWA). MBWA was made famous by Tom Peters and Robert Waterman after their visit to Hewlett-Packard in the late 1970s and later discussed in their book *In Search of Excellence*. Peters and Waterman (1982) defined MBWA as "the business of staying in touch" (p. 288). The idea behind an MBWA program is to get a manager out of the office and onto the floor to make contact with employees (Amsbary and Staples 1991). If you have ever watched the popular television show *Undercover Boss*, you have witnessed this technique. A high-ranking executive in a company (often the president or the CEO) alters her appearance and gains an alias so she can work in an entry-level position within the organization for a week. During this time, the boss works in various areas of company operations and with many employees, often with a different job and at a different location each day. This gives the undercover boss a better appreciation for the work being done by her staff. At the end of the show, the undercover boss summons these employees to the corporate office, at which time her true identity is revealed. In the end, the boss learns more about the day-to-day operations of the company and either rewards hardworking employees through promotion or financial rewards or provides additional training or better working conditions. The idea here is that event managers should be critically involved in the operations of the event. In other words, by employing MBWA, the event manager knows whether concession employees are serving hot and high-quality foods, and they can monitor the length of time it takes to wait in line at a concession stand. Furthermore, the event planner can monitor whether ushers and ticket takers are friendly, helpful, and reliable.

Another way to conduct staff evaluation is to administer a quantitative or qualitative survey to consumers of the event. Some of the questions should measure customer service components such as employee helpfulness, product knowledge, empathy, caring, friendliness, reliability, responsiveness, and assurance. Other items on the questionnaire may measure whether employees keep the facility clean and can also gauge consumer perceptions related to the atmosphere of the facility. This type of quantitative analysis can help identify service touchpoints where consumers are dissatisfied or highly satisfied. It can also help reveal areas where the event may experience a service failure.

Finally, qualitative questionnaires can provide event planners with more in-depth knowledge of areas where consumers are experiencing satisfaction or dissatisfaction. This type of questionnaire asks for more detailed information from the consumer, and often the questions are open-ended (figure 13.1). An open-ended question might be, "How can the sporting event be improved?" or "What was your favorite part of the event?"

Management Evaluations

The evaluation of an event should not focus only on the performance of frontline staff such as ushers, concession workers, and ticket takers; it should also examine the management of these employees and the processes for helping them complete their work. For example, sales staff may be responsible for selling event inventory such as signage, broadcast commercials, print ads, and other forms of sponsorship, but management evaluations may pertain more directly to the effectiveness of staff members

POSTEVENT EVALUATION SURVEY

Thank you for attending our recent event. We'd like to hear your impression of the various aspects of the event so we can continually improve the experience for all attendees.

1. Overall, how would you rate the event?
   Excellent
   Good
   Fair
   Poor
   Terrible
2. Please rate the following aspects of the event:

	Excellent	Good	Fair	Poor	Terrible
Scheduling and timing					
Entertainment					
Food and beverages					
Parking and directions					
Invitations and guest list					
Choice of facility or venue					
Cost and pricing					
Vendor management					

3. Based on your experience at this event, how likely are you to attend future events?
   Very likely
   Somewhat likely
   Not likely
4. What was your favorite part of the event?
5. What was your least favorite part of the event?
6. Do you have any other suggestions or comments to help us improve future events?

FIGURE 13.1 Postevent evaluation survey.
Adapted by permission from Web Survey Master. Available: http://www.websurveymaster.com/t/29/

such as the director of marketing, who supervises these employees. Areas of evaluation may include the following:

- How well does the supervisor communicate with employees under her supervision?
- Does the supervisor provide employees with the necessary resources to perform their jobs in an effective manner?
- Is the manager clear in communicating the expectations for the position?
- Does the manager possess strong leadership skills that help her motivate subordinates?
- Is the manager knowledgeable about the organization and its various products and services?
- Does the manager present a strong vision for the event to subordinates?

Event managers should also consider conducting 360-degree evaluations, which allow subordinates to see themselves from multiple perspectives. Weigelt and colleagues (2004) describe a 360-degree evaluation as a self-assessment and an assessment by coworkers (peers), staff supervised by the person, and the people who supervise the person. Formal feedback is provided to the person from all sources of evaluation. The program should invest 20 percent in data and 80 percent in designing, training, and coaching.

Budget Evaluations

As Allen (2009) suggests, do not wait until you get to the end of the event to find out that you have exceeded your budget projections. The budget should be reconciled throughout the event process and updated each time you receive new costs or make adjustments or changes. One way to evaluate the event is to compare its cost to its usefulness or value in monetary benefits, which is commonly referred to as the event's ROI (Myhill and Phillips 2010). Destination Marketing Association International (DMAI), an association for destination marketing organizations, provides an event impact calculator that measures the economic value of an event and calculates its ROI (DMAI 2012). DMAI is currently working on a sports calculator that will provide a more valid and reliable estimate of economic impact for sports commissions across the United States.

The term **return on event (ROE)** was coined by Aggarwal and Goldblatt to identify the percentage of earnings returned to an organization sponsoring an event based on marketing efforts (Goldblatt 2014). Goldblatt suggests that if you increase attendance by 25 percent through e-marketing strategies for a small event of 100 persons, you may save a significant amount of money and generate a sizable net profit that can be attributed directly to this e-marketing activity. See figure 13.2, which illustrates how to measure the return on event.

Hanson (2010) suggests that successful budgeting is dependent on the amount of detail put into the budget, and managers must continually ask the question "What other expenses can I expect?" Hanson claims that "clumping" and "miscellaneous" are two of the most common mistakes made by managers. *Clumping* means that 12 to 15 possible expenses are put into one administrative category rather than being broken into separate line items. Allocating a number of items to a miscellaneous or other category is also easy to do, but it often becomes too large and not very beneficial to the manager. Following are some common budget categories that Hanson outlines for events:

- Accommodations
- Administrative
- Ceremonies
- Contingency
- Exhibitions or trade shows
- Food service
- Hospitality
- Insurance
- Marketing
- Media and public relations
- Medical
- Merchandise
- Officials
- Participant services

	Year 1	Year 2
Expenses		
Advertising • Newspaper • Radio • Television	 $30,000 $25,000 $65,000	 $40,000 $30,000 $80,000
Direct mail • Design and printing • Postage	 $3,000 $7,000	 $4,000 $8,000
Internet	$8,000	$10,000
Promotions	$3,500	$4,500
Public relations	$4,500	$5,500
Subtotal	**$146,000**	**$182,000**
Income		
Ticket sales	$125,000	$150,000
Sponsorships	$50,000	$50,000
Subtotal	**$175,000**	**$200,000**

FIGURE 13.2 Measuring the return on event.

- Printing
- Rights fee
- Salaries
- Site visits
- Transportation
- Venue
- Volunteers

Attendance Evaluations

Attendance can be a valuable form of evaluating the success of an event. For a single one-off event, the event planner can compare attendance from year to year. Events with multiple activities may also be evaluated based on the attendance at each of the separate activities.

Two common ways to count attendance at a sporting event are paid attendance and turnstile counts. Paid attendance or paid registration counts every person who bought a ticket or registered for the sporting event, regardless of whether they attended or not. Thus, a sport event that sold 25,000 tickets in 2017 and 50,000 tickets for the same event in 2018 could be said to have doubled its attendance in a year. However, evaluating an event based solely on paid attendance does not indicate how many people were actually at the event and thus contributed to the atmosphere of the event. In contrast, turnstile counts measure how many people actually attended. Many event planners employ turnstile counts using bar-code scanners or the more antiquated system of having a ticket taker manually use a clicker as each spectator enters the facility. More recently, sports teams such as the Houston Astros and Houston Rockets are using paperless tickets that allow consumers to simply swipe their credit cards at the gate upon entry.

Although attendance can be an effective way to evaluate an event's success, some precautions are necessary. First, event planners representing the rights holder of the event should be sure they have control over any public announcement of the attendance. Second, there does not seem to be an industry standard for the correct way to count attendance. Some teams include both paid attendance and the turnstile count, which inflates the numbers. Many professional and collegiate teams have been known to inflate their numbers in this way to appeal to sponsors. Third, simply calculating attendance without considering other relevant factors can be misleading when evaluating an event. For example, consider the impact of the following scenarios on attendance:

- The event was held at the same time as another big event in the area.
- Inclement weather prevented many people from attending the sporting event.
- The event was held on a religious holiday.
- The event was rushed, and there was inadequate time for marketing and advertising.
- The sport does not have a large following in the geographic area where the event was held (for example, lacrosse is widely popular in the northeastern regions of the United States but less popular in other areas).

Evaluating Outcomes and Objectives

Event planners are increasingly using **return on objectives (ROO)** as a more comprehensive measure of event effectiveness than ROI. Instead of calculating the impact of the event based solely on revenues, ROO measures success based on whether key objectives for the event are met. Arnold (2012) provides some guidelines for measuring ROO:

1. Talk with key stakeholders, and ask them some of the following questions:
    - Why are you holding the event?
    - What type of outcome do you want from the event?
    - Who do you expect will attend? Are they the right people?
    - At the end of the day, how will you measure success? This may vary for each stakeholder. For example, success for sponsors may be related to name recognition, but success for the rights holder is winning the contest.
    - What is unique about this event? Consider the Kentucky Derby, which is branded as "the most exciting two minutes in sport." Not many sporting events can make this claim.
    - If something could go wrong, what is it?
2. Next, analyze the conversations with stakeholders and come up with a few succinct objectives. It is important to keep in mind the SMART acronym. Whereas goals are normally broad statements, objectives should be specific, measurable, achievable, realistic, and timely.
3. Determine how your objectives translate into monetary deliverables. The more business-related your objectives, the easier you will be able to translate them into dollars. Although ROO is not focused solely on revenues, all events must be cognizant of the bottom line.
4. Factor in the fact that every dollar spent on the event should somehow be tied to the objectives of the event.
5. Using quantitative or qualitative measures, set up a simple and consistent way of measuring success based on your objectives.

Measuring Economic Impact

Measuring the economic impact of an event is a somewhat controversial but very important topic in the industry. Event planners must have a keen understanding of this topic because of the political nature of economic impact. Many scholarly studies have shown that bringing an event to a certain destination does not always equate with enhanced economic impact for the region. However, at the same time, economic impact is widely used by both event planners and government officials to sell key stakeholders on bidding for and hosting an event in their region because of the positive impact the event will have through economic growth of local businesses, increased job growth, enhanced infrastructure, and overall community pride.

There are a number of ways to measure economic impact in the sport event industry.

The total estimated economic impact of a sporting event is made up of the direct, induced, indirect, and implicit benefits (Depken 2011). According to Depken, **direct spending** refers to money spent specifically because of the event; it reflects only money that would not have been spent but for the event, called *new spending*. Direct spending may include lodging, food, local transportation, access to the event, and other spending in the local market for tourism and entertainment venues. The new spending on hosting the event that would not have occurred if the event had not taken place is called **induced spending** and is generally undertaken by entities such as a sports franchise, a convention bureau, a sports commission, or a host city. For example, the city of Beijing spent considerable money on facilities such as Beijing National Stadium (referred to as the Bird's Nest) at a cost of $423 million for the primary purpose of hosting the Olympic and Paralympic Games.

The money consumers spend outside of the local economy is called **leakage**. Some events (e.g., mega-events such as the Super Bowl) employ the use of multipliers when calculating economic impact. Depken suggests that multipliers account for the additional spending created after the direct and induced spending has been completed. It is important to use a multiplier of correct magnitude. The appropriate multiplier for direct spending is different from that for induced spending based on factors related to leakages and tax structures. Economists suggest that multipliers be less than two, but some studies use multipliers as high as five.

The indirect benefits of hosting a sporting event may include additional tourism to a destination or enhanced reputation. **Implicit benefits** are those that enhance the destination's image and may include quality of life advancements, civic pride, and advertisements for the destination. Such benefits add value to the host destination and are difficult to measure.

Summary

After all the planning and the actual implementation of an event, it's natural to expect that event planners can relax at the event's conclusion. However, a number of important activities must take place even after the event is complete. This chapter discusses the importance of cleanup and breakdown as well as postevent media coverage. Sponsors must be contacted, and some time must be set aside to review the strengths and weaknesses of the event. Postevent evaluation is critical to the success of future events and must not be dismissed. Evaluation allows the event planner to identify whether objectives were met and to provide feedback to stakeholders who are vitally involved in the event.

LEARNING ACTIVITIES

1. Think of a recent event you attended. Using a form of participant observation, evaluate the event by describing what you liked and did not like.
2. Once again, consider a recent event you have attended. Now think about any money that you spent on the event that can be considered direct spending. Make a list of the money you spent and calculate it.
3. Describe some objectives for an event such as the Super Bowl.

CASE STUDY: 2018 FIFA WORLD CUP AND RUSSIA

The FIFA World Cup is one of the largest sport mega-events in the world and its global appeal is unmatched short of the Olympic Games. The worldwide audience is estimated to be around 160 million viewers. The 2018 FIFA World Cup ran from June 14 to July 15 and was hosted by Russia in 12 stadiums across 11 cities, including Moscow, St.

Petersburg, and Sochi. In the end, France defeated Croatia on July 15 in the final game by a score of 4 to 2. France took home $38 million in prize money and Croatia won $28 million. Contributions to fund the 2018 World Cup totaled some $791 million, which was an increase of 40 percent from the previous tournament in 2014. This money is given to each country's national FIFA federation, which determines how it is distributed. While France and Croatia walked away with the largest earnings, each team that advanced to the group stage received a minimum of $8 million plus $1.5 million to cover preparation costs. As the winner, France received a trophy valued at $20 million; and while they don't get to keep it indefinitely, it is difficult to estimate the value that derives from this fame and publicity, which leads to corporate sponsorships, advertising deals, and social and economic impacts for the winning country, not to mention other contracts.

Hosting the most expensive FIFA World Cup in its history, Russia was reported to have spent approximately 883 billion rubles (USD $14.2 billion), or around 1 percent of Russia's GDP over the last five years. Of this amount, around $6.11 billion was spent on transportation infrastructure, $3.45 billion on stadium construction, and $680 million on facilities for accommodation. Economics research on sport mega-events suggests that spending on these types of events does not result in the economic benefits that are normally touted by politicians and event planners. The event lasted one month, and while the economics are mega, the economic stimulus of hosting the event is small in comparison to the size of Russia's $1.3 trillion economy.

Another metric often touted as an advantage of hosting a sport mega-event is an increase in tourism. Inbound tourism arrivals to Russia were projected to compound at an annual growth rate of 4 percent by 2022, reaching 37.5 million trips. As a direct result of hosting the World Cup tournament, a 1.4-percent increase in the number of total arrivals to Russia was forecast. More than three million fans attended the 64 total matches and stadiums averaged around a 98 percent occupancy rate. Russian officials expected approximately 570,000 foreign fans and 700,000 Russians to attend World Cup matches.

While the numbers speak for themselves, it is difficult to measure some of the social impacts of a sport mega-event such as the FIFA World Cup. FIFA president Gianni Infantino was reported to have told Russian president Vladimir Putin that the world was "in love" with the Russian hosts, and he praised Putin for overcoming negative stereotypes about the country. Alexei Sorokin, director of Russia's World Cup organizing committee claimed that "the World Cup exceeded the expectations of even the organizers. I was amazed by the atmosphere that gripped our country."

So, how does one evaluate the success of a sport mega-event such as the FIFA World Cup? Is it based on economics, tourism, social factors or expectations of government officials and fans? Russia as a host of the tournament was criticized for its lack of midtier accommodation facilities, safety concerns, relatively high visiting costs, and burdensome visa regulations.

In addition, there was concern about recent political tension between Russia and the U.K., and economic sanctions imposed on Russia by the United States, the European Union and several other countries following its annexation of Crimea in 2014. Russian relations with the West were also strained by the Kremlin's alleged meddling in the 2016 U.S. election and suspected involvement in an attack on a former Russian spy. Finally, there were concerns that hooliganism between Russia and England fans at the last major European soccer tournament in 2016 might carry over.

Case Study Application

1. How would you evaluate the 2018 World Cup from an economic perspective? How would you measure the success or lack of success from an economic perspective?
2. The case study talks about the potential for France to capitalize on additional sponsors. Do some research on the Internet to see whether you can find any information about new sponsors for France's national team.
3. Describe some of the social benefits that arise from a sport mega-event like the FIFA World Cup.

GLOSSARY

10 Ps—The necessary elements to create a successful sport marketing plan: purpose, product, projecting the market, position, players, package, price, promotion, place, promise.

acceptance—The act of agreeing to the terms offered in a contractual agreement; a contract is typically considered to have been accepted when a signature is attached.

accessible—Describes ease of access for someone who is disabled.

activation—The process of actively marketing and managing the sponsor's partnership with an event.

advertising—Paid, nonpersonal, clearly sponsored messages.

aftermarketing—The process of providing continuing satisfaction and reinforcement to a past or current customer in order to create a lasting relationship.

AIDA—The intent of promotion is to move the consumer through these four phases: awareness, interest, desire, action.

Americans with Disabilities Act (ADA)—A federal law that prohibits discrimination on the basis of disability in employment, state and local government, public accommodations, commercial facilities, transportation, and telecommunications.

ancillary event—An activity designed to support the primary event.

benchmarking—A systematic approach through which organizations can measure their performance against best-in-class organizations.

bid document—Thorough accounting of the site's key assets and how they conform to bid requirements.

bilateral contract—A promise for a promise; a reciprocal agreement.

brainstorming—A group discussion designed to produce ideas or solve problems.

brand—The combination of names, symbols, slogans, or logos that identifies a product and distinguishes it from other products.

capacity—The ability to enter into a contract legally (minors cannot do so).

cash flow—The amount of money being transferred in and out of the event.

cast list—A roster identifying the various people or groups involved in an event and listing their roles or functions.

cause-related marketing—A partnership of not-for-profit and for-profit entities that share mutually beneficial goals in an effort to increase attention and facilitate action.

clearance—The process of obtaining permission to use an artist's work; for example the use of music in the event industry.

communication plan—A summary of the methods you will utilize to communicate with employees, attendees, and the media during a crisis or emergency situation.

consideration—The leader's concern for member well-being and warm and friendly relations within the group.

consideration (monetary)—Each party must provide consideration; some value or benefit (typically, money) must be given or given up by each party.

constraint—A factor that may limit attendance or participation.

contingency allowance—Funds reserved for emergencies, cost overruns, or unforeseen expenses.

contingency plan—A plan designed to account for and respond to future possibilities.

contract—A tool that protects the interests of all parties and helps foster partnerships between the various entities critical to producing events.

coordination phase—The phase during which the event planner synchronizes and integrates activities, responsibilities, and organizational structures to make sure that resources are used efficiently so as to achieve organizational objectives.

crisis management plan—The part of the risk management plan that covers any hazard that could harm your event.

critical Rs—To grow your media relationships, you need to relate, retain, repair.

cross-cultural event—An event that involves interactions between members of different cultural groups.

cross-promotion—A partnership where two (or more) businesses join forces to engage in joint promotion.

crowd control—Your plan for managing crowds to maintain order, such as by the use of barriers, barricades, and cones.

crowd management plan—Your plan for managing and facilitating the masses for access and egress and moving around your event.

destination marketing organization (DMO)—any organization responsible for the marketing of an identifiable destination.

DIM process—A three-step process that helps you implement your risk plan.

direct spending—Refers to money spent specifically because of the event.

distribution—Decisions related to how, where, and when the product is made available to the consumer.

dropout rate—The percentage of youth under the age of 18 who no longer participate in organized sport.

economic impact—The net change in the economy as a result of hosting a sporting event.

egress—How individuals exit a facility.

emergency action plan—An outline of how you will respond to an emergency (typically a medical emergency).

employee orientation—The degree to which a leader is concerned with human relations on the job.

evaluating sponsorship—A means of measuring the success of your efforts.

evaluation phase—The phase during which the event planner determines whether the event objectives were met, and provides guidance for planning future events.

event budget—An estimate of revenues and expenses over the life of an event.

event logistics—Detailed organization and implementation of the event.

event rundown—A document detailing the sequence of activities that will happen during an event.

event timeline—A sequential listing of all the tasks and duties associated with an event.

event triangle—Represents the important stakeholders (event, fans, sponsors) who must be satisfied for the event to be a success.

exclusivity clause—Protects the event manager from the talent's scheduling another event close by that could affect the event's success.

expense—A cost incurred from doing business.

feasibility study—An assessment of how successfully an event can be completed.

flat organizational structure—Describes an organization with fewer management levels and a broader span of control.

force majeure—A contract provision that allows a party to suspend or terminate the performance of its obligations when certain circumstances beyond its control arise, making performance inadvisable, commercially impracticable, illegal, or impossible; for example, a hurricane, a tornado, or an earthquake.

Gantt chart—A chart illustrating a project's tasks and timelines.

goal—A broad, qualitative statement that provides direction in support of the event's mission.

governing body—An organization that has a regulatory or sanctioning function, for example over sports.

guarantee—Monies promised to a team to play another team; found in game contracts.

hospitality—Providing service to a guest.

implicit benefits—Benefits that enhance the destination's image; these may include quality-of-life advancements, civic pride, and advertisements for the destination.

induced spending—New spending on hosting a sport event that would not have occurred if the event had not taken place.

ingress—How individuals enter a facility.

initiating structure—The leader's concern for the effective performance of the group's tasks.

in-kind—Nonmonetary partnerships that provide a service or product to an event in exchange for sponsorship recognition.

insurance—Protection against financial loss resulting from a hazard.

integrated marketing communication (IMC)—A technique for making sure that all promotional efforts work in concert by linking all the promotional pieces.

international federation—An organization that serves as a nongovernmental governing body for a given sport and administers its sport at a world level.

league—A group of athletic teams organized to promote mutual interests and to compete chiefly among themselves.

leakage—Money that consumers spend outside of the local economy.

legality—Refers to a contract following the law; of or pertaining to something legal; that both state and federal laws must not be broken in the formation of a contract.

leveraging an event—This phrase refers to the activities surrounding a sport event itself that seek to maximize the long-term benefit of the event.

local organizing committee—An organization of stakeholders formed to organize and execute events.

market segment—A group of consumers or potential consumers with similar attributes, attitudes, or behaviors.

marketing plan—A document detailing the marketing activities that need to happen for an event to reach its objectives.

media promotion—The integration of various communication strategies to convey the organization's message.

media relations—Working with the media to convey messages to the public; one arm of public relations.

mega-event—A large short-term, high-profile event capable of having a significant impact on its host community or country (Hiller 2000).

miscellaneous expense—A cost typically too small to need its own category.

moment of truth—Any time a customer comes into contact with the company and has the opportunity to make an evaluation.

motivation—An individual's inner drive to satisfy needs and wants.

naming rights—A type of sponsorship/partnership that can take the form of a legacy gift, title sponsorship of an event, or a long-term partnership. (Rights to a legacy gift.)

negligence—Unintentional wrongdoing that leads to injury or harm to a person, property, or reputation.

niche market—A typically small, focused segment whose needs may not be currently served by larger events.

O&O—Owned and operated.

objective—A specific, quantitative statement that serves as a measurable indicator of whether or not the organization is meeting its goals.

offer—A conditional promise to do or refrain from doing something in the future.

organizational chart—Displays the structure of an organization.

outsourcing—Procuring goods and services from external suppliers.

participant liaison—The primary point of contact with event participants.

personal seat license—A contractual right acquired for a fee that allows the person to purchase tickets for a specific seat; no one else may acquire tickets for that seat as long as the PSL contract is in effect.

positioning—Gaining a prominent place in the mind of the consumer in hopes that they will act.

preliminary budget—A budget developed during the early phase of the event planning process.

production orientation—The degree to which the leader is concerned about the technical aspects of the job and about productivity.

production schedule—A tool that highlights all of the activities at the event facility.

project management—The process of organizing and managing resources to achieve the project objectives.

promotion—All the activities that you use to convey positive messages and images about your event; communicating with and persuading defined user groups.

promotional mix—A combination of all the elements you use to promote your event.

request for proposal (RFP)—A document soliciting proposals or bids to host a sporting event.

research phase—The phase during which the event planner gathers data that will help in planning the event.

return on event—The percentage of earnings returned to an organization sponsoring an event based on marketing efforts.

return on investment (ROI)—Effectiveness of the investment in monetary terms.

return on objectives—The measurement of success based on whether key objectives for the event are met.

return on opportunity (ROO)—Effectiveness of the investment in helping to achieve established sponsorship goals.

revenue—Income generated before costs or expenses are deducted.

rider—An amendment that spells out the requirements of the talent.

rights fee—An agreement whereby a broadcaster pays for the rights to broadcast an event and its associated content.

rights-holder organization (RHO)—An organization that owns the rights to a sporting event.

risk—The possibility of loss or injury; someone or something that creates or suggests a hazard.

risk management planning—The process whereby you identify hazards, identify a remedy, and create a guide for handling or treating the identified hazards.

risk matrix—used to help identify the risk level of a situation based on the probability of the occurrence happening against the severity of the occurrence.

sales promotion—Activities designed to add value or increase demand.

service—An act, deed, performance, or effort.

situational (SWOT) analysis—A method used to analyze both the internal environment (strengths and weaknesses) and the external environment (opportunities and threats).

small-scale sport event—Includes regular season sport competitions that use existing infrastructure and need less public support for hosting (Gibson, Kaplanidou, and Kang 2012).

social media—Various interactive platforms for two-way communication that allows the sharing and creating of messages.

SOP—Standard operating procedure; the outcome of your risk management plan that outlines how you are to respond to the various hazards that you identified (plan of action).

sponsor follow-up—Meeting with the sponsor after an event to determine whether goals and objectives were met.

sponsorship—Acquisition of rights to affiliate or directly associate with a product, person, organization, team, league, or event for the purpose of deriving benefits related to that affiliation or association.

sponsorship level—A specific level of involvement, or a package, ranging from minimal investment to full-blown rights of ownership.

sponsorship proposal—The research, pitch, and ask of sponsorship; a package of information that will help a potential sponsor decide whether they want to partner with your event.

sport tourism—Leisure-based travel that takes individuals temporarily outside of their home communities to play, watch physical activities, or venerate attractions associated with these activities (Gibson 1998).

sports commission—a nonprofit or governmental entity designed to attract and assist sporting events.

sports information director (SID)—The individual (usually within the sport organization) who establishes the relationship with the media and provides them with information to use.

stakeholder—An individual or a group with an interest in the event.

subsidy—Funds granted governmental or other public agencies to assist in conducting an event.

supervision—Overseeing a particular division or group; providing guidance.

sustainability—The ability to act with minimal long-term impacts on the environment.

symbiotic relationship—A mutually beneficial relationship between two entities working together for success.

tall organizational structure—Describes an organization with many levels of management, whereby managers have many ranks and a narrow span of control.

target market—A segment to which the event will be marketed.

team—A group of people who unite to accomplish a common mission or objective.

threat—An identified hazard that could result in harm to your event, employees, attendees, or supporters.

touchpoint—Any interaction between the consumer and the event or the organization running the event.

transactional leadership—Involves an exchange between a leader and a subordinate in which they influence one another, each deriving something of value.

transformational leadership—The process of influencing major changes in the attitudes and assumptions of organization members and building commitment for major changes in the organization's objectives and strategies.

trolling—The anonymous sending of threats, insults, or other harassment, usually online, from a distance.

unilateral contract—A promise by one of the parties to perform.

viral marketing—Techniques encouraging consumers to share information with others.

waiver—Releases the organization from liability should the participant become injured during the event.

working budget—A budget that is updated as revenues and expense categories are realized.

REFERENCES

Aaker, D. 1991. *Managing Brand Equity*. New York: Free Press.

ABM. 2018. "Ensure a High Quality Surface & Enhance Visual Aesthetic: Athletic & Sports Field Maintenance." https://www.abm.com/sports-entertainment/athletic-field-maintenance.

Adgate, B. 2018. "The Sports Bubble Is Not Bursting." *Forbes* (January 16). www.forbes.com/sites/bradadgate/2018/01/16/the-sports-bubble-is-not-bursting

All-American Soap Box Derby. 2009. What is the SBD? aasbd.org. www.soapboxracing.com/about.htm.

Allen, J. 2009. *Event Planning: The Ultimate Guide to Successful Meetings, Corporate Events, Fundraising Galas, Conferences, Conventions, Incentives and Other Special Events*. 2nd ed. Mississauga, ON: Wiley.

Allen, J., W. O'Toole, I. McDonnell, and R. Harris. 2002. *Festival and Special Event Management*. 2nd ed. Queensland, AU: Wiley.

Allen, J., W. O'Toole, R. Harris, and I. McDonnell. 2011. *Festival and Special Event Management*. 5th ed. Queensland, AU: Wiley.

Allmers, S., and W. Maennig. 2009. "Economic Impacts of the FIFA Soccer World Cups in France 1998, Germany 2006, and Outlook for South Africa 2010." *Eastern Economic Journal* 35:500-19.

Amador, L., P. Campoy-Muñoz, M.A. Cardenete, and M.C. Delgado. 2017. "Economic Impact Assessment of Small-Scale Sporting Events Using Social Accounting Matrices: An Application to the Spanish Football League." *Journal of Policy Research in Tourism, Leisure and Events* 9 (3): 230-46.

Ambrose, C. 2010. "Negotiating Vendor Contracts." www.gartner.com/it/initiatives/pdf/KeyInitiativeOverview_NegotiatingVendorContracts.pdf.

American Footgolf League. 2018. "About Us." https://www.footgolf.us/about-footgolf.

American Staffing Association. 2018. "Staffing Employment Steady in 2017." https://americanstaffing.net/posts/2018/03/22/staffing-employment-steady-in-2017.

Ammon, R., R. Southall, and M. Nagel. 2010. *Sport Facility Management: Organization Events and Mitigating Risks*. 2nd ed. Morgantown, WV: Fitness Information Technology.

Ammon, R., R. Southall, and M. Nagel. 2016. *Sport Facility Management: Organization Events and Mitigating Risks*. 3rd ed. Morgantown, WV: Fitness Information Technology.

Amsbary, J.H., and P.J. Staples. 1991. "Improving Administrator/Nurse Communication: A Case Study of 'Management by Wandering Around.'" *Journal of Business Communication* 28 (2):101-12.

Arnold, K. 2012. "How to Create a Return on Objectives (ROO) for Your Next Meeting." *Official Newsletter of the Arizona Sunbelt Chapter of Meeting Professionals International*. www.naylornetwork.com/maz-nwl/articles/?aid=16810&projid=1243.

Ashley, S., and R. Pearson. 1993. "Fundamentals of Risk Management." www.sashley.com/downloads/articles/fundamentalsofriskmanagement.pdf.

Attiany, M. (2009). "The Role of Benchmarking in Improving Institutional Performance of the Jordanian Pharmaceutical Firms," Unpublished PhD dissertation. Arab Academy forBanking and Financial Sciences, Amman, Jordan.

Attwood, E. 2014. "Tech Upgrades Boost Sports Concessions Operations." *Athletic Business*. (June). www.athleticbusiness.com/apps-software/technology-upgrades-boosting-sports-venue-concessions-operations.html.

Avolio, B.J., F.O. Walumbwa, and T.J. Weber. 2009. "Leadership: Current Theories, Research, and Future Directions." *Annual Review of Psychology* 60:421-49.

Axzo Press. 2002. "Advanced Interpersonal Communication." http://proquestcombo.safaribooksonline.com/book/communications/0619075996/firstchapter.

Bahr, C. 2015. "Flashback Massive Earthquake Interrupts 1989 World Series." *Fox Sports*. https://www.foxsports.com/mlb/story/san-francisco-giants-oakland-athletics-world-series-earthquake-bay-area-candlestick-park-101715.

Barker, M. 2016. "ShotTracker, Klay Thompson Renew Virtual Basketball Camp." *Sports Illustrated*. https://www.si.com/tech-media/2016/07/19/shot-tracker-klay-thompson-virtual-basketball-camp.

Barringer, P. 2006. "Risk Matrix: Know When to Accept the Risk. Know When to Reject the Risk." www.barringer1.com/nov04prb_files/Risk-Matrix.pdf.

Barron, D. 2009. "$1.15 Billion Stadium Gives the Cowboys Braggin' Rights." *Houston Chronicle*. August 21. www.chron.com/sports/texans/article/1-15-billion-stadium-gives-the-Cowboys-1730035.php.

Bartner, A. 2017. "College Football Playoff Announces Indianapolis as Host Site for 2022." *IndyStar.com* (November 2). https://www.indystar.com/story/sports/college/2017/11/01/indianapolis-host-2022-college-football-playoff-national-championship-game/822320001/.

Bass, B.M. 1985. *Leadership and performance Beyond Expectations*. New York: Free Press.

Bass, B.M. 1990. *Bass & Stogdill's Handbook of Leadership: Theory, Research, and Managerial Applications*. 3rd ed. New York: Free Press.

Beese, J. 2014. "Learn How Sports Brands Are Scoring Big With Hashtag Campaigns." *Sproutsocial*. www.sproutsocial.com/insights/sports-brands-scored-big-popular-hashtag-campaigns.

Bell, S.T. 1995. "Legal Issues Affecting Event Management at Colleges and Universities." Deland, FL: Stetson University.

Belson, K. 2018. "In Atlanta, Concessions Prices Go Down and Revenue Goes Up." *New York Times* (January 25). www.nytimes.com/2018/01/25/sports/football/nfl-concessions.html

Bendapudi, N., and R.P. Leone. 2002. "Managing Business-to-Business Customer Relationships Following Key Contact Employee Turnover in a Vendor Firm." *Journal of Marketing* 66:83-101.

Benson, A. 2018. "F1 & TV Rights—What Does the Future Hold?" *BBC* (January 25). www.bbc.com/sport/formula1/42816877.

Berkowitz, S. 2017a. "This Year's 'Guarantee Games' Worth $150 Million for College Football Programs." *USA Today*. https://www.usatoday.com/story/sports/ncaaf/2017/08/29/guarantee-games-worth-150-million-college-football-programs/608668001.

Berkowitz, S. 2017b. "Canceling Football Games Due to Hurricane Irma Brings Financial Complications for Schools." *USA Today*. https://www.usatoday.com/story/sports/ncaaf/2017/09/08/canceling-football-games-due-hurricane-irma-brings-financial-complications-schools/646699001.

Berlonghi, A. 1994. *The Special Event Risk Management Manual*. Rev. ed. Dana Point, CA: Berlonghi.

Berry, L. 1980. "Services Marketing Is Different." *Business* 30 (May/June): 24-29.

Bissell, K. 2011. "Most Ridiculous PGA Tour Tournament Names in History." *Bleacher Report* (November 14). http://.bleacherreport.com/articles/940985-most-unwieldy-pga-tour-tournament-names-in-history.

Black's Law Dictionary. 2nd ed. http://www.freelawdictionary.org.

Bladen, C., J. Kennell, E. Abson, and N. Wilde. 2012. *Events Management: An Introduction*. New York: Routledge.

Bladen, C., J. Kennell, E. Abson, and N.Wilde. 2018. *Events Management: An Introduction*. 2nd ed. New York: Routledge.

Bogle, M.J. 2008. "A Premier Family Event: The National Soccer Festival." *BusinessPeople*. www.highbeam.com/doc/1P3-1458467711.html.

Boteler, C. 2018. "Waste Management Phoenix Open Aims to Again Be World's Largest 'Zero Waste' Event." *Waste Dive*, January 31. https://www.wastedive.com/news/waste-management-phoenix-open-world-largest-zero-waste-event/515984.

Breen, T.H. 2010. "Horses and Gentlemen: The Cultural Significance of Gambling Among the Gentry of Virginia." In *Sport in America: From Colonial Leisure to Celebrity Figures and Globalization* (vol. 2), edited by D. Wiggins. Champaign, IL: Human Kinetics.

Brickley, S.D., and Gottesman, B.M. 2017. *Business Law Basics*.

Bullas, J. n.d. "48 Significant Social Media Facts, Figures and Statistics Plus 7 Infographics." www.jeffbullas.com/2012/04/23/48-significant-social-media-facts-figures-and-statistics-plus-7-infographics.

Burden, W., and M. Li. 2009. "Minor League Baseball: Exploring the Growing Interest in Outsourced Sport Marketing." *Sport Marketing Quarterly* 18 (3):139-49.

Burton, T. 2008. *Naming Rights: Legacy Gifts and Corporate Money*. Hoboken, NJ: Wiley.

Bussell, L.A. 2011. "Media relations." In *The Encyclopedia of Sports Management and Marketing*, 890-91. Thousand Oaks, CA: Sage.

Butcher, D. 2010. "Tissot Swiss Watches Activates NASCAR Sponsorship with QR codes." *Mobile Marketer* (October 8). www.mobilemarketer.com/cms/news/advertising/7668.html.

Carbonell, C. 2012. "Social Media: Six Ways to Build Your Brand." *SportsEvents* 9 (1):12.

Carlisle, K.G. 2006. "Taming the Registration Beast." In *Professional Meeting Management: Comprehensive Strategies for Meetings, Conventions and Events*, edited by G.C. Ramsborg, 359-74. Dubuque, IA: Kendall/Hunt.

Carlzon, J., and T. Peters. 1987. *Moments of Truth*. Cambridge, MA: Ballinger.

Carp, S. 2018. "Glasgow to Host 2019 European Athletics Indoor Championships. *SportsPro* (February 28). http://www.sportspromedia.com/news/glasgow-2019-european-athletics-indoor-championships.

Case, W., and S. Welsh. 2018. "Here Are the New Food, Beer Options at Oriole Park at Camden Yards for 2018." *Baltimore Sun*. March 29. http://www.baltimoresun.com/entertainment/dining/baltimore-diner-blog/bs-fe-orioles-food-camden-yards-20180328-story.html.

Center for Disease Control (n.d.) "Foodborne Illnesses and Germs." https://www.cdc.gov/foodsafety/foodborne-germs.html

Chalip, L. 2004. "Beyond Impact: A General Model for Sport Event Leverage." In *Sport Tourism: Interrelationships, Impacts and Issues*, edited by B.W. Ritchie and D. Adair. Tonawanda, NY: Channel View Publications.

Chavez, C. 2017. "Hurricane Irma Tracker: Dolphins College Football Games Affected Due to Storm." *Sports Illustrated*. https://www.si.com/nfl/2017/09/06/hurricane-irma-sporting-events-effected-miami-buccaneers-dolphins.

Chavis, S. 2008. "Multi-Sport Festivals: Broader Events, Bigger Returns. *SportsEvents* 5 (May):69.

Chelladurai, P. 2005. *Managing Organizations for Sport and Physical Activity: A Systems Perspective*. 2nd ed. Scottsdale, AZ: Holcomb Hathaway.

Clapp, B. 2017. "Unique Strategies for Using Social Media in Sports Marketing." *Workinsports.com* January 31. htpps://www.workinsports.com/blog/unique-strategies-for-using-social-media-in-sports-marketing.

CNN.com. 2003. "At Least 96 Killed in Nightclub Inferno." February 21. http://articles.cnn.com/2003-02-21/us/deadly.nightclub.fire_1_attorney-general-patrick-lynch-nightclub-stampede-rhode-island-nightclub?_s=PM:US.

Coates, D. 2008. "A Closer Look at Stadium Subsidies." *The American*. April 28. www.american.com/archive/2008/april-04-08/a-closer-look-at-stadium-subsidies.

Cole, N. 2018. "Officials Say There Likely Will Be Another 'Battle at Bristol' College Football Game." *SECcountry.com* January 22. htpps://www.seccountry.com/sec/officials-say-likely-will-another-battle-bristol-college-football-game.

Collier, M. 2018. "Red Bull creates better content than you do, here's how they do it." *MackCollier.com* (February 1). www.mackcollier.com/red-bull-content-marketing.

"Commonwealth Games: Birmingham Announced as Host of 2022 Event." 2017. *BBC* (December 21). https:// www.bbc.com/sport/commonwealth-games/42437441.

"Countries by number of registered ice hockey players in 2017/18." *Statista.com*. https://www.statista.com/statistics/282349/number-of-registered-ice-hockey-by-country/.

Cornelissen, S. (2004). "Sport Mega-Events in Africa: Processes, Impacts and Prospects." *Tourism and Hospitality Planning & Development* 1(1):39-55.

Cornell Law School. n.d. "Mailbox Rule." https://www.law.cornell.edu/wex/mailbox_rule.

Cotten, D., and J. Wolohan. 2012. *Law for Recreation and Sport Managers*. 5th ed. Dubuque, IA: Kendall/Hunt.

Cotten, D., and J. Wolohan. 2017. *Law for Recreation and Sport Managers*. 7th ed. Dubuque, IA: Kendall/Hunt.

Country Club Services. 2018. "About." http://www.countryclubservicesinc.com/about.php

Cowan, A.L. 1988. "*Advertising; Ad Clutter: Even in Restrooms Now*." *New York Times*. [Online]. (February 18). Available: www.nytimes.com/1988/02/18/business/advertising-ad-clutter-even-in-restrooms-now.html.

Crisp, E. 2014. "SU Settles Lawsuit Over Accessibility Complaints." *Advocate*. http://www.theadvocate.com/baton_rouge/news/education/article_40cc6f3e-dc40-5b4c-9943-2a2c788ac2f7.html.

Culpeper, J.E. 2017. "Hurricane Irma: Football Games Cancelled, Moved by Storm." *Atlanta Journal-Constitution*. https://www.ajc.com/sports/hurricane-irma-football-games-canceled-moved-storm/cTSrjsLzTu-MOjrsNGMMHOM.

Cummins, L. 2012. "The Social Media Smackdown." *Band Digital*. April 10. http://banddigital.com/node/222.

Cuskelly, G., R. Hoye, and C. Auld. 2006. *Working with Volunteers in Sport: Theory and Practice*. New York: Routledge.

Cutter, C. 2009. "Youth, High School Events May Be Next Sports Thrust." *Indianapolis Business Journal* 29 (52):16.

D'Ambrosio, D. 2014. "Burton Rides Trends from Vermont to China." *Burlington Free Press* (June 19). https://www.burlingtonfreepress.com/story/money/2014/06/19/burton-snowboards-trends-vermont-china/10790125.

Danigelis, A. 2018. "Super Bowl Zero-Waste Rush2Recycle Program Results Are In." *Environmental Leader* (February 22). https://www.environmentalleader.com/2018/02/super-bowl-zero-waste-results.

deLisle, L. 2009. *Creating Special Events*. Champaign, IL: Sagamore.

deLisle, L.J. 2014. *Creating Special Events*. 2nd. ed. Champaign, IL: Sagamore.

DeMarco, K.A. 2014. "In for the Win/Win: How to Negotiate Facility Contracts." http://www.sportsdestinations.com/management/services/winwin-how-negotiate-facility-contracts-8093.

DeMille, D. 2018. "How St. George Ironman Helped Southern Utah Become Endurance Sport Destination." *The Spectrum* (May 2). https://www.thespectrum.com/story/news/local/2018/05/02/st-george-ironman-evolution-southern-utah-tourism-focus/573067002/.

Depken II, C.A. 2011. "Economic Impact Study." In *Encyclopedia of Sports Management and Marketing*, edited by L.E. Swayne and M. Dodds, 428-35. Thousand Oaks, CA: Sage.

Destination Marketing Association International. 2012. "About the Industry." www.destinationmarketing.org/page.asp?pid=21

Destination Marketing Association International. 2012. "Event Impact Calculator." www.destinationmarketing.org/page.asp?pid=417.

Diaz, E. 2015. "Leading the Majors: The Man Behind the D-Backs Hispanic Sports Marketing Initiative." *The Nativa*. November 13. www.thenativa.com/blog/hispanic-sports-marketing-jerry-romo-arizona-diamondbacks.

Donnor, M.E. 2012, February 14. "Kings and Dodgers Team for Cross Promotion." www.examiner.com/article/kings and dodgers team for cross promotion.

Dremann, S. 2009. "2009 Senior Games: Senior Games a Winner with Local Merchants." *Palo Alto Weekly*. www.almanacnews.com/news/show_story.php?id=4591.

Drosos, M. 2011. "Using Facebook to Engage With your Fans, Alumni . . . and Your Recruits!" *Tudor Collegiate Strategies*. February. www.dantudor.com/2011/02.

Dwyer, L., R. Mellor, N. Mistilis, and T. Mules. 2000. "A Framework for Assessing 'Tangible' and 'Intangible Impacts' of Events and Conventions." *Event Management* 6:175-89.

"Economic Impact of the Valley's Big Sporting Events is $1.3 Billion." 2018. *AZ Big Media* (February 24). htpps://www.azbigmedia.com/economic-impact-valleys-big-sporting-events-1-3-billion/.

Ernst & Young. 2017. "Sports in India." www.ey.com/Publication/vwLUAssets/ey-sports-newsreel/$File/ey-sports-newsreel.pdf.

ESPN News Services. 2008, March 15. "Storm That Damaged Georgia Dome, Atlanta was a Tornado." http://www.espn.com/mens-college-basketball/champweek2008/news/story?id=3295046.

Etchells, D. 2018. "Taipei 2017 Sumer Universiade Generates Economic Impact of More Than $150 Million." *Inside the Games* (April 21). htpps://www.insidethegames.biz/articles/1064177/taipei-2017-summer-universiade-generates-economic-impact-of-more-than-150-million.

Eugenio-Martin, J.L. 2003. "Modelling Determinants of Tourism Demand as a Five-Stage Process: A Discrete Choice Methodological Approach." *Tourism and Hospitality Research* 4 (4):341-54.

"F1 Corporate Hospitality Packages." 2019. *Grand Prix Events*. www.grandprixevents.com/f1-corporate-hospitality.

Fairley, S. 2003. "In Search of Relived Social Experience: Group-Based Nostalgia Sport Tourism." *Journal of Sport Management* 17:284-304.

Fell, A. 2003. *A Study of Modeling Crowd Dynamics*. Unpublished senior project. www.sxs.carelron.ca/~arpwhite/documents/honoursProjects.

Fiedler, F.E. 1967. *A Theory of Leadership Effectiveness*. New York: McGraw-Hill.

FIFA. 2018. "Impact and Legacy of 2018 FIFA World Cup Russia: Facts and Figures." www.fifa.com/worldcup/news/y=2017/m=2/news=impact-and-legacy-of-2018-fifa-world-cup-russia-facts-and-figures-2867772.html.

Finley, M. 2016. "Churchill Downs Racetrack Targets $16 Million Clubhouse Renovation." *Louisville Business First*. October 18. https://www.bizjournals.com/louisville/news/2016/10/18/churchill-downs-racetracktargets-16-million.html.

Fireupacure.com. 2018. https://www.fireupacure.com/about.

Fisher, E. 2018. "Satisfi to Provide Minor League Baseball with Bilingual Chatbots." *New York Business Journal*. May 15. https://www.bizjournals.com/newyork/news/2018/05/15/satisfi-to-provide-minor-league-baseball-with.html.

Foster, J.S. 2006. "Facility Contracts in the Meetings Industry." In *Professional Meeting Management: Comprehensive Strategies for Meetings, Conventions and Events*, edited by G.C. Ramsborg, 627-48. Dubuque, IA: Kendall/Hunt.

Francisco, J.M. 2007. "How to Create and Facilitate Meetings That Matter: Learn How to Plan and Run a Successful Meeting Using Crucial Checklists." *Information Management Journal* 41 (6):54-57.

Fried, G. 2009. *Managing Sport Facilities*. 2nd ed. Champaign, IL: Human Kinetics.

Fried, G. 2015. *Managing Sport Facilities*. 3rd ed. Champaign, IL: Human Kinetics.

Frost, S. 2012. "Top 10 Reasons a Business Should Use Social Networking in Its Promotional Plan." *Houston Chronicle*. January. http://smallbusiness.chron.com/top-10-reasons-business-should-use-social-networking-its-promotional-plan-20337.html.

Fruin, J.J. 1984. "Crowd Dynamics and Auditorium Management." *Auditorium News (May)*.

Gameday Security. 2018. "On the Fly: Are Sports Security Professionals Truly Prepared for the Enormous Threat Unmanned Aerial Vehicles Pose to All Sporting Events?" Summer https://www.ncs4.com/knowledgeportal/gameday-security.

Gems, R.R., L.J. Borish, and G. Pfister. 2008. *Sports in American History: From Colonization to Globalization*. Champaign, IL: Human Kinetics.

Gerber, S. 2011. How to Negotiate Vendor Contracts. April 1. www.huffingtonpost.com/scott-gerber/young-entrepreneur-counci_1_b_843800.html.

Getz, D. 2005. *Event Management and Event Tourism*. New York: Cognizant Communication Group.

Gibson, H.J. 1998. "Sport Tourism: A Critical Analysis of Research." *Sport Management Review* 1 (1):45-76.

Gibson, H.J., Kaplanidou, K., and Kang, S.J. 2012. "Small-Scale Event Sport Tourism: A Case Study in Sustainable Tourism." *Sport Management Review* 15(2):160-70.

Glover, W.H. 2009. "Waivers and Releases Regarding Sports Activities With Forms." http://williamhgloverjd.wordpress.com/2009/03/11/waivers-and-releases-regarding-sports-activities-with-forms.

Goldblatt, J. 2008. *Special Events: The Roots and Wings of Celebration*. 5th ed. Hoboken, NJ: Wiley.

Goldblatt, J. 2011. *Special Events: A New Generation and the Next Frontier*. Hoboken, NJ: Wiley.

Goldblatt, J. 2013. *Special Events: The Roots and Wings of Celebration*. Hoboken, NJ: Wiley.

Goldblatt, J. 2014. *Special Events: Creating and Sustaining a New World for Celebration*. 7th ed. Hoboken, NJ: Wiley.

Gordon, K.O. 2013. "Emotion and Memory in Nostalgia Sport Tourism: Examining the Attraction to Postmodern Ballparks Through an Interdisciplinary Lens." *Journal of Sport & Tourism* 18(3):217-39.

Goss, N. 2011. "Bowling Green Video: Watch Falcon's Stroh Center Rap Video." *Bleacher Report*. October 22. https://bleacherreport.com/articles/905768-bowling-green-video-watch-falcons-stroh-center-rap-video.

Graham, S., L.D. Neirotti, and J.J. Goldblatt. 2001. *The Ultimate Guide to Sports Marketing*. New York: McGraw-Hill.

GrantSpace. 2012. http://.grantspace.org/tools/knowledge-base/funding-resources/corporations/cause-related-marketing.

Green, H.G. 2009. *More Than a Minute: How to Be an Effective Leader and Manager in Today's Changing World*. Franklin Lakes, NJ: Career Press.

Greenwell, T.C., J. Lee, and D. Naeger. 2007. "Using the Critical Incident Technique to Identify Critical Aspects of the Spectator's Service Experience." *Sport Marketing Quarterly* 16:190-98.

Gwinner, K.P., D.D. Gremler, and M.J. Bitner. 1998. "Relational Benefits in Services Industries: The Customer's Perspective." *Journal of the Academy of Marketing Science* 26 (2):101-14.

Haase, N. 2017. "U.S. College System Responsible for Developing World's Top Women's Hockey Talent." *SI.com* (April 7). https://www.si.com/nhl/2017/04/07/division-i-womens-hockey-international-team-usa-canda.

Hanson, B. 2010. "Budgeting for Sports Events—Part 2." http://sportscommissions.wordpress.com/2010/10/25/budgeting-for-sports-events-part-2.

Harrison, K. n.d. "Focus on What You Can Do for a Potential Sponsor Rather Than What They Can Give You." *CuttingEdgePR.com*. www.cuttingedgepr.com/articles/what-you-can-do-for-potential-sponsor.asp.

Harrison, K. n.d. "How to Calculate Sponsorship Fees." *CuttingEdgePR.com*. www.cuttingedgepr.com/articles/sponsorship_calculate_fee.asp.

Hartnett, J. 2017. "Wimbledon: Adapting to Technological Change." *Drum* July 19. http://www.thedrum.com/opinion/2017/07/19/wimbledon-adapting-technological-change.

Hepburn, S. 2010. "The Panthers Purrsuit Is On—A Social Media Challenge!" *Media Merging*. September 2. www.mediaemerging.com/2010/09/02/the-panthers-purrsuit-is-on-a-social-media-challenge.

Higham, J.E.S., and T.D. Hinch. 2003. 'Sport, Space, and Time: Effects of the Otago Highlanders Franchise on Tourism.' *Journal of Sport Management* 17:235-257.

Hiller, H.H. 2000. "Mega-Events, Urban Boosterism and Growth Strategies: An Analysis of the Objectives and Legitimations of the Cape Town 2004 Olympic Bid. *International Journal of Urban and Regional Research* 24 (2):449-58.

Hixon, T. 2005. "Price and Non-Price Promotions in Minor League Baseball and the Watering Down Effect." *The Sport Journal* 8 (4). www.thesportjournal.org/article/price-and-non-price-promotions-minor-league-baseball-and-watering-down-effect.

Honigman, B. 2012. "How Sports Brands Are Using Stars and Social Media." *Businessinsider.com*. April 23. http://articles.businessinsider.com/2012-04-23/news/31385406_1_twitter-and-facebook-brand-audience.

Hoogendoorn, S., and P.H.L. Bovy, 2003. "Simulation of Pedestrian Flows by Optimal Control and Differential Games." *Optimal Control Applications and Methods* 24 (3):153-72.

Houghtailing, J. 2018. "Flooding Sets Back Dick's Sporting Goods Open Events." August 14. http://spectrumlocalnews.com/nys/binghamton/news/2018/08/15/flooding-sets-back-dick-s-sporting-goods-tournament-open-events.

House, R.J. 1971. "A Path-Goal Theory of Leader Effectiveness." *Administrative Science Quarterly* 16:321-38.

Howard, D.R., and J.L. Crompton. 2014. *Financing Sport*. 3rd ed. Morgantown, West Virginia: FIT.

HowTo.gov. 2012. "How to Blog." www.howto.gov/social-media/blogs/writing.

Hoyle, L. 2002. *Event Marketing*. Hoboken, NJ: Wiley.

Hums, M.A., and J.C. MacLean. 2017. *Governance and Policy in Sport Organizations*. 3rd ed. Scottsdale, AZ: Holcomb Hathaway.

Hunsucker, A. (2017, September 8). Irma cost ULM $1 million buyout. *The News Star*. https://www.thenewsstar.com/story/sports/college/ulm/2017/09/08/irma-costs-ulm-1-million-buyout/647419001/.

International Events Group (IEG). 2012 "IEG's Guide to Why Companies Sponsor." Chicago, IL: IEG. http://stjude.org/SJFile/alsac_ieg_guide_why_companies_sponsor.pdf.

Irwin, R.L., W.A. Sutton, and L.M. McCarthy. 2002. *Sport Promotion and Sales Management*. Champaign, IL: Human Kinetics.

Irwin, R.L., W.A. Sutton, and L.M. McCarthy. 2008. *Sport Promotion and Sales Management*. 2nd ed. Champaign, IL: Human Kinetics.

Isenberg, M. 2018. "Top Ten Media Tips for Athletes and Coaches." http://coachgeorgeraveling.com/top-ten-media-tips-athletes-coaches.

Jackson, J. 2012. "Social Media and Sports: Natural Teammates." *Time.com*. January 26. www.techland.time.com/2012/01/26/social-media-and-sports-natural-teammates.

Jacobs, S. 2015. "Making Meetings Accessible and Inclusive for All." www.smartmeetings.com/magazine_article/ada-accessible-inclusive-meetings.

Jagler, S. 2016. "Hospitality at the U.S. Open Will Have a Wisconsin Flavor." October 22. https://www.msgpromotions.com/hospitality-at-the-u-s-open-will-have-a-wisconsin-flavor.

Johnson, C. 2006. "Cutting Through Advertising Clutter." *CBSNews.com* February 11. www.cbsnews.com/stories/2006/09/17/sunday/main2015684.shtml.

Jones, M. 2018, October 16. "Using cross-promotion to strengthen your digital product brand." https://easydigitaldownloads.com/blog/using-cross-promotion-to-strengthen-brand/

Kansas State High School Activities Association. 2012. *Media Relations Guide: Tips on Working With the Media and Increasing Awareness of Your School Activities Program.* www.kshsaa.org/Media/Media%20Guide.pdf.

Kaplan, D. 2017. "ESPN Deepens Its Investment in Wimbledon." *SportsBusiness Journal* (May 22). www.sportsbusinessdaily.com/journal/issues/2017/05/22/media/wimbledon.aspx.

Kaylor, J. 2017. "How Much Money Will It Cost NFL Fans to Attend Super Bowl 51?" *Sports Cheat Sheet* February 3. htpps://www.cheatsheet.com/sports/cost-attend-super-bowl-51.html/?a=viewall.

Kear, J. 2017, January 17. "How to get sponsors for your events in 14 simple steps." https://blog.planningpod.com/2017/01/26/how-to-get-sponsors-for-events-in-14-simple-steps/

Kell, J. 2017. "Exclusive: Adidas to Sponsor World OutGames." *Fortune.com* (April 26). www.fortune.com/2017/04/26/adidas-sponsors-world-outgames.

Kelly, J. 2000. "Looking to Sports for Development Dollars." *American City & County* 115:20-21.

Kentucky Derby. 2018. "Official Kentucky Derby Programs." www.kentuckyderby.com/party/derby-party/cocktails-recipes-and-more/official-kentucky-derby-programs

Kercheval, B. 2011. "Updated: Miami LB Taken to Hospital for Heat Exhaustion." *NBC Sports*. November 15. http://collegefootballtalk.nbcsports.com/2011/11/15/miami-player-taken-to-hospital-for-heat-exhaustion.

Kim, M., and H. Bang. 2012. "Volunteer Management in Sport." In *Handbook of Sport Management*, edited by L. Robinson, P. Chelladurai, and P. Downward. New York: Routledge.

Kirchen, R. 2018. "PGA Swings Into Push to Market 2020 Ryder Cup Hospitality Suites to Regional Businesses." *Milwaukee Business Journal* (July 23). www.bizjournals.com/milwaukee/news/2018/07/23/pga-swings-into-push-to-market-2020-ryder-cup.html.

Klara, R. 2018. "PGA Tour Retires 20-Year-Old Slogan and Stresses Fans as Much as Players in New Campaign." *Adweek* April 10. http://www.adweek.com/brand-marketing/pga-tour-retires-20-year-old-slogan-and-stresses-fans-as-much-as-players-in-new-campaign.

Knox, T. 2017. "Ohio State Has Third-Highest Athletic Marketing Deal in U.S." March 13. https://www.bizjournals.com/columbus/news/2017/03/13/ohio-state-has-third-highest-athletic-marketing.html.

Kokemuller, N. n.d.. "Advertisement vs. Sponsorship." *Small Business - Chron.com*. http://smallbusiness.chron.com/advertisement-vs-sponsorship-17459.html.

Kotler, P. 1975. "Marketing for Nonprofit Organizations." Englewood Cliffs, NJ: Prentice Hall.

Kozlowski, J.C. 1996. "Can You Say 'Exculpatory Agreement'?" *NRPA Law Review*. March 1996. http://classweb.gmu.edu/jkozlows/p%26r396.htm.

Krupa, G. 2017. "Detroit Committee Hunting for Super Bowl and More." *Detroit News* (October 25). htpps://www.detroitnews.com/story/sports/2017/10/25/detroit-committee-target-marquee-sporting-events/106991170.

Kuhnert, K.W., and P. Lewis. 1987. "Transactional and Transformational Leadership: A Constructive/Developmental Analysis." *Academy of Management Review* 12 (4):648-57.

Kurtzman, J., and J. Zauhar. 1998. "Sport Tourism: A Business Inherency or an Innate Compulsion?" *Visions in Leisure and Business* 17 (2):21-30.

Kurtzman, J., and J. Zauhar. 2003. "A Wave in Time: The Sports Tourism Phenomena." *Journal of Sport Tourism* 8 (1):35-47.

Kuse, K.R. 2012. "Vendor Contracts: What Are They and Do You Need Them?" http://integratedgeneralcounsel.com/vendor-contracts-what-are-they-and-do-you-need-them.

Kushner, S. 2017. "Pelicans' Struggles Slow Franchise's Momentum, but Team Executives Say They're Committed to New Orleans." *The Advocate*. March 11. http://www.theadvocate.com/new_orleans/sports/pelicans/article_448da1e4-069f-11e7-b622-1b9407a8cff3.html.

Kyriakos, A. 2015. "Sports & media: A symbiotic relationship." *Fan to Friend*. www.fromfantofriend.wordpress.com/2015/03/10/sports-are-social-anyways-the-history-of-sports-and-media.

Lage, L. 2004. "Pacers-Pistons Game Halted by Brawl." *USA Today*. November 19. http://usatoday30.usatoday.com/sports/basketball/games/2004-11-19-pacers-pistons_x.htm.

Lavidge, R.A., and G.A. Steiner. 1961. "A Model for Predictive Measurements of Advertising Effectiveness." *Journal of Marketing* 25 (6):59-62.

Lawrence, H., and M. Wells. 2009. "Event Sponsorship." In *Event Management Blueprint*, 119-26. Dubuque, IA: Kendall/Hunt.

Lees, I. 2011. "Building Teams for Performance." *Keeping Good Companies* 63 (9):562-65.

Limpert, R. 2012. "BB&T to Extend Sports Sponsorships with Atlanta Tennis Championships." *RickLimpert.info* April 23. http://ricklimpert.squarespace.com/journal/2012/4/23/bbt-to-extend-sports-sponsorships-with-atlanta-tennis-champi.html.

Lissau, R. 2017. "Girls Are Flocking to Ice Hockey Across Illinois and the Nation." *Dailyherald.com* (December 3). http://www.dailyherald.com/news/20171202/girls-are-flocking-to-ice-hockey-across-illinois-and-the-nation.

Lizandra, M., and J.M. Gladden. 2015. "International Sport." In *Principles and Practice of Sport Management*. 2nd ed., edited by L.P. Masteralexis, C.A. Barr, and M.A. Hums, 166-94. Sudbury, MA: Jones and Bartlett.

Lombardo, J., and M. Smith. 2009. "Ga. Tech Hands Ticket Sales to Aspire Group." *Street and Smith's SportsBusiness Journal*, May 25.

Lough, N.L., R.L. Irwin, and G. Short. 2000. "Corporate Sponsorship Motives Among North American Companies: A Contemporary Analysis." *International Journal of Sport Management1* (4):283-95.

Lussier, R.N., and D.C. Kimball. 2009. *Applied Sport Management Skills*. Champaign, IL: Human Kinetics.

Lynde, T. 2007. *Sponsorships 101*. Mableton, GA: Lynde & Associates.

Lyons, M. 2018. "From Juleps to Fascinators, the Kentucky Derby Is Good for Small Businesses Across the U.S." *NBC News* (May 5). htpps://www.nbcnews.com/business/business-news/juleps-fascinators-kentucky-derby-good-small-businesses-across-u-s-n871501.

Mandel, J.R. 2012. "Top 10 Negotiation Tips." *MeetingsNet*. September 4. http://meetingsnet.com/negotiatingcontracts/top-10-negotiation-tips.

Manning, A. 2012. "Noise Ordinances Can Be Bigger Headaches for Communities Than Noise Itself." *Columbus Dispatch*. April 23. www.dispatch.com/content/stories/local/2012/04/23/noise-ordinances-can-be-big-headaches-for-communities.html.

Markazi, A. 2018. "Vegas a College Hoops Destination, Despite NCAA Cold Shoulder." *ESPN.com* (April 1). http://www.espn.com/chalk/story/_/id/22956217/las-vegas-forbidden-home-march-madness.

Martens, R. 2001. *Directing Youth Sport Programs*. Champaign, IL: Human Kinetics.

Mashable Entertainment. 2012. "How Social Media Is Changing Sports." http://mashable.com/2012/04/27/sports-social-media-2.

Maskeroni, A. (2018, September 21). Bud Light unlocks coolers full of free beer around Cleveland as Browns win first game since 2016. Ad Age. https://adage.com/article/creatives-08/bud-light-unlocks-free-beer-fridges-cleveland-browns-win/315011/.

Masteralexis, L.P., C.A. Barr, and M.A. Hums. 2015. *Principles and Practice of Sport Management*. Sudbury, MA: Jones and Bartlett.

Masterman, G. 2009. *Strategic Sports Event Management*. 2nd ed. Oxford, UK: Butterworth-Heinemann.

Masterman, G. 2009. *Strategic Sports Event Management: Olympic Edition*. Oxford: Elsevier.

Masterman, G. 2014. *Strategic Sports Event Management*. 3rd ed. New York: Routledge.

Matthews, D. 2008. *Special Event Production: The Process*. Oxford, UK: Butterworth-Heinemann.

Mavros, A. 2015. "Five Tips to Fine-Tune Your Media Relations in Sports PR." *The Edge: PRSA*. http://prnewpros.prsa.org/five-tips-to-fine-tune-your-media-relations-in-sports-pr.

Mazique, B. 2018. "ONE Championship's Major Success Attributed to Timing and the Collaboration of 3 Harvard Grads." *Forbes* April 7. https://www.forbes.com/sites/brianmazique/2018/04/07/one-championships-major-success-can-be-attributed-to-timing-and-the-collaboration-of-3-harvard-grads/#4c59ce3c5902.

McCarthy, E.J. 1960. *Basic Marketing: A Managerial Approach*. Homewood, IL: Irwin.

McCue, B. 2016 "What to Include in Your Event Sponsorship Proposal." htpps://www.winmo.com/sponsorship/what-to-include-in-your-event-sponsorship-proposal.

MCG. 2012. "MCG Light Towers." www.mcg.org.au/The%20MCG%20Stadium/Facts%20and%20Figures/Light%20Towers.aspx.

McKnight, M., and G. Bishop. 2018. "Inside the Dark World of Trolling." *Sports Illustrated*. March 29. https://www.si.com/more-sports/2018/03/29/twitter-internet-trolls-sports-athletes.

Mickle, T. 2009. "Gatorade's Name on Amateur Tour." *Street and Smith's SportsBusiness Journal*, March 23:6.

Mickle, T. 2012. "Sponsors Activate for Winter Youth Olympic Games." *Street and Smith's SportsBusiness Journal* (January 2) 7.

Miller, R.K., and K. Washington. 2012. *Sports Marketing 2012*. Loganville, GA: Richard K. Miller & Associates.

Ministry of Youth Affairs and Sports. 2018. Department of Sports. https://yas.nic.in/sports.

Mol, M.J. 2007. *Outsourcing: Design, Process and Performance*. Cambridge, UK: Cambridge University Press.

Morrison, P. 2014. "The Real Reason to Go to Sporting Events: Being with Other Americans." *Los Angeles Times* June 12. http://www.latimes.com/opinion/opinion-la/la-ol-sports-fan-american-community-20140612-story.html.

Moutinho, L. 2001. "Consumer Behaviour in Tourism." *European Journal of Marketing* 21 (10):5-44.

MSG Promotions. 2012. "Events Portfolio." www.msgpromotions.com/MSG/events.html.

Mullin, B.J., S. Hardy, and W.A. Sutton. 2007. *Sport Marketing*. 3rd ed. Champaign, IL: Human Kinetics.

Mullin, B.J., S. Hardy, and W.A. Sutton. 2014. *Sport Marketing*. 4th ed. Champaign, IL: Human Kinetics.

Myhill, M., and J. Phillips. 2006. "Determine the Success of Your Meeting Through Evaluation." In *Professional Meeting Management: Comprehensive Strategies for Meetings, Conventions and Events*, edited by G.C. Ramsborg, 17-48. Dubuque, IA: Kendall/Hunt.

Myhill, M., and J. Phillips. 2010. "Determine the Success of Your Meeting Through Evaluation." In *Professional Meeting Management: Comprehensive Strategies for Meetings, Conventions and Events*, edited by G.C. Ramsborg, 691-710. Dubuque, IA: Kendall/Hunt.

National Association of Sports Commissions. 2016. "Sport Tourism: A State of the Industry Report." www.sportscommissions.org/Portals/sportscommissions/Documents/Reports/ST_report_16_to_print2.pdf.

National Association of Sports Commissions. 2017. "About NASC: Who We Are." www.sportscommissions.org/about.

National Association of Sports Commissions (NASC). 2018. "About Us." www.sportscommissions.org/about-NASC.

National Oceanic and Atmospheric Administration. 2018 https://www.nws.noaa.gov/om/hazstats.shtml.

National Oceanic and Atmospheric Administration. n.d. "Preparing Venues and Large Events for Severe Weather." http://www.crh.noaa.gov/Image/dtx/web/PreparingVenues.pdf.

NBA. 2016. "NBA to Debut Interactive Basketball Fan Event at All-Star 2016 in Toronto." http://www.nba.com/2016/news/01/11/interactive-fan-event-all-star-2016-official-release.

Nelson, B. 1999. "Low-Cost Ways to Build Employee Commitment." *Inc.* December 1. www.inc.com/articles/1999/12/16412.html.

New Bundesliga Television Deal Worth 4.64 Billion Euros. 2016. *Dw.com* (June 9). www.dw.com/en/new-bundesliga-television-deal-worth-464-billion-euros/a-19318613.

"The NHL Has Two Ridiculous Contingency Plans for a Rainy Winter Classic." 2017. *SI.com* (January 2). https://www.si.com/nhl/2017/01/02/blues-blackhawks-winter-classic-rain-scenarios-plans-shootout.

O'Connor, J.T. 2018. "Our 13th Annual State of the Industry Report." *SportsEvents* (March):30-42.

O'Connor, J.T., and M. Martin. 2009. "2009 Market Report: Stability & Optimism." *SportsEvents* 6 (March):26-33.

Olenski, S. 2012. "The Lines Between Social Media and Sports Continue to Blur." *Forbes.com*. February 13. https://www.forbes.com/sites/marketshare/2012/02/13/the-lines-between-social-media-and-sports-continue-to-blur/#348f9d2f2d5f.

Osborn, R.N., and J.G. Hunt. 1975. "An Adaptive-Reactive Theory of Leadership. The Role of Macro Variables in Leadership Research." In *Leadership Frontiers*, edited by J.G. Hunit and L.L. Larson. Kent, OH: Kent State University.

Ourand, J. 2018. "The Escalation of Sports-Rights Fees Can Be Traced to a 2008 ESPN Deal." *New York Business Journal* (May 3). www.bizjournals.com/newyork/news/2018/05/03/escalation-of-sports-rights-fees-traced-to-espn.html.

Owen, D.G. 2007. "The Five Elements of Negligence." *Hofstra Law Review* 35 (4):1671-86.

Paddock, M. 2018. *Fox 40*. "The Dicks Open Champions Tour Won't Let Rain Slow Them Down." August 15. http://www.wicz.com/story/38892373/the-dicks-open-champions-tour-wont-let-rain-slow-them-down.

Parkhouse, B. 2005. *The Management of Sport: Its Foundation and Application*. New York: McGraw-Hill.

Peltier, E. 2017. "Paris Won the 2024 Olympics by Learning From Its Mistakes." *New York Times* (September 17). htpps://www.nytimes.com/2017/09/17/world/europe/olympics-2024-paris.html.

Perez, A.J. 2017. "NBC Sports, Snapchat Debut NHL Playoff Beard Filter." *USA Today* April 27. https://www.usatoday.com/story/sports/nhl/2017/04/27/stanley-cup-nhl-playoff-beards-snapchat-nbc-sports/100969480.

Perez, C. 2017, February 21. Social media is changing how sports franchises an fans interact. USC Anneberg School of Communication DSM News. https://annenberg.usc.edu/communication/digital-social-media-ms/dsm-today/social-media-changing-how-sports-franchises-and-fans.

Performance Research. n.d. "Loyal NASCAR Fans Please Stand Up." www.performanceresearch.com/nascar-racestat.htm.

Perkins, T. 2018. "Report shows Grand Prix will have one-third of the economic benefit Penske claims." *Detroit Metro Times* (April 30). https://www.metrotimes.com/news-hits/archives/2018/04/30/report-shows-grand-prix-will-have-one-third-of-the-economic-benefit-penske-claims.

Perry, J.L., D. Mesch, and L. Paarlberg. 2006. "Motivating Employees in a New Governance Era: The Performance Paradigm Revisited." *Public Administration Review* (July/August):505-14.

Peters, T., and R. Waterman. 1982. *In Search of Excellence*. New York: Harper & Row.

PGAtour.com. 2012. "Tournament Schedule." www.pgatour.com/r/schedule.

Phillips, H. 2011. "Will Outsourcing Become the New Normal?" *SportsTurf* 27 (7):32-35.

Pitts, B. G., and D.K. Stotlar. 2002. "Fundamentals of Sport Marketing." 2nd ed. Morgantown, WV: Fitness Information Technology.

Plunkett Research 2018. "Sports & Recreation Business Statistics Analysis, Business and Industry Statistics." www.plunkettresearch.com/statistics/sports-industry.

Plunkett Research, Ltd. 2015. Sports Industry Overview. Houston, TX.

Qualman, E. 2009. *Socialnomics: How Social Media Transforms the Way We Live and Do Business* . Hoboken, NJ: John Wiley & Sons.

Qualman, E. 2018. *Social Media Revolution*. https://www.youtube.com/watch?v=3SuNx0UrnEo.

Rader, B.G. 2009. *American Sports: From the Age of Folk Games to the Age of Televised Sports*. 6th ed. Upper Saddle River, NJ: Pearson Education.

Ramshaw, G. 2014. "Too Much Nostalgia? A Decennial Reflection on the Heritage Classic Ice Hockey Event." *Event Management* (December 9):473-77.

Reddy, T. 2015. "10 Ways Stadiums & Venues Are Using Technology to Delight Fans & Keep Them Coming Back." September 29. https://www.umbel.com/blog/publishers/10-ways-stadiums-are-using-technology-to-delight-fans.

Reibel, J. (2010, December 1). Using social media to generate team revenue. Coach and AD. https://coachad.com/articles/using-social-media-to-generate-revenue/

Reichard, K. 2017. "NFL Stadiums, Listed Oldest to Newest." September 15. https://footballstadiumdigest.com/2017/09/nfl-stadiums-listed-oldest-to-newest.

Reisinger, Y. 2001. "Concepts of Tourism, Hospitality, and Leisure Services." In *Service Quality Management in Hospitality, Tourism, and Leisure*, edited by J. Kandampully, C. Mok, and B. Sparks. Binghamton, NY: Haworth Hospitality Press.

Research and Markets. 2018. "Global Sports Tourism Market 2017-2021." www.researchandmarkets.com/research/93pwbp/global_sports.

Reuters News Agency. 2018 (May 8). "Freak Hailstorm Halts MTV Movie and TV Awards Red Carpet." https://www.theweathernetwork.com/us/news/articles/us-weather/california-los-angeles-mtv-awards-hail-storm-rain-wind-red-carpet/82076.

Rigby, D. 2011. "The Future of Shopping." *Harvard Business Review*. www.hbr.org/2011/12/the-future-of-shopping.

Rivals. 2012. "About Us." http://highschool.rivals.com/content.asp?CID=36178.Shonk, J.H. 1982. *Working in Teams: A Practical Manual for Improving Work Groups*. New York: AMACOM.

Robinson, T., and S. Gammon. 2004. 'A Question of Primary and Secondary Motives: Revisiting and Applying the Sport Tourism Framework.' *Journal of Sport Tourism* 9 (3):221-33.

Sanchez, J. 2017. "History 'n' the shaking: Cards-Bucs, Bravo!" *MLB.com* (August 21). https://www.mlb.com/news/history-made-in-first-little-league-classic/c-249481446.

Sanserino, M., and D. Todd. 2014. "Federal Aviation Administration Investigating Drone Over PNC Park." *Pittsburgh Post-Gazette*. June 28. http://www.post-gazette.com/business/2014/06/27/FAA-investigating-drone-over-PNC-Park/stories/201406270183.

Sawyer, T.H. 2013. *Facility Design and Management for Health, Physical Activity, Recreation, and Sport*. 13th ed. Urbana, IL: Sagamore.

Schmader, S.W., and R. Jackson. 1997. *Special Events: Inside and Out*. 2nd ed. Urbana, IL: Sagamore.

Schoettle, A. 2012. "City Leaders Determined to Use Global Super Bowl Spotlight to Build Cachet." *Indianapolis Business Journal*. January 30. www.indianaeconomicdigest.com/Main.asp?SectionID=31&SubSectionID=121&ArticleID=63766.

Shafer, S. 2007. "Let the Games Begin." *Louisville Courier-Journal*. Retrieved June 22, 2018, from www.courier-journal.com/apps/pbcs.dll/article?aid=2007706220446.

Shank, M.D. 2009. *Sports Marketing: A Strategic Perspective*. 4th ed. Upper Saddle River, NJ: Pearson.

Shank, M.D. 2014. *Sports Marketing: A Strategic Perspective*. 5th ed. Upper Saddle River, NJ: Pearson.

Sharp, L., A. Moorman, and C. Claussen. 2014. *Sport Law: A Managerial Approach*. 2nd ed. Scottsdale, AZ: Holcomb Hathaway.

Sharrow, R. 2009. "Not Kids Play: Youth Sports Eyed to Boost Maryland Tourism." *Baltimore Business Journal*. http://baltimore.bizjournals.com/baltimore/stories/2009/08/03/focus2.html.

Shock, P.J. 2006. "Food and Beverage Arrangements." In *Professional Meeting Management: Comprehensive Strategies for Meetings, Conventions and Events*, edited by G.C. Ramsborg, 399-417. Dubuque, IA: Kendall/Hunt.

Shonk, D.J. 2011. "Event Logistics." In *The Encyclopedia of Sports Management and Marketing*, edited by L.E. Swayne and M. Dodds, 482-84. Thousand Oaks, CA: Sage.

Shonk, D.J., and G. Bravo. 2010. "Interorganizational Support, Commitment, Cooperation and the Desire to Maintain a Partnership: A Framework for Sporting Event Networks." *Journal of Sport Management* 24 (3):272-90.

Shonk, D.J., and P. Chelladurai. 2008. "Service Quality, Satisfaction and Intent to Return in Event Sport Tourism." *Journal of Sport Management* 22:587-602.

Shonk, J.H. 1992. *Team-Based Organizations: Developing a Successful Team Environment*. Homewood, IL: Business One Irwin.

Shortridge, D. 2009. Delaware Set to Plunge into Youth Sports Market. *News Journal*. www.delawareonline.com/article/20090817/business/908170329/1006/news.

Siegel, J. 2011. "High School Football Player Dies; Sixth Athlete Death This Summer." *ABC News*. September 3. http://abcnews.go.com/Health/high-school-football-player-dies-sixth-athlete-death/story?id=14442856#.T57kWvUw8TA.

Silvers, J.R. 2004. *Professional Event Coordination*. Hoboken, NJ: Wiley.

Silvers, J.R. 2007. "Return on Objectives (ROO)." October 27. www.juliasilvers.com/embok/return_on_objectives.htm.

Singh, V. 2009. "Sponsorship Proposals: 10 Ideas That Will Get You Cash in This Recession." January 30. www.allaboutpresentations.com/2009/01/sponsorship-proposals-10-ideas-that.html.

Skildum-Reid, K. 2010. "Top Ten Tips for Sponsorship Seekers." Sydney, Australia. www.powersponsorship-downloads.com/powersponsorship/TopTenTipsForSponsorshipSeekers.pdf.

Skildum-Reid, K. 2011, April 5. K.I.S.S—Keep It Simple, Sponsors. http://blog.powersponsorship.com/index.php/2011/04.

Skildum-Reid, K., and A.-M. Grey. 2008. *Sponsorship Seeker's Toolkit*. 3rd ed. Sydney: McGraw-Hill.

Smith, M. 2009. "Ohio State Lands $110M Deal." *Street and Smith's SportsBusiness Journal*, March 30.

Solomon, J. 2002. *An Insider's Guide to Managing Sporting Events*. Champaign, IL: Human Kinetics.

Spanberg, E. 2017. "Hammer Time for Charlotte's PGA Championship." *Charlotte Business Journal* (March 19). https://www.bizjournals.com/charlotte/news/2017/03/19/hammer-time-for-charlottes-pga-championship.html.

Special Olympics (2018). "Mattel." https://www.specialolympics.org/Sponsors/Mattel.aspx.

Spendolini, M.J. 1992. *The Benchmarking Book*. New York: AMACOM.

Spengler, J.O., D.P. Connaughton, and A. Pittman. 2016. *Risk Management in Sport and Recreation*. 2nd ed. Champaign, IL: Human Kinetics.

Spengler, J.O., P.M. Anderson, D.P. Connaughton, and T.A. Baker III. 2016. *Introduction to Sport Law*. 2 ed. Champaign, IL: Human Kinetics.

Spoelstra, J. 1997. *Ice to the Eskimos*. New York: Harper Business.

SponsorMap. 2008. "Understanding Sponsorship." www.sponsormap.com/defining-sponsorship.

Sport England. 2012. "The Scale of Sports Volunteering in England in 2002. Summary Report of the Findings of the Sports Volunteering Study Commissioned by Sport England from the Leisure Industries Research Centre, Sheffield, October 2003." www.sportengland.org.

Standeven, J., and P. DeKnop. 1999. *Sport Tourism*. Champaign, IL: Human Kinetics.

Statista (2018). "Global Market Size of Outsourced Services from 2000 to 2017 (in billion U.S. dollars). https://www.statista.com/statistics/189788/global-outsourcing-market-size.

Statista. 2018. "Global Sports Market - Total Revenue from 2005 to 2017 (in Billion U.S. Dollars). www.statista.com/statistics/370560/worldwide-sports-market-revenue.

Steinbach, P. 2008. "Concessions: Concessions Contracts Capitalizing on Consumers' Brand Loyalty." *Athletic Business* 32 (8). www.athleticbusiness.com/articles/article.aspx?articleid=1838&zoneid=37.

Steinbach, P. 2010. "Colleges Use Social Media to Sell Sports Tickets." *Athletic Business*. August. www.athleticbusiness.com/articles/article.aspx?articleid=3599&zoneid=40.

Stim, R. n.d. "Contract Negotiation: 11 Strategies." www.nolo.com/legal-encyclopedia/contract-negotiation-11-strategies-33340.html.

Stoldt, G.C., S.W. Dittmore, and S.E. Branvold. 2012. *Sport Public Relations: Managing Stakeholder Communication*. 2nd ed. Champaign, IL: Human Kinetics.

Stotlar, D. 2005. *Developing Successful Sport Sponsorship Plans*. 2nd ed. Morgantown, WV: Fitness Information Technology.

Streibel, B.J. 2007. *Plan and Conduct Effective Meetings: 24 Steps to Generate Meaningful Results: The Employee Handbook for Enhancing Corporate Performance*. New York: McGraw-Hill.

Struna, N.L. 2009. American Sports, 1607-1860. In *Encyclopedia of Sports in America: A History from Foot Races to Extreme Sports* (vol. 1), edited by M.R. Nelson. Westport, CT: Greenwood Press.

Super Bowl XLVII New Orleans Host Committee. 2012. "Frequently Asked Questions." www.nolasuperbowl.com/FAQ.php#Q3.

Supovitz, F. 2005. *The Sports Event Management and Marketing Playbook*. Hoboken, NJ: Wiley.

Supovitz, F. 2014. *The Sports Event Management and Marketing Playbook*. 2nd ed. Hoboken, NJ: Wiley.

Supovitz, F., and R. Goldwater. 2014. *The Sports Event Marketing and Management Playbook*. 2nd ed. Hoboken, NJ: Wiley.

Swaddling, J. 1999. *The Ancient Olympic Games*. Austin: University of Texas Press.

Swanson, R.A., and B. Spears. 1995. *History of Sport and Physical Education in the United States*. Boston: McGraw-Hill.

Sweeney, M. 2017. "Amazon Outbids Sky to Win Exclusive ATP Tour Tennis Rights." *Guardian* (August 1). www.theguardian.com/media/2017/aug/01/amazon-outbids-sky-to-win-exclusive-atp-tour-tennis-rights.

Swenson, M. 2017. "5 Things you need to know about Sioux Fall, South Dakota." *Connect Sports*. htpps://www.connectsports.com/feature/5-things-need-know-sioux-falls-south-dakota/.

Sympson, T. 2010. "How E-Mail and Other Online Technology Impact Contract Issues." http://www.sbnonline.com/article/how-e-mail-and-other-online-technology-impact-contract-issues-courtney-d-tedrowe-novack-and-macey-llp.

Tabakoff, N. (2018). "Champagne companies bubbling with enthusiasm for sport." *Australian* (August 2). www.theaustralian.com.au/sport/champagne-companies-bubbling-with-enthusiasm-for-sport/news-story/44a03b73a66f250f1b1c27252e102537.

Tabi. 2010. "Top 10 World's Largest Sport Stadiums." *The Wondrous*. April 2. http://thewondrous.com/top-10-worlds-largest-sports-stadiums.

Taillier, S. 2014. Triathlete Injured as Drone Filming Race Falls to Ground. *ABC News Australia*. April 7. http://www.abc.net.au/news/2014-04-07/triathlete-injured-as-drone-filming-race-drops-to-ground/5371658.

Target. 2017. "Target's $14-Million Move Will Help More Kids Play Youth Soccer." https://corporate.target.com/article/2017/08/youth-soccer.

Tarlow, P. 2002. *Event Risk Management and Safety*. New York: Wiley.

Taylor, T., S. Darcy, R. Hoye, and G. Cuskelly. 2006. "Using Psychological Contract Theory to Explore Issues in Effective Volunteer Management." *European Sport Management Quarterly* 2 (6):123-47.

Thorpe, H. 2017. "Action Sports, Social Media, and New Technologies: Towards a Research Agenda." *Communication & Sport* 5 (5):554-78.

Thwaites, D., and S. Chadwick. 2005. "Service Quality Perspectives in Sport Tourism. *Sport in Society* 8:321-37.

Ticketmaster. 2012. "Our History." www.ticketmaster.com/history/index.html?tm_link=abouttm_history.

Tomko, M. 2011. "College Athletic Departments Use Social Media to Increase Fan Engagement." October 19. http://news.medill.northwestern.edu/chicago/news.aspx?id=190560.

Tosi, H.L., and N.P. Mero. 2003. *The Fundamentals of Organizational Behavior: What Managers Need to Know*. Oxford: Blackwell Publishing.

Tourism on the Edge Travel Blog. 2014 April 10. "10 great places in India for adventure sports." https://www.tourismontheedge.com/get-extreme/india-adventure-sports.

Townley, P. 2017. "USA Hockey Reports Increase in Participation." *Sports Events Magazine*. https://sportseventsmagazine.com/2017/09/27/usa-hockey-reports-increase-in-participation/..

Truettner, H. 2017. "Event Marketing: How to Successfully Promote an Event." *Brandwatch*. December. www.brandwatch.com/blog/event-marketing-how-to-promote-an-event.

Trump, K. 2009. "Columbine's 10th Anniversary Finds Lessons Learned." *District Administration*. April 1. www.districtadministration.com/article/columbine%E2%80%99s-10th-anniversary-finds-lessons-learned.

Tucker, T. 2018. "Leadoff: Super Bowl hospitality packages now on sale." *Atlanta Journal-Constitution* (June 7). www.ajc.com/sports/leadoff-super-bowl-hospitality-packages-now-sale/VKlmlvNsq9TKFY7Z3rxDOK.

Tucker, T. 2018. "Leadoff: Why MLB Chose Dodger Stadium, Not SunTrust Park, for All-Star Game." *Atlanta Journal Constitution* (April 12). htpps://www.ajc.com/sports/leadoff-why-mlb-chose-dodger-stadium-not-suntrust-park-for-all-star-game/tvSCqf5exA8hwotBTD54PM.

Tuckwell, K.J. 2011. *Integrated Marketing Communication: Strategic Planning Perspectives*. Toronto: Pearson.

Turchi, M. 2018. "Is Today the Worst Weather in Boston Marathon History? It Depends on How You Define 'Worst.'" April 16. https://www.boston.com/sports/boston-marathon/2018/04/16/worst-boston-marathon-weather-history.

Turco, D.M., R. Riley, and K. Swart. 2002. *Sport Tourism*. Morgantown, WV: Fitness Information Technology.

Ukman, L. 2012. "Sport Sponsorship." In *Principles and Practice of Sport Management*. 4th ed., edited by L.P. Masteralexis, C.A. Barr, and M.A. Hums, 362-389. Sudbury, MA: Jones & Bartlett Learning.

Ukman, L. 2012. *IEG's Guide to Sponsorship*. 29th Annual Sponsorship Conference. Chicago: IEG.

Ukman, L. 2018. *IEG's Guide to Sponsorship*. 35th Annual Sponsorship Conference. Chicago: IEG.

UNANIMA-International. n.d. "Human Trafficking and Major Sporting Events." https://www.unanima-international.org/wp-content/uploads/11_13HTMajor-Sporting-Events-FINAL.pdf.

U.S. Department of Justice. 2012. "Accessible Stadiums." www.ada.gov/stadium.txt.

U.S. Department of Labor Bureau of Labor Statistics. 2016. "Volunteering in the United States—2015." February 25.

USTA.com. 2012. "BB&T Agrees to Naming Rights Deal for Atlanta Tennis Championships." April 23. www.bbtatlantaopen.com/news/bbt_agrees_to_naming_rights_deal_for_atlanta_tennis_championships.

VanDen Heuvel, D. 2009. "Marketing Classics: The Hierarchy of Effects Model." June 16. www.marketingsavant.com/2009/06/marketing-classics-the-hierarchy-of-effects/trackback.

Van Der Wagen, L., and B. Carlos 2005. *Event Management for Tourism, Cultural, Business and Sporting Events*. Upper Saddle River, NJ: Pearson Prentice Hall.

van Mierlo, M., and S. van der Laarse. 2010. "Philips' Sports Lighting at South African Stadiums Set to Enhance Viewing Experience." June 10. www.newscenter.philips.com/main/standard/news/press/2010/20100610_wc_africa.wpd.

Vladem, E. 2018. "Northwestern Mutual's First CMO on Partnering with March Madness." *Chiefmarketer.com* (March 28). www.chiefmarketer.com/northwestern-mutuals-first-cmo-partnering-march-madness.

Volunteer Canada (2017). "Recognizing Volunteering in 2017: Summary Report." https://volunteer.ca/.

Vomiero, J. 2018. "Hosting the Olympics Has Become the Contest No One Wants to Win, and the IOC is Worried." https://globalnews.ca/news/4029340/hosting-olympics-ioc-worried-expensive.

Wagner, K. 2017. "This Is How the NBA Makes Exclusive Shows for Millions on Snapchat." *Recode.net* June 6. https://www.recode.net/2017/6/6/15739092/nba-snapchat-story-video-finals-warriors-cavaliers.

Wakefield, K. 2007. *Team Sports Marketing*. Oxford: Elsevier.

Walton, P. 2014. "DuPage County Wins USBC Bid." *Connect Sports* (February 26). htpps://www.connectsports.com/news/dupage-county-wins-usbc-bids.

Wann, D.L., B. Allen, and A.R. Rochelle. 2004. "Using Sport Fandom as an Escape: Searching for Relief from Under-Stimulation and Over-Stimulation." *International Sports Journal* 8 (1):104-13.

Washington Nationals. 2012. "Premium Seating." http://washington.nationals.mlb.com/was/ticketing/premium_seating.jsp.

Watkins, S. 2017. "U.S. Bank Arena Wins Bid to Host NCAA Men's Basketball Tournament Games." *Cincinnati Business Courier* (April 18). htpps://www.bizjournals.com/cincinnati/news/2017/04/18/u-s-bank-arena-wins-bid-to-host-ncaa-men-s.html.

Wayman, S. n.d. "Don't Be Afraid, Be Prepared! How to Prepare for Severe Weather." *OTEMS*. April 25. http://otems.com/dont-be-afraid-be-prepared-how-to-prepare-for-severe-weather.

Weed, M., and C. Bull. 2004. *Sports Tourism: Participants, Policy and Providers*. Oxford, UK: Elsevier Butterworth-Heinemann.

Weigelt, J.A., K.J. Brasel, D. Bragg, and D. Simpson. 2004. "The 360-Degree Evaluation: Increased Work With Little Return?" *Current Surgery* 61 (6):616-26.

White, L. 2017. "Stadium Foodservice Sports the Latest Trends." *Foodservice Equipment & Supplies*. (January 31). http://www.fesmag.com/departments/segment-spotlight/14174-sporting-the-latest-trends.

Winick, T.J., R. Claiborne, K. Gray, and D. Schabner. 2011. "Indiana State Fair Death Toll of 5 Could Go Higher After 'Fluke' Storm Fells Stage." *ABC* News. August 14. http://abcnews.go.com/US/indiana-state-fair-death-toll-higher-fluke-storm/story?id=14302288.

Witthaus, J. 2018. "Houston Texans to Add AI, Text Messaging Service to Gameday Experience." *Houston Business Journal*. February 15. https://www.bizjournals.com/houston/news/2018/02/15/exclusive-houston-texans-to-add-ai-service-to.html.

World Flying Disc Federation (WFDF). 2018. "Event Hosting." *Wfdf.org*. www.wfdf.org/events/event-hosting.

World Travel and Tourism Council. 2018. "Travel & Tourism: Economic Impact 2018: Foreword."

WRTV. 2012. "Softball Player Improving After Lightning Strike." March 16. www.theindychannel.com/news/softball-player-improving-after-lightning-strike.

Yukl, G., and D.D. Van Fleet. 1992. "Theory and Research on Leadership in Organizations." In *Handbook of Industrial and Organizational Psychology*, vol. 3, edited by M.D. Dunnette and L.M. Hough, 147-97. Palo Alto, GA: Consulting Psychologists Press.

Yukl, G.A. 1981. *Leadership in Organizations*. Englewood Cliffs, NJ: Prentice Hall.

Zhukovsk, L. 2017. "Major Sports Events: Are They Worth It?" *Theconversation.com* (August 9). htpp://www.theconversation.com/major-sports-events-are-they-worth-it-80691.

INDEX

Note: The italicized *f* and *t* following page numbers refer to figures and tables, respectively.

A
AAR (After Action Report) 139
accessibility 132
ADA. *See* Americans with Disabilities Act (ADA)
Adkins, Mandy 160, 161
administrative costs 69
admission policies 208
advertising 104*t*. *See also* marketing
advisory boards 105-106
AED (automated external defibrillator) 143
After Action Report (AAR) 139
aftermarketing 221
AIDA process 112
alcohol policies 125, 149
All-American Soap Box Derby 17
Americans with Disabilities Act (ADA) 132-133, 193, 208
ancillary events 40-41
apps 217
artificial intelligence 216
assessment. *See* evaluation
athletes. *See* participants
AT&T 118
attendance
  constraints to 98
  evaluation 229-230
  total cost of 95
attorneys 131-132, 151, 152
Audi Field 197-198
automated external defibrillator (AED) 143
awards ceremonies 72, 196

B
Baby Boomers 3
Barbetto, George 94
barriers 98
barter 68
behavioral theories of leadership 169
benchmarking 226
#BeTheFan 118
bidding
  competitive advantage 49, 54-56
  documents 54-56, 55*t*
  events seeking bids 49*t*
  feasibility studies 53-54
  financial considerations 53
  industry profile on 48
  requests for proposals 52, 53
  requirements 52
  tips for winning bids 56
bilateral contracts 126
blogs 172
blood-borne pathogens 146
brainstorming 29-30
brands 100, 118
Braslow, Neil 131
breach 151
broadcast agreements 68
broadcast partners 33
budgeting. *See also* costs; revenue
  benefits of 61
  categories 228-229
  clumping 228
  development 60
  for equipment 60
  financial statements 61
  and goals 61
  industry data 62, 64
  industry profile on 60
  postevent evaluation 228, 229*f*
  preliminary versus working budgets 61
  process 61-64
  projections 63
  research 61-62
  template 63*f*
  tips 73
Burton US Open Snowboarding Championships 32

C
capital investments 70-71
cardiopulmonary resuscitation (CPR) 143
career paths 6-7, 9
career qualifications 7-9
cash flow 74
cash management 74
cast lists 164
cause 151
cause-related marketing 90
ceremonies 72, 196
certifications 4, 7
certified sports event executives 7
chain of command 206
charitable causes 33
checklists 202, 203*t*-204*t*
Churchill Downs 12, 17, 66, 191, 216
cleanup 187, 188, 221
clearance 128
Clemons, Michael 26
Cleveland Rocks 121
closing ceremonies 72
Coca-Cola 90
collaboration tools 31
college athletics 60, 176, 180, 218
College Football Playoff National Championship 50
commercialism 5, 6
communication
  active listening 215
  apologies to customers 215
  crisis communications 114, 209
  on event day 202, 207
  face-to-face 172
  interpersonal 172
  lines of 207
  on-site 173
  with participants 211-212, 211*t*
  plans 141
  promotional methods 102, 112
  of risk management plans 143
  skills 8
  social media 172-173
  with spectators 209
  with staff 172-173, 216
  with target audience 112
  tools 31, 102
community partners 33
community support 105
competitive advantage 54, 62, 97, 195, 215
conceptual planning 27
concessions 65-66, 184, 185-186
conduct policies 130
consumers
  constraints 98
  expectations of 98-99
  feedback from 103
  motivation 97
  retention 214
  surveys of 226, 227*f*
  touchpoints 196, 216
  understanding 97-99, 215
contact lists 202, 204*t*
contingencies
  action plans for 41
  allowances in budget 72-73
  identifying potential issues 41

contingencies *(continued)*
overlooking 43
planning for 41-42, 201
updating plans 42
contracts 125
acceptance 126
addenda 131
assignments 132
attorney's perspective on 131-132
bilateral versus unilateral 126
boilerplate form 131
capacity 126
clauses 126, 127, 132, 136
clearance 128
coaches 136
consideration 126
definition 125
details 124, 126
digital signatures 134
entertainment contracts 127
essential elements 126-127
exclusivity clauses 127
facility contracts 126-127
food and beverage services 128-129
force majeure 136
game contracts 127
guarantees 135
industry profile on 124-125
language in 124, 221
legality 126
media contracts 128
negotiating tips 124, 131
offers 126
personal services 132
purpose of 125
releases 129
riders 127
security services 128
sponsorship agreements 127-128
and technology 134
terms 126
third party 128
tips for managing 126
types of 126-130
waivers 129
convention and visitors bureaus (CVBs) 2
coordination phase 182
corporate hospitality 66-67, 71-72, 184, 187
costs
administrative 69
capital investments 70-71
contingency allowances 72-73
controlling 60, 73-74
equipment for competition 60, 69
estimating 62-63
of event attendance 95
event presentation 72
facility-related 69-70
fixed 69
guest management 71-72
insurance 70
marketing 71
medical 69
miscellaneous expenses 72
officials 69
operations costs 69
player-related 70
promotions 60, 71
services for competition 69
sponsor fulfillment 71
sponsorships 83-84, 88
staffing 60, 69
variable 69
CPR (cardiopulmonary resuscitation) 143
Crawford, Scott 60
creative services 162
crisis communications 114
crisis management plans 141, 152
critical dates calendar 164*t*
critical Rs 113
cross-cultural events 14
cross-promotions 90
crowd control 148-149, 150, 151, 191
crowd management plans
alcohol policies 149
crisis situations 152
evacuation procedures 149
issues addressed by 149
movement theory 149
signage 150
staff training 150
crowds
demographics 149
dynamics 149
expectations 149
cultural differences 9
custodial services 187-188
customers. *See* consumers
customer service 195-196, 200
benefits of 214-215
moments of truth 215-216
proactive 215
quality of 195
reactive 215
CVBs (convention and visitors bureaus) 2

D

damage 151
data management systems 217
dates 36-37
D.C. United 197, 198
Deaflympics 16
debriefing 224
decision-making 28-29, 182
delegating 201
DeMeo, James A. 138, 139, 140
demographics 99, 149
departures 208, 212
Destination Marketing Association International 228
destination marketing organizations (DMOs) 12, 13, 166
details 43, 124, 202
Dew Tour 14
differentiation 27, 89, 100, 114-115, 215
DIM process 141
direct spending 231
disabled participants 14, 16, 57
discussion forums 173
distribution 101-102
DMOs (destination marketing organizations) 12, 13, 166
documentation 74
Dodge National Circuit Finals Rodeo 164, 165*t*
Donna's Hope 90
donors 67
drones 147-148
dropout rates 5
due diligence 134, 146
duty of care 139, 146, 150-151

E

Eastern Michigan University 124, 125
e-commerce 134
economic impact 2, 3
counting costs 51
direct spending 231
estimate examples 50-51
formulas for calculating 50
implicit benefits 231
induced spending 231
leakage 51, 231
of mega-events 18
multipliers 50, 231
objectivity 51
overstatements 51
postevent measurement 230-231
spending by locals 51
sport tourism 10
visitor spending 10, 13, 50, 51, 231
egress 208
Electronic Signatures in Global and National Commerce Act 134
e-marketing 228
emergencies
action plans 141, 150, 152
budgeting for 72
communications during 209
reporting 207
types 41, 143, 156

employees. *See* staff
employment 6-7, 9
employment agencies 166
Encyclopedia of Sports Management and Marketing (Bussell) 113
entertainment contracts 127
equipment
  budgeting for 60
  costs 69
  inventories 221
  liability 146
  postevent management 221
  safety inspections 134, 146
esport 12
e-ticketing 208, 216
evacuation procedures 149
evaluation
  attendance 229-230
  budget performance 228
  consumer surveys 227*f*
  economic impact 230-231
  industry profile on 220
  in-game 225
  levels of 224-225
  of management 227-228
  objectives 230
  by participants 212-213, 213*f*
  phase 182
  as planning stage 28
  and promises 115
  purposes of 183
  qualitative 225-226, 227
  quantitative 225, 226
  social media for 220
  by spectators 209-210, 210*f*
  of sponsorships 90-91, 214, 223-224
  of staff 226-227
  street-intercept method 225
  of success 119-120
  360-degree 228
event conceptualization. *See also* planning
  brainstorming 29-30
  choosing event type 33
  common mistakes 43
  creativity 38-39
  decision-making 28-29
  industry profile on 26-27
  leadership 28
  missions 35-36
  purpose of events 32-33
  setting goals and objectives 36
  sustainability 39-40
  uniqueness 27, 38-39
event day
  anticipation 201
  apps 217
  checklists 202, 203*t*-204*t*
  communication during 202
  contact lists 202, 204*t*
  contingency plans 201
  delays 202
  delegating 201
  details 202
  industry profile on 200
  plans of action 201
  rehearsals 201-202
  rundowns 164, 204, 204*t*-205*t*
  schedules 202
  staff management 205-208
  technologies 216-217
  tools 202, 205
  training for 201-202
event management 13-14
event rundown 164, 202, 204, 204*t*-205*t*
events. *See also* sport events
  for causes 32, 33
  dates for 36-37
  destination-specific factors 162
  differentiation 27, 89, 100, 114-115, 215
  duration 37-38, 163
  location 37, 38, 101
  naming 100
  nonsporting 9-10
  presentation 72
  registration 183
  scripts 205
  timelines 26, 42-43, 118, 181-183, 182*f*
  time of 37, 101, 163
  types 9-10, 14-20, 15*t*, 33, 162
  uniqueness 38-39
event triangle 80
exclusivity clauses 127
expenses. *See* costs
extreme sports 14
Extremity Games 16

F

Facebook 103, 117, 172
facilities
  access credentials 211
  aesthetic value 190
  briefing staff on 206
  case study 197-198
  cleanup 187-188, 221
  contracts 126-127
  costs 69-70
  easements 190
  entrances 208, 209
  feasibility studies 190
  hotel availability 194-195
  ingress and egress 208
  inspection checklist 153*f*-155*f*
  lighting 189
  locker rooms 212
  maintenance 166
  management 13-14
  parking 66, 189, 191, 192*f*
  public versus private 13
  recreational opportunities 190
  regulations 190
  renovations 216
  restroom facilities 191
  seating 192-193, 208
  selection 190-191
  sound considerations 193-194
  traffic flow 191, 192*f*
  zoning 190
facility managers 13-14
family events 16-17
fandemonium 152
fastpitch softball 218
feasibility studies 53-54
federal legislation 132-133
feedback 61-62, 103, 119, 168
Fiedler, F.E. 169
field maintenance 166
FIFA World Cup 17, 18, 54, 231-232
financial statements 61
Fire Up a Cure 32
first aid 143
fixed costs 69
fixed events 17
flat organizational structures 161
focus groups 226
food and beverage services
  concessions operations 185-186
  considerations 186
  contracts for 128-129
  licensing 185
  meals for participants 184-185
  offerings 66, 185
  outsourcing 66, 166
  revenue from 65
  types of 184
food safety 147*f*
Footgolf 5
force majeure 136
Formula One 67
functional areas 162
fundraising for causes 32, 38, 75

G

gambling 4
game contracts 127
Gantt charts 43*f*
Gatorade Free Flow Tour 14
general admission 208
goals 36, 61, 99
golf tournaments 67, 75-76, 82, 87, 110, 187
governing bodies 7, 20, 33

grants 67
Greater Grand Junction Sports Commission 48
green practices 39-40
guarantees 135
guest management 71-72
guest services 162. *See also* hospitality

H
hashtags 118
heat-related illnesses 144
Herzberg, Frederick 167
hierarchy of effects model 82*t*, 115
hierarchy of needs 167
Homeland Security 146
hospitality 71-72
  corporate 66-67, 184, 187
  sponsors 214
  suites 187, 192
host sites 18, 49, 54
hotel availability 194-195
House, R.J. 169
Houston Texans (NFL) 216
human trafficking 148
Hunt, G. 169

I
illnesses 143, 144, 147
image promotion 32
implementation stage 27-28
implicit benefits 231
India, sport in 21-22
Indianapolis, Indiana 50, 119, 120
Indiana State Fair 133
induced spending 231
industry trends 62
Infield Chatter 223
information gathering 61-62
ingress 208
In Search of Excellence (Peters and Waterman) 226
insurance 70, 146-147
integrated marketing communications 82, 102, 112
intermediaries 101, 102
international events 17
international federations 7
International Ice Hockey Federation 44-45
International Olympic Committee (IOC) 18, 161, 187
Internet 68, 134, 172, 173
interpersonal skills 8
interviews 226
intramural sports 130
inventory 64-65
IOC (International Olympic Committee) 18, 161, 187
Ironman events 51

J
James, Lebron 117
jobs 6-7, 9
Jones, Daron 200

K
Kabbadi (sport) 21
Kansas Collegiate Athletic Conference 60
Kansas State High School Activities Association 112
Kentucky Derby 17, 51, 66, 191, 216, 230
Kidd, Al 2
knowledge 7-9

L
lawyers 131-132, 151, 152
leadership 28
  consideration 169
  definitions 168
  employee orientation 169
  environmental factors 170
  initiating structure 169
  personal style 169
  production orientation 169
  transactional 170
  transformational 170
leadership theories
  adaptive-reactive 169-170
  behavioral 169
  contingency model 169
  path-goal theory 169
  situational 169-170
  trait theories 169
Leadoff Classic 218
leagues 4, 5
leakage 231
legacy gifts 87
legal issues. *See also* contracts
  federal legislation 132-134
  industry profile on 124-125
  liabilities 124
legislation 125, 132-134
leveraging 13
liabilities
  and contract language 124
  equipment 146
  insurance 146-147
  and negligence 151
  supervision 146
  transferring to third party 141
licensing 65
lighting 189
lightning safety 144
Little League Baseball 32
local organizing committee (LOC) 28
locations 37, 38, 101, 162
locker facilities 212
logistics 26, 36-38, 181, 210-211
losses 63, 64
Louisiana State University 118
Louisville Sports Commission (LSC) 26

M
mailbox rule 134
maintenance services 166
Major League Baseball 32
Major League Soccer 197
management by wandering around (MBWA) 226
management evaluations 227-228
management meetings. *See* meetings
marketing 4, 5. *See also* promotions
  advertising 104*t*
  assessment 96
  branding 100
  cause-related 90
  communicating messages 80
  competition 97
  consumer research 97
  costs 71
  data 96
  demographic segmentation 99
  distribution 101-102, 115
  environment considerations 97
  event characteristics 97
  four Ps 115
  as functional area 162
  industry profile on 94
  marketing mix 114-115
  and motivation 97
  niche markets 100
  omnichannel marketing 116, 117
  placing 115
  plan development 95-96
  plan implementation 96
  plans 95-96
  positioning 115
  pricing 100-101
  and product benefits 99
  and product usage 99
  psychographic segmentation 99
  research 96-97, 96*t*
  setting goals and objectives 96, 99
  and sponsorships 80
  of sporting events 95
  tactics 96
  target markets 96, 99-100
  10 Ps 115
  understanding consumers 97-99
  viral marketing 103-104
market segments 99
Maslow, Abraham 167
Mattel, Inc. 163
Mayo, Elton 167
media contracts 128

media coverage
broadcast agreements 68
broadcast partners 33
news conferences 222
postevent 221
social media impact 222-223
tips when talking to media 222
media promotion 111. *See also* promotions
media relations
critical Rs 113
definition 111
industry profile on 110-111
relating 113-114
repairing 114
retaining favor 114
symbiotic relationships 112, 113
media rights 67-68, 166
medical attention 143
medical costs 69
Mediterranean Games 18-19
meetings
action items 172
attendees 170-171
conducting 171
documentation 171
follow-up 171-172
preparation 171
mega-events 17-18, 54
memberships 64
merchandising 65
microblogs 172-173
Millennials 3
minor league baseball 116, 216
minors 129, 130
miscellaneous expenses 72
missions 26, 35-36, 43, 52, 215
mobile point-of-service 216
mobile technology 102, 173
moments of truth 215-216
motivation
consumers 97
of event staff 166-168
incentives 168
participant 97
theories on 167, 168
of volunteers 174
movement theory 149
mud runs 39, 44
multiple-location events 19
multisport events 18-19
music 128, 194

N

naming rights 14, 87-88, 92
National Association for Stock Car Auto Racing (NASCAR) 81, 116
National Association of Sports Commissions 2 National Basketball Association 103, 216
National Fastpitch Coaches Association 218
National Football League 118, 216
National Hockey League 39, 103
National Oceanic and Atmospheric Administration (NOAA) 144, 145
National Soccer Festival 17
National Weather Service 144, 146
National Wheelchair Basketball Tournament 40-41
natural disasters 148
NBC Sports 103
NCAA championships 17, 33
NCAA Final Four 161
negligence 139
assumption of risk 151
breach 151
cause 151
damage 151
definition 150
duty 150-151
liability laws 151, 152
networks 163, 172
New Orleans Pelicans 216
news conferences 222
NFL Tennessee Titans 78-79
niche markets 100
noise ordinances 194
nonfixed events 17
nonsporting events 9-10
nostalgia sport tourism 11

O

objectives
for marketing 99
return on 26, 230
setting 36
Occupational Health and Safety Act 133
Occupational Health and Safety (OSHA) 133-134, 146
officials 69
Olympic Games 14, 17, 18, 54, 90
omnichannel marketing 116, 117
ONE Championship 103
online communities 173
opening ceremonies 72
operational planning 27, 42
operations 162
organizational charts 29*f*, 161-162
organizational structures 161
Osborn, R.N. 169
OSHA guidelines 133-134, 146
outsourcing 66, 165-166
owned and operated (O&O) market 3

P

Panhellenic Games 4
Paralympic Games 14, 16
parking 66, 189, 191, 192*f*
participants
area logistics 210
arrival 210
communication with 211-212
credentials 211
departure 212
evaluation by 212-213, 213*f*, 220
information sheet for 211*t*
legal representation 131
liaisons 212
locker rooms 212
meals for 184-185
observation 225
refreshments 185
risk assumption 151
surveys of 213*f*, 220
tracking systems 217
traveling parties 212
unsportsmanlike conduct policy 130
pay-per-view 68-69
pay-to-play 2, 3
pedestrian traffic 191
permits 190
personal seat licenses 183
personal traits 3-4, 7-9
personnel. *See* staff
Peters, Tom 226
petty cash 74
PGA Tour 110-111
Phillips 66 Big 12 Men's Basketball Championship 40
photo sharing 173
Pinstripe Bowl 38
planning
ancillary components 40-41
blunders 43
for contingencies 41-42
details 43
logistics 26, 36
need for 27
operational planning 27, 42
phase 182
process 26, 27
project management approach 30-32
resources 33*t*
in risk management 141
stages 27-28
SWOT analysis 34-35, 35*f*
timelines 42-43
play 3
player costs 70
point-of-service 216

polar bear plunge 38
positioning 115
postevent. *See also* evaluation
  breakdown 221
  cleanup 221
  debriefing 224
  media coverage 221-223
  promotions 221
  reporting 71
  sponsor follow-up 223-224
  staff debriefing 207-208, 224
preliminary budgets 61
presentation
  costs 72
  functions 162
press conferences 222
price promotions 105
pricing 65, 100-101, 101*t*
problem resolution 207
production management 162
production orientation 169
production schedules 164, 165*t*
professional associations 62
professional athletes 5
Professional Disc Golf Association 53
professional sports 5, 192
profits 63, 64
programs 66
project management 30, 42, 163
project tracking software 31
promotional mix 114-115
promotions
  advertising 104, 104*t*
  AIDA process 112
  communication tools 102
  community support 105
  costs 60, 71
  creativity 116
  cross-promotions 90
  definition 114, 115, 221
  end users 102
  and event purpose 32
  events as 40
  image promotion 32
  messages 102
  objectives for 102
  postevent 221
  price promotions 116
  sales promotion 105, 116
  social media 103, 118
  sponsors 214
  tools 115-117
  value-added 105, 116
  viral marketing 103-104
  websites 102-103
public address systems 41, 164, 194, 212
publications 66
publicity 113-114

Q
qualitative data 182, 225-226, 227
quality 195
Qualman, E. 117
quantitative data 182, 225, 226
quick-response codes 90
quidditch 12

R
radio 68
receipts 74
Red Bull Cliff Diving World Series 14
referrals 118
registrations 64, 183
rehearsals 201-202
releases 129
requests for proposals 52, 191
research phase 182
reserved seating 208
resources 27, 33*t*
restroom facilities 191
return on event 228, 229*f*
return on investment 81, 90-91, 225, 228
return on objectives 26, 115, 230
return on opportunity 81, 91
revenue
  concessions 65-66
  corporate hospitality 66
  donations 67
  estimating 62
  generation 4
  grants 67
  licensing 65
  media rights 67-69
  memberships 64-65
  merchandising 65
  parking 66
  publications 66
  registrations 64*t*, 65
  sponsorships 65
  in sport tourism 10
  subsidies 67
  tickets 64-65
Rhino Sports & Entertainment Services 176-177, 180-181
Richards, Chris 110-111
rights fees 68, 165
rights-holder organizations (RHOs) 4, 12, 13
rights holders 67-68, 87-88
risk management
  buy-in 143
  communication of 143
  crowd control 148-150
  definition 140
  DIM process 141
  evaluation after event 143
  industry profile on 138-140
  lessons learned 139
  and liability 125
  managing the plan 143
  negligence 150-152
  plan development 142-143
  plan implementation 143
  process 141
  and social media monitoring 139
  standard operating procedures 141
risk matrix 142*f*, 143
risks 140
  assessment 141, 142*f*
  assumption of risk 151
  classifying 141, 142-143
  identification 141, 142
  potential threats 41, 139, 143-148, 151, 156-157
  treatment 141, 143
Rivals (website) 173
Robarge, Dennis 180, 181
Rose Bowl 32
rundowns 164, 204, 204*t*-205*t*
running events 26-27, 38, 39, 107, 195, 213
Rush2Recycle program 40
Russia case study 231-232
Ryder Cup 67

S
safety
  equipment inspections 134, 146
  negligence 150-152
  security service contracts 128
sales
  promotion 105
  techniques 106*t*
  tickets 183
San Antonio Sports Commission 160, 161
Sanders, Deion 222-223
satellite radio 68
scheduling
  critical dates calendar 164*t*
  lists 202
  parallel 163
  production schedules 164, 165*t*
  serial 163
  software 31-32
  staff 163-165
  timelines 26, 181-183
  time of event 37, 101, 163
scientific theory of management 167
scripts 205
Scully, Patrick 78, 79
seating 192-193, 208
security
  at admissions 208
  personnel 138-139, 177

physical measures 138
proactiveness 140
service contracts 128
and technology 138
threats 139
for traffic flow 191
training for 138, 139, 140
self-service kiosks 216-217
senior events 19
Senior Games 19
service 195
ShotTracker 9
signage 150, 209, 213
situational analysis (SWOT) 34-35, 35*f*
situational theories of leadership 169
skills 3-4, 7-9
small-scale sport events 19
SMART goals 36, 230
Snapchat 103
social media
audience 103
blogs 172
branding opportunities 118
connectivity 117, 118
cost-effectiveness 117
discussion forums 173
for evaluation 220
for event promotion 103, 220
flexibility 118
hiring through 118
microblogs 172-173
monitoring for threats 139
photo sharing 173
postgame coverage 222-223
promotional opportunities 118
reach 117-118
referrals 118
and risk management 139
sales through 103
sites 5
strategies 103
timeliness 118
trolling 223
types of 172
video sharing 173
web traffic 118
Social Media Revolution (Qualman) 117
social networks 172
SOPs (standard operating procedures) 141
sound considerations 193-194
Spartathlon 100
specialization 3
Special Olympics 16, 163
spectators 4
admission policies 208
communicating with 209
evaluations by 209-210, 210*f*
ingress and egress 208
risk assumption 151
survey 210*f*
sponsor liaisons 71, 214
sponsorships 81-82
activation 71, 89-90
agreements 127-128
benefits of 32-33, 88-89
and commercialism 6
components of 83
costs to corporations 83-84
costs to event organizers 88
definition 80, 81
deliverables 214
evaluation 90-91, 214, 223-224
event triangle 80-81
expectations 213
follow-up 223-224
fulfillment 71
hierarchy of effects model 82*t*
hospitality 214
industry profile on 78-79
in-kind 83
integrated marketing communications 82
levels 85, 86*t*, 87
meeting objectives 32
naming rights 87-88
postevent reporting 71
potential offerings 88
promotions 214
proposals 84-85
retaining 213
revenue from 65
signage 213
in youth sports 20
sport
definition 10
origins of 4
terminology 4
sport event industry
careers in 6-9
changes in 3, 6
components 5
future of 5, 6
growth 3, 5
industry trends 62
revenues 5
size of 2-3
sport event management 13-14
sport identity 5
sporting events
creating new 26
differentiation 27, 38-39, 48
historical perspective 4
leveraging 13
versus nonsport events 9-10
rights holders 13
role of 4
types of 14-20, 15*t*, 33
sport marketing. *See* marketing
sport participation 4
sport promotion 32
sports commissions 2, 6, 7
funding from 67
industry profile on 160-161
missions of 52
sports information directors 114
sportsmanship 130
sport tourism
actors in 12-13
description 10
economic impact 10
motivation for 12
types of 11-12
spreadsheets 73
staff
arrival 205
autonomy 168
benchmarking 226
breaks 207
briefing 205-206
buy-in 143
case study 176-178
chain of command 206
check-in 205
communication with 172-173, 207, 216
costs 60, 69
emergency reporting 207
evaluations 165, 226-227
feedback 61-62, 165, 168
hiring 118
industry profile on 160-161
involvement 168
job performance 166
management tips 207
managing 166-167, 205-208
morale 215
motivating 166-168
needs identification 162-163
organizational charts 29*f*, 161-162
orientation 169
outsourcing 165-166
positional assignments 180, 206-207
postevent debriefing 207-208, 224
preevent tasks 163-164
problem resolution 207
providing information 168
recognition 168
responsibilities 201, 206
rewarding 215
rotation 168, 207
scheduling 163-165
screenings 146
security personnel 138-139

staff *(continued)*
  staffing during events 164
  team building 175
  team introductions 206
  training 139, 140, 146, 150, 201, 215
stakeholders 27
  assessment questions 32, 230
  and decision-making process 28-29
  meetings with 170-171
  needs of 32-33
standard operating procedures (SOPs) 141
St. Jude Children's Research Hospital 106
Stoll, Jennifer 48
StormReady 146
strategic plans 34, 182
subsidies 67
Super Bowl 18, 39, 40, 67, 119, 146
supervision 146
surveys. *See* evaluation
sustainability 39-40
SWOT analysis 34-35, 35*f*
symbiotic relationships 112, 113
syndication 68

T

Taipei 2017 Summer Universiade 51
tall organizational structures 161
target markets 99
Taylor, Frederick 167
team building 175
technical production 162
technology
  communication tools 216
  and contracts 134
  event day 216-217
  media 6
  point-of-service 216
  for security measures 138
  skills 8-9
  software 8, 31-32
  ticketing 208, 216
  touch-screen kiosks 216-217
television broadcasts 67-68, 100
temporary employment agencies 166
terrorist threats 139
Texas Christian University volleyball 117
third party contracts 128
threats 41, 143
  blood-borne pathogens 146
  drones 147-148
  equipment 146
  food handling 147*f*
  heat-related illnesses 144
  human trafficking 148
  insurance 146-147
  medical attention 143
  natural disasters 148
  social media monitoring 139
  supervision 146
  terrorism 139
  violence 138, 139, 151, 156-157
  weather issues 144-146
Ticketmaster 166
tickets
  mobile ticketing 208, 216
  outsourcing 165, 166
  personal seat licenses 183
  pricing 65
  revenue 64
  sales 183
  secondary markets 183, 184
  for sponsors 71
  types 208
time buy 68
timelines 26, 181-183, 182*f*
time management 8, 21
touchpoints 196, 216
touch-screen kiosks 216-217
tourism. *See* sport tourism
tourism sport 12
trade publications 62
traffic flow 191, 192*f*
training
  security procedures 138-139
  staff 139, 140, 146, 150, 201
  volunteers 175
traits 3-4, 7-9
trait theories of leadership 169
transactional leadership 170
transformational leadership 170
transportation services 188-189
triathlon events 51
trolling 223
Twitter 117, 118, 172-173, 222, 223

U

Undercover Boss (television show) 226
Unified Sports & Entertainment Security Consulting 138, 139, 140
Uniform Electronic Transactions Act (UETA) 134
unilateral contracts 126
United States Tennis Association (USTA) 36
University of Florida 104
University of Louisville 94
University of Wisconsin 142*f*, 200
Urban Bourbon Half Marathon 107
U.S. Army All-American Bowl 32
USA Weightlifting 52

V

variable costs 69
vendors. *See also* contracts
  mobile point-of-service options 216
  relationships 189-190
  researching for budgeting 62
venues. *See* facilities
video 128, 173
violence 138, 151, 156-157
VIPs 162, 208-209
viral marketing 103-104
Virginia Amateur Sports 220
Virginia Tech 176-177, 180
visitor spending 10, 13, 50, 51, 231
volunteers
  finding 173-174
  interviewing 174, 175
  statistics on 173
  training 146, 175
  working with 160, 161, 174-175

W

waivers 129, 130*f*, 151
Waldron, Charity 220
waste management 187
Waterman, Robert 226
weather issues
  climate 9
  contingency plans 26, 35, 41, 145
  heat-related illnesses 144
  lightning safety 144
  natural disasters 145, 148
  and safety 133-134
  severe weather potential 144, 145
  StormReady program 146
  time of year for events 37
websites. *See also* social media
  job boards 7
  marketing on 102-103
  ticket sales 183, 184
  traffic 118
wheelchair rugby 57
will call 209
Wimbledon 103
women's ice hockey 44-45
Women's Tri-Fitness 36
word of mouth 104, 214-215
working budgets 61
World Wrestling Entertainment (WWE) 40, 118

X

X Games 14

Y

youth sport
  costs 5
  dropout rates 5
  economic impact 2-3, 20
  governing bodies 20
  market 19-20
  sponsors 20
YouTube 173

Z

zero waste events 40
Zonder, Erica 124, 125

ABOUT THE AUTHORS

Courtesy of Chris Greenwell.

T. Christopher Greenwell, PhD, is a professor in the department of health and sport science at the University of Louisville in Kentucky. He has taught event management since 2002 and has published several articles on unique aspects of the service environment at sporting events and how these can be used as an effective marketing tool.

Greenwell has direct experience as an event manager, having planned and coordinated the event management, promotions, and game operations for all athletic events in an NCAA Division I athletic program. Events under his management set attendance records in men's and women's basketball, volleyball, and women's soccer. Greenwell was also an event volunteer for major events such as the Super Bowl, the PGA Championship, the Ryder Cup, NASCAR races, and the World Equestrian Games.

Greenwell and his wife, Donna, reside in Louisville. In his free time, he enjoys watching mixed martial arts and playing fantasy football.

Courtesy of Leigh Ann Danzey-Bussell.

Leigh Ann Danzey-Bussell, PhD, is an associate professor of sport management at Trevecca Nazarene University in Nashville. She has taught event and facility management courses since 2006. In 2008, she was named Outstanding Professor of the Year by Sigma Phi Epsilon, Gamma Chapter, at Ball State University in Muncie, Indiana.

Danzey-Bussell has over 25 years of experience working in the sport industry in various capacities in NCAA Division I, II, and III programs and NAIA programs as well as in the nonprofit sector. She has served as the executive director of Team Clydesdale International, a nonprofit organization responsible for hosting national and world championships in various events. She also worked as the media relations coordinator for the United States Golf Tour, and she was a sport information director responsible for event management and promotion at the University of Alabama, University of South Alabama, and Northeast Louisiana University. Danzey-Bussell serves as the chair of the North American Society for Sport Management's Teaching & Learning Fair. A former member of the finance committee for the North American Society for the Sociology of Sport, she is currently a member of the Drake Group and the Nashville Sports Council and is a TN Promise mentor.

Danzey-Bussell has volunteered for local, regional, and national sporting events, including American Heart Association walks, Southeastern Conference gymnastics championships, two NCAA Final Fours (Indianapolis and Atlanta), NCAA swimming and diving championships, the 2018 NCAA men's basketball tournament (rounds 1 and 2) in Nashville, the 2018 Music City Bowl, the 2012 Super Bowl in Indianapolis, the 2019 Super Bowl in Atlanta, the 2019 Southeastern Conference men's basketball tournament, and the 2019 NFL draft. She also served the University of Alabama as the alumni chapter president for the state of Indiana for 10 years.

Danzey-Bussell enjoys attending and watching sporting events, sharing movies with her family, and cooking. She and her husband, Timothy, and daughter, Sophie Grace, reside in Nolensville, Tennessee.

Courtesy of David Shonk.

David J. Shonk, PhD, is an associate professor in the School of Hospitality, Sport, and Recreation Management at James Madison University in Harrisonburg, Virginia, where he conducts research in sport event management and has taught a course in sport facility and event management. Shonk has worked as a meeting and event planner in both professional sports and the nonprofit sector since 2003. During that time he was responsible for planning a range of conferences, tours, and events, including concerts, on-field promotions, and special events such as the Carolina League All-Star Game. He also worked as marketing director of the Salem Professional Baseball Club and director of development at DECA, Inc.

In 2011, Shonk founded the all-volunteer organization Harrisonburg-Rockingham Sports Commission, where he serves as the executive director. He also currently serves as associate editor for the *Sport Management Education Journal*.

Shonk lives in Harrisonburg with his wife, Jennifer, and their children, Ashley and Ryan. He is an active board member with Valley Fellowship of Christian Athletes and enjoys traveling with his family.